Modernity, Memory and Identity in South-East Europe

Series Editor
Catharina Raudvere
Department of Cross-Cultural and Regional Studies
University of Copenhagen
Copenhagen, Denmark

This series explores the relationship between the modern history and present of South-East Europe and the long imperial past of the region. This approach aspires to offer a more nuanced understanding of the concepts of modernity and change in this region, from the nineteenth century to the present day. Titles focus on changes in identity, self-representation and cultural expressions in light of the huge pressures triggered by the interaction between external influences and local and regional practices. The books cover three significant chronological units: the decline of empires and their immediate aftermath, authoritarian governance during the twentieth century, and recent uses of history in changing societies in South-East Europe today.

Catharina Raudvere • Petek Onur
Editors

Neo-Ottoman Imaginaries in Contemporary Turkey

palgrave
macmillan

Editors
Catharina Raudvere
Department of Cross-Cultural and
Regional Studies
University of Copenhagen
Copenhagen, Denmark

Petek Onur
Department of Cross-Cultural and
Regional Studies
University of Copenhagen
Copenhagen, Denmark

ISSN 2523-7985 ISSN 2523-7993 (electronic)
Modernity, Memory and Identity in South-East Europe
ISBN 978-3-031-08022-7 ISBN 978-3-031-08023-4 (eBook)
https://doi.org/10.1007/978-3-031-08023-4

© The Editor(s) (if applicable) and The Author(s), under exclusive licence to Springer Nature Switzerland AG 2023
This work is subject to copyright. All rights are solely and exclusively licensed by the Publisher, whether the whole or part of the material is concerned, specifically the rights of translation, reprinting, reuse of illustrations, recitation, broadcasting, reproduction on microfilms or in any other physical way, and transmission or information storage and retrieval, electronic adaptation, computer software, or by similar or dissimilar methodology now known or hereafter developed.
The use of general descriptive names, registered names, trademarks, service marks, etc. in this publication does not imply, even in the absence of a specific statement, that such names are exempt from the relevant protective laws and regulations and therefore free for general use.
The publisher, the authors, and the editors are safe to assume that the advice and information in this book are believed to be true and accurate at the date of publication. Neither the publisher nor the authors or the editors give a warranty, expressed or implied, with respect to the material contained herein or for any errors or omissions that may have been made. The publisher remains neutral with regard to jurisdictional claims in published maps and institutional affiliations.

This Palgrave Macmillan imprint is published by the registered company Springer Nature Switzerland AG.
The registered company address is: Gewerbestrasse 11, 6330 Cham, Switzerland

Contents

1. "I am the Granddaughter of the Ottomans": Gender, Aesthetics and Agency in Neo-Ottoman Imaginaries—An Introduction 1
   Catharina Raudvere and Petek Onur

2. Neo-Ottomanism versus Ottomania: Contestation of Gender in Historical Drama 33
   Murat Ergin and Yağmur Karakaya

3. Lovers of the Rose: Islamic Affect and the Politics of Commemoration in Turkish Museal Display 57
   Torsten Janson

4. Between Memory and Forgetting and Purity and Danger: The Case of the Ulucanlar Prison Museum 99
   Courtney Dorroll

5. Architectures of Domination? The Sacralisation of Modernity and the Limits of Ottoman Islamism 125
   Kerem Öktem

6. Claiming the Neo-Ottoman Mosque: Islamism, Gender, Architecture 155
   Bülent Batuman

7 Commemorating the First World War and Its Aftermath: Neo-Ottomanism, Gender, and the Politics of History in Turkey   175
Nazan Maksudyan and Hilal Alkan

8 The New Ottoman Henna Nights and Women in the Palace of Nostalgia   209
Petek Onur

9 Post-truth and Anti-science in Turkey: Putting It into Perspective   237
Hande Eslen-Ziya

10 Mixed Marriage Patterns in Istanbul: Gendering Ethno-religious Boundaries   257
Özgür Kaymak

11 Neo-Ottoman Intersections: The Politics of Gender in a Transforming Turkey—An Afterword   285
Nora Fisher-Onar

Index   313

Notes on Contributors

Hilal Alkan is a researcher at the Leibniz-Zentrum Moderner Orient (ZMO). She received her PhD in Political Science from The Open University, UK. She was a EUME (Europa im Nahen Osten – Der Nahe Osten in Europa) Fellow of Forum Transregionale Studien in Berlin in 2016–2017, Georg Forster Fellow of the Alexander von Humboldt Foundation in 2017–2020, and the receiver of Potsdam University's Voltaire Award for Tolerance, International Understanding and Respect for Difference in 2017. Her work focuses on gender, migration, and social welfare, through the lenses of anthropology and citizenship studies. Her most recent publications include 'Syrian Migration and Logics of Alterity in an Istanbul Neighbourhood' (2020), 'The gift of hospitality: (un)welcoming Syrian migrants in Turkey' (2021), *Urban Neighbourhood Formations: Boundaries, Narrations, Intimacies* (ed. with N. Maksudyan) (2020), and *The Politics of the Female Body in Contemporary Turkey: Reproduction, Maternity, Sexuality* (ed. with A. Dayı, S. Topçu and B. Yarar) (2021).

Bülent Batuman is an associate professor of architecture at Bilkent University with joint appointment at the Department of Urban Design and Landscape Architecture and the Department of Architecture. He studied at the Middle East Technical University and received his PhD in History and Theory of Art and Architecture from State University of New York–Binghamton. His research areas include social production and politics of built environment, history and theory of modern architecture and urbanism, and urban politics. His recent work focuses on the relationship between Islamism and the built environment. He is the author of *New Islamist Architecture and Urbanism: Negotiating Nation and Islam through Built Environment in Turkey* (Routledge, 2018) and editor of *Cities and Islamisms: On the Politics and Production of the Built Environment* (Routledge, 2021).

Courtney Dorroll is associate professor in the Religion Department at Wofford College. Courtney co-coordinates the Middle Eastern and North African Studies Program on campus. Her work focuses on Turkish Studies, Scholarship of Teaching and Learning, and Self-Care in the Academy. She edited the volume *Teaching Islam during the Age of ISIS, Islamophobia, and the Internet*. She blogs on self-care pedagogy on vocationmatters.org. She is currently writing a book titled *Radical Care* that documents adding in intentional care to one's life and profession.

Murat Ergin is associate professor of Sociology at Koç University, Istanbul, and received his PhD from the University of Minnesota. His research interests include nationalism, race, and ethnicity; cultural boundaries, consumption and popular culture; science and technology; crime and deviance; and death. He co-published "Between Neo-Ottomanism and Ottomania: Navigating State-Led and Popular Cultural Representations of the Past" in together with Yağmur Karakaya in *New Perspectives on Turkey* (2017). In 2016 he published the monograph *Is the Turk a White Man?: Race and Modernity in the Making of Turkish Identity* with Brill.

Hande Eslen-Ziya is professor of Sociology at the University of Stavanger and director of the Populism, Anti-Gender and Democracy Research Group at the same institution. She has an established interest in gender and social inequalities, transnational organisations, and social activism, and has a substantial portfolio of research in this field. Her research has been published in *Gender, Work and Organisation; Emotion, Space and Society; Social Movement Studies; European Journal of Women's Studies; Culture, Health and Sexuality; Leadership; Men and Masculinities;* and *Social Politics* as well as in other internationally recognized journals. Currently she is working on how right-wing populist ideologies, by creating alternative troll-scientific discourses, oppose scientific facts and gender theory.Dr. Eslen-Ziya has also authored a book that investigates how men construct their identities throughout their developmental trajectories—*The Social Construction and Developmental Trajectories of Masculinities*—published at Istanbul Bilgi Üniversitesi Yayınları (2017) and another one entitled *Politics and Gender Identity in Turkey: Centralized Islam for Socio-Economic Control*, published by Routledge, that looks at how illiberal regimes use discursive tools and governmentalities rather than actual public policies to foster human capital. Currently she co-edited the book titled *The Aesthetics of Global Protest: Visual Culture and Communication* published by Amsterdam University Press. Eslen-Ziya is the Co-I of Covid-19 project funded by the Norwegian Research Council (2020–2022). The project titled "Fighting pandemics with enhanced risk communication: Messages, compliance and vulnerability during the COVID-19 outbreak" aims to uncover the correlation between risk communication and social vulnerability in the context of the Covid-19 outbreak.

Nora Fisher-Onar is an associate professor of international studies at the University of San Francisco. Her research interests include the theory and practice of international relations, foreign policy analysis, comparative area studies (Turkey; Middle East; Europe), political ideologies, gender, and history/memory. She received her doctorate from Oxford and holds master's and undergraduate degrees from Johns Hopkins (SAIS) and Georgetown universities, respectively. Fisher-Onar is editor of the volume *Istanbul: Living With Difference in a Global City* (2018 with Rutgers University Press). Her forthcoming *Pluralism in Turkey: Islam, Liberalism and Nationalism* will be published by Cambridge University Press.

Torsten Janson is senior lecturer at the Centre for Theology and Religious Studies and affiliated with the Advanced Centre for Middle Eastern Studies, Lund University. During the past decade, he has served as co-coordinator and principal investigator of the Swedish national research program *The Middle East in the Contemporary World* (MECW). He has published widely on Islamic mission (*daʿwa*) and religious socialisation through cultural production, with a particular focus on children's culture. Among his publications are *Your Cradle Is Green: The Islamic Foundation and the Call to Islam in Children's Literature* (Almqvist & Wiksell 2003) and contributions to the volumes *Images of the Child and Childhood in Modern Muslim Contexts* (Duke University Press 2012), *New Words about Pictures: Current Research on Picturebooks and Visual/Verbal Texts for Young People* (Routledge 2017), and *Handbook of Islamic Education* (Springer 2018). He is currently principal investigator for the three-year project, *Beyond Sacred/Secular Cities: Politics of Memory, Space, and Religion in Middle Eastern Nationalisms*.

Yağmur Karakaya is visiting assistant professor at Hamilton College, Clinton NY. Her dissertation research, "Imperial Daydreaming: Disentangling Contemporary Ottoman Nostalgia in Turkey", examines Ottoman nostalgia in contemporary Turkey, focusing on both popular and political settings, through a multi-method qualitative analysis. The thesis was examined at the University of Minnesota in 2020. Karakaya's article "The Conquest of Hearts. The Central role of Ottoman Nostalgia within Contemporary Turkish populism" was published 2020 in the *American Journal of Cultural Sociology*. She co-published "Between Neo-Ottomanism and Ottomania. Navigating State-Led and Popular Cultural Representations of the Past" with Murat Ergin in *New Perspectives on Turkey* (2017).

Özgür Kaymak completed her PhD in the Department of Public Administration and Political Science, Istanbul University,, in 2016 with a dissertation titled "The Socio-Spatial Construction of Istanbul's Rum, Jewish and Armenian Communities". She has published in the fields of ethnic and religious minorities, identity construction of social groups, state-minority relations, women's studies, and gender, including three books, book chapters, and journal articles, as well as opinion pieces. She is the author of *İstanbul'da Az(ınlık) Olmak: Gündelik Hayatta Rumlar, Yahudiler, Ermeniler* (Being a Minority in Istanbul: Rums, Jews, Armenians in the Daily Life) in 2017 and co-author of "A study on Identity Perception of Arabic-Speaking Rum from Antioch and Their Relationality with the Istanbul Rum Community" in *The Arabic-speaking Eastern Orthodox: An Ancient Community in the Shade of Three Nationalisms* ed. Haris Rigas, istos Publishing, 2018, and *Kısmet Tabii. İstanbul'un Rum, Yahudi ve Ermeni Toplumlarında Karma Evlilikler* (Mixed Marriages in Rum, Jewish and Armenian Communities of Istanbul) also published by istos (2020). Kaymak currently works on a project in collaboration with the Gulbenkian Foundation about the Armenian image in modern politics and society. She is also involved in the Women's Library and Information Centre Foundation, Istanbul. Her academic interest areas are ethno-religious minorities, memory studies, family and marriage studies, gender, and feminist theories.

Nazan Maksudyan is Einstein Guest Professor at the Freie Universität Berlin and a research associate at the Centre Marc Bloch, Berlin. She was a EUME Fellow 2009–2010 at the Wissenschaftskolleg zu Berlin and an

Alexander von Humboldt Stiftung Postdoctoral Fellow at the ZMO in 2010–2011. Her fields of expertise are Ottoman and modern Turkish history with additional academic training and research experience in children and youth studies, gender studies, global history, Armenian Studies, intellectual history, and history of science. Her publications include *Orphans and Destitute Children in the Late Ottoman Empire* (2014); (ed.) *Women and the City, Women in the City: A Gendered Perspective to Ottoman Urban History* (2014); *Ottoman Children & Youth during WWI* (2019); (ed. with Hilal Alkan); and *Urban Neighbourhood Formations: Boundaries, Narrations and Intimacies* (2020).

Kerem Öktem is professor of International Relations at Ca' Foscari University of Venice, Department for Linguistics and Comparative Cultural Studies. Before his call to Venice, he held the chair of Southeast European Studies and Contemporary Modern Turkey at the University of Graz where he studied and taught the politics and international relations of Turkey and the field of Islam and Muslims in the Balkans. Since his PhD at the University of Oxford in 2006 and his residence as a research fellow at the European Studies Centre at St Antony's College Oxford, Dr. Öktem has published extensively on these and related topics, beginning with *Turkey's Engagement with Modernity. Conflict and Change in the Twentieth Century* (Palgrave Macmillan 2009, with Celia Kerslake and Philip Robbins) and his monograph *Angry Nation. Turkey since 1989* (Zed Books, 2011). His more recent volumes examine Turkey's autocratisation under successive Justice and Development Party governments, for instance, *Exit from Democracy: Illiberal Governance in Turkey and Beyond* (Routledge 2018, with Karabekir Akkoyunlu) and the shrinking space for non-Muslim communities in AKP Turkey in the collection *Turkish Jews and Their Diasporas* (Palgrave Macmillan 2021 with Ipek Yosmaoğlu). Dr. Öktem is the founding Chair of the Consortium for European Symposia on Turkey (CEST) and alumnus of the Mercator-IPC Fellowship Programme. He serves as an editorial board member of the *Journal of Muslims in Europe* and the *Journal of Southeast European and Black Sea Studies* and as a member of the advisory board for the series New directions in Turkish Studies at Berghahn Books.

Petek Onur is a postdoctoral researcher at the Department of Cross-Cultural and Regional Studies, University of Copenhagen. She had her PhD from Department of Sociology at Middle East Technical University, Turkey with the thesis entitled "Changing Discourse on Women and Islam in Turkey in Ethnographic Studies". She received Sabancı University, Gender and Women's Studies Center of Excellence, 2018 Şirin Tekeli Research Award with her research "Yeni Osmanlı Kına Geceleri ve Saray Nostaljisi içinde Kadınlar" ("New Ottoman Henna Nights and Women in Palace Nostalgia"). She is the author of "The Politics of Nostalgia: The New Urban Culture in Ankara's Historic Neighbourhoods" in *The Politics of Culture in Contemporary Turkey* edited by P. Hecker, I. Furman and K. Akyıldız, published by Edinburgh University Press (2022). Her current project "Gendered Nostalgia: Neo- Ottomanism in Islamist Women's Media in Turkey" is funded by EC Horizon 2020 Marie Skłodowska-Curie Individual Fellowships. Her fields of research include gender, Islam, nostalgia, urban culture and neo-Ottomanism.

Catharina Raudvere is professor of History of Religions at the University of Copenhagen and manages its research centre "Many Roads in Modernity: South-East Europe and its Ottoman Roots" (modernity.ku.dk). Her publications include the monograph *The Book and the Roses: Sufi Women, Visibility and Zikir in Contemporary Istanbul* (I.B. Tauris, 2002) and the co-edited volumes *Religion, Politics, and Turkey's EU Accession* (with Dietrich Jung, Palgrave Macmillan, 2008), *Sufism Today: Heritage and Tradition in the Global Community* (with Leif Stenberg, I.B. Tauris, 2009) and *Rethinking the Space for Religion: New Actors in Central and Southeast Europe* (with Krzysztof Stala and Trine Stauning Willert, Nordic Academic Press, 2012). Among her publications are also *Islam: An Introduction* (I.B. Tauris, 2015) and the edited volume *Contested Memories and the Demands of the Past: History Cultures in the Modern Muslim World* (Palgrave Macmillan, 2016). Most recently she edited *Nostalgia – Loss and Creativity: Political and Cultural Representations of the Past in South-East Europe* (Palgrave Macmillan, 2018) and she published "Between Religiosity, Cultural Heritage and Politics: Sufi-oriented Interests in Contemporary Bosnia and Herzegovina" in Jamal Malik and Saeed Zarrabi-Zadeh (ed.) *Sufism East and West*. (Brill, 2019) and "Instructive Speech among Bosnian Muslim Women" in Elisabeth Özdalga and Simon Stjernholm (ed.) *Modern Muslim Homiletics* (Edinburgh University Press, 2020).

List of Figures

Fig. 3.1	Public, ritual, and pedagogic commemorations in school displays and student crafts, cross-referencing Islamic ritual, Prophet devotion, and global Valentine Day's aesthetics	73
Fig. 3.2	A "Trip to the Age of Felicity" arranged in Istanbul 2015. Models and narratives drawing on sacred geography and historiography suspended mundane time and space in the midst of urban public space	74
Fig. 3.3	Inner courtyard (*left*) and one exhibit room (*top right*) in the Hilye-i Şerif ve Tesbih Museum. *Bottom right*: Sacred Trusts exhibit in Tünel Metro station, Istanbul 2017	76
Fig. 3.4	Components of the *hilye-i şerif* (*left*), as developed by master scribe Hafız Osman (d. 1698) (model designed by author, following Derman 1998b; Uzun 1998). The panel by Gürkan Pehlivan (*right*), displayed at Hilye-i Sṃerif ve Tesbih Museum, strictly follows Hafız Osman's scheme. (Photograph by author)	79
Fig. 3.5	Variations of the rose of Muhammad in contemporary *hilye-i şerif*, by Ferhat Kurlu (*left*), İbrahim Halil İslam (*top right*), and Levent Karaduman detail (*bottom right*). (Photographs by author)	82
Fig. 3.6	Creative re-appropriations of the *Hilye-i şerif* tradition through references to sacred geography, nationalism, and cosmology. Panels by Fatima Ali (*top left*); Abdullah Güllüce (detail, *top right*); Gürkan Pehlivan (*mid left*); Ebubekir Altıok (*mid right*); Levent Karaduman (*bottom left*); Ömer Şen and Said Abuzeroğlu (*bottom right*). (Photographs by author)	83

xiv   LIST OF FIGURES

Fig. 3.7   Two award-winning panels. Cevan Huran and Emel Türkmen (*left*) provide a lexicon of Muhammad nomination, in fairly close compliance with Master Osman's scheme. The structurally more inventive design by Avni Nakkaşm and Emel Selamet (*right*) invokes the Prophet as the defender of monotheism, through extensive Quran quotations and symbolic/textual cosmic references   86
Fig. 4.1   Ulucanlar courtyard. (Photograph by author)   106
Fig. 4.2   Mugs for sale in the prison museum giftshop. Pictured on the mug is Nazım Hikmet, modern Turkey's most famous poet who was a political prisoner in Turkey during his lifetime. (Photograph by author)   116
Fig. 4.3   Wax figure display of prisoners in a communal cell inside the museum. (Photograph by author)   119
Fig. 5.1   *Top left*: The Mausoleum of the state founder Atatürk (Anıtkabir), *Top right*: Hacıbayram Mosque and plateau, *Bottom left*: Streets in the Hacıbayram neighbourhood, *Bottom right*: View from Hacıbayram to lower-middle-class neighbourhoods. (The source of all figures is the author)   133
Fig. 5.2   *Top left*: Ulus Square, *Top right*: Melike Hatun Mosque, *Bottom left*: Gençlik Park Entrance, *Bottom right*: Melike Hatun Mosque seen from the north   134
Fig. 5.3   *Top*: Taksim Mosque, *Bottom*: Taksim Mosque and commemoration of Atatürk's death   139
Fig. 5.4   *Top left*: North Ankara Mosque Complex, general view, *Top right*: North Ankara Mosque Complex park, *Bottom*: North Ankara Mosque Complex Hacıbayram University   142
Fig. 5.5   *Top*: Çamlıca Mosque, general view, *Bottom*: View to central Istanbul from the plateau   145
Fig. 5.6   *Top left*: General view of the Presidential Complex, *Top right*: Mosque of the Nation (Millet Camii), *Bottom left*: Forecourt of the Library of the Nation (Millet Kütüphanesi), *Bottom right*: Main reading hall of the library   147
Fig. 6.1   *Left*: The original proposal for Kocatepe Mosque designed by Vedat Dalokay and Nejat Tekelioğlu. (Source: Vedat Dalokay Archive). *Right*: Kocatepe Mosque dominating the skyline of Ankara. (Photograph by author. The reversion to classical Ottoman mosque architecture represented by this project involved not only the reproduction of the external image. The interior organisation, as well as traditional decorations, also strictly followed classical examples, and this approach henceforth defined the mainstream in mosque architecture endorsed by the Presidency of Religious Affairs)   158

Fig. 6.2	The Ahmet Hamdi Akseki Mosque inside the Diyanet compound, designed by Salim Alp. (Photograph by author. Located along the main road tying Ankara to Eskişehir, the mosque rises as a landmark visible to everyone approaching the city from the western suburbs)	161
Fig. 6.3	The Ahmet Hamdi Akseki Mosque inside the Diyanet compound, designed by Salim Alp: early stage and the actual building. Note the change in the main entrance to the mosque. (Source: Salim Alp Mimarlık and author)	162
Fig. 6.4	The Mimar Sinan Mosque designed by Hilmi Şenalp. (Photograph by Gülse Eraydın. Located in Ataşehir, a rapidly growing district in the Anatolian part of Istanbul, the mosque is situated at the north-western corner of a large park surrounded by two highways and a busy street. To the west of the park lies an upper-class mixed-use compound of high-rise blocks. Thus, although it is huge in size, the mosque is unavoidably dwarfed by the blocks towering over it)	166
Fig. 6.5	The Çamlıca Mosque, designed by Hayriye Gül Totu and Bahar Mızrak: (*left*) under construction with Erdoğan's posters surrounding the site in August 2016; (*right*) view from across the Bosphorus in January 2017. (Photographs by author. The billboards, part of mobilisation efforts following the failed coup, read, "Whatever they do, it is futile/There is [This is] a divine judgement coming from heaven")	169
Fig. 7.1	Soldier with the "historical uniform" of the First World War Ottoman infantry. (Sibel Hürtasm, "Çankkale ve Öteki Şehitler" (Çanakkale and other martyrs), *Al-Monitor*, 27 March 2015, https://www.al-monitor.com/pulse/tr/originals/2015/03/turkey-gallipoli-war-other-m.html#)	182
Fig. 7.2	Poster for the centennial Sarıkamışm commemorations prepared by the Ministry of Youth and Sports. The poster slogans read, "Asım's generation at the March of the Century"; "Sky Allahuekber, Earth Allahuekber"	186
Fig. 7.3	*Top left:* The memorial of Atatürk and Şerife Bacı in Kastamonu, sculpted by Tankut Öktem between 1985 and 1990; the memorial stands in the city centre ("Atatürk ve Şehit Şerife Bacı Anıtı" [Atatürk and Şerife Bacı Monument], Kastamonu Belediyesi, https://www.kastamonu.bel.tr/v2/portfolio/ataturk-ve-sehit-serife-baci-aniti/ (7 July 2020)). *Top right and bottom right:* Nene Hatun Memorial, with the rifle (1994–2018) (https://www.haberturk.com/yerel-haberler/haber/53573170-tarihe-adini-kahramanligiyla-yazdiran-nene-	

	hatunun-heykeli-tartismaya-neden-oldu) and with the axe (as of 2018) (https://www.hurriyet.com.tr/seyahat/vatan-savunmasini-gormek-icin-nene-hatuna-akin-ettiler-41340809). *Top right and bottom right*: Nene Hatun Memorial, with the rifle (1994–2018) and with the axe (as of 2018) (https://www.hurriyet.com.tr/seyahat/vatan-savunmasini-gormek-icin-nene-hatuna-akin-ettiler-41340809). *Bottom left:* Monument of Gördesli Makbule in Gördes, Manisa, courtesy of Hilal Alkan, 20 May 2019	196
Fig. 7.4	A widely circulating picture of Kara Fatma, Fatma Seher Erden ("Kurtuluş Savaşının Kahraman Kadın Askeri: Kara Fatma" [The heroic female soldier of the Independence War: Kara Fatma], *CNN Türk*, 28 April 2017, https://www.cnnturk.com/yasam/kurtulus-savasinin-kahraman-kadin-askeri-kara-fatma?page=4)	200
Fig. 7.5	Halime Çavuş in a photograph published in the national newspaper *Milliyet* on 30 August 2004. The photo caption reads, "Halime Çavuş tells her memories of the 'Independence War' to her visitors"	202
Fig. 8.1	The current outlook of Hamamarkası, with its rebuilt mansions, is in stark contrast with the demolished neighbourhood preceding it: an area of urban decay with neglected houses, poverty, and high crime rates. (Photograph by author)	217
Fig. 8.2	Interiors of henna houses in Hamamarkası compete with one another in adopting imageries of Ottoman luxury and authenticity. (Photograph by author)	218
Fig. 8.3	Ihlamur Kasrı bears a very strong resemblance to the Ottoman-Seljuk architectural projects of the AKP era. (Photograph by author)	220
Fig. 8.4	A velvet sofa with satin pillows is preferred here as the bride's throne. (Photograph by author)	221
Fig. 8.5	*Top*: The opening dance show in Ihlamur Kasrı. The bride has taken her place on the gilt throne surrounded by other gilt Turco-Islamic ornaments. The large screen at the back welcomes the guests with a photograph of red roses and candles. (Photograph by author). *Middle*: Couple dancing after the henna ceremony to an Ankara folk song. (Photograph by author). *Bottom*: Filiz and her husband are joining a Romani dance. (Photograph by Uygar Bulut)	225

CHAPTER 1

"I am the Granddaughter of the Ottomans": Gender, Aesthetics and Agency in Neo-Ottoman Imaginaries—An Introduction

Catharina Raudvere and Petek Onur

"Happy birthday, Muhammed!" a woman exclaims, celebrating the birthday of her youngest child at a café together with her elder daughters. She continues, "I gave birth to three girls to have you." In the documentary film, *Osmanlı Torunu (Granddaughter of the Ottomans)* (2019), Kadriye Mercan introduces herself as a motorcycle courier in Istanbul.[1] Dressed in

---

[1] *Osmanlı Torunu* (*Ottoman Granddaughter*) was produced by the media publisher 140journos in 2019 and is published on https://www.youtube.com/watch?v=zx3F_W2lr7M. Accessed on 28 April 2021.

C. Raudvere (✉) • P. Onur
Department of Cross-Cultural and Regional Studies, University of Copenhagen, Copenhagen, Denmark
e-mail: raudvere@hum.ku.dk; petek.onur@hum.ku.dk

© The Author(s), under exclusive license to Springer Nature Switzerland AG 2023
C. Raudvere, P. Onur (eds.), *Neo-Ottoman Imaginaries in Contemporary Turkey*, Modernity, Memory and Identity in South-East Europe,
https://doi.org/10.1007/978-3-031-08023-4_1

headscarf, leather jacket and a badge with the Turkish crescent, she articulates her complete identification with the Ottoman past:

> —I ruled the world! I sometimes meet people who say, "I'm Yugoslavian," "I'm Kosovan" and the like, exactly like this. I say, "You are nuts. Those places are ours; you are my sibling. I haven't given away those places." Think of Palestine or anywhere up to Venice. I did not give my territories away in my heart. This is what the procedure requires. We are standing by.
> —Will we take them back one day? [the interviewer asks]
> —I want to, if I don't die.

The sense of ownership and the ambition to reclaim are, in Kadriye's worldview, connected to the morals of our time. In the following scene, the family have a picnic and Kadriye expresses in a high voice her ideas about women's honour, sexual indecency and the corrupted gender relations which to her stand out as the hallmark of the modern era: "Let me give these women some lessons in honour, OK? Those shameful women… Be decent!"[2] She moves on to reject homosexuality as sinful before returning to her views on lineage by outlining her own family's background:

> We really come from the Kayı tribes [that founded the Ottoman Empire]. … I proudly say, "I'm a granddaughter of the Ottomans; my grandfather was born in the Ottoman period. I'm the granddaughter of a grandfather who died in the first years of the Republic. Should I deny my ancestry now? These territories, these seas, this ground, this sky. All of them are mine."

Further on in the film, Nilhan Osmanoğlu Vatansever, one of the great-granddaughters of Sultan Abdülhamid II, introduces herself by saying, "I'm married. I have two children, Mehmet Vahdettin [the name of the last sultan] and Hanzade." With this, she sets a tone of traditional family values and bonds with the past. She has studied communication and business administration and is now the owner of the brand Nilhan Sultan which "transfers the seal of the past to the present day; the beauty, knowledge, science and culture to the present day and explains them to people." This combination of history, aesthetics and identity does not simply serve as a privileged position of interpreting an envisioned past; rather, the commodities offer a tangible link to the world of the sultans accessible for

---

[2] *Adam olsunlar* literally translates to "Be a man!" which refers to being a decent person.

those who can afford it. Her business includes a café and a store selling Ottoman-style souvenirs in a historic mansion in Istanbul.

Both women emphasise the glory of the Ottoman Empire and express a strong sense of connectedness with Ottoman history and culture, as well as sympathy for the imperial mode of governance, the latter reflected in Nilhan Osmanoğlu Vatansever's claim, "There is no such thing in life as absolute freedom." History is thus perceived in a deterministic mode and the future as a matter of rediscovery of bonds rather than visions of change. This kind of essentialism in the comprehension of the values of the past is recognisable in many facets of neo-Ottoman discourse in the cultural sphere. Being a descendant, an *Osmanlı torunu*, is fundamental to both women's way of presenting themselves and in both cases directly connected to a moral stance.

A Desirable Past, Homogeneous Fellowships and Fixed Roles

Although the two women come from very different social backgrounds, both are capable professionals and economically independent. Their extensive use of Ottoman imaginary in their self-definitions and means of communication raises the issue of the rhetorical effects gained from such historical references. While the portraits in this film perhaps are on the exceptional side, they nevertheless point to a recognisable form of argument wherein a personal narrative connects with a glorious long-term past. As this volume shows, the various agents constructing neo-Ottoman imaginaries instil a sense of ownership of history through an idiom inspired by trust in what is conceived as authentic when selectively claiming back segments of the past. The women's mode of communication is in many ways revealing: the metaphors, the ways of telling, the disciplining ambition, the commercial side and, not to forget, the vivid imaginaries. The latter serve as a reminder not to reduce neo-Ottoman trends merely to mass consumerism only. The popular indeed plays a crucial part, but the cases discussed in the chapters of this volume demonstrate that there are other modes of articulation. The boundaries between the popular and the exclusive appear to be as blurred as ever.

References to the Ottoman period in contemporary Turkey are not only frequently present in verbal communication, but also highly perceptible in visual manifestations and designs. Yet, as these are products of numerous agents active in diverse arenas, it is difficult to piece together the overall picture, while the employment of Ottoman imaginary as a favoured present past is often explicit, the objectives can most often remain obscure. Political and religious intentions vary, and popular culture takes many directions, as do the more elaborate Aesthetic programmes envisaged in architecture, design and life-style media. Even when limiting the analysis to the sphere of culture, neo-Ottomanism is a problematic concept to use beyond the descriptive level, with references to the occurrence of certain figurative expressions.

This volume presents gendered readings of cultural manifestations that relate to the Ottoman era as a preferred past and a model for the future. By means of claims of authenticity and the distribution of imaginaries of a homogenous heritage based on a pure religion, agents in the neo-Ottoman field construct a desirable alternative to everyday concerns, as well as invoking an imperial past at the national level. In this mode of thinking, shaped around a polarised worldview, Republican ideals serve as a counter-image to the promoted splendour and harmony of the Ottomans. Yet, the stereotypical gender roles inextricably linked with this neo-Ottoman imaginary remain largely unacknowledged, dissimulated in the construction of the desire of an idealised past. Our adaption of a cultural studies perspective in this volume puts special emphasis on agency, gender and authority. It provides a shared ground for the interrogation, through the contributions comprising this project of knowledge production about the past in light of what constitutes acceptable legitimacy in interpreting not only the canonical literature, but history at large. In her chapter in this volume, Nora Fisher-Onar presents a valuable overview of academic analyses of the politics of gender in Islamist discourses in the age of neoliberalism and with the necessary reflection over the discussions during the past decades.

Ottoman themes have been an essential part of the Islamist mobilisation since 1995, featuring with steadily increased intensity in the discourse animating them (Lord 2018a, 241–284; Arat and Pamuk 2019,125–129; Yavuz 2020, 144–178). After gaining governmental power in 2002, the ambition of the ruling Adalet ve Kalkınma Partisi (Justice and Development Party, hereafter AKP) has been to distance the country from Republican historiography and to formulate an alternative and more homogeneous past—a goal that increased in prominence after the elections in 2007 (Fisher-Onar 2018; Göçek 2018). This cultural policy was implemented through extensive state sponsoring of large-scale projects as well as the government's ideological involvement in educational institutions (Lüküslü 2016). The AKP's cultural programme emphasises that the party will "make the greatest effort in the field of conserving and developing national values" and claims that a true modern cultural atmosphere can be created by "preserving the essential structure and style of our culture" and supporting the party's interactions with universal values (Yavuz 2020, 162–166).[3] It is a telling example of the recurring tension between what is defined as nationally specific and the universal Islamic ideals. Relating to a multi-cultural and multi-religious past has, however, been a complicated matter. Or rather a question of silence. As Ceren Lord (2018a, 241) remarks in her book on religious politics in Turkey, "the religious majoritarianism of the state involving the elevation of Sunni Muslim Turks as the base of the nation-state" has made Muslim diversity less visible and practically marginalised the lives of other denominations.

In the context of the present volume, neo-Ottomanism is regarded as an umbrella term to which the chapters relate in different ways and with different chronologies. *Neo-Ottoman Imaginaries in Contemporary Turkey* does not address the contested use of the term in foreign politics discussions on the ambitions of Turkish leadership in the Muslim world, the involvement in South-East European politics or Turkey's role in the Syrian conflict. This collection of analyses of the neo-Ottoman currents in contemporary Turkey largely focus on the phenomenon in terms of social-conservative political ideology and cultural and historical policies formulated by the ruling AKP. Discussions about the place and use of neo-Ottoman references in popular media are also on the rise, especially after the international success of the TV series *Magnificent Century*. These chapters, however, have been collected with the ambition to understand neo-Ottomanism not solely as relating to constructions by the Turkish state, but, rather, to emphasise that connected processes also work in other realms of life. Thus, the volume offers examinations of cultural manifestations within neo-Ottoman trends with a specific emphasis on their gendered features. It analyses how these imaginaries envision ideal life-styles, taste and knowledge production, and the resulting impact on Turkish society. The chapters highlight the articulation of Ottoman visions by actors in the Turkish media-scape, art world and museums. With this, the authors move away from regarding neo-Ottomanism as only ideological

---

[3] AK Parti Programı, https://www.akparti.org.tr/parti/parti-programi/. Accessed on 30 April 2021

governance, and open discussions about creativity in which high and low culture are not always distinguishable entities. The result is eleven chapters that explore the ambitions of a variety of actors and investigate the conditions for individual as well as collective agency. The chapters include analyses of architecture, uses of public space and media, ritual events, post-truth in science, minority politics, memorialisation of the near and more distant past, museum cultures and heritage claims.

Several variations of the expression "neo-Ottomanism" have been introduced in the academic literature over the past decade that shed light on the phenomenon, all based on dissatisfaction with the term's ungainly character and having the objective of indicating the variation in the form and content of a many-sided history culture. The problematic suffix "-ism" evokes ideology and policy making, which are undoubtedly at the core of the matter, but overshadows the many other ways in which the Ottoman paradigm is promoted. The bulk of the literature on Turkish neo-Ottomanism deals with actualised and failed foreign politics moves. There are also a number of important studies of the cultural aspects of the neo-Ottoman trends, ranging from analyses of the political to the aesthetic. Some contributions have been pivotal for this introduction and for the following chapters and should therefore receive special mention.

In *Nostalgia for the Empire: The Politics of Neo-Ottomanism*, Hakan Yavuz provides a full section on literary and artistic expressions that carry the counter-identity ideals significant for neo-Ottoman nostalgia (2020, 68–106). Taking his examples from writers as varied as Yahya Kemal, Ahmed Hamdi Tanpınar and Orhan Pamuk,[4] the author discusses how the Ottoman world has been presented in Turkish literature, albeit transposed to new eras. Yavuz notes in his chapters on the political application of neo-Ottomanism that references to a glorious past have even been activated in attempts to overcome the deep ethnic conflicts in the country. He further examines how the Islamic element in President Erdoğan's political programme has evolved and Islamic heritage has been positioned as the foundation of the nation (2020, 156–166), quoting one of Erdoğan's early addresses: "Presiding over the heritage of our ancestors, the Ottoman State that ruled the world for 600 years, we will revive the Ottoman consciousness again" (2020, 155). The president's personal attachment to the sultans plays a crucial role in Yavuz' analysis. Abdülhamid II in particular stands out in the interpretation by Necip Fazıl Kısakürek (1904–1983),

[4] A theme developed at length by Johanna Chovanec (2021).

one of the chief ideological inspirations for the revivalist thought of a future Islamic government, who called attention to this sultan as the model pious leader who defended the Muslim world against Western influences (2020, 146–155). Abdülhamid II is also the main character in the highly controversial TV series *Payitaht* (meaning "The Capital" 2017–2021, but distributed with the English title *The Last Emperor*), one nevertheless commended by Erdoğan. As this production addresses a historical period that is closer in time than other major contemporary Ottoman series, depicting the decades prior to World War I, the "enemies" are more easily translated into the present day: Westernists, Zionists and secularists.

Ceren Lord's contributions to the examination of the roots and routes of Islamist mobilisation in Turkey avoid any simplistic dichotomies between the secular and the Islamic (2017, 2018a, b). Rather than specifically focusing on neo-Ottomanism, her interest is directed more generally toward the uses of history; thus, she points to the role of nationalism as a driving force among groups with diverse agendas. Her comprehensive study, *Religious Politics in Turkey. From the Birth of the Republic to the AKP* (2018a), examines the great variety within the category conventionally labelled "the Islamists". Lord follows the development of the AKP as a religio-political movement which she characterises as practising "a type of identity politics geared toward political action" (2018a, 5), thereby navigating away from any Turkish exceptionalism and equating references to Islam and historical imaginaries with evolving authoritarianism in Europe and globally. Lord's arguments open a fruitful discussion about how Turkish Islamists connect to Turkey's Ottoman roots in terms of theological and ideological positions, as well as being part of a contemporary global wave of authoritarianism seeking legitimacy in the authentic, pure and unalloyed.

In 2016 Stefano Taglia edited a special issue of *Die Welt des Islams*, "Ottomanism Then and Now: Historical and Contemporary Meanings," which combines analyses of past and present Ottomanisms. Taglia underlines that from the last decades of the nineteenth century Ottomanism comprised a critique of state-initiated reform ambitions with transnational implications, positioned on an Islamic foundation that gave the sultan his legitimacy. It was, despite the many thematic similarities, a diverse elitist and intellectual project far from today's populism, using quite another spectrum of communicative means.

Finally, on a related, methodological note, Jeremy F. Walton, dissatisfied with memory as an analytical concept, edited a special issue of *History and Anthropology* that "approaches memory as a medium and discourse that embodies and entails the effects of past powers" (2019, 355). Taking his point of departure in the work of Walter Benjamin, Walton argues in favour of "textured historicity," a term which can encompass an ambivalent span of emotions and attitudes.

These studies, as well as the chapters in this volume, all in their own way present cases from the neo-Ottoman sphere and identify a semantic field of concepts that recur in art, popular culture, political discourse and media: Islamic symbols blended with references to loss, home, authenticity, return, rebuilding, remembrance, safety, purity, splendour and the legitimacy of worldly and religious authorities. Such concepts can be connected to notions of historical imagery and nostalgia and have proven to be most efficient tools in public communication.

Based on fieldwork in the 1990s, two anthropological studies paved new ways in the academic discussions about Turkish history cultures and the transformation of collective memory in local life; both of them with a keen eye on the ritualisation of historic events and everyday life as a battleground for ideological conflicts. In *Faces of the State* (2002) Yael Navaro-Yashin discusses "state phantasies" as an umbrella term for the Kemalistic efforts to implement narratives and rituals for unifying identities. An important part of this study focuses on cultural politics as means of exclusion as well as creativity which resonates well with the chapters in this volume. Esra Özyürek, in her *Nostalgia for the Modern* (2006), investigates the growing tensions between state secularism and Islamism in the transformation of what narratives were successful in the early AKP era in terms of mobilisation, identity construction and appealing imaginaries. The force of the historic visions in the Islamic movement(s) soon became an emerging theme in following academic studies.

For example, Defne Karaosmanoglu (2010) speaks of the neo-Ottomanism of "Ottomanness" to underline the construction of belonging when indicating how references to "authentic Islam" are formulated. This provides an important reflection on how new spatial forms are constructed to include—rather than exclude, as one might initially think—on nationalistic, rather than religious common ground (2010, 287–288). She illustrates this with a discussion of publicly funded nostalgia spaces for Ramadan festivities in Istanbul in which commodification has played an equally large part as practiced piety. The visions inherent in these spaces of nostalgia were carried forward by the grand scale of the celebrations, which turned out to be more attractive than the ideological thinking of political Islam. Karaosmanoglu concludes by regarding them as shared ground whereby, as she put it, "a utopian future is inscribed through an imagined past"—although a past not necessarily associated with the sphere of religion, but, rather, with general sentiments toward national history. Her observations from a decade ago are important as they point to the risk of interpreting discourses comprising strong Islamic rhetoric as essentially religious when their background in commercial and national interest is as significant.

In his investigation of the long-term evolution of the concept, Hakan Ö. Ongur (2015) argues in favour of the plural form, "Ottomanisms", to encompass the variety of ideological, theological and cultural stands taken since the late nineteenth century. Ongur's emphasis on the contextualisation of the usage of the term opens a discussion about analytical specifications: whether neo-Ottomanism and its equivalents refer to a distinct set of ideas or are better described as discursive trends with significant impact on practice and material representations. In both cases, historicising the concept clearly demonstrates its heterogeneous background, often springing from revivalist ambitions in conflict with one another. Alp Eren Topal (2021) argues from a conceptual history perspective in the same direction and debates even the use of the term Ottomanism in historical studies.

Murat Ergin and Yağmur Karakaya's differentiation between "neo-Ottomanism" and "Ottomania" also indicates a need to distinguish between discussions about ideology on the one hand and developments in popular culture on the other (2017). In their chapter in the present volume this discussion is further developed to problematise the border between mainstream culture and what are supposed to be expressions of more subtle aesthetic programmes. Obviously, they do not claim to identify such a border either, but the dynamics in popular culture and the uses of Ottoman tropes are clearly contextualised and the creative side of neo-Ottoman trends are recognised. Instead of taking Islamic rhetoric at face value, Ergin and Karakaya point to wider connections where Turkish social-conservatism, neo-liberalism and nationalism have been implemented with the help of Islamic rhetorical visions of the past. Taken together, this blend operates as a connecting link to ensure possible centre-right support in the political arena.

Chien Yang Erdem argues in a similar direction when introducing "Ottomentality" as a form of governmentality and a term for the new developments in contemporary Turkey taking place in the border zone between politics, consumption culture and religion (2017, 718–720.). The changes in neo-Ottoman trends over the past ten years become apparent when comparing Karaosmanoglu's emphasis on nationalistic elements (that are still very much there) with Yang Erdem's point that neo-liberal and social-conservative rationalities converge with shared references to Islam. These allusions to Islamic culture are not religious in the conventional sense, but refer to a set of images that indicate assumptions of shared norms, fellowship and a history to look back on. According to Yang Erdem, from this follows an emphasis on the production of knowledge in a Foucauldian sense: the power to govern what is generally accepted as truth. For the central Islamic administration as well as its local staff, there is a certain challenge to tying the traditional Medina model—based on interpretations of canonical texts, with universal moral ideals to endeavour to attain—to Ottoman imaginaries. The multi-religious character of the empire remains problematic to these homogenising interpretations. Our use of the term "cultural neo-Ottomanism" in this introductory chapter does not signify the ambition to promote yet another term, but is intended to underline that the point of departure for the chapters in this volume is a keen interest in agents, practices and modes of communication—or, in short, how neo-Ottomanism is mediated in various modes and with various objectives. Yang Erdem argues that such a large-scale project is a matter of governmentality, namely, "the multiple and intersecting political rationalities, strategies and policies of cultural governance" (2017, 724). Yet Ottomentality does not exclude the operational involvement of commercial, religious and private agents. On the contrary, these actors contribute to this process and produce "tangible practices and objects that are commodified and consumed as commercial products in everyday life" (Yang Erdem 2017, 717).

Imaginaries of a Future Past

The term "imaginaries" is here used in the plural in order to emphasise that cultural references to an Ottoman past subsume a broad scope of narratives, norms and codes that embrace the Ottoman era as a shared background, although seldom with more exact periodisation and with Muslim identities taken for granted. In the subtext of these imaginaries lie tools for inclusion and exclusion that call for investigations of the rationalities of governance and dominating discourses. By displaying pictures of a heritage ventured for consumption and on claims authenticity, these figures construct a sense of inclusion for larger groups through narratives of luxury, military success and an ordered society. All this is in marked contrast to the everyday life of most people. Therefore, issues of transmission and communication are at the core of several of the chapters in the volume. Certainly, such an ideological current could not have such enduring influence on the general public without powerful depictions. The impact is reinforced by the desires for glory, prestige and authority induced in the consumers. Consequently, the embedded gender constructions are manifested in preferred masculinities and femininities.

Cultural neo-Ottomanism in its many facets can be regarded as an example of what Svetlana Boym has termed "restorative nostalgia" (2001), a longing for a lost home that can be successfully constructed with claims of absolute truth and tradition. Boym writes, "The past is not supposed to reveal any signs of decay; it has to be 'freshly painted' in its 'original image' and remain eternally young" (2001, 49). Nationalist and religious revivalists utilise nostalgia as an important element of their appeal and tend to benefit from conspiracy theories. Restorative nostalgia is, for example, an essential part of the remembrance activities constructed by Turkish Islamists to provide shelter, safe space and stability in the disorder of the contemporary world, thereby promoting a sense of belonging among those who are willing to share the same imaginary.

Many creative agents of cultural neo-Ottomanism have effectively constructed a notion of an Ottoman home which includes a vision of a traditional family, gender roles and life style: a set of customs and traditions which are embedded in religious practices. Moreover, this home becomes the lens through which to see and comprehend contemporary Turkey and the world. Heritage, as François Hartog suggests,

> makes visible and expresses a certain order of time, in which the dimension of the past is the most important. More precisely, it is a past that the present cannot or does not want to relinquish entirely, whether the bond to it takes the form of celebration, imitation, banishment, reflected glory, or, simply, the possibility of visiting it. (2015, 152)

Thus, its "visible embodiment is important for the present," Hartog continues. By underlining the cultural aspects of neo-Ottomanism, we suggest that the politics of Ottoman heritage dominate by framing the heritage as Turkish, Islamic, victorious and glamorous; such a worldview reinforces attempts to create social cohesion based on references to Ottoman society. Visual expressions play a vital role in the communication of Ottoman ideals and the aesthetic preferences promoted are transforming cityscapes in urban areas. Ayşe Öncü has illustrated how Ottoman heritage was communicated by Istanbul's AKP-governed municipality through a number of initiatives: the celebration of "the tulip year" in 2006, inspired by the Tulip Era; the Miniatürk Museum which displays replicas of monuments in Turkish and Ottoman history; the organisation of Ramadan fairs as proper cultural activities for families; and the dissemination of narratives of a peaceful multi-cultural past (Öncü 2010). Meanwhile, a similar urban policy was being pursued in Ankara with the construction of a grandiose theme park Wonderland Eurasia (Tunc and Tunc 2020) and urban regeneration of the historic district Hamamönü (Onur 2022). Drawing attention to the Turco-Islamic definition of the Ottoman heritage by the AKP regime, Edhem Eldem also underlines that there has been a "re-Ottomanization of the country starting with the former imperial capital, Istanbul," not with historical accuracy in mind, but by "retro-projecting the values of a nation-state to a multi-ethnic empire" (Eldem 2015, 87). Kalaycı (2021) discusses the interconnections between how the AKP uses its political and economic power to diffuse neo-Ottoman ideology into Turkish football through stadium projects, renaming and founding teams and fan clubs.[5] Conquest fests and re-enactments of the conquest of the city were the high points of the trend until 2020 when the Hagia Sophia Museum was converted into a mosque in a clear rejection of the building's Christian history. This shift in attitude toward anything outside Sunni Orthodoxy has been noted by several scholars (Lord 2017, 2018b) and is an illustration of what Nora Fisher-Onar has termed civilisational nationalism, which she defines as "a form of cultural nationalism which invokes an imagined imperial golden age of religious and racial purity" (Fisher-Onar 2021, 388).

Religion, Heritage and Belonging

References to Islam in the neo-Ottoman discourse are both obvious and difficult to pinpoint as these currents cover areas at very different scales: from national politics and ideological concepts to individual engagement,

---

[5] For another discussion on football, nationalism and Islamic authoritarianism in contemporary Turkey, see Evren (2022).

with all the possibilities of public space in between. It can be tempting to regard these references to religion only as a means of ideological hammering without further identifying the spaces for commitment beyond the political. Islamic allusions play a crucial role in both recent and historical Ottoman visions (Ongur 2015), although not necessarily in terms of religious practices or theological doctrines. Rather, they have provided the material for cultural goals. Many studies have analysed Islam as a trope in nationalistic discourses, identity politics and as a key rhetorical tool when mobilising (Lord 2018a), but—as pointed out in this volume by Petek Onur and Torsten Janson—there is an engagement in the consumption of Ottoman imaginaries beyond governmental initiatives in the lives of individuals.

The adherents of the AKP's cultural politics have made use of an Ottoman past in a multiplicity of configurations that have appealed to diverse groups embracing an Islamic past. This usage has highlighted that there are players on the neo-Ottoman scene other than the party. As discussed above, aesthetic creativity in the 2020s and the many channels for popular culture are effectively employed in the transmission of historical tropes, with two themes dominating academic discussions on neo-Ottomanism: ideological aspects on the one hand and popular culture and consumerism on the other. These two trajectories extend to how Islam and Muslim life is perceived and expected to be conducted.

The conversion of the Kariye Museum (formerly the Chora Church) into a mosque in 2019 and discussions about the intentional dilapidation of Byzantine churches in places like Trabzon and Izmir paved the way for strong reactions both in and outside Turkey when Hagia Sophia was declared a mosque. Hardly a recent issue, the status of Hagia Sophia (a museum since 1934 and made a UNESCO world heritage site in 1985) has been a theme in nationalistic discourse throughout the Republican era. It was, therefore, more of the fulfilment of a long-term campaign promise than a surprise when President Erdoğan formalised a decree to let domestic politics develop into foreign policy, with momentous implications, as also discussed in Kerem Öktem's chapter.

The chain of events in July 2020 was a cautiously staged process from decision making to the return of Muslim prayers at the historical site. The museum status of Hagia Sophia was first annulled by court decision that made it possible for President Erdoğan to place the premises under the legislation of Diyanet (Eldem 2021; Sofos 2021; Yosmaoğlu 2021). On Friday, 24 July, Erdoğan participated in the Friday prayer that manifested the changed status of the building which Spyros Sofos has discussed in terms of "the emotional topography of populism" (Sofos 2021, cf. Sofos 2022). Led by the president of Diyanet, Ali Erbaş, the prayer attracted large crowds that filled the courtyard and adjoining streets; many of the participants carried Turkish and Ottoman flags; nationalist symbols appeared on t-shirts, badges and placards. The Ottoman references operating during the event were further emphasised when Ali Erbaş climbed the stairs of the pulpit for his sermon with an Ottoman sword in his hand: the core symbol at the inauguration ceremony of the sultans and an allusion to the founder of the Ottoman dynasty, Osman. In order to accentuate the Ottoman allusions, Erdoğan continued after the service to visit the tomb (*türbe*) of Mehmet the Conqueror at the mosque that bears his name, the Fatih Mosque. On site, Erdoğan proclaimed Mehmet "the real owner" of Hagia Sophia.

The significance of the event was not only visible in the massive presence of Ottoman symbols and the invisibility of the Christian history of the place, but in the exaggerated mode of communication, which was not substantially different from Islamo-national discourse in general, but even more aggressive in its rhetoric. Words, acts and visual representations spoke of victory, conquest and reconnection to (parts of) earlier history. The issue of rightful ownership was the central theme and embedded in a tone of combat. The crowds outside represented more than attendance at a Friday prayer; the gathering had a character that was equally celebration and demonstration. The forceful emotional involvement linked to the martial tone of the communication inside the now mosque. It was a highly male business. Furthermore, by choosing to visit the *türbe* as a finale to this public manifestation, Erdoğan connected very directly to Ottoman ritual practices when Sufi saints, sultans and war heroes defending Islam (*gazi*) were venerated at their tombs. President Erdoğan hereby stood out as an heir to the sultans and the *gazi*s and a man who had rightfully recaptured what had been lost: a demonstration of restorative nostalgia in Boym's vocabulary and an effective marker of diverging stands on historical matters in Turkish society.

Islamist understandings of the Ottoman era dominate popular conceptualisations of the past, but they are not without competitors (Akturk 2009; Barkey 2012). How to relate to a multi-cultural and multi-religious past has, however, remained a complicated matter, difficult to integrate into the Islamic vision and one confined to silence. The Ottoman Empire was diverse not only in terms of ethnicities and denominations. The varied regional conditions, the social differentiation within local communities, the contrasts between life in urban areas and that in small towns and rural regions were considerable, as were the differences in what were conceived as Muslim traditions. This, in combination with the possibilities for social mobility, made encounters and cooperation inevitable. Under the present Sunni hegemony, the situation works differently: where some find arguments in favour of diversity, others espouse a vision of homogeneity.

Since its establishment in 1924, the Presidency of Religious Affairs (Diyanet İşleri Başkanlığı, hereafter Diyanet) has been the major agent establishing and guarding Sunni orthodoxy in the Republic as the singular line of interpreting Islam (Gözaydın 2006; Öztürk 2016, 2018; Lord 2017, 2018a, 92–102, 111–126, 2018b; Mutluer 2018; Adak 2020). This homogenisation has been systematically implemented marginalising and supressing differences within the Turkish Muslim communities. Large groups like the Alevis and to some extent the traditional Sufi orders, as well as the neo-Sufi orders, have been denied official recognition. Through its theological clergy (*ulema*)—functioning as civil servants, employed on their theological credentials—Diyanet has for long influenced the standard understanding of religion by means of its publications, weekly distributed sermons and the advice provided by its Department of Legal Consultancy (Öztürk 2016, 2018; Lord 2017, 2018b; Akturk 2018)— and the image of the Ottoman era as multi-religious or even marked with Muslim variation has never been a prominent trope in its history writing. Diyanet's conformist ambitions also have been working through its appointment of imams and the control it has over local mosques. In recent decades the conditions for its work have radically changed. Its budget and institutional domains have significantly expanded and Diyanet has gradually become tied to the legitimation of the nationalist and Islamist policies of the AKP governments thus occupying an important position in the development of contemporary neo-Ottoman discourses.

Throughout the heterogeneous media flow of Ottoman imaginaries, there are strong claims of authenticity striving to offer reconnections to what is conceived to be a Muslim past accessible to all "true" Turks (Karaosmanoglu 2010, 287, 290). This kind of restorative nostalgia serves as a tool to identify contemporary flaws and wrongs as well as making religion the foremost identity marker. With the exception of cases such as the ones provided in Torsten Janson's chapter, the popular imagery of Ottoman life only to a limited extent includes detailed depictions of religious practices. Rather, under an umbrella of a nationalist conservative perception of what it means to be a Turkish Muslim, these images are projected through a modern lens of religious understanding (Lord 2018a).

As discussed in several of the chapters of this volume, the multi-ethnic and multi-religious character of Ottoman society is a disturbing fact to many supporters of neo-Ottoman ideals. With urban trading centres hosting citizens and visitors of different denominations dotted around the empire, meeting grounds between ethnicities and religious groups were inevitable. The empire's non-Muslim citizens were organised in nations (*millet*), in what Karen Barkey phrases "the management of diversity" (2012); by regulating religious communities, although recognising far from all groups, the state could maintain governance. The *millet* administration has a complicated history. Despite only being used for a limited time, the concept has become central in a significant segment of academic discourse and has come to underline the perception of strict separations of homogeneous Ottoman religious communities.

The *millet* system as a trope takes a prominent place in neo-Ottoman visions of a "natural" order when it comes to the position of minorities in contemporary Turkey. Views on Ottoman diversity are perhaps a point where neo-Ottomanism with Islamist inclinations can be distinguished from a more or less conservative inclination for the past more broadly. Sener Aktürk has pointed to the lingering importance of Sunni Islam as essential to national identity throughout the history of the Turkish Republic and how the organisation of religious communities came to mean the nation in modern Turkey (2009; cf. Lord 2018a; Yavuz 2020; Topal 2021). The concept, along with its essentialist and fixed understanding of religious belonging, is adopted by Islamists in their arguments in favour of clear-cut borders between religious communities, as also discussed in Özgür Kaymak's chapter. Today, for some ideologists, dealing with Islamic diversity is perhaps more problematic than countenancing the presence of non-Muslim groups.

The vision of an era when Islamic institutions enjoyed authority at all levels of society for the majority of the population offers an essentialist view of religion, where identity is inborn and not a matter of choice. The wish for distinct borders between different religious communities—which diverges markedly from contemporary Turkish legislation or historical realities—is not so much a question of the organisation of everyday life and civil matters, but, rather, the conceptualisation of religious communities as homogenous and easily defined. Differences within communities are of no interest from this perspective. Furthermore, and perhaps more importantly, belonging to such imaginary *millet* communities is regarded as unalterable and defines an individual. The contrast with contemporary hybrid identities is striking. Once born into a *millet*, according to the Islamist perception, the individual is positioned within the community's internal hierarchies, with little or no space to define individual conceptions of what it means to be an Istanbul Jew or a Kurdish Sunni Muslim. Nor, according to such visions of *millet* life, is it possible to change identities or cherish multiple identities; conceptualisations of the *millet* system only envision broad units of recognised religious groups.

The link between neo-Ottoman trends and Islam is obvious yet elusive. The claims of authenticity, with their references to an Islamic past, are powerful rhetorical means, but hard to apply on contemporary living conditions. Instead, conservative and national understandings of religion as the core of individual and collective identities prevail.

Gender During the AKP Regime

Neo-Ottoman discourses not only frame Turkish history and culture as pioneering elements in the history of Islam, they also highlight the patriarchal power of the sultans, legitimised by their status as caliphs, leaders of the Islamic world. The unquestionable authority of the male sovereign invested with the glory of military victories and conquests constructs a model for hypermasculinity affirmed by history, religion and traditions. Such an ideal has become desired and normalised and is a widely accepted way of being a man in contemporary Turkey. In parallel, a model for womanhood is defined by acceptance of male privilege along with the limitations of women's role as mothers and spouses. Defining gender within such a framework has meant that neo-Ottoman imaginaries have increasing impact on gender policies under AKP governance—and the status of women in Turkey has not improved. This turned out to be part of strategic moves to evade the notion of gender equality and replace it with gender justice, as discussed in Eslen-Ziya's chapter.

Neo-Ottoman nostalgia defines women's primary place as the domestic sphere. Thus, a gradual decrease in women's representation, presence and power in public life—most significantly in the fields of law and governance—has become apparent. This nostalgia moots the sphere of the home as the harem of the sultan and, motivated by the consumption of Ottoman fashion and design, women are offered a sense of satisfaction, self-indulgence and pride in this idealised and aestheticised segregation, as

Onur shows in her chapter. Consumption is a sphere where the ideas and imaginaries of Ottoman history are put into practice through tangible objects in everyday life, as well as ceremonial events and celebrations. The phenomenon of Islamic fashion has been part of many pious urban women's lives since the 1990s, during which time the Islamic fashion industry has evolved from a small market with a few companies into a large sector which offers modest fashion in a wide range of tastes, styles and preferences. The heyday of neo-Ottoman cultural trends inspired this sector to adopt Ottoman clothes and symbols. The *ferace* (a long dress which women used to wear when they went out) in casual outfits and the kaftan in festive clothing (see Onur's chapter) have become prominent pieces. The signatures of sultans, views of Istanbul and the palaces, golden tones and numerous other iconic symbols started to be widely printed or embroidered on scarves, clothes and accessories.[6]

However, modest fashion is only a part of the world of consumption where this trend may be observed. As Akçaoğlu (2020 [2018]) and Alimen (2018) show, for the newly emerging Islamic upper-middle class, having elegant and distinctive taste which is also religiously acceptable and displaying it through their lifestyles, particularly their home and office decor, have become increasingly important. Islamic fashion and lifestyle magazines offer guidelines and have become highly influential among the newly rich Islamic upper class and the lower classes which aspire to the same upward mobility. As well as adherence to Turco-Islamic values, nostalgic and glamorous references to the Ottoman era have become symbols of status.

While domestic spaces and daily life were being redesigned with touches of neo-Ottoman nostalgia and imageries of harem life, urban spaces have also been under major transformation. The public space policy of the AKP governments started to become a strategy to counter Republican architectural symbols and create an urban habitus for the Islamist way of life (Batuman 2018). As Batuman and Öktem discuss in this volume, numerous mosques, state buildings and emblematic squares and other public spaces in Ankara and Istanbul have been have been erected in a short period and with substantial impact on the cityscapes. Or are suggested as part of reconstruction plans. The Ottoman-Seljuk style is not only

---

[6] Based on the data from Petek Onur's ongoing research project "Gendered Nostalgia: Neo-Ottomanism in Islamist Women's Media in Turkey" funded by H2020-MSCA-IF-2019.

prevalent in state projects but widely adopted in other sectors, such as new residential areas and tourism enterprises. The Ottoman home, imagined by AKP governance to have been lost with the Republican era, is to be rebuilt. The grandiose constructions evoke emotional connections with the imperial past and sultan ancestors and create a public memory (Tokdoğan 2019, 167–220; Çınar 2020, 92–95). Walton also draws attention to the recent attempts of the AKP governments and Erdoğan to unify Istanbul. Hereby aiming to homogenise its identity by erasing its multicultural, fragmented, heterogeneous heritage and memory (Walton 2021). However, with an intentional exclusionary attitude, the decisions for these major transformations and constructions are made without the involvement of civil society and most of the time against the will of a large part of the country's inhabitants as well as diaspora. Furthermore, they are unsuccessful in building public spaces that are safe and easily accessible for women, non-Muslims, ethnic minorities and other disadvantaged groups; therefore, they are not meaningful and fail to generate a sense of belonging.

Back in 2002, lifting the headscarf ban in public spaces was among the election promises of the newly founded AKP. The ban, which prevented women state employees from wearing a headscarf when on duty and women university students when on campus, was a long-term dividing line in Turkish society. It reached its turning point when Erdoğan, then Prime Minister, fulfilled his promise on 3 October 2013, eleven years after he came to power. To Erdoğan, this was the end of a dark time, "a step towards normalization,"[7] and toward increased professional opportunities for women, along with full access to higher education. In the meantime, the plain *tesettür* clothing of the 1980s and early 1990s had given way to a colourful and diversified world of modest fashion offering stylish solutions to the participation of veiled women in public life. The discussions about veiled women being victims of the strict secular regime were gradually replaced by discussions of boundaries of religiously appropriate and acceptable veiling (Sandıkçı and Ger 2010; Alimen 2018; Sayan-Cengiz 2018).

The transformation of state institutions responsible for women's issues and gender equality is yet another significant indicator of the AKP approach to gender in Turkey. For twenty years (1991–2011), the Ministry

---

[7] *Aljazeera*, "Turkey Lifts Decades Old Ban on Headscarves" https://www.aljazeera.com/news/2013/10/8/turkey-lifts-decades-old-ban-on-headscarves, Accessed on 4 November 2020.

of State for Women and Family was expected to develop gender policies and gender equality, but was replaced by the Ministry of Family and Social Policy in the years 2011–2018. President Erdoğan explained the institutional change by saying, "We are a conservative democratic party. It is the family that is important to us."[8] In 2018 this administrative body was transformed into the Ministry of Family, Labour and Social Services and women's issues are currently the responsibility of the ministry's special General Directorate of Woman's Status.[9] The shrinking administrative structure signifies both the decreasing importance attributed to the problems of women's empowerment and equal rights and the increasing emphasis on prioritising family over women, family being defined on the basis of Turkish and Islamic traditions and values. In addition to the ministry, Diyanet started to take a more active role in gender and family issues by reaching out to women and youth via its Family and Religious Guidance Bureaus and female preachers in the field. These endeavours certainly take their references for women's roles as mothers and wives from those defined by Sunni Islam (Yilmaz 2015, 2017; Kocamaner 2017, 2018; Adak 2020, 5).

What concerns and priorities characterise the last decade of gender policies and government discourse in Turkey? Forming heterosexual, religious, nationalist, patriarchal families which also involve a pronatalist ethics, and defining women's status within this family, are the clearly expressed missions of the party, particularly since 2011, a year which marks the authoritarian turn in the political sphere (Cindoglu and Unal 2017). In the following years statements by Erdoğan, high-ranking state officials, AKP members and the coalition partner, the Nationalist Movement Party (Milliyetçi Hareket Partisi, MHP), regarding the control of women's sexuality, women's rights and violence against women, which had drastically increased, should be understood within this framework. Prominent figures of radical Islamist and nationalist groups support and contribute to the discourse and even, in some cases, criticise it because they find it too moderate or Western. Turkey was the first country to sign The Council of Europe Convention on Preventing and Combating Violence against

---

[8] *Bianet*, "Kadın Bakanlığı Kaldırıldı, Kadın Örgütleri Öfkeli" https://bianet.org/bianet/kadin/130585-kadin-bakanligi-kaldirildi-kadin-orgutleri-ofkeli. Accessed on 25 May 2021.

[9] On 21 April 2021, with a presidency decree, the ministry was changed into The Ministry of Family and Social Service. For the whole history, see Aile ve Sosyal Hizmetler Bakanlığı "Tarihçe" https://www.aile.gov.tr/bakanlik/hakkinda/tarihce/. Accessed on 30 April 2021.

Women and Domestic Violence, widely known as the Istanbul Convention, in 2011; yet, less than a decade later there was wide public debate, initiated by Erdoğan, about the country's withdrawal, using the argument that it targets traditional Turkish family structure. In the end, Turkey withdrew by presidential decree on 19 March 2021.

Erdoğan, in response to Abdurrahman Dilipak, a radical Islamist columnist who insulted the Woman and Democracy Association (*Kadın ve Demokrasi Derneği*, KADEM) for their support for the Istanbul Convention, stated:

> I believe that we have sufficient potential to create original and free texts which exalt humans and human honour, put family in the centre and are suitable for our social texture. Instead of translated texts now we need to determine our own framework. Instead of saying Copenhagen Criteria, we will say Ankara Criteria and pursue our way. I think that the last discussion is deliberately fuelled. If the ones who fan the flame think that we will take even one step back from the struggle against violence against women and providing human rights for women, they should know that they will be disappointed. I believe that we will put out this fire of instigation.[10]

This statement also openly opposes the EU accession criteria known as the Copenhagen Criteria and reveals a change in direction away from the EU membership process, which also delineates a roadmap for achieving equality on the basis of universal human rights for candidate states. Yet, despite the promises and the official statements, no progress has been made toward preventing male violence and establishing gender equality in the country.[11]

The shift from the aim of establishing gender equality to providing gender justice for women at the discursive and institutional level was made possible by several factors. Firstly, KADEM, one of its founders being Erdoğan's daughter Sümeyye Erdoğan Bayraktar (discussed by Eslen-Ziya, this volume), encourages civil societal and academic discourse by disseminating the term, especially through its organisation of annual

---

[10] *Haber 7*, "Erdoğan'ın Sözlerinin Perde Arkası Ortaya Çıktı! Bazı Maddeler Değişiyor", https://www.haber7.com/guncel/haber/3004137-erdoganin-sozlerinin-perde-arkasi--ortaya-cikti-bazi-maddeler-degisiyor Accessed on 10 November 2020.

[11] According to the 2020 Global Gender Gap Index of World Economic Forum Turkey's rank among 153 countries is 130. http://www3.weforum.org/docs/WEF_GGGR_2020.pdf Accessed on 10 November 2020.

gender justice conferences.[12] Secondly, educational policy has a conservative agenda to raise a religious generation in terms of representations of traditional gender roles and the stereotypes in text books, increasing the number of imam-hatip high schools, expanding the place of religious education in schools and opening a women's university in 2021.[13] Thirdly, women's gains under the civil code and penal code have been under continuous attack by claims of the negative impact of empowering women on increasing divorce rates and detrimental changes in the traditional Turkish family (Kandiyoti 2019, 90). These factors work simultaneously to define and legitimise women's and men's gender roles according to their nature (*fıtrat*), Islam and the postulated authentic Turkish culture. Further, and more important, the changes and issues discussed above should be seen as being in direct opposition to the secular principles that guide women's emancipation in the Republican regime founded by Atatürk. The mission of creating a new gender ideology that aims to rebuild the ties with pre-Republican history, identity and culture seems to be the intersection point of all these endeavours. In the final chapter Nora Fisher-Onar provides an overview of how all these symbolic acts of AKP governments can be understood in relation to the women question in Turkey in the light of gender studies discourse and the roots and transformation of Ottomanist nostalgia.

COMMUNICATING HERITAGE AND HISTORY, BUILDING IDENTITIES

The impact of neo-Ottomanism would not be so widespread without being creatively transmitted in various media, among which television has been the leading medium. As Çelik clearly demonstrates, television still has the primary role in Erdoğan's retention of power and the support of

---

[12] KADEM, https://kadem.org.tr/zirve-ve-kongreler/uluslararasi-toplumsal-cinsiyet-adaleti-kongresi/. Accessed on 11 November 2020.

[13] The decision to open a women's university is announced in the 2021 Annual Plans of the Presidency: Türkiye Cumhuriyeti Cumhurbaşkanlığı Strateji ve Bütçe Başkanlığı (2020) *2021 Yılı Cumhurbaşkanlığı Yıllık Programı*, 272.

the voters of the AKP (Çelik 2020).[14] Due to the conglomerations in the AKP period, the mainstream television channels and print media are owned by pro-AKP business groups and mostly constitute a univocal choir of party propaganda, particularly the news and debate shows. Besides, the state's strict control and censorship have weakened, if not silenced, alternative voices and discourses in Turkey, thus facilitating the post-truth communications of the party. The leading agents in the mainstream and conservative media, namely the columnists, use conspiracy theories to mobilise the masses with the aim of maintaining the status quo, especially in times of crises. They adopt a strategy that actively creates certain links with the past, expands the borders of the present and tells the masses what to remember, how to remember and what to forget. The discourse of conspiracy theories is mostly based on an emphasis on dualities, polarities of us versus them and hostilities that create or define enemies and stress the notion of victimhood (Tangün and Parlak 2020). Consequently, the age-old dichotomies like Islamic/secular, conservative/modern, Eastern/Western, Sunni/Alevi, Turkish/Kurdish, Turkish/Armenian, Muslim/non-Muslim and Ottoman/Republican never lose their power in either political discourse or mainstream media, becoming an essential part of public memory.

Media support has a fundamental route of transmission and communication of the AKP governments' gender perspective. Islamist and other pro-AKP women columnists come to the fore as "a bridge between their conservative community and secular feminists" (Arat 2016, 127). The statements of these popular and influential female figures do not challenge the ideology but celebrate the politics of the government and Erdoğan. However, as Arat shows in her analysis covering the period 2011–2013, on certain subjects such as abortion, women's employment and domestic violence, they make arguments for women's empowerment and gender equality by using references drawn from both Islam and secular feminism. For these pioneering figures—insiders of the Islamic community and forerunners of the headscarf struggle—criticising the patriarchal policies of the

---

[14] Despite the increasing prevalence of social media, television continues to be the most consumed medium. The Association of Radio and Television Broadcasters (Radyo Televizyon Yayıncıları Meslek Birliği, RATEM) reported in 2018 that Turkey ranks first in the world in terms of daily consumption with 5.5 hours a day (Çelik 2020, 341). 81% of AKP voters do not use Internet as their news source (KONDA 2018, 61) and 56% are not Internet users (KONDA 2014, 25). The state channels and the mainstream pro-AKP channels are the most watched and trusted choices of this group.

government is a matter of courage which may cost them their jobs, as Arat contends (2016, 206, 128).

The place of neo-Ottomanism in popular culture, particularly in television productions, can be understood within these dynamics. The pioneering example of the portrayal of the Ottoman Empire on television has been *Magnificent Century* (*Muhteşem Yüzyıl*), aired on a private TV channel, which narrates the sixteenth-century reign of Süleyman the Magnificent. As Carney argues, the series portrays Süleyman "as a great hero of the time and yet also treats his character subjectively, exploring his human side and allowing viewers to form a bond with him" (Carney 2014, 9). It was not only Süleyman's character but also the depiction of Hürrem Sultan, his legendary love and harem life that enabled the audience to build a new bond with history and the Ottoman heritage that replaces the previous unidimensional heroic narratives. Coloured with Oriental exotic imageries and soap opera intrigues, the series succeeded in reaching millions in Turkey, the Balkans and the Middle East. Yet it was targeted by then Prime Minister Erdoğan for its underrepresentation of the campaigns and victories of the Sultan and the overemphasis on his love life.[15]

The following popular production, the movie, *Conquest 1453* (*Fetih 1453*), narrated the conquest of Istanbul by Sultan Mehmet II. In contrast to *Magnificent Century* the movie's storyline is a "black and white representation of history" and "Mehmed's character is largely one-dimensional: he is young, ambitious and clever, and will stop at nothing in his quest to conquer the city" (Carney 2014, 9). The film ends with images and messages of tolerance which aim to provide the concept of conquest with new meaning that can be interpreted as the AKP's populist mission of "conquest of the hearts" (Karakaya 2018). Strong heroism, chauvinism, valorisation of violence and a lack of a humanised presentation of history were the points that were brought into discussion by columnists in liberal and oppositional newspapers (Carney 2014, 10). Furthermore, as Koçak and Koçak argue, the film "solidifies a longing for a golden age" and "puts forward a Muslim-Turkish identity in place of secular Turkish identity" (Koçak and Koçak 2013, 73).

The involvement of the Turkish state television (TRT) in bringing Ottoman nostalgia to the screen with big budget productions began with the series *Resurrection Ertuğrul* (*Diriliş Ertuğrul*), which narrates the

---

[15] *Hürriyet*, "Erdoğan Zafer Havalimanını Açtı", https://www.hurriyet.com.tr/gundem/erdogan-zafer-havalimanini-acti-22010262. Accessed on 10 November 2020.

story of the Kayı tribe's founding of the Ottoman state. The series achieved top rankings in ratings, being watched by millions of viewers in Turkey and abroad and had its audience highly engaged with its characters and messages.[16] Due to the fact that it depicted a period in history less known to the wider public, it had the opportunity to fill the gaps in public memory by communicating ideological messages in line with the political standpoint of the ruling government. Predictably, the series soon gained the admiration of Erdoğan, who visited the set in person with his wife.[17] As Carney discusses, the use of the notion of resurrection is also very common in AKP discourse and election propaganda, where it references a rebirth of Islamic politics and a return to Ottoman identity in contemporary Turkey (Carney 2018). Furthermore, while *Magnificent Century* was blamed for misrepresenting history, *Resurrection* has been praised for its respect for the so-called authentic Turkish culture, particularly by the nationalist-Islamist audience.

It was with another TRT production—*Payitaht Abdülhamid*, about the late nineteenth-century Ottoman Empire and Sultan Abülhamid's struggle against the Western world as the empire declined—that echoes of the contemporary ruling ideology became most visible; indeed, "as one watches *Payitaht*, it becomes hard to distinguish whether it's the state-sponsored news bulletin, a conspiratorial debate show or an artefact of popular culture" (Bulut and İleri 2019, 246).

Even though there are numerous other representations of Ottoman history on both private and state television channels, these have been the most debated and influential. The use of popular culture and media in building a neo-Ottoman identity serving, or in line with, the hegemonic power of the AKP had its golden years in the last decade but it still continues with new productions. Ultimately, except for *Magnificent Century* to a large extent, this media discourse has been created on the basis of a conspiracy theory of polarities and enmities, along with the exaltation of militarism, masculine heroism, violence and feelings of victimhood and

[16] The viewers shared their photographs of watching the series in costumes, toy swords, guns and knives in their hands: *Onedio*, "Diriliş: Ertuğrul Dizisini İzlerken Kendini Biraz Fazla Kaptıran Vatandaşlarımızdan 15 Komik Fotoğraf'", https://onedio.com/haber/dirilis-izlerken-ecdaninin-davasini-evinde-yasayan-cilgin-torunlardan-15-komik-fotograf-806126. Accessed on 19 November 2018.

[17] "Cumhurbaşkanı Erdoğan, 'Diriliş Ertuğrul' Dizisinin Setini Ziyaret Etti" https://www.tccb.gov.tr/haberler/410/32612/cumhurbaskani-erdogan-dirilis-ertugrul-dizisinin--setini-ziyaret-etti.html. Accessed on 19 November 2018.

revenge. The effects that this has had on the masses have been to build new links with the past and ancestors and a new notion of Ottoman identity based on Turkish and Islamic roots. On the other hand, with the wide range of themed merchandise available on the market, these series offer the playfulness of accessible glamour, heroism and historical symbols of Ottoman identity, status and power to be consumed in the everyday life of their fans. All these media productions also provide temporary escapism by offering a safe space for the masses who have to deal with the impacts of social, economic and political crises in their daily lives. They address feelings, thus bringing the emotional side of neo-Ottoman imaginary into being, for better or worse, during and after these moments of escape.

Interest in depictions of history on screen is not unique to Turkey though. The popularity of these productions should also be considered in relation to an on-going, globally popular, culture trend in historical dramas such as *Rome* (2005–2007), *The Tudors* (2007–2010) and *Vikings* (2013–). *Game of Thrones* (2011–2019) can also be included to this genre despite being based on a mythical story. All of them have an aestheticised way of narrating history and post-imperial nostalgia, enabling their audiences to be further attracted to their stories no matter which country of origin or where they are watching them. The neo-Ottoman imaginaries are emotional and accessible, finding a place (in time and space) and providing glamour in everyday life, be it fashion, social status or an identity confirmed by the past.

Neo-Ottomanism's Elusive Cultural Authority

By way of conclusion, we can note that even if other matters are on the agenda in contemporary Turkey, the cultural consumption of neo-Ottoman imaginaries is still prevalent. President Erdoğan stated in 2017[18] and 2020[19] that his governance had failed to establish a cultural and intellectual authority: "We have been in power for 14 years, but there are problems with being in social and cultural power." Interpreted as his ambitions to live and rule in accordance with a perceived Ottoman legacy,

---

[18] *Sputnik Türkiye*, "14 Yıldır İktidarız ama Sosyal ve Kültürel İktidar Olma Konusunda Sıkıntılar Var" https://tr.sputniknews.com/turkiye/201705281028639872-erdogan-ensar-vakfi-genel-kurulu/. Accessed on 23 November 2020.

[19] *Euronews Türkçe*, "18 Yılda Arzu Ettiğimiz İlerlemeyi Sağlayamadık" https://tr.euronews.com/2020/10/19/cumhurbaskan-erdogan-18-y-lda-egitimde-arzu-ettigimiz-ilerlemeyi-saglayamad-k Accessed on 23 November 2020.

the President here refers to the weakening bonds of the younger generations with Turco-Islamic identity which he explains with the continued influence of Western and global culture, and of other ways of thinking about religion than following in the footsteps of Diyanet (Bilici 2018). State-governed attempts to imitate the glory of the Ottoman era and enact the imagined golden age of Turkish and Islamic history did not achieve a long-term success, after a brief heyday in the 2010s. Popular culture, consumerism and transnational media proved stronger and ready to take on new themes, while authoritarian politics and nationalistic discourse remained in the sphere of state governance.

Yet the political turbulence attending the transformation of Hagia Sophia—as discussed in several of the chapters—offers a multi-layered example of how the combination of nationalism and Sunni Islamic hegemonic claims still functions as a forceful tool. The Friday prayer, which marked the denominational shift, brought about the intended responses, in both domestic and international politics. Inclusionary and exclusionary family metaphors have appeared along with a self-understanding that presents the Republican period in parentheses. If Ottomania has lost some of its medial attraction, Ottomentality lingers in the construction of collective memory and the politics of belonging.

The peak of the neo-Ottoman media trends seems to have passed. Internal affairs and foreign policy have taken other directions and Turkish popular culture presents new themes, like psychological dramas on TV and Turkish rap in the music industry: a reminder of how the dynamics, creativity and speed of popular culture provides an immediate adaptability to shifting conditions that political top-down strategies lack. The neo-Ottoman imaginaries of the past carry with them hegemonic pictures of life-style models, gendered norms and aesthetic preferences promoted as modes of relating to the present. The elusive character of these varying, and sometimes conflicting, visions is at the core of the discussions in this volume.

References

140journos. 2019. *Osmanlı Torunu.* Accessed May 18, 2021, from https://www.youtube.com/watch?v=zx3F_W2lr7M.
Adak, Sevgi. 2020. Expansion of the Diyanet and the Politics of Family in Turkey under AKP Rule. *Turkish Studies* 22: 1–22.

Aile ve Sosyal Hizmetler Bakanlığı. Tarihçe, Accessed April 30, 2021. https://www.aile.gov.tr/bakanlik/hakkinda/tarihce/.

AK Parti. *Parti Programı.* Accessed April 30, 2021. https://www.akparti.org.tr/parti/parti-programi/.

Akçaoğlu, Aksu. 2020 [2018]. *Zarif ve Dinen Makbul: Muhafazakar Üst-Orta Sınıf Habitusu.* İstanbul: İletişim.

Akturk, Şener. 2009. Persistence of the Islamic Millet as an Ottoman Legacy: Mono-Religious and Anti-Ethnic Definition of Turkish Nationhood. *Middle Eastern Studies* 45 (6): 893–909.

———. 2018. One Nation under Allah? Islamic Multiculturalism, Muslim Nationalism and Turkey's Reforms for Kurds, Alevis, and non-Muslims. *Turkish Studies* 19 (4): 523–551.

Alimen, Nazlı. 2018. *Faith and Fashion in Turkey: Consumption, Politics and Islamic Identities.* London: I.B. Tauris.

Aljazeera. 2013. Turkey Lifts Decades Old Ban on Headscarves, August 8. Accessed November 04, 2020. https://www.aljazeera.com/news/2013/10/8/turkey-lifts-decades-old-ban-on-headscarves.

Arat, Yeşim. 2016. Islamist Women and Feminist Concerns in Contemporary Turkey: Prospects for Women's Rights and Solidarity. *Frontiers: A Journal of Women Studies* 37 (3): 125–150.

Arat, Yeşim and Şevket Pamuk. 2019. *Turkey between Democracy and Authoritarianism.* Cambridge: Cambridge University Press.

Barkey, Karen. 2012. Rethinking Ottoman Management of Diversity. What Can We Learn for Modern Turkey? In *Democracy, Islam, and Secularism in Turkey*, ed. Ahmet Kuru and Alfred Stepan, 12–31. New York: Columbia University Press.

Batuman, Bülent. 2018. *New Islamist Architecture and Urbanism.* London: Routledge.

Bianet. 2011. Kadın Bakanlığı Kaldırıldı, Kadın Örgütleri Öfkeli, June 8. Accessed May 19, 2021. https://bianet.org/bianet/kadin/130585-kadin-bakanligi-kaldirildi-kadin-orgutleri-ofkeli.

Bilici, Mucahit. 2018. The Crisis of Religiosity in Turkish Islamism. *Middle East Report* 288, Fall: 43–45.

Boym, Svetlana. 2001. *The Future of Nostalgia.* New York: Basic Books.

Bulut, Ergin and Nurçin İleri. 2019. Screening Right-Wing Populism in 'New Turkey': Neo-Ottomanism, Historical Dramas, and the Case of Payitaht Abdulhamid. *The Routledge Companion to Global Television*, 244–255. London: Routledge.

Carney, Josh. 2014. Re-creating History and Recreating Publics: The Success and Failure of Recent Ottoman Costume Dramas in Turkish Media. *European Journal of Turkish Studies* 19: 1–21.

Carney, Josh. 2018. Resur(e)recting a Spectacular Hero: Diriliş Ertuğrul, Necropolitics, and Popular Culture in Turkey. *Review of Middle East Studies* 52 (1): 93–114.

Çelik, Burce. 2020. Screening for Erdoğanism: Television, Post-truth and Political Fear. *European Journal of Communication* 35 (4): 339–354.

Chovanec, Johanna. 2021. The Ottoman Myth in Turkish Literature. In *Narrated Empires Perceptions of Late Habsburg and Ottoman Multinationalism*, ed. Johanna Chovanec and Olof Heilo. London: Palgrave.

Çınar, Reyhan Ünal. 2020. *Ecdadın İcadı: AKP İktidarında Bellek Mücadelesi*. İstanbul: İletişim.

Cindoglu, Dilek and Didem Unal. 2017. Gender and Sexuality in the Authoritarian Discursive Strategies of New Turkey, *European Journal of Women's Studies* 24 (1): 39–54.

Eldem, Edhem. 2015. Cultural Heritage in Turkey: An Eminently Political Matter. In *Essays on Heritage, Tourism and Society in the Mena Region*, ed. Dieter Haller, Achim Lichtenberger and Meike Meerpoh, 67–91. Paderborn: Ferdinand Schöningh.

———. 2021. The Reconversion of the Hagia Sophia into a Mosque: A Historian's Perspective. *Journal of the Ottoman and Turkish Studies Association* 8 (1): 243–260.

Ergin, Murat and Yağmur Karakaya. 2017. Between Neo-Ottomanism and Ottomania: Navigating State-Led and Popular Cultural Representations of the Past. *New Perspectives on Turkey* 56: 33–59.

Euronews Türkçe. 2020. 18 Yılda Arzu Ettiğimiz İlerlemeyi Sağlayamadık, October 19. Accessed May 20, 2021. https://tr.euronews.com/2020/10/19/cumhurbaskan-erdogan-18-y-lda-egitimde-arzu-ettigimiz-ilerlemeyi-saglayamad-k.

Evren, Can. 2022. United against the Referee: Competitive Authoritarianism, Soccer, and the Remaking of Nationalism in Erdoğanist Turkey. In *Politics of Culture in Contemporary Turkey*, ed. Pierre Hecker, Ivo Furman and Kaya Akyıldız, 111–129. Edinburgh: Edinburgh University Press.

Fisher-Onar, Nora. 2018. Between Neo-Liberalism and Neo-Ottomanism: The Politics of Imagining Istanbul. In *Istanbul: Living with Difference in a Global City*, ed. Nora Fisher-Onar, Susan C. Pearce and E. Fuat Keyman, 1–21. New Brunswick, NJ: Rutgers University Press.

———. 2021. Afterword: Remembering Empire: Between Civilizational Nationalism and Post-National Pluralism. In *Narrated Empires: Perceptions of Late Habsburg and Ottoman Multinationalism*, ed. Johanna Chovanec and Olof Heilo, 387–398. London: Palgrave Macmillan.

Göçek, Fatma Müge (ed.). 2018. *Contested Spaces in Contemporary Turkey*. London: Bloomsbury.

Gözaydın, İştar B. 2006. A Religious Administration to Secure Secularism: the Presidency of Religious Affairs of the Republic of Turkey. *Marburg Journal of Religion* 11 (1): 1–8.
Haber 7. 2020. Erdoğan'ın Sözlerinin Perde Arkası Ortaya Çıktı! Bazı Maddeler Değişiyor, August 15. Accessed November 10, 2020. https://www.haber7.com/guncel/haber/3004137-erdoganin-sozlerinin-perde-arkasi-ortaya-ciktibazi-maddeler-degisiyor.
Hartog, François. 2015. *Regimes of Historicity: Presentism and Experiences of Time*. New York: Columbia University Press.
Hürriyet. 2012. Erdoğan Zafer Havalimanını Açtı, November 25. Accessed November 10, 2020. https://www.hurriyet.com.tr/gundem/erdogan-zafer-havalimanini-acti-22010262.
Kadın ve Demokrasi Derneği (KADEM). Uluslararası Toplumsal Cinsiyet Adaleti. Accessed November 11, 2020. https://kadem.org.tr/zirve-ve-kongreler/uluslararasi-toplumsal-cinsiyet-adaleti-kongresi/.
Kalaycı, Hüseyin. 2021. A Not-So-Friendly Match Between 'Old Turkey' and 'New Turkey': Turkish Football and Stadiums as a Domain of Hegemonic Struggle. *Asian Journal of Middle Eastern and Islamic Studies* 15 (4): 519–535.
Kandiyoti, Deniz. 2019. Against All Odds: The Resilience and Fragility of Women's Gender Activism in Turkey. In *Gender, Governance and Islam*, ed. Deniz Kandiyoti, Nadja Al-Ali and Kathyryn Spellman Poots, 80–100. Edinburgh: Edinburgh University Press.
Karaosmanoglu, Defne. 2010. Nostalgia Spaces of Consumption and Heterotopia: Ramadan Festivities in Istanbul. *Culture Unbound* 2 (2): 283–302.
Karakaya, Yağmur. 2020. The Conquest of Hearts: The Central Role of Ottoman Nostalgia within Contemporary Turkish Populism. *American Journal of Cultural Sociology* 8:125–157.
Koçak, Dilek Özhan and Orhan Kemal Koçak. 2013. Glorifying the Past on Screen. In *Bringing History to Life through Film: The Art of Cinematic Storytelling*, ed. Kathryn Anne Morey, 71–88. Plymouth: Rowman & Littlefield.
Kocamaner, Hikmet. 2017. Strengthening the Family through Television: Islamic Broadcasting, Secularism, and the Politics of Responsibility in Turkey. *Anthropological Quarterly* 90 (3): 675–714.
———. 2018. The Politics of Family Values in Erdogan's New Turkey. *MERIP*, 288, Fall.
KONDA. 2014. *Kitle İletişim Araçlarının Etkisi*. Accessed May 19, 2021. https://konda.com.tr/tr/rapor/kitle-iletisim-araclarinin-etkisi/.
———. 2018. *Seçmen Kümeleri: AK Parti Seçmeni*. Accessed May 19, 2021. http://konda.com.tr/tr/rapor/secmen-kumeleri-ak-parti-secmenleri/.
Lord, Ceren. 2017. Between Islam and the Nation: Nationbuilding, the Ulama and Alevi Identity in Turkey. *Nations and Nationalism* 23 (1): 48–67.

———. 2018a. *Religious Politics in Turkey: From the Birth of the Republic to the AKP.* Cambridge: Cambridge University Press.
———. 2018b. The Story behind the Rise of Turkey's Ulema. *MERIP*, 2.
Lüküslü, Demet. 2016. Creating a Pious Generation: Youth and Education Policies of the AKP in Turkey. *Southeast European and Black Sea Studies* 16 (4): 637–649.
Mutluer, Nil. 2018. Diyanet's Role in Building the 'Yeni (New) Milli' in the AKP Era. *European Journal of Turkish Studies* 27: 1–24. Accessed August 11, 2022. https://journals.openedition.org/ejts/5953
Navaro-Yashin, Yael. 2002. *Faces of the State. Secularism and Public Life in Turkey.* Princeton: Princeton University Press.
Öncü, Ayşe. 2010. Narratives of Istanbul's Ottoman Heritage and Competing Political Claims to its Present. In *Spatial Conceptions of the Nation: Modernizing Geographies in Greece and Turkey*, ed. Nikiforos Diamandouros, Caglar Keyder and Thalia Dragonas, 205–228. London: IB Tauris.
Onedio. 2018. Diriliş İzlerken Ecdadının Davasını Evinde Yaşayan Çılgın Torunlardan 15 Komik Fotoğraf, January 23. Accessed May 20, 2021. https://onedio.com/haber/dirilis-izlerken-ecdaninin-davasini-evinde-yasayan-cilgin-torunlardan-15-komik-fotograf-806126.
Ongur, Hakan Ovunc. 2015. Identifying Ottomanisms: The Discursive Evolution of Ottoman Pasts in the Turkish Presents. *Middle Eastern Studies* 51 (3): 416–432.
Onur, Petek. 2022. The Politics of Nostalgia: The New Urban Culture in Ankara's Historic Neighbourhoods. In *Politics of Culture in Contemporary Turkey*, ed. Pierre Hecker, Ivo Furman and Kaya Akyıldız, 253–276. Edinburgh: Edinburgh University Press.
Öztürk, Ahmet Erdi. 2016. Turkey's Diyanet under AKP Rule: From Protector to Imposer of State Ideology? *Southeast European and Black Sea Studies* 16 (4): 619–635.
———. 2018. Transformation of the Turkish Diyanet both at Home and Abroad: Three Stages. *European Journal of Turkish Studies* 27:1-27. Accessed August 10, 220. https://journals.openedition.org/ejts/5944
Özyürek, Esra. 2006. *Nostalgia for the Modern: State Secularism and Everyday Politics in Turkey.* Durham, NC: Duke University Press.
Sandıkçı, Özlem and Güliz Ger. 2010. Veiling in Style: How Does a Stigmatized Practice Become Fashionable? *Journal of Consumer Research* 37 (1): 15–36.
Sayan-Cengiz, Feyda. 2018. Eroding the Symbolic Significance of Veiling? The Islamic Fashion Magazine Âlâ, Consumerism, and the Challenged Boundaries of the 'Islamic Neighborhood'. *New Perspectives on Turkey* 58: 155–178.
Sofos, Spyros. 2021. Space and the Emotional Topography of Populism in Turkey: The Case of Hagia Sophia. *Cogent Social Sciences* 7 (1): 1–15.

———. 2022. *Turkish Politics and 'The People'. Mass Mobilisation and Populism.* Edinburgh: Edinburgh University Press.

Sputnik Türkiye. 2017. 14 Yıldır İktidarız Ama Sosyal ve Kültürelİktidarız Olma Konusunda Sıkıntılar Var, May 28. Accessed May 20, 2021. https://tr.sputniknews.com/turkiye/201705281028639872-erdogan-ensar-vakfi-genel-kurulu/.

Taglia, Stefano. 2016. Ottomanism Then and Now: Historical and Contemporary Meanings: An Introduction. *Die Welt des Islams* 56 (3–4): 279–289.

Tangün, Yağız Alp and İsmet Parlak. 2020. Politik Söylemin 'Komplo Teorisi Formu'na Özdeş Sınırları: Kanaat Teknisyeni, Habitus ve İktidar Stratejileri. *Mülkiye Dergisi* 44 (2): 287–320.

Tokdoğan, Nagehan. 2019. *Yeni Osmanlıcılık: Hınç, Nostalji, Narsizm.* İstanbul: İletişim.

Topal, Alp Eren. 2021. Ottomanism in History and Historiography: Fortunes of a Concept. In *Narrated Empires, Modernity, Memory and Identity in South-East Europe*, ed. Johanna Chovanec and Olof Heilo, 77–98. London: Palgrave Macmillan.

Tunc, Tanfer Emin and Gokhan Tunc. 2020. Wonderland Eurasia: Theme Parks and Neo-Ottoman Identity Politics in Ankara, Turkey. *Popular Entertainment Studies* 11 (1–2): 93–113.

Türkiye Cumhuriyeti Cumhurbaşkanlığı, Haberler. Cumhurbaşkanı Erdoğan, 'Diriliş Ertuğrul' Dizisinin Setini Ziyaret Etti. Accessed May 20, 2021. https://www.tccb.gov.tr/haberler/410/32612/cumhurbaskani-erdogan-dirilis-ertugrul-dizisinin-setini-ziyaret-etti.html.

Türkiye Cumhuriyeti Cumhurbaşkanlığı Strateji ve Bütçe Başkanlığı. 2020. *2021 Yılı Cumhurbaşkanlığı Yıllık Programı.*

Walton, Jeremy F. 2019. Introduction: Textured Historicity and the Ambivalence of Imperial Legacies. *History and Anthropology* 30 (4): 353–365.

———. 2021. Silhouettes and Submersions: Istanbul's Past from Above and Below. *Journal of the Ottoman and Turkish Studies Association* 8 (1): 11–22.

World Economic Forum. *2020 Global Gender Gap Index.* Accessed November 10, 2020. http://www3.weforum.org/docs/WEF_GGGR_2020.pdf.

Yang Erdem, Chien. 2017. Ottomentality: Neoliberal Governance of Culture and Neo-Ottoman Management of Diversity. *Turkish Studies* 18 (4): 710–728.

Yavuz, M. Hakan. 2020. *Nostalgia for the Empire: The Politics of Neo-Ottomanism.* Oxford: Oxford University Press.

Yilmaz, Zafer. 2015. 'Strengthening the Family' Policies in Turkey: Managing the Social Question and Armoring Conservative–Neoliberal Populism. *Turkish Studies* 16 (3): 371–390.

———. 2017. The AKP and the Spirit of the 'New' Turkey: Imagined Victim, Reactionary Mood, and Resentful Sovereign. *Turkish Studies* 18 (3): 482–513.

Yosmaoğlu, İpek Kocaömer. 2021. History, Memory, and the Hagia Sophia Controversy. *Journal of the Ottoman and Turkish Studies Association* 8 (1): 235–242.

CHAPTER 2

Neo-Ottomanism versus Ottomania: Contestation of Gender in Historical Drama

Murat Ergin and Yağmur Karakaya

Over the past few decades, contemporary Turkey has witnessed a growing interest in Ottoman history, part of which has manifested itself in popular culture and consumption (Ergin and Karakaya 2017), with Ottoman-themed cultural products becoming best sellers, both in Turkey and the countries surrounding it. TV series displaying the intrigues of the Ottoman palace have been a driving force behind this industry, as well as movies, music, and other forms of entertainment. Shopping malls display items that "represent" Ottoman tastes, such as jewellery, clothing, and

---

The authors are listed alphabetically, as each is an equal co-author.

M. Ergin (✉)
Koç University, Istanbul, Turkey
e-mail: muergin@ku.edu.tr

Y. Karakaya
Yale University, New Haven, CT, USA
e-mail: yagmur.karakaya@yale.edu

© The Author(s), under exclusive license to Springer Nature Switzerland AG 2023
C. Raudvere, P. Onur (eds.), *Neo-Ottoman Imaginaries in Contemporary Turkey*, Modernity, Memory and Identity in South-East Europe,
https://doi.org/10.1007/978-3-031-08023-4_2

33

souvenirs. Restaurants have responded to the trend by re-inventing Ottoman cuisine for a twenty-first-century, highly globalised society. The *hamam*, or public bathhouse, a widely forgotten Ottoman institution, has made an impressive comeback to health clubs and five-star hotels. Ottoman history has become an item for consumption reminiscent of postmodern pleasures that brought distinct historical symbols and artifacts together in unprecedented cultural pastiches. These playful appropriations have made the Ottoman past cool, but their irreverence, or at least indifference, to historical figures and events that were imbued with sacredness reveal an underbelly of potential controversy.

Pleasure-oriented popular culture is not the end of story, as made visible in the backlash from those who revere the Ottoman Empire and everything it represented. Ottoman history has also become manifest as a form of governance and an actual blueprint for making sense of the contemporary world, both in domestic and foreign affairs (Murinson 2006; Fisher Onar 2011; White 2013; Yang Erdem 2017; Tokdoğan 2020): the current Turkish government uses the Ottoman past as a source of legitimacy; a number of public venues and museums celebrate the Ottoman past in heroic terms; and the education system increasingly emphasises a particular version of Ottoman history at the expense of the previous narratives of heroism associated with Turkish nationalism and secular modernisation (Çayir 2009). Domestic reminders of the reclaiming of the Ottoman past are also appearing in public spaces as the state attempts to recreate the grandeur of the classical Ottoman period with public renovation projects and construction works. The re-conversion of the Hagia Sophia Museum into a mosque, and the subsequent mass Friday prayer in July 2020 amidst the Covid-19 pandemic, exemplify the practices of this form of cultural governance. The government is openly protective of this more conservative and masculine interpretation of Ottoman history, lambasting the others as examples of false history sacrificing truth for the sake of popular pleasure.

Thus, Ottoman nostalgia involves two separate but related tracks: commercialised, irreverent, and pleasure-oriented *Ottomania*, and masculine, "truth"-oriented, and state-led *neo-Ottomanism*. In this chapter, using two TV series, the controversial *Magnificent Century* (*Muhteşem Yüzyıl*) and a product of the conservative backlash, *Resurrection: Ertuğrul* (*Diriliş: Ertuğrul*), we investigate how these nostalgic forms intermingle, cooperate, and clash, and the different gender paradigms they employ. Ottomania refers to the way in which popular culture appropriates and recirculates the

Ottoman past in a vast array of gratifying consumption items and practices; neo-Ottomanism, on the other hand, is an assemblage of discourses that position Turkey as the legitimate heir to the perceived glories of the Ottoman Empire. Clearly, Ottomania and neo-Ottomanism are intertwined in their attempts to rewrite history from the standpoint of present concerns; however, it is important to establish their conceptual autonomy, as popular cultural representations of the Ottoman past can be at odds with the neo-Ottomanist vision of the Turkish state.

NEO-OTTOMANISM VERSUS OTTOMANIA

If neo-Ottomanism is a political project that involves the state's rewriting of history to address its contemporary ideological prerequisites, then its development needs to be traced to the immediate aftermath of the Ottoman period. The republican regime confronted the history of its predecessor in particular ways. The main goal was to distinguish the newly established republic from its Ottoman legacy and limit the appeal of the latter for the population, while salvaging whatever glory was left over from the defunct imperial past. Both Western publics and domestic perceptions associated the empire with Islam; memories of the Ottoman sultan serving as the Caliph, or the spiritual leader of Sunni Muslims, were still fresh. Thus, the desire to secure autonomous governmental legitimacy along secular and nationalist lines led to efforts to seek Turkish ethnic origins in a prehistoric past much earlier than the Ottomans. This allowed the construction of the Ottoman period as an intermediary hiatus, marked by decline and degeneracy, in a broader Turkish history, although, as the argument went, the essence of Turkishness remained intact throughout the period, making national reawakening possible. This lukewarm stance towards the Ottomans allowed the republican modernisers to retain claims on Ottoman achievements without complete commitment to uniformity. All the achievements of the empire could be claimed as Turkish triumphs while the skeletons in the historical closet could be written off as the side effects of a long but temporary process of degeneration.[1]

The end of the single-party period in 1950 made it easier for succeeding conservative governments to reinterpret the Ottoman past in more Islamic ways. Until the 1950s, one-party rule maintained a collective memory vision that kept the Ottoman past at bay, but the transformation

---

[1] For a critique see Sönmez (2020).

to a multi-party state changed how the Ottoman past was seen. The economic policies of the Turkish Republic—as guardian of economic security and facilitator of industrial modernisation—prioritised national self-reliance and development under state control. By the 1950s, new roads were being built, linking villages to towns and cities. Along these new roads, peasants began to move to cities in search of jobs, fuelling urbanisation.

In this climate, the Turkic narrative of the nomadic steppes slowly started to give way to a more sympathetic approach to the Ottoman past, as those left at the margins of society were now gaining power, and the newly urbanising masses needed a more enchanting narrative than one of Central Asian origins. In 1953—the quincentennial of the Conquest of Constantinople—a demand for public commemoration emerged. A committee established by the new Democratic Party government organised commemorative activities spanning ten days, which placed considerable emphasis on Istanbul as an Islamic City and Mehmed II as a Muslim sultan. The central celebration was a parade into the city through the gate by which Mehmed II had first entered, led by a lookalike in period costume. Sacrificial slaughter of sheep, a Quran recital on the radio, and Friday sermons at the Fatih Mosque were all geared towards remembering this auspicious event (Brockett 2014, 198).

The transformation to a multi-party democracy also coincided with harsh economic hardships including the Oil Crisis and triple-digit inflation with a massive debt to the IMF, which sparked multiple coups. The 1980 military coup marked the beginning of dramatic changes in the infrastructure that contributed to yet another revolutionary transformation in Turkey in the following decades, radically reshaping the political landscape. Turkey's predominantly state-led, import-substitution, industrialisation economy opened up to export-led growth and global market competition. The late 1980s witnessed the deregulation of the media and the rise of multiple private TV and radio stations, cable, and other technologies that the state was not able to control, which allowed the appearance of Islamic radio shows and television stations. As a result, Islamist political parties emerged in the 1990s (White 2013, 7–8). Businesses owned by pious Muslims benefited tremendously from the economic opening. Now named the Anatolian Tigers, their wealth created a market for bourgeois products suitable for Islamic lifestyles and tastes, which Jenny White identifies as a "Muslim cultural renaissance in fashion, lifestyle, leisure activities, novels, media, and music" (2013, 8).

In this context, if the 1953 commemoration—fuelled by the centennial—was a blip, the 1990s saw the first full manifestations of the neo-Ottoman spirit in public and local governance. By 1994, with Recep Tayyip Erdoğan winning the Istanbul municipality, the narrative of the re-conquest of Istanbul made its first appearance. Beginning with that of 1996, major commemorations marked the conquest, not organised by the state but by several youth organisations, and—at least before it was shut down—the Welfare Party. Unlike the earlier small-scale commemorations, populated by a few army officials and characterised by a formal and solemn recognition of the military success and achievements of Mehmed the Conqueror, this version involved an enthusiastically mobilised audience, predominantly comprising young people. This moment is the decisive beginning of neo-Ottoman nostalgia. The 1996 rally was so influential that the 2016 commemoration rally was also, in a way, a memory and a re-enactment of it—this time dominated, perfected, and successfully hegemonised by the state (Karakaya 2018). The major shift in the 1990s and 2000s was towards a re-evaluation of the Ottoman heritage in a much more positive light. With the declining pressure from secularist policies to construct a pre-Islamic origin story, the Ottoman past was absorbed into practices of governing as an autonomous force that defined the fundamental values of the republic.

A parallel stream to neo-Ottomanism was Ottomania, the integration of the Ottoman heritage into the commercial popular culture of the 1990s, which fit with the neo-liberalisation sweeping the country, with its emphasis on consumption. Until the 1990s, popular culture was much more political in the sense that a hegemonic state controlled cultural production and consumption as devices for modernisation. The relative success of this tutelary approach had to do with the fact that the state enjoyed virtual monopoly on TV and radio broadcasting. The economic liberalisation of the post-1980 period corresponded with the spread of private media companies and, later, internet technologies. The state began to retreat from culture in the neo-liberal 1990s, making it possible to turn Ottomania into a commercialised product which embraced popular culture with an emphasis on the consumption of a wide spectrum of products, from *hamam* packages, through belly-dancing courses (Potuoğlu-Cook 2006), to television series. Earlier attempts to represent the Ottoman past foregrounded historical "truth" as their main objective; the logic of consumption, however, puts more emphasis on entertainment and commercial value. These two streams of Ottoman nostalgia coexisted as two distinct but related approaches. "Neo-Ottomanism" maintained the search for the truth and essence—Turkish, Islamic, or multicultural—of the imperial past, whereas "Ottomania" offered an irreverent mishmash of historical images for consumption in an increasingly commercialised popular culture.

A Feminised-Private Sphere: Gender Anxieties in Ottomania and Neo-Ottomanism

Projects of nationhood come with specific conceptualisations of "manhood" and "womanhood" (Yuval-Davis 1997; Altınay 2004), with women's behaviour and their proper place in society weighing heavily in this conceptualisation. Yuval Davis (1997) argues that as a response to various modernisation projects around the world, groups who were at the social margins came up with alternative fundamentalist constructions of nationhood as they gradually became contenders for hegemony. These groups envision and impose an "alternative fundamentalist construction of the 'true' cultural essence of their collectivity" (1997, 64) in which women occupy the role of the "carriers of tradition" rather than being symbols of change (1997, 67). They are constructed as "the cultural symbols of the collectivity, of its boundaries, as carriers of the collectivity's honour and as its intergenerational reproducers of culture" (Yuval-Davis 1997, 69).

Both Ottomania and neo-Ottomanism promote particular gender paradigms. Ottomania associates gender with conspicuous consumption, leisure, and a certain type of femininity linked with Oriental belly dancing, sensuous *hamams*, and pleasures like luxurious fabrics, scents, and jewellery. Palace women in popular TV series become role models for consumption and shape the fashion choices of their contemporary counterparts. In Ottomania, the past represents a postmodern consumption item; decontextualised images and products circulate the consumption world and are juxtaposed with other items in an endless mishmash. Neo-Ottomanism, on the other hand, rests on a discourse of sober masculinity, Islam, and heroism. This hegemonic Turkish masculinity frowns upon consumption as frivolous and limits space for women's self-expression. Yet neo-Ottoman insignia are far from absent. The *tughra* (the sultan's seal in Arabic script) has become a ubiquitous symbol, and a perfect example of Baudrillardian simulacra. An identity assertion, if not a fashion statement, it adorns male rings, features as stickers on cars and small shop windows, and appears as framed versions on office walls. As Çınar argues, "the dramatization of the conquest and the activities around it abundantly employed various symbols that concertedly constructed a national subject performed as Ottoman, Islamic, and male" (Çınar, 2005, 154). The two TV series, *Magnificent Century* and *Resurrection: Ertuğrul*, display these conflicting anxieties connected with gender and history.

What made *Magnificent Century* so controversial for the regime and a segment of the Turkish public is what we call the feminised-private sphere created by the domestic setting of the show, bolstered by the conspicuous consumption depicted in endless feasts, the indulgence of carnal satisfactions, and the identity turmoil of characters from which even the sultan is not exempt. The feminised-private feeling is enhanced through the portrayal of women consuming frivolous luxury, searching for romance, and fighting for a strong man's attention. Gender seclusion in the palace where women are shown to predominantly socialise with other women feeds into this perception. It is this feminised-private sphere that *Resurrection: Ertuğrul* repudiates by relying on the cinematography of the vast steppes, modest tents, and horsemen riding to their next heroic adventure. Unlike the feasting, dancing, and indulgent emotions that *Magnificent Century* fosters, *Resurrection* dwells on famine, hardships, and the Christian enemies against which the strong men and the modest subdued women of the steppes fight so diligently.

Truth, Pleasure, and Anxieties

The tensions between Ottomania and neo-Ottomanism reveal how pleasure, power, and historical truth operate in constructing alternative visions of the past. In this section, we expand on the two case studies, *Magnificent Century*, a controversial 2011 soap opera depicting Ottoman harem intrigues, and *Resurrection: Ertuğrul*, a state-endorsed 2014 show that portrays the nomadic beginnings of the Ottoman Empire. As we examine how Ottomania and neo-Ottomanism interact, we situate gender as one of the central sites of the tense relationship between these two discourses. We argue that, ultimately, neo-Ottomanism attempts to co-opt Ottomania and solidify its own gendered interpretation through *Resurrection: Ertuğrul*.

Historical "truth" marks one of the central points of tension between Ottomania and neo-Ottomanism. One of the charges that conservatives regularly made against *Magnificent Century* was its misrepresentation of historical facts. The anxieties generated by this perceived falsity were so great that even defenders of the show succumbed to these critiques by responding that *Magnificent Century* was only intended for entertainment and did not aim to be a serious study of history. In a previous work, we found that, to gauge truth and authenticity, audiences frequently projected their contemporary views onto evaluations of a mysterious past (Ergin and Karakaya 2017). Many viewers accepted the Ottomans as the representatives of the golden age of Islam, reasoning, therefore, that one would not expect powerful women and rampant sexuality in the soap opera. Others imagined an ethnic Turkish past and rejected the multi-ethnic origins of the Ottoman ruling class as fiction. Despite, or because of, the high entertainment value of the show, the tensions between "truth" and "pleasure" generated intense levels of anxiety among viewers.

If *Magnificent Century* stood for guilty pleasures in viewing historical exaggeration and falsity, *Resurrection: Ertuğrul* represented a conservative attempt at correction, depicting a putatively true history cleansed of all impurities. When *Magnificent Century*—the epitome of Ottomania in ascent—aired, its feminised-private sphere, created through the genre choices, character development, and depiction of gender, stirred up multiple anxieties and sources of embarrassment deeply embedded in, and relationally articulated by, the Turkish public. Rather than providing the imagery of belligerent, heroic men swinging their swords in places far from the bounds of the domestic sphere, *Magnificent Century* predominantly depicted the domain of the palace, with women exchanging jewellery and expensive fabrics, fighting for the love of the sultan, and crying over the loss of his attention. This portrayal, in line with stereotypes of extravagant female consumption of frivolous luxury, the constant search for romantic love, and the need for a strong man's attention, is germane to fostering the feminised-private sphere. Even the theme songs of the two shows signal the differences in approach. *Magnificent Century* opens with a lush orchestral arrangement by Fahir Atakoğlu, a composer with an education in the classical Western tradition. The theme song has the feeling of a cinematic piece with a strong presence of Western classical strings and multi-layered polyphonies. The theme song in the opening sequence of *Resurrection: Ertuğrul*, however, is melodically simpler and features local instruments. The heavy reliance on percussive instruments and intense rhythm, coupled with the frequent cuts to men on horseback, combine to create a masculine groove.

The feminised-private sphere of *Magnificent Century* generates multi-layered anxieties in three domains: (a) ethnicity and religion; (b) gender and sexuality; (c) conspicuous consumption. An important anxiety has to do with the complex heritage, portrayed especially in regard to religious conversion. If the sacred sultans, the highly revered torchbearers of Islam, are themselves the sons of converts and former Christians, where does this leave the general public? The second unease is spurred by the display of *mahrem*, or the secrecy and privacy of the Ottoman court and the harem, which was rife with tragedy, the pursuit of power, and ambitious women (Peirce 1993). For a segment of Turks, it was not only the amount of female cleavage that was shocking, but also the scenes of women fighting for power and ultimately ruling the empire. It seemed hard for the public not to mourn one of the commonly cited clichés for the decline of the empire that frequently appeared in high school history textbooks: "palace women gained too much power". This period in the seventeenth century, dubbed the "sultanate of women", was part of the official history textbooks' explanations for Ottoman decline for decades (Gemalmaz 2004). Lastly, the conspicuous consumption of luxury items, including jewellery and expensive fabrics, raised questions about the authenticity of the "empire on TV", as it went against the modesty of the ideal Ottoman in the minds and hearts of the public.

On the other hand, *Resurrection: Ertuğrul*—the response of neo-Ottomanism to Ottomania—portrays a severe divide between Christianity and Islam, unlike the anxiety-inducing, fluid boundaries depicted in *Magnificent Century*. The moral structure of the series' universe is strongly anchored in traditional authority and shaped around Ertuğrul as an honourable yet lonely hero, a fierce warrior, fighting against the West at the expense of being perceived as not looking after his own interests. Moreover, the way women are displayed is very different from their representations in *Magnificent Century*'s Ottomania. In *Resurrection: Ertuğrul*, women are modest, hardworking, and unassuming, unlike the outspoken and enticing women of *Magnificent Century*, with their claims to power. Finally, there is no room for conspicuous consumption in the nomadic context. In a nutshell, *Magnificent Century* offered the opportunity to question the Ottoman past through the lens of light-hearted consumption, but *Resurrection: Ertuğrul* closed this window, easing anxieties by presenting a triumphalist and easy-to-digest narrative of silent women, strong men, and traditional authority standing firm against the Christian world.

Magnificent Century: Popular Gone Wrong

Magnificent Century is a prime-time soap opera based on the lives of the Ottoman Sultan Süleyman the Magnificent (r. 1520–1566) and his wife Hürrem (also known as Alexandra or Roxelana in the West), a Ukrainian slave who became one of the most powerful female figures in Ottoman history. Süleyman's reign is popularly seen as the zenith of the Ottoman Empire. *Magnificent Century* focuses on his love life with Hürrem and on harem intrigues. During the show's four-season run (2011–2014) it reached a large audience both in Turkey and abroad, causing a great uproar and triggering debates in Turkey—what Öncü calls "public chatter"—concerning the historical accuracy of personalities and events (Öncü 2000, 2011). The public was mesmerised by such questions as whether or not it was appropriate to depict a sultan's personal life in such detail and whether or not concubines actually wore such low-cut dresses. Meanwhile, the current president Recep Tayyip Erdoğan and his political allies condemned the show for falsely depicting the Ottoman "forefathers" spending their lives involved in harem intrigues rather than fighting on horseback. Several high-ranking members of the ruling party asked the producers, the Taylan Brothers, to discontinue the show. Both the then screenwriter, Meral Okay, and the Taylan Brothers emphasised that they did not align themselves with any politics or ideology in relation to the Ottoman past, and that what they were doing was creating characters inspired by history and thus ultimately creating historical fiction (*NTV Tarih* 2011). Okay also argued that she faced extensive criticism because of her gender, stating that a man in her position would probably not have been criticised as much or as heavily (Ergin and Karakaya 2017).

Despite Erdoğan's condemnation of the show, and the radical Islamist sect İsmailağa's protesting the series by throwing eggs at the production crew, many Turks watched it with guilty pleasure, if not titillating disgust or shame, as keenly observed by a YouTube user: "this is a series of series! Everyone watches it secretly without telling anyone, everyone watches it from the beginning till the end, but they hide it because they are embarrassed."[2] We take this embarrassment seriously and argue that the

---

[2] *Muhteşem Yüzyıl: 5. Bölüm* https://www.youtube.com/watch?v=lzjIC9p87D4&lc=UggZ1Dk7nvtswngCoAEC. Accessed on 17 May 2021.

"feminised-private sphere" that the show fostered caused this general response. Based on a discursive reading of the first five episodes, we identified three distinctive features associated with some of the conflicting feelings that are induced by watching the *Magnificent Century*. The first has to do with the depiction of the complex inner lives of historic persona, and their multicultural past, which created controversy because the public largely codes these characters as sacred. The second is generated by confronting strong women from the past who have a stake in power. The show broke new ground given that textbooks present Ottoman women's involvement in politics as one of the causes for Ottoman decline. Lastly, the drama includes high levels of conspicuous consumption of luxury items, including jewellery and expensive fabrics, which made the public uneasy and raised questions about authenticity.

Complex Characters

Let us begin with the first characteristic: the complex depiction of these historical characters' inner life worlds, and their constant identity crises. Many of the characters in the show have ambivalent pasts and personalities as a result of conversion from Christianity to Islam. Religious conversion poses a threat to neo-Ottomanism's essentialist interpretations of historical personas. Unlike superhuman depictions in the popular imagination, even the sultan is not shown as infinitely self-assured, but as a person who questions his acts every step of the way. Take this scene, for example, where we see Süleyman in a potent moment, yet clouded by his self-doubt about future justice:

> While gazing at the stars and the Bosphorus, the sultan is presented with a nervous concubine, too shy even to look at him. He chuckles as she drops to her knees to kiss his kaftan. They stare at each other in a very suggestive way for a few seconds, with tension-building music. In the next scene, as the girl exits the room, we gather from the sultan's satisfied yet existential look that they had sex. His strong arms spread out on his knees, Süleyman becomes buried in thought, and we hear his inner monologue, "I am scared, father, of being covered in blood, becoming a cruel tyrant. What if the power and the sound of being in power muffles my conscience? Don't keep your breath off me. Dear Allah, please don't make me afraid to look myself in the mirror." (Episode 1, 2011)

Süleyman on the screen is potent and seems to be enjoying moments of submission from his subjects, but we also understand that his power is not infinitely self-assured. At a vulnerable moment, we hear his doubts, and his wish to not abuse his power. The show portrays Sultan Süleyman as a complex character. He has a front-stage persona which he dons when attending a state meeting, and a back-stage one which we hear during private moments as an inner monologue, when chatting with Ibrahim of Parga, and later on with Hürrem, the "love of my life".

Similarly, Süleyman's loyal friend and falconer—and later *hasodabaşı* (Sultan's right-hand, the person who takes care of the Sultan's personal life)—İbrahim of Parga, has a fluid identity, as he was uprooted from his Christian village to be raised as a Muslim boy and conscripted into the Ottoman Palace. Even though his uprooting eventually resulted in his ascent to power, he constantly engages in inner musings about his heritage, meditating about his identity. While Giddens (1991) attributed reflexivity to modern subjects, the inner monologues of these historical TV personas are not short of the musings of a reflexive individual; prevalent throughout the series, they seem to be projections of our modern anxieties. These historical characters seem to construct who they are in an autobiographical way, being made anxious by the prospect of not having a linear biography, and remembering their convoluted and multicultural beginnings:

> İbrahim stands on the palace balcony, with his own fair share of life-questioning inner pondering. He sighs and thinks, "I am Ibrahim, the son of Rum fisherman Manolis of Parga, and a Venetian woman named Sofia. Ibrahim of Parga, who was recruited, and converted at the age of ten. What was my name? What my name meant in what language, I forgot. Forgetting frees you. Or else, the language of your given name, the soil you learned to walk on, does not leave your heart." (Episode 1, 2011)

These character depictions unsettle the neo-Ottomanist visions of an unproblematic Ottoman past represented as the culmination of Turkish and Muslim historical achievements. The long-held assumptions about the Ottoman past deny the multicultural nature of Ottoman society, yet complex character building in the show directs attention to the "murky" roots of Turkishness, raising the potential for anxiety:

I am Ibrahim the convert, conscripted from Parga, at the age of ten. What is it like to convert [to turn]; what do you turn to [convert to]? Where does one turn to? Where is it that one turns? Is there any turning back? Is it possible? Or does destiny only point forward? Is where you turned from, where you came from, still there? Does it wait for you? Would you be able to see it if you looked? Does your heart become your compass when you are turning? Can you go back home, without forgetting the roads you travelled from? Or are you still only a "convert" in there where you think you turned to, and changed to, in that language, and in that religion you said you converted to? Is converting not a talent but a requirement, Ibrahim? (Episode 1, 2011)

These inner musings imbue the characters with fluidity and ambiguity, and leave the audience anxious. Ibrahim is a multicultural and complex personality. Valide Sultan (the "legal mother" of the sultan) speaks Russian. Hürrem, the new favourite of the sultan, dreamt of Christ during her first night under the Ottoman dome. In addition to the general public chatter crystallised in disbelief of how much cleavage the palace women flaunted, the discord also has to do with this titillating encounter with the multicultural past, and an unease about converts who might still be missing their homes or be in a secret alliance with Christianity. Furthermore, the background of these characters also had the potential to direct attention to the convoluted roots of Turkishness. When the *Magnificent Century* aired, media debates raged around the unease with cleavages; however, an even greater source of transgression was the acknowledgement of complex heritage, which caused deep anxiety.

Powerful Women

The second controversial characteristic of the show is its depiction of powerful palace women. Although the *Magnificent Century* presents the tragic rivalries and harem intrigues of the age, this reality of female power seems to disturb many people in Turkey for whom Ottoman history is supposed to be masculine and sacred as opposed to women fighting for a sultan's love and personal political power. Female agency, depicted most often through interpersonal conflict, is a profane reminder—in both the Durkheimian and colloquial sense of the word—of women's political power, which tarnishes the neo-Ottoman vision of a pure and masculine Ottoman past. In the following scene, ready to build her own destiny, Hürrem deliberately takes the first step towards her fate with the Sultan:

One day a queue of girls is moving through the palace, encountering the sultan by accident. They have to bow their heads and wait, peacefully and respectfully, for him to pass. However, Alexandra has a different idea. She yells, "Sultan Sülüman!" in a funny accent and gets his attention, to the others' astonishment. There is a deafening silence as he approaches her, and they look at each other for a few seconds. The sultan looks very stern, as one of his eyebrows is furrowed in anger. Then Alexandra falls into his arms, showing him her beautiful green eyes before once again saying his name wrongly, "Sülüman", and fainting in his arms. He shouts for bystanders to help find out what's wrong with the girl. After this slow-motion, meet-cute[3] scene, the sultan gathers himself and sternly walks off—in the wrong direction. He is surely under her spell! (Episode 1, 2011)

Instead of being a passive harem girl, Alexandra is full of life and tricks, while the sultan seems to lose his way after the encounter. The contemporary Turkish public, disturbed by power-hungry queens, mirror their sixteenth-century counterparts who—unable to comprehend unprecedented changes—found resolution for their astonishment in blaming Hürrem for bewitching the sultan (Peirce 1993) because—lodged in the palace—she became a crucial political agent. She acted as political confidante to the sultan, which is especially evident in the letters she wrote to Süleyman when he was absent from Istanbul on military campaigns, a role that was unfathomable for an Ottoman public.

Conspicuous Consumption and Authenticity

The third characteristic that contributed to a feminised sphere is the coupling of conspicuous consumption and authenticity concerns. The show displays immense riches, ornate clothing, and exquisitely decorated rooms with luxurious carpets and furniture. The production boosted and encouraged consumption of history. Jewellery was one of the most significant consumption areas alongside the furniture, kitchen gadgets, hair products, Turkish delight, lavish *hamam* visits, and home decor. The sale of jewellery was particularly successful as Süleyman is depicted as a jeweller in many scenes, frequently crafting rings and other jewellery. People in the palace are constantly exchanging pieces of jewellery, giving them as gifts,

---

[3] In film and television, a meet-cute is a scene in which the two people who will form a future romantic couple meet for the first time, typically under unusual, humorous, or "cute" circumstances.

and selecting and wearing an assortment of different items throughout the many episodes; indeed, one cannot help but notice the different types of jewellery as most of the episodes are shaped around them. The ring that Süleyman gives Hürrem as a gift becomes the subject of scandal when it is stolen by Mahidevran, Hürrem's arch-rival; it is stolen again in subsequent episodes. The series even gave rise to a court battle over sponsorship between the most powerful jewellery producers in Turkey, demonstrating the flourishing domestic, Middle Eastern, and Arab market for these items engendered by the show.

In our previous work (Ergin and Karakaya 2017), we have argued that the Turkish public found the conspicuous consumption of luxury fostered by *Magnificent Century* inauthentic, as Ottomans are usually equated with a pious modesty. Further, imitation is not highly regarded, and the public passes negative judgement on people who want to appear like TV characters. Similarly, some of our respondents claimed that popular culture waters down "historical truth" and disseminates "false history". Most of the respondents paired their criticisms of historical inaccuracy with arguments relating to guilty pleasures, coupling reports of their own anxious enjoyment of Ottomania with claims that these products of popular culture are harmful for others. Meanwhile, staunch critics of popular representations of Ottoman history were quick to point out that historical truth would not sell. One common refrain, a pleasure-centred defence of popular culture, was that television series are not documentaries. In other words, audiences in Turkey enjoyed Ottomania with their cultural shields up. Combining a social view of historical degeneration with an individual view of pleasure, consumers of Ottomania absolved their immersion in popular culture, believing that their critical stance makes them impervious to intrusions of the so-called false history. For them it was others, not as aware as they were, who were at risk.

The most frequently questioned issue was revealing clothing. By articulating their concerns and embarrassment about the depiction of the Ottoman palace women, the public did not only talk about history, but also signalled where they stand with regard to gender roles, women's sexuality, and moral boundaries (Ergin and Karakaya 2017). Based on the embarrassment expressed by some of the audience, we claim that frivolous luxury consumption and issues of authenticity, the constant lingering on a complex past by the converts, and domestic rivalry between palace women, congealed into a "private feminised sphere" which disturbed the audience because the "Ottoman" has overwhelmingly been coded as a masculine public domain. A domestic family setting which the Turkish TV viewer is accustomed to watching in other shows proved disturbing when it involved the lives of the sacred sultans, who were coded as belligerent yet just rulers who carried the torch of Islam. Resonating with the work of Berlant and Warner (1998), Lauren Berlant (1997, 2000, 2008), Michael Herzfeld (2005), and Martin Stokes (2010), we suggest the series contributed to a distinct cultural intimacy—a sense of togetherness that can result from encountering a common object of embarrassment.

This togetherness—shaped around a titillating embarrassment and anxiety—did not sit well with Erdoğan. As we mentioned earlier, he condemned the show by asserting that he did not recognise the sultan depicted on TV and asked for its cancellation, a moment that underlined where the president stands vis-à-vis Ottomania. When Erdoğan pushed for a belligerent Süleyman, a warrior who spent forty years on military campaigns, he was urging the series creators to remove attention from the sultan's devotion to a woman who played a significant role in Ottoman rule, and her drive to come to power.

In 2014, a peculiar thing happened. TRT (the government's official broadcasting channel) came up with its own nostalgic series, this time going back to the founding moment of the Ottoman Empire. This show is emblematic in showing how the nation state learns from the popular, making it serve its own purposes by tweaking the discourses, but still benefiting from the nostalgic allure.

Resurrection: Ertuğrul: State-Endorsed Popular

Resurrection: Ertuğrul aired between 2014 and 2019, and was an instant hit domestically; Netflix USA now airs the show, indicating its global appeal. Most recently, Egypt has banned *Resurrection: Ertuğrul*, among other Turkish series, because, it is claimed, Erdoğan's propaganda is directed at reviving the Ottoman Empire in the region. An in-depth analysis of the first two episodes of *Resurrection: Ertuğrul* proves fruitful in establishing its significance for neo-Ottomanism, what it did to Ottomania, and how it differs from it.

The show counters the feminised-private sphere in *Magnificent Century* in several ways. First, it portrays a severe divide between Christianity and Islam, unlike the anxiety-inducing fluid boundaries shown through the character development in *Magnificent Century*. For example, the narrative in the first episode is woven around the rigidly clashing forces of Islam and

Christianity. Moreover, a duality of the oppressor and the oppressed maps perfectly unto Christianity and Islam. The moral structure of the series' universe is strongly anchored in traditional authority and shaped around Ertuğrul as an honourable yet lonely hero. He is depicted as a fierce warrior who is constantly portrayed in neo-Ottomanist discourse as fighting against the West at the expense of being perceived as not looking after his own interests. Ertuğrul seeks justice, rejects siding with the oppressor, and follows tradition even when that is the hardest route. Second, there is not much room for conspicuous consumption in *Resurrection: Ertuğrul*. The nomadic settlement, arranged with tents and workstations amidst a famine, is joyous but simple. It always seems to be sunny and busy with hard work: women are always weaving, smiths relentlessly hammer iron, and people cook or carry water. And third, most importantly, the way gender roles are displayed is very different from *Magnificent Century*'s Ottomania. In *Resurrection: Ertuğrul*, women are modest, hardworking, and unassuming, unlike the outspoken and enticing women of *Magnificent Century*. In the following section we scrutinise this topic further by looking at how gender operates through these two distinctive heteronormative imaginaries, and how the public interprets the difference between the two paradigms.

Meet-Cute

Essentially, the pilots of both *Resurrection* and *Magnificent Century*, are an extended meet-cute. The following excerpt shows how Halime and Ertuğrul meet, signalling the prevalent themes of the series:

> Ertuğrul, a keen, proud warrior with no interest in power and politics, gathers his insatiable warrior posse of three, and gallops away on a hunt as an admiring young woman beams at him. As Ertuğrul pursues a gazelle, whose beautiful eyes feature in a close-up, he hears the cries of a girl, and his hunt is interrupted. The look on the gazelle's face and the girl's eyes are identical. Magically and auspiciously, Ertuğrul and his men emerge from the bushes at the exact moment the girl's father calls for mercy and help from Allah. Here the audience gets treated to an eight-minute fight scene where Ertuğrul smilingly slashes, chops, axes, and swings his sword against the Christian soldiers, killing them all. In contrast to the grim and gloomy Christian figures, Ertuğrul has a constant mischievous, proud, and handsome smile on his face. He manages to save the girl from imminent rape and rescues her brother and her father. The wide-eyed girl looks on, helpless, throughout

the whole scene, even though she had been able to kick a horse and kill a man to escape, minutes before Ertuğrul arrived. The genial yet belligerent Ertuğrul saves the day. Yet the girl is coy and does not want to leave with Ertuğrul; she is proud and hesitant. Ertuğrul's sidekicks say, "It's easy to defeat a herd of crusaders, but Ertuğrul looks like he is losing against this girl", adding, "It is easy to defeat a crusader brigade; Ertuğrul is done for now", and "Well, God has mercy on those who are defeated [by love]". (Episode 1, 2014)

Even though the circumstances under which Ertuğrul and Halime meet do not necessarily count as "cute", they are certainly unusual. In this scene, Halime almost gets raped by Christian soldiers, but thanks to proud warrior Ertuğrul, she escapes this scenario. Unlike Hürrem, the lead female character in *Magnificent Century*, Halime is presented as shy and quiet while Ertuğrul does not have an overt sexual appetite like Sultan Süleyman. Ertuğrul saves the girl out of a sense of duty, and it is his friends, not him, who make the observation that he might be falling for her. As you might recall, Hürrem made Süleyman notice her by screaming "Sülüman" inappropriately, and then fainting in his arms; Halime is not agentic that way. Similarly, in this scene of nostalgic heteronormativity, Ertuğrul's masculinity, unlike Süleyman's, features as duty rather than desire. The love interest, Halime, is an unassuming, shy woman, who is potentially a hidden princess. Ertuğrul is her saviour. Halime is not aware of her assets as a woman, such as her beauty. Unlike Hürrem, she does not speak unless spoken to, and does not show power or agency without permission. In this following excerpt Aykız, her female friend, asks Halime if she has a sweetheart:

Halime: "No there is nobody in my life. After my mother passed away all I did was look after my brother Yigit and keep my father company. Also, what man would want a girl like...?" (indicating that she is not worthy or beautiful enough to be loved).
Aykız: "Don't be silly, guys would fight for you and move mountains for you. When was the last time you looked at yourself in the mirror?" (She gives her a dagger, so she can see her beautiful reflection.) (Episode 1, 2014)

Halime, unlike Hürrem, has not been in love before. She does not even think she is worthy of love. We understand from her questions, however, that she might now be thinking about a warrior in these terms, and also that she might be the worrying kind. In fundamentalist responses to nationhood, rather than being symbols of change, women are constructed as the reproducers of culture (Yuval-Davis 1997). Accordingly, both Halime and Ertuğrul's mother, Hayme Hatun, in *Resurrection: Ertuğrul* are coded as modest carriers of tradition. Unlike Ertuğrul and other men who are destined to change the world—flaunting their agency on horseback—and unlike Hürrem, who had the guts to throw herself into the sultan's arms, the women in *Resurrection* show an agency bound to *oba*, the pastoral land, visible in their patience, hard work in weaving and cooking, and in their unassuming, pure appearance. Furthermore, even though they display a melancholic beauty, they are not aware of it—it is passive. Men act on the world, where women are coded as culture and the bearer of pastoral tradition.

In *Resurrection: Ertuğrul*, the *oba*-bound pastoral women garbed in ethnic clothing, coupled with their wise and patient demeanour, recall depictions of land—in this case *oba*—as a woman, which Kolodny (1975) labels the "pastoral impulse". These nurturing, receptive, and gratifying women are like the soil, nurturing the seed that the agentic men provide and giving birth to life. Carol Delaney (1991) argues that this "pastoral impulse", which likens women to fertile soil and nature, "glorif[ies] the receptivity of women, but deprive[s] her of creativity" (1991, 35). Neo-Ottomanism, disturbed by agentic palace women who fought for power, once again relegates the place of women to that of passive carriers of tradition, bound to an eternal pastoral.

In follow-up interviews[4] we found that the feminised-private sphere created in *Magnificent Century* was further consolidated. People equated the harem it depicts with women and feminine intrigue. Moreover, they asserted a gendered division in viewership, underlining that more women watched *Magnificent Century* because they like intrigue, and men watched *Resurrection: Ertuğrul* as they are into "belligerent stuff". In line with this, Carney (2019) documents how *Resurrection* garnered a new form of re-enactment in which sword-wielding male viewers mimic Ertuğrul's fights in real time. These highly popular, almost exclusively male fanfare videos on YouTube, full of jubilant cheering and cursing, further consolidate the show as a male domain. Some informants claimed that *Resurrection*

[4] These data come from Karakaya's dissertation work. She conducted follow-up interviews to investigate the shift between 2012 and 2017.

is a great propaganda tool that motivates people, that when international politics do not seem to be going well, people escape into its winning world and find solace in its atmosphere. In other words, the show wove daily international politics into its fabric, thereby also operating as a release valve. When people felt underwhelmed by Turkey's performance in the political arena, or felt that a country had "insulted" Turkey, they resorted to boosting their morale by watching *Resurrection: Ertuğrul*, a practice attesting to the way in which TV series have been absorbed into neo-Ottomanist state propaganda (Karakaya 2020).

Conclusion

In this chapter we have unpacked the overlaps and differences between neo-Ottomanism and Ottomania, two different veins of Ottoman nostalgia which are in continuous discord, even though they rely on the same past for their inspiration. Based on our comparative reading of the two nostalgic shows, it is apt to argue that neo-Ottomanism further defined and consolidated itself as a rival paradigm to Ottomania after 2014 by mobilising its own popular cultural interpretations of the past. An entertaining, titillating, and potentially subversive show, *Magnificent Century* became the yardstick used by neo-Ottomanism to hammer home, once again, what it is not. Gender, in this process—as always—became a sphere of contestation. *Magnificent Century*'s feminised-domestic sphere circumvented a more conservative culture industry to reclaim what its proponents deem the true history of the authentic and patriarchal Ottomans. Neo-Ottomanism co-opted Ottomania, a potentially light-hearted, cosmopolitan engagement with the Ottoman past, and made it "his" by hardening its fluid boundaries into rigidly heteronormative and overly self-assured categories.

Yet this is not the end of story. As *Resurrection: Ertuğrul* and *Magnificent Century* aired simultaneously between 2014–2017, some *Magnificent Century* fans stopped watching it, as they started to feel that the show was moving in a more conservative, neo-Ottoman, direction. This association of Ottoman symbols with a conservative interpretation of the Ottoman past led a segment of people to distance themselves from their popular cultural pleasures. Cultural power is very complicated, and the relationship between the more fragmented commercial nostalgia and the state-led populist project is not one which is completely controllable, even by cunning political players. People who left *Magnificent Century* and Ottomania remind us that mobilising culture will not always lead to the intended outcome, pointing to the ultimate instability of hegemony. No matter how vast the resources are, mobilisation will not necessarily lead to the expected result: complete interpellation. This reminds us once again that culture is a social force on its own.

Magnificent Century begins every episode with the proviso, "This series has been inspired by history." *Resurrection: Ertuğrul* has a seemingly similar, but meaningfully different message, "This series has been inspired by OUR history." As these two statements indicate, a history war in Turkey is being fought over nostalgic TV series. The president watches, comments on, and commissions series, having realised that he can create a strong hybrid by combining aspects of fun, entertainment, and light-hearted commercial nostalgia, with the mobilising, unifying, and collective effervescence induced by neo-Ottoman discourse. With *Resurrection*, the techniques and tropes of popular culture are co-opted to create a rigid history that is marked by authoritarian populist binaries (Karakaya 2018) of "us" versus "them", the "infinitely good" and the "horribly bad". Once again, the ownership of the "true" Turkish history is consolidated and forced onto people. Different interpretations, potential contestations, and recognitions of flaws and ambiguities are cut off right where they might most be expected to spring forth.

References

Altınay, Ayşe Gül. 2004. *The Myth of the Military Nation: Militarism, Gender, and Education in Turkey*. New York: Palgrave Macmillan.

Berlant, Lauren Gail. 1997. *The Queen of America Goes to Washington City: Essays on Sex and Citizenship*. Durham, NC: Duke University Press.

———. 2000. *Intimacy*. Chicago: University of Chicago Press.

———. 2008. *The Female Complaint: The Unfinished Business of Sentimentality in American Culture*. Durham, NC: Duke University Press.

Berlant, Lauren, and Michael Warner. 1998. Sex in Public. *Critical Inquiry* 24 (2): 547–566.

Brockett, Gavin D. 2014. When Ottomans Become Turks: Commemorating the Conquest of Constantinople and Its Contribution to World History. *The American Historical Review* 119 (2): 399–433.

Carney, Josh. 2019. ResurReaction: Competing Visions of Turkey's (Proto) Ottoman Past in Magnificent Century and Resurrection Ertuğrul. *Middle East Critique* 28 (2): 101–120.

Çayir, Kenan. 2009. Preparing Turkey for the European Union: Nationalism, National Identity and 'Otherness' in Turkey's New Textbooks. *Journal of Intercultural Studies* 30 (1): 39–55.

Çınar, Alev. 2005. *Modernity, Islam, and Secularism in Turkey: Bodies, Places, and Time*. Minneapolis: University of Minnesota Press.

Delaney, Carol Lowery. 1991. *The Seed and the Soil: Gender and Cosmology in Turkish Village Society*. Berkeley: University of California Press.

Ergin, Murat and Yağmur Karakaya. 2017. Between Neo-Ottomanism and Ottomania: Navigating State-Led and Popular Cultural Representations of the Past. *New Perspectives on Turkey* 56: 33–59.

Fisher-Onar, Nora. 2011. Constructing Turkey Inc.: The Discursive Anatomy of a Domestic and Foreign Policy Agenda. *Journal of Contemporary European Studies* 19 (4): 463–473.

Gemalmaz, Mehmet Semih. 2004. Evaluation of Data Concerning Human Rights Criteria Obtained from a Survey of Textbooks. In *Human Rights Issues in Textbooks: The Turkish Case*, ed. Deniz Tarba Ceylan and Gürol Irzık, 9–48. Istanbul: Tarih Vakfı Yurt Yayınları.

Giddens, Anthony. 1991. *Modernity and Self-Identity : Self and Society in the Late Modern Age*. Stanford, CA: Stanford University Press.

Herzfeld, Michael. 2005. *Cultural Intimacy: Social Poetics in the Nation-State*. 2nd ed. New York & London: Routledge.

Karakaya, Yağmur. 2018. The Conquest of Hearts: The Central Role of Ottoman Nostalgia within Contemporary Turkish Populism. *American Journal of Cultural Sociology* [online].

———. 2020. Imperial Daydreaming: Disentangling Contemporary Ottoman Nostalgia in Turkey. Unpublished doctoral dissertation. University of Minnesota, Twin Cities.

Kolodny, Annette. 1975. *The Lay of the Land: Metaphor as Experience and History in American Life and Letters*. Chapel Hill: University of North Carolina Press.

Muhteşem Yüzyıl: 5. Bölüm. n.d. Accessed 17 May 2021. https://www.youtube.com/watch?v=lzjIC9p87D4&lc=UggZ1Dk7nvtswngCoAEC.

Murinson, Alexander. 2006. The Strategic Depth Doctrine of Turkish Foreign Policy. *Middle Eastern Studies* 42 (6): 945–964.

Öncü, Ayşe. 2000. The Banal and the Subversive: Politics of Language on Turkish Television. *European Journal of Cultural Studies* 3 (3): 296–318.

———. 2011. Representing and Consuming 'the East' in Cultural Markets. *New Perspectives on Turkey* 45 (3): 49–73.

Peirce, Leslie Penn. 1993. *The Imperial Harem: Women and Sovereignty in the Ottoman Empire*. Oxford: Oxford University Press.

Potuoğlu-Cook, Öykü. 2006. Beyond the Glitter: Belly Dance and Neoliberal Gentrification in Istanbul. *Cultural Anthropology* 21 (4): 633–660.

Sönmez, Erdem. 2020. A Past to Be Forgotten? Writing Ottoman History in Early Republican Turkey. *British Journal of Middle Eastern Studies* 47 (1): 1–17.

Stokes, Martin. 2010. *The Republic of Love: Cultural Intimacy in Turkish Popular Music*. Chicago: University of Chicago Press.

Tokdoğan, Nagehan. 2020. Reading Politics through Emotions: Ontological Ressentiment as the Emotional Basis of Current Politics in Turkey. *Nations and Nationalism* 26 (2): 388–406.

White, Jenny B. 2013. *Muslim Nationalism and the New Turks*. Princeton, NJ: Princeton University Press.

Yang Erdem, Chien. 2017. Ottomentality: Neoliberal Governance of Culture and Neo-Ottoman Management of Diversity. *Turkish Studies* 18 (4): 710–728.

Yuval-Davis, Nira. 1997. *Gender and Nation*. Sage: London.

CHAPTER 3

Lovers of the Rose: Islamic Affect and the Politics of Commemoration in Turkish Museal Display

Torsten Janson

REVIVING ART, CONTESTING THE PRESENT

"Our principal guide in shaping our future is undoubtedly our history and this civilization of the heart and love that we have inherited." With these words, President Erdoğan opened his foreword to the "Aşk-ı Nebi" (Love for the Prophet) exhibition of calligraphy, held in Istanbul in 2013. Elaborating on the "revival of classical and traditional arts", Erdoğan contended that calligraphic art today demonstrates a striking revitalisation, after being "hidden away in the dusty chests of history". Collectors used to come to Istanbul to acquire classic works; now they come for new calligraphy. While rooted in tradition, calligraphers "present a unique contemporary face of our classical arts" and "a new leap forward". The

T. Janson (✉)
Lund University, Lund, Sweden
e-mail: torsten.janson@ctr.lu.se

© The Author(s), under exclusive license to Springer Nature Switzerland AG 2023
C. Raudvere, P. Onur (eds.), *Neo-Ottoman Imaginaries in Contemporary Turkey*, Modernity, Memory and Identity in South-East Europe,
https://doi.org/10.1007/978-3-031-08023-4_3

"essence, spirit and understanding" we find in art will "show us the way and become an inherent part of our lives" (Hilye-i Şerif Catalogue 2013, 10–11).

Erdoğan's words capture the interconnection (and institutionalisation) of memory, aesthetics, and devotion in Turkish cultural politics under the auspices of the AKP (Adalet ve Kalkınma Partisi, Justice and Development Party) government. The showcasing of the Ottoman past provides more than a claim on a cherished artistic heritage. Compounding cultural, virtuous, and affective values, it provides a paradigm for the present as well as the future. Between the lines, the President denounces secularist Kemalism for neglecting Turkey's Islamic-Ottoman artistic and civilisational heritage. He positions himself and the AKP government as devoted to rectifying this neglect, as patrons of living Ottoman-Islamic art forms and cultural practices. This feeds into a memory-political construction of a Turkish, socio-conservative nationalism in continuity with an (imagined) Ottoman past (Eickelman and Piscatori 1996; Çınar 2005; Tokdoğan 2018; Janson and Kınıkoğlu 2021).

Notably, here the President does not refer to an Ottoman cultural heritage or Islamic art tradition in general, but the devotional-calligraphic genre of *hilye-i şerif*: "the noble description" of Prophet Muhammad.[1] The *hilye* has deep roots in Islamic theology, literature, and Prophet devotion. Lyrically describing the physical and moral attributes of Muhammad, *hilye* poetry has a central role in the yearly *mevlid* rituals, commemorating the birth of the Prophet. As described in detail by art historian Christiane Gruber, during Ottoman times *hilye* poetry was rendered into calligraphic form as "verbal icons" (Gruber 2019, 285ff), establishing *hilye-i şerif* as a distinct genre of visual-devotional art. Its central motif has been the love (*aşk*) and longing felt for the departed Prophet, and the aspiration to re-establish affective and redemptive proximity through visual representation (Gruber 2017; Schick 2011).

---

[1] A note on spelling and transliteration: the Arabic word *hilya* literally means description, or *hilye* in Turkish. During the Ottoman period, the calligraphic artform in focus for this essay was often referred to as *hilye-i şerife*. In the following, however, I refer to it as *hilye-i şerif*, following recent conventions and—most notably—the print material of the exhibitions here discussed. I use Turkish forms of Islamic concepts only in direct quotes, and Ottoman-Turkish spelling only for technical concepts relating to the components of *hilye-i şerif* (*âyet*, *hilâl*, etc.). Otherwise, I apply simplified Arabic forms for proper names and Islamic/Quranic concepts, excluding diacritical signs (Muhammad, Ali, Kaba, Quran, *masjid*, etc.).

In *hilye* poetry and calligraphy, a central metaphor for this affective conjuring of the Prophet has been the sweet-smelling, pink rose. It developed in the late Ottoman period into a fully-fledged devotional doctrine known as "the rose of Muhammad", compounding the Prophet's human-bodily nature (coded red) with the supra-corporeal (white/golden) light of divine revelation (Gruber 2017, 2019). "The rose of the Prophet", Gruber contends, "is one of the most significant metaphors expressive of Muhammad's supernatural beauty that blossomed under the aegis of mystical-devotional traditions during the late Ottoman period." (Gruber 2017, 225).

During the past decade, such themes have been central in the grand *hilye-i şerif* exhibitions created as part of ever-aggrandising, state-organised *mevlid*. Such exhibitions have repeatedly been organised in Hagia Sophia (Ayasofya) and Topkapı Palace Museum, contributing to a (re)sacralisation of secular and museal memory sites. Erdoğan's enthusiasm for the "revival of classical and traditional arts" hence finds shape in the context of memory-political contest, ritual *mevlid* celebrations, and museal-cum-devotional practice. To draw on Paul Connerton (1989), social memory finds shape in (museal exhibitions of) a chosen past, commemorated in the present. Political-nationalist imaginations surface in inscribed (textual, visual) as well as incorporated (ritual, performative) memory practice.

As shall be developed below, academia has devoted a keen interest to the importance of museums and heritage sites in the construction of social memory, nationalism, and public values. Even so, little work has explored the bourgeoning museal landscape of Turkey as a visual-performative form for political contest (for notable exceptions, see Shaw 2002; Yilmaz and Uysal 2007; Karahasan 2015; Bozoğlu 2020; Janson and Kınıkoğlu 2021; Kınıkoğlu 2021). Devotional art exhibitions, I shall argue, provide an important modus for promoting a cultural-nationalist heritage politics.

Yet memory politics transcend museal institutional orchestration. The sacralisation of Turkish memory emerges in a nexus of cultural institutionalism, pedagogics, consumption, and a ritualisation of public space. The metaphors of Prophet devotion are appropriated (and recast) in diverse aesthetic formats and performances, ranging from "high-cultural", museal art exhibitions to pre-school pedagogics. A touch stone in such appropriation has been the rose of Muhammad, endlessly varied in public display, ritual commemoration, and student crafts. Beyond its focus on *hilye-i şerif* exhibitions, therefore, this essay aims at probing the multimodality of the politics of commemoration and Islamic affect—inside and outside of museums buildings. It explores the broader cultural trajectories of heritage politics, museal display, ritual performance, and religious-conservative nationalism in contemporary Turkey.[2]

My argument will be developed in four sections. The first discusses museums as spaces for exhibiting nationalism, and the growing interest in religion and affect within a new museology. The second section explores how Turkish museums have appropriated aspects of such a new museology, accommodated to current state interests. Inspired by the theoretical perspectives of Paul Connerton (1989), it demonstrates how museal display has co-occurred with a religious-performative ritualisation of public space, and interventions in contested memory sites. In the process, Islam and the Ottoman past is re-constructed, re-imagined, and re-spatialised, not only as a national-cultural heritage, but as a matrix for social life.

The following two sections delve into recent *hilye-i şerif* exhibitions in the context of such memory-political processes. In dialogue primarily with Christiane Gruber's (2017, 2019) work on floral metaphors in Prophet devotion, the third section explores how the rose of Muhammad is negotiated and developed in contemporary *hilye-i şerif* design. The final section develops this into a synthesising reflection on Turkish memory-politics as it surfaces in museal-cum-ritual display. Ultimately, the exhibitions of *hilye-i şerif* invite an Islamic-nationalist, pious gaze, with the prophetic body of Muhammad as its affectively imagined, calligraphically inscribed, and ritually exhibited object.

Museums, Nationalism, and Religion: Key Issues and Recent Trends

Nationalism emerges through the imagination of communities, symbolically organised around invented traditions and rituals. Images of the past are part and parcel of aspirations to produce popular cohesion and political legitimacy in the present (Anderson 1983; Hobsbawm 1983;

---

[2] This essay is partly based on fieldwork in Topkapı Palace Museum, Panorama 1453 History Museum, MiniaTürk, and Hilye-i Şerif ve Tesbih Museum (2004 and 2016–2019); partly on analysis of calligraphies and print material from temporary exhibitions of *hilye-i şerif* (2010–2015) and Hilye-i Şerif ve Tesbih Museum. The sections on Topkapı Palace Museum and Holy Birth Week/Mevlidi Nebi largely rely on my collaboration with Neşe Kınıkoğlu (see Janson and Kınıkoğlu 2021). I wish to express my gratitude to Mehmed Çebi, collector and patron of contemporary *hilye-i şerif* for his kind permission to reproduce works from his collections, which have provided the basis of several recent exhibitions.

Connerton 1989). In this context, national museums have played a central role, one that coincided with the rise of nationalism (Duncan 1991). Typically located in public city centres, modern museums became the material-cum-symbolic embodiments of state power. Exhibitions were assembled to show and tell national history, rhetorically incorporating citizens as national subjects within the processes of the state (Bennett 1988, 99; Hetherington 2011). This is not to say that national identities were constructed as stable or static. On the contrary, museums "are always in the process of becoming national or (so to speak) of un-becoming and re-becoming national" (Bennett 2015/2018, 85).

In the ambition to foster national identity, traditional museal display tended to be authoritarian and monological. Cultural and artistic heritage exhibits literally became the objective manifestations of national historiography and state authority. Public museums produced utopian space, offering "a seductive vision of harmonious existence and communal values" (McClellan 2008, 8). Hence museal space was devised to instil a sense of grandeur and awe as "the temples of our times" (Duncan 1991; Buggeln 2017, 11). In other words, public museums make the state *look good*: "progressive, concerned about the spiritual life of its citizens, a preserver of past achievements and a provider for the common good" (Duncan 1991: 93). In this sense, museal engagement with time is ambivalent, simultaneously forging images of past, present, and future (Zuanni 2017, 63).

Religion has assumed an ambiguous role in such state orchestrations of nationhood. European nationalism was ideologically constructed on representations of religion as modernity's archaic and irrational other (Van der Veer and Lehmann 1999; Petersen and Walhof 2002). While national museums are filled with religious artefacts and motifs, displays have traditionally been organised according to an aesthetic, secular-rational, and chronological taxonomy (Paine 2013; Bennett 2015/2018). Anthropology museums have more actively engaged with popular devotion, meanwhile representing religious objects as artefacts of "culture" in demystified (and colonial) displays (Paine 2013, 3; Bennett 2015/2018; Roberts 2017; Byrne 2017).

Importantly, however, in many formerly colonised nation-states, such an othering dualism has been less pronounced. Middle Eastern nationalisms have often incorporated religion as a patriotic and unifying national duty—if one that is relieved of (alleged) popular and heterodox practices (Petersen and Walhof 2002, 8; Gelvin 2002; Shaw 2002). Hence religion has served as a discursive and ritual template for nationalism (Petersen and Walhof 2002: 9). Middle Eastern nationalism has drawn (and continues to draw) on the pool of resources of religious traditions (Connerton 1989; Eickelman and Piscatori 1996, 29; Van der Veer and Lehmann 1999; Chelkowski and Dabashi 1999).

The secular Turkish Republic is a case in point. Wendy Shaw (2002) has demonstrated how secular nation-builders claimed and represented Islamic artefacts in museums as vestiges of a "Turkish heritage": religion was appropriated to forge the idea of secular-national-historic-cultural unity. In the process, Islamic objects were set apart (Zubaida 2011), both from their ritual contexts and contemporary significance. Such efforts notwithstanding, Turkish museums remain sites of contesting readings and practices. Devout visitors continue to invest locales and objects with sacred significance, sometimes turning secular museums into destinations for pilgrimage (Shaw 2002; Janson and Kınıkoğlu 2021). Recent academic scholarship has devoted increasing attention to such non-conformity versus secular museal display (Paine 2013; Buggeln et al. 2017; Roberts 2017; Zuanni 2017; Britton 2017; Byrne 2017).

A New Museology: Critical Perspectives on Subjectivity, Materiality, Affect, and Representation

Museums and museum studies have seen an immense expansion in recent decades, along with an emergent new museology. Central themes have been the multiplicity of historiographies; the power mechanisms (and colonial regimes) of state-organised representation; and the subversion of uniform national identity narratives of heritage, culture, ethnicity, class, gender, and sexuality (Karp et al. 1990, 1992; Stern Hein 2007; Mills 2008).

Traditional museology has been devoted to collecting, documenting, preserving, exhibiting, and interpreting objects, with a hierarchical, authoritarian, Euro/Americano-centric, and male voice, universally defining cultural-aesthetic values. In contrast, a new museology emerging from the late 1980s had a focus on social subjects and museums as social/political actors. Museums do not display objects—museums display ideas (Weil 1990). This shifted the perspective to the experiences of visitors and museums' commitments to local communities. It highlighted questions of relevance, meaning, and access (Harrison 2005), suggesting that museums should scrutinise their representations of society, culture, and history.

Since museums are involved in forging social memories, norms, and relations (Stam 2005, 57), they should aspire to democratic, inclusive, empowering, and multi-vocal displays (Ames 1992, 161; Harrison 2005, 48).

This has implications for the very notion of museums as public. Jennifer Barrett (2012), for example, scrutinises Habermas' notion of the public sphere from a museal perspective, exploring museums' ability to stage various forms of being in the public (Barrett 2012, 16). Today, multiple and contesting publics have stakes in display and historical representation (Kidd 2014; Fraser 1992). Furthermore, museums need not be confined to a museum building but may involve public space more broadly. Such perspectives have had profound effects on pedagogics. Museums increasingly emulate a theme-park model, while retaining their ambitions to stimulate learning, which requires that they understand themselves as fundamentally performative and theatrical (Kidd 2014, 4). This, in turn, means engaging with the present (and hence with popular culture), not only to spice up dusty exhibits, but as the very objective (and subject) of display: "the present is an integral part of any story the 'new' museum will tell", as Harrison (2005, 47) observes.

Parallel with the emphasis of a new museology on subjects, the material turn in culture studies has renewed (and recast) an interest in objects, analysing materiality in its social and political context (Harrison 2005, 46–47). If the new museology turned its attention from objects to actors and ideas, material studies explore how ideas and social relations are hosted in and structured by objects (Appadurai 1986). The material perspective highlights the performativity of subjects vis-à-vis material objects: people "do things with *things*", as Paine (2013, 9) has put it.

In the wake of such theories, and in response to community interests, there is a burgeoning (public, academic, as well as curatorial) interest in religious objects in museums. Should museums accommodate the "needs" of religiously/emotionally/politically invested visitors? A longstanding resistance to such accommodation is currently being reconsidered in curational practice and academic discussion (Paine 2013; Buggeln et al. 2017; Classen 2016). This goes hand in hand with the questioning of univocal historiography, sensitivity to community relations, and museal engagement with popular culture, but it is also a reflection of pedagogical reconsideration. How are museums to engage their audiences, in the context of multicultural society, globalisation, consumerism, and identity political awareness? Such questions are particularly pertinent for displays considered sensitive. Holocaust museums and victim memorials often have redemptive and theodical aspirations, dealing with trauma through narratives on historical meaning, resilience, and triumph in "a metahistorical, metaphysical resolution of good versus evil" (Buggeln 2017, 18).

Hence, historiographic and affective representations often merge in contemporary display, moving far beyond the detached taxonomies of traditional museology. "The emotional museum" radically reconceptualises the museal mission. Museums may assume ownership of affect, and actively pursue both emotional and cognitive learning (Kidd 2014, 11; Drago 2014). Such ambitions render conventional display "hopelessly inadequate" (Byrne 2017) for representing objects (regarded as) alive with supernatural potency or affective significance. Recognising the limitations of narrative/visual display, many museums create immersive environments to build a multi-sensory historical experience (Turek 2017, 61). As an ultimate side-lining of the artefact, some history museums even create "experience spaces" without any actual artefacts at all, geared at claiming a heritage by creating "a feel" for a crucial historic moment through bodily sensations (Classen 2016). On display are not artefacts of history, but a subjective-affective experience of (redemptive) history itself.

Despite such recent appeals to multi-sensory experiences, however, an "empire of sight" still largely rules museal display (Classen 2016; Bennett 2015/2018, 100), although museums worldwide are re-inviting touch, sound, and bodily movement to boost visitor experience. Ambient soundscapes and creative lighting routinely animate historical displays. Even silent art museums commonly provide immersive soundscapes in audio guides, while "regional music" and videos of "local life" often accompany ethnographic exhibits. On the other hand, "It would be novel for an exhibition of Renaissance art to feature videos of period houses and a soundtrack of barking dogs and rumbling carriages …. Such display strategies would be seen as trivialising great works in order to cater to plebeian tastes" (Classen 2016, 140).

Despite aspirations towards diversifying representation, broadening access, and inviting multi-sensory experiences, museal practices hence remain marred by class distinctions and notions of "high" versus "low culture", colonial regimes, and skewed representations of culture and society. Since the 1980s, museums have diversified in terms of reflecting the previously denigrated experiences of women, minorities, children, youth, and various class positions. Yet representation remains deeply imbalanced. The artists whose work appears in US art collections, for instance, are 87%

male and 85% white, according to a report from the Public Library of Science (2019), while in 2018 a mere 11% of the acquisitions of 26 prominent American museums were works by female artists (Halperin and Burns 2019). In view of such figures, the critical perspectives of film critic Laura Mulvey (1975) remain valid for many exhibitions. As in cinema, the visitor's perspective is largely locked into a male gaze, focusing on, and following active, male protagonists. Conversely, women in art museums tend be depicted as passive and inward-looking objects of (mostly male) attention and desire. Or as John Berger already noted in *Ways of Seeing* (1972): "Men look at women. Women watch themselves being looked at" (Berger 2008/1972, 47).

In order to break with such representational patterns, critical feminist and queer perspectives suggest a foundational retheorisation of museal display. Robert Mills (2008) reflects on how a queer museum may be theorised, given the subversive perspectives of queer theory vis-à-vis the utopian/unifying ambitions of (conventional) museums. Similarly, Hilde Stern Hein (2007) argues that museal mis- and underrepresentation reflects something deeper than a mere imbalance. Museums are predicated on (and uphold) an order of display wherein subjects, neutralised as visitors, walk among objects of value, gazing and marvelling, under the sway of the authoritative voice of the museum. Critical perspectives challenge the very economy of ownership and entitlement which defines the subject's relation to the object (whether observed, desired, cultivated, possessed, tamed, conquered, or revered) (Stern Hein 2007, 32). Visitors are never neutral, but carriers of (gendering, sexual, racialising, class-related) discourses and positions. Conversely, objects on display are not "simply there" as vestiges of "our" history, religion, or artistic tradition. They are carriers of constructed and reified narratives on identity, historical moments, systems of classification, and artistic individuality.

Hence a critical museology subverts the very notions of "the masterpiece" or "individual ingenuity". Art museums may be organised to exhibit processes of relational, contingent, and collective creativity. Science museums may turn away from the notion of "scientific breakthroughs" and create displays of how we explore and understand the world. And instead of adulating the reified "historic moment", history museums may represent history as broad (non-linear, non-teleological) processes of change, from the vantage point of "common people" rather than political, cultural, or religious elites. In short, museums may disengage with insular historical moments, individual genius, and tangible objects-under-our-gaze, in exchange for "the depiction of practices and processes that vitalise societies" (Stern Hein 2007, 39). Or with Mills: theorising a queer museum "affords an opportunity to think museums themselves radically *other*wise." (Mills 2008, 50).

THE SACRED AND THE CITY: ISTANBUL AS A RITUAL-MUSEAL MEMORY SITE

As noted, much recent scholarship on religion in museums has focused on the responsibility to diversify representation and counteract exclusion: to "see through the eyes of the devotee" and to accommodate devotional needs (Paine 2013, 10). Yet, as pointed out by Tony Bennett (2015/2018), there is a shortage of studies on how relations with religion in museums reflect "wider changes in the organisation of particular regimes of power and authority" (Bennett 2015/2018, 86). Studies of the management and governance of museums of Islam and Islamic art remain scant (Guidi 2019). And the ambiguous relationship between religion, secularity, and museal display in/of the Middle East and Islam begs particular attention (Eldem 2013a; Bennett 2015/2018).

Accordingly, we need to explore how devotional accommodation in museal practice may feed into state interests (Wedeen 1999; Janson and Kınıkoğlu 2021). The representational and pedagogic principles of a new museology may be appropriated in affective idealisation and sacralisation of an authoritarian state apparatus—a far cry from the ideals of criticality, democratisation, and empowerment. This may showcase (rather than subvert) the reification of defining historical moments and contribute to a further adulation of individualistic brilliance, in turn incapacitating nuanced and balanced museal representation. Similarly, the inclusion of community interests in public displays in no way guarantees representational diversity and critical historiography. On the contrary, it can be a vehicle for supplanting one (reified) historic-national narrative with another. The following sections explore such tendencies in recent Turkish museal display.

Re-Narrating, Ritualising, and Redeeming History in Turkish Memory Space

Istanbul carries a particular importance in Turkish, Islamic-Ottoman memory (Çınar 2005; Koyuncu 2014). Turkish memory production has recently re-engaged with religion in (and beyond) museal space in the construction of a contesting nationalist narrative. Ritual performance and establishment (or re-representation) of museal memory institutions contribute to a sacralisation of urban public space, in turn reinforcing Istanbul as a nucleus for Islamic-political imagination (Janson and Kınıkoğlu 2021). With Paul Connerton (1989), we may think of this as a juxtaposition of inscribed cultural memory and incorporated ritual practice, rendering contemporary Turkish museal-ritual practice mnemonically powerful and politically significant.

Literary canon, political and legal tracts, scholarship, education, and memory institutions such as museums are essential repositories of inscribed social memory. Yet, Connerton surmises, memory is also conveyed through incorporated ritual practice, not least commemorative ceremonies, constructing nationalist imagination in the social re-enactment of central moments and personae of the past (Connerton 1989, 4–5; 62). In so doing, commemorative space ambiguously engages with time. Ritual-performative re-enactment of the past suspends mundane time; participants become contemporaneous with defining moments; and relics become consubstantial with paradigmatic personae (Connerton 1989, 42–43).

Commemorative rituals are distinctly social (and political), in at least two ways. They are porous, thereby affecting non-ritual behaviour and mentality in mundane social life, and they reflect group affiliation, determining what pasts are worthy of commemoration (Connerton 1989, 20). Remembering "is not a matter of reproduction but of construction; it is the construction of 'schema,' a coding, which enables us to distinguish and, therefore, to recall" (Connerton 1989, 27). Hence, commemorative ritual constructs the past as non-contingent and forward-looking; it carries meaning and purpose with relevance for the present (Connerton 1989, 42–43). Socially commemorated past is redemptive (Buggeln 2017, 18).

Topkapı Palace and Hagia Sophia stand out as particularly significant memory-political sites. They attract some three to four million visitors annually, second in Turkey only to the Atatürk mausoleum/museums of

Anıtkabir in Ankara. With the 1923 establishment of the Turkish Republic, they were among the primary targets of a republican politics of forgetting. As the symbolic centres of Ottoman power, administration, and piety, both sites were converted into secular museums. Today, they are subject to intense contestation and re-narration: Hagia Sophia as an object of religious sentiment; Topkapı Palace as hosting objects of religious significance, vestiges of an idealised religio-political past.

The relics collection of the Topkapı Palace Museum remained closed until 1962, illustrating the public obscurity of Islam under Kemalist rule (Shaw 2010, 129). Once opened, objects were displayed according to a secular, more or less random, and emotionally detached display. With the 1997 and 2007 reorganisations, however, the exhibit was provided with a distinct ritual ambience (sonically immersed in Quran recitation) and a carefully crafted Islamic-thematic narrative. The visitor symbolically enters the cradle of humankind and monotheism (thematised by the Kaba sanctuary of Mecca). Guided through the material vestiges of Quranic prophets, the visitor ultimately reaches the epitome of Muhammad (represented by his Blessed Mantle, Hırka-i Saadet) and Islamic society under the Caliphate (represented by the swords of the Prophet's Companions, al-Rashidun). Even so, the exhibit underscores the materiality of the artefacts and establishes distinct disciplinary boundaries: relics should be approached with modesty and affect, but not (allegedly) improper, popular veneration (Janson and Kınıkoğlu 2021).

The thematic reorganisation thus accommodates several traits of a new museology; yet subsumes the display under an Islamic-ideological historiography. It immerses the visitor in a ritual-affective soundscape and thematically narrates history as non-contingent and forward-looking. It appeals to (and constructs) the devotional sentiments of a faith community, while disciplining the visitor according to Sunni-orthodox mores. The reorganised exhibition ambiguously negotiates a secular-rational and religious-affective taxonomy by chronologically re-arranging the artefacts according to sacralised historiography, as vestiges of creation, prophethood, and religious-political order. It hence invites a commemoration of the past as a redemptive paradigm for social, political, and religious order, intertwining a sacred past with the present: Islamic order was established by the Prophet, carried through the Caliphate, claimed by the Ottoman Empire, and is currently patronised under AKP rule. In short, the display concomitantly makes claims on an Ottoman heritage, spatialises sacred history, and symbolises contemporary Turkish space as a carrier of (purportedly) sound Sunni-Islamic orthopraxy.

Significant as the sacralisation of the museal space of Topkapı Palace may be, it has attracted far less attention than the status of Hagia Sophia. For decades, strong interests have advocated the museum's reversion to a formal mosque (Hürriyet 25 March 2019). Debates reached an apex (or nadir) with the official decision for its reversion during the summer of 2020. Even before this, however, Hagia Sophia had been subject to a process of gradual Islamic ritualisation. During the 2015 celebrations of Holy Birth Week (to which I return below), *hilye-i şerif* exhibits were organised in Hagia Sophia as well as the Topkapı Palace Museum, thus appropriating secular museums for ritual-commemorative displays. Ritualisation was further accentuated when the first Quran recitation in 85 years was performed in the building during the grand opening of the *hilye-i şerif* exhibition (Daily Sabah 2015-04-11). Henceforth, prayer calls and Quran recitations were repeated on several occasions (*Hürriyet* 2 July 2016).

Notably, the Islamic signification of Hagia Sophia has been interconnected with the reification and iconising of the Ottoman conquest of Istanbul, commemorated yearly on Istanbul Day (May 29). Istanbul Day has grown into a carefully ritualised public event, more spectacularly celebrated than any republican fixture (Bozoğlu 2020, 107). The Ottoman conquest hence has emerged as an alternative foundational moment for the Turkish nation (Çınar 2005). When Hagia Sophia again staged Quran recitations during the 2020 celebration of Istanbul Day (*Hürriyet* 31 May 2020), the event was politicised in polemic rhetoric within the Islamic movement. Fatih Erbakan, leader of the New Welfare Party (Yeniden Refah Partisi) agitated for the reversion as a fulfilment of the conquest, announcing, "Ayasofya testifies that Istanbul is Islamic land and will remain so until the Day of Resurrection." Hagia Sophia is "the symbol of superiority over the West" and its re-opening as a mosque will be "the seal of the conquest" (*Yeni Akit* 29 May 2020).

We see in the reversion discourse a contestation of the very notion of the secular museum. Hagia Sophia is considered a mosque and a living ritual space, not a museum of an Islamic (let alone Christian) past. Not only the Ottoman conquest, but the *Islamisation* of Hagia Sophia is reified as the defining moment for the Turkish nation. To the extent Hagia Sophia should be commemorated, it testifies to the historic and civilisational triumph of Islam. The museum thus transcends its spatial as well as temporal nature. If we are to think of museums as the "temples of our time" (Duncan 1991), the reverted Hagia Sophia not only re-accentuates its religious, templar significance. It redefines the very conception of "our time" thus sanctified. Hagia Sophia does not house "Western", republican time, as conceptualised by secular Kemalism. It neither exhibits the Ottoman heritage in any nostalgic or "cultural" display. Hagia Sophia is the living temple of an Islamic-modern present, in civilisational continuity with a reclaimed Ottoman past, and carrier of the socio-conservative virtues and values of the AKP government (and other segments of the Islamic movement).

The establishment in 2009 of the Panorama 1453 Museum, with its dramatic graphic/aural representation of the Ottoman conquest, has contributed to further institutionalising this contesting Islamic-Ottoman national narrative. In her study of the politics of display and visitor experiences of the museum, Gönül Bozoğlu demonstrates how visitors tend to accept the idealised historical narrative of the display. The museum thus primarily appeals to, reinforces, and animates already nurtured political-religious-affective predispositions. Many come to the museum to "exercise emotion and to practice their membership of a memory community" (Bozoğlu 2020, 184). Or formulated with Connerton (1989): the construction of memory in the Panorama museum reflects and co-constructs group-affiliation and pours into the present. The museum experience animates a sense of socio-political victimhood: visitors charge "the republicans" with enforcing historical amnesia and suppressing religious rights. Commemoration in the museum not only looks forward. It feeds into distinct ideological processes that support state interests:

> [P]eople's *reflective* nostalgic expressions lamenting the demise of the Ottoman regime often prefaced *restorative* statements about the need to recapture (perceived) Ottoman values and to replicate Ottoman achievements in the present ..., often directly linking to the AKP and sometimes to Erdoğan himself. ... [It] was the AKP who were bringing back the "forgotten" and "real" past and history. (Bozoğlu 105; 107)

We find a different yet related manifestation of restorative nostalgia in the architectural miniature park of MiniaTürk (established in 2003), which celebrates Turkey in 122 monuments at a scale of 1:25. Notably, most of the models replicate Ottoman heritage sites and, while 22 of the models showcase Istanbul, there are only two Ankara monuments. Furthermore, 13 of the miniaturised Ottoman monuments are situated beyond current

Turkish borders. Hence Miniatürk represents Turkey less as a political entity, and more as a civilisational realm (or dream). Transcending a mere recreational space for family leisure, Miniatürk provides an interpretive framework and restorative-architectural map of Turkish-Ottoman grandeur, physically inscribed on the Golden Horn (Yilmaz and Uysal 2007, 123).

Expanding Memory Spaces: Visual-Ritual Commemoration in Public Space

The memory-cultural re-narration of Turkish history under the auspices of the AKP government is not confined to museal institutions. It has coincided with a sacralisation of urban public space and secular education, appropriated for Islamic-ritual commemoration. Of particular importance have been the state-orchestrated celebrations of *mevlid*, the birthday of Prophet Muhammad. As analysed in a different context (Janson and Kınıkoğlu 2021), *mevlid* celebrations were provided with a national platform in 1989. Reconceptualised as Holy Birth Week (Kutlu Doğum Haftası), during the 1990s and 2000s, it developed into a massive ritual-educational event, disconnected from *mevlid* proper. Its public success notwithstanding, the celebration incurred growing critique from various quarters: some criticising it as subverting secular education; others as an un-Islamic invention (*bida*) or "Westernised" quasi-Christmas; yet others as connected with the Gülen movement. In response, the celebrations were reconceptualised once again in 2017, now as Mevlid-i Nebi (The Prophet's Birth), and ritually as well as temporarily realigned with traditional *mevlid*.

The nationalised *mevlid* celebrations prompted a wave of religious-pedagogical creativity, and unprecedented incursions of Islamic signifiers into Turkish secular public space. Inside and outside of museums, exhibitions of Islamic art and crafts were organised, juxtaposing the inscription and incorporation of memory in performative practice and display, the most prominent symbol of which became the rose of Muhammad. On Rose Day (Gül Günü), religious officials distributed long-stemmed red roses among the citizens, and political officials (representing parties across the political spectrum) posed in media with red roses in their hands. Centralised organisation, in turn, stimulated locally organised, impromptu (and sometimes problematic) manifestations: red roses dropped from a hot-air balloon, rosewater sprayed over pedestrians with the water-cannon of an armoured police car, a Quran-shaped and rose-decorated birthday cake—the latter incurring a formal investigation within the Presidency of Religious Affairs.

Schools were the primary scene for the celebrations, accommodating ritual commemoration to educational-cum-nationalist discourse and practice. In 2011, Holy Birth Week was included in the national curriculum and by 2017 more than 30,000 events were organised nationally, the vast majority targeting school children. Educational *mevlid* films were produced for national television, ceremonially screened in public schools, and circulated through social media. In glossy visuals, haughty narrative, and dichotomies of social virtues and vices, the films appeal to Islam as an affective ethics of citizenship. Elaborate student performances, contests, and displays of commemorative crafts were organised in schools across Turkey, endlessly variating the rose motif.

In such accommodations, the references to Prophet devotion often eclectically intersected with sacred geography, Islamic scripture, and ritual orthopraxy, but also with globalised Valentine's Day and birthday aesthetics (Fig. 3.1). In a set of poetic "Happy Mevlid" cards, the rose of Muhammad sprouts from a poem as "the crown of love", promising the scent of roses for "the one who remembers Muhammad" (Pinterest 2017a-10-26). A preschool wall is decorated in the shape of a prayer niche (*mihrab*). Rather than indicating the direction towards Mecca, however, the niche "points" towards the Prophet himself. Marked with the calligraphic "Muhammad" above, it is composed of red and white paper roses, and covered with garlands of Valentine hearts (Pinterest 2017b-10-26). A religious high school installation references the Prophet through red rose petals, strewn in front of a Quran stand, surrounded by candlelight symbolising revelation. A sign reads "Recite!" (*Oku!*), the first word revealed for the Prophet (Quran 96: 1), and the blackboard showcases abundant references to Islamic creed. Above it we read, "The Lord of Roses Muhammed" (Güllerin Efendisi Hz. Muhammad) (Ayşe-Kemal İnanç School 2019-11-12).

Holy Birth Week also became the framework for inventive exhibits commemorating sacred history and geography in the midst of urban space. In the Üsküdar district of Istanbul in 2015, a religious-educational theme park was erected, called "A Trip from Üsküdar to the Age of Felicity" (Üsküdar'dan Asr-ı Saadet'e Yolculuk) (Fig. 3.2, top). The name invokes the notion of *asr-ı saadet*, the ideal, pristine society of the Prophet's early Caliphs. As vehicles for this trip into sacrosanct space-time, the park

3 LOVERS OF THE ROSE: ISLAMIC AFFECT AND THE POLITICS... 73

Fig. 3.1 Public, ritual, and pedagogic commemorations in school displays and student crafts, cross-referencing Islamic ritual, Prophet devotion, and global Valentine Day's aesthetics

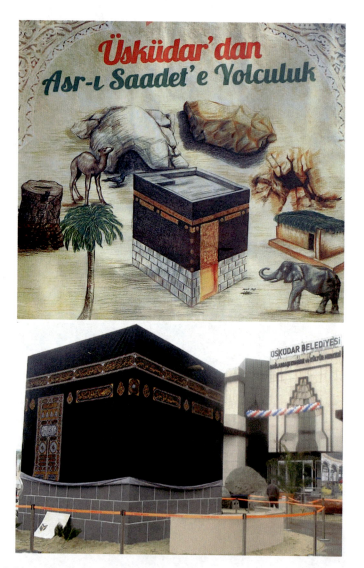

Fig. 3.2 A "Trip to the Age of Felicity" arranged in Istanbul 2015. Models and narratives drawing on sacred geography and historiography suspended mundane time and space in the midst of urban public space

displayed models illustrating central events and places in the Prophet's life, the most conspicuous (and controversial) of which was a 4–5-metre-high replica of the Kaba sanctuary (Fig. 3.2, bottom). The models were accompanied with didactic stories, combining appeals to miracle and wonder with lessons about the origin of religious institutions and central events in the formation of Islamic creed, as is common in Islamic children's literature (Janson 2012).

To draw on Connerton, the park performatively—if playfully and pedagogically—staged a suspension of mundane time. Or to quote the opening speech of Mayor Hilmi Türkmen: "We call our Üsküdar the land of Haram, the land of Kaba (*Üsküdar'ımıza Harem toprağı Kabe toprağı diyoruz*)" (Üsküdar Municipality Website: 8 October 2015). It re-enacted a paradigmatic past, staging visitors as contemporaneous with defining moments; and models as (only too!) consubstantial with sacred geographies and ritual monuments. This is not to suggest that all accepted the pious script of the Mayor. To the very contrary, the display became subject for satire, ridicule, and solemn debate. In response to stunts of mock pilgrimage to the mini-Kaba, the Presidency of Religious Affairs was compelled to issue a statement that circumambulation of the model was strictly forbidden, and the model was discretely removed from the exhibition (*Hürriyet Daily News* 21 April 2015).

It thus appears that the Üsküdar theme park went over the top, transgressing boundaries for the theologically acceptable. It is therefore not surprising that the commemorative exhibitions increasingly have become aligned with formal memory institutions since the 2017 realignment with traditional *mevlid*. In recent years, photographic exhibits of the Islamic relics of Topkapı Palace Museum have been organised in public space across Turkey; from the Eyüpsultan Mosque in Istanbul to small urban squares in Anatolia; from state museums to Tramway stations (Fig. 3.3, bottom right). As vestiges of prophethood and revelation, the relics appeal to similar affective-devotional registers (Gruber 2019) as the theme park, yet safely within the confines of institutional memory.

In conclusion, the many recent examples of public-visual and ritual-commemorative practices discussed in this section illustrate that sacralised (museal, educational, and public) space functions as something more than a setting for devotion: it incorporates citizens as national subjects within the processes of the state (Bennett 1988). It does so by crafting an image of the Turkish state (and the ideal Turkish citizen) as one centred on Islam—not understood as a national-cultural heritage, but as a matrix for

Fig. 3.3 Inner courtyard (*left*) and one exhibit room (*top right*) in the *Hilye-i Şerif ve Tesbih* Museum. *Bottom right*: Sacred Trusts exhibit in Tünel Metro station, Istanbul 2017

social life and political authority. And while the display of sacred past expands beyond the walls of museum buildings, formal memory institutions remain a central repository for social memory. In the following two sections, I shall turn my attention to the establishment of one such memory institution: the museal showcasing of *hilye-i şerif* as a visual-devotional, and quasi-national, Turkish art form.

HILYE-I ŞERIF: COMMEMORATION, AFFECT, AND NATIONALISM IN CALLIGRAPHIC INCORPORATION

As part of the state-run Holy Birth Week celebration, grand exhibitions of *hilye-i şerif* calligraphy and *tesbih* (rosaries) recurred annually from 2010. They were conceptualised as Aşk-ı Nebi (Love for the Prophet), hence explicitly drawing on religious-affective imageries. The exhibitions became permanent with the establishment of the Hilye-i Şerif ve Tesbih Museum in 2016, housed in a restored Ottoman *medrese* building in the Süleymaniye neighbourhood of Istanbul (Fig. 3.3, left and top right). Contemporary *hilye-i şerif* art (and its relation to a classic Ottoman art) remains a largely uncharted field, worthy of systematic historical, artistic, and theological analysis beyond the scope of this essay.[3] The following is intended to probe museal exhibitions as artistic-devotional-political events. I shall tentatively explore how artistic inscription, performative practice, and political imaginations intersect in cultural production and memory institutions commemorating the Ottoman past. How have the exhibits been organised as events within a ritual-commemorative of *mevlid* and Prophet devotion? What tendencies may be discerned in contemporary *hilye-i şerif* art vis-à-vis an Ottoman artistic-devotional legacy in general, and the rose theme in particular?[4] And how do the museal exhibitions of contemporary *hilye-i şerif* relate to broader trajectories of AKP memory politics?

Negotiating a Devotional Art Tradition in Contemporary Display

With roots in Arabic literature and theology, the *hilye* tradition developed in Ottoman times into a particular form of Sunni-Sufi religiosity. Poetry and visual art came to function as "visual-textual proxies" for the Prophet (Schick 2008; Gruber 2017, 2019). Floral metaphors served to interweave theological-devotional themes with chromatic and olfactory references, developing into a full-fledged devotional-mystical doctrine known as the rose of Muhammad (*gül-i Muḥammed*) (Gruber 2017, 224f). To

---

[3] For discussions of the classical *hilye-i şerif* tradition, see further Derman 1998a; Derman 1998b; Zakariya 2003/ 2004; Schick 2008; Gruber 2017; Gruber 2019. Selim Deringil (1993) offers important perspectives on the invention of tradition in late-Ottoman nationalism and its symbolic expression, providing interesting historical parallels to the contemporary tendencies discussed in this essay, worthy of further exploration. For critical perspectives on the modern reception of Ottoman artistic and architectural traditions, see Eldem 2010, 2013a, b; Ersoy 2016. Christine Gruber (2019, 2020) is one of few scholars to explore how classical/devotional art traditions are subject to contemporary negotiation (and commodification) in Turkey (and beyond).

[4] I should underscore that this chapter does not engage in any exhaustive or systematic discussion of the calligraphic techniques or scripts employed in contemporary *hilye-i şerif*. For some observations in this regard, see Schick 2011. The purpose of the following is to probe the graphic composition and theological references in some recent work, as it negotiates a classical-devotional *hilye* tradition.

this day, Mehmet Hakani's (d. 1606) beloved poem *Hilye-i Şerif* (The Noble Description) remains a centrepiece of Turkish *mevlid* ritual. The poem builds on the description (*hilye*) of Muhammad's physical features and moral character as rendered in hadith—most important among which is the description attributed to Ali ibn Abi Talib (the Prophet's cousin and son-in-law). Hadith literature describes the Prophet's complexion as reddish. In Hakani's lyricism, this is transformed into a rosy pink, as the Prophet's persona is conjured through elaborate floral metaphor:

> In his pietistic verses, for example, Hakani tells us that Muhammad's body was of medium height, much like the rose buds (*nahl-i gül*) in the garden of paradise (*bâğ-ı cinan*), that his round and wide-open face resembled the rose (*gül-rüyu*), and that nobody had smelled anything more beautiful than his body's rose scent (*ten-i gül-büyu*). (Hakani's *Hilye-i saadet*, cited by Gruber 2017, 234)[5]

In development of such imagery, the colour pink itself became an analogy for Muhammad's prophethood, chromatically compounding his (red) human nature with the (white/golden) light of divine revelation. The pink rose, Gruber concludes, "visually recalls the Prophet's graceful composition and harmonious complexion while concurrently giving visual expression to his otherwise trans-human character. In brief, the rose connotes Muhammad's insubstantial and thus inappreciable qualities" (Gruber 2017, 227).

The literary *hilye* tradition was converted into calligraphic form by the master scribe Hafiz Osman (d. 1698), most likely as a visual interpretation of Hakani's poem (Fig. 3.4). The textual, visual, affective, and ritual commemoration of the Prophet thus remain closely interconnected and interreferential. As İrvin Cemil Schick underscores in a text written for the 2011 exhibition, Hafiz Osman created his *hilye-i şerif* format not only as a calligraphic panel but "as a devotional object to be visited by believers, to occasion a nexus with the Prophet" (Schick 2011, 14), calligraphically carrying the Prophet's promises, as rendered in Hakani's poem:

---

[5] A caveat: the grammar forms in this quote appear somewhat irregular, as I have been advised by colleagues versed in Ottoman-Turkish. Rather than aspiring to linguistic correctness, however, they are meant to illustrate the floral/cosmological metaphors in Hakani's opus and other Prophet devotional sources discussed in Gruber's empirically rich and illuminating article.

Fig. 3.4 Components of the *hilye-i şerif* (*left*), as developed by master scribe Hafız Osman (d. 1698) (model designed by author, following Derman 1998b; Uzun 1998). The panel by Gürkan Pehlivan (*right*), displayed at Hilye-i Şerif ve Tesbih Museum, strictly follows Hafız Osman's scheme. (Photograph by author)

> Whoever sees my pure Hilye
> Will be as though he has seen my beautiful countenance.
> If he becomes passionate the more he sees it,
> In short, if he comes to love my beauty,
> Then he will be spared the fire of Hell
> And will enter Heaven by the grace of God. ...
> (Hilye-i Şerif Catalogue 2011a, 13)

As a vehicle for such visual-affective visits, Master Osman's calligraphic *hilye* conjured a symbolic prophetic body from textual and visual components (Fig. 3.4). The head section (*baş makam*) contains the *bismillah* ("In the name of Allah, the Gracious, the Merciful"). The panel's centre is dominated by the circular belly or omphalos (*göbek*), containing the first part of Ali's *hilye*. The belly and the crescent (*hilâl*) form a cosmic metaphor of sun and moon. Around this cosmic omphalos hover al-Rashidun, the four first Sunni caliphs: Abu Bakr (Ebübekir), Umar (Omer), Uthman (Osman), and Ali. The lower register carries the verse (*âyet*, or belt, *kuşak*) from the Quran, praising the Prophet. It usually cites 21:107 ("And we did not send you, but for a mercy to the world") or 68:4 ("And indeed you are of a great moral character"). Under the verse follows the second part of the *hilye* in the foot or skirt (*etek*), framed on each side by a sleeve (*koltuk*). The body, finally, is encapsulated by an inner and outer sill or moulding (*iç pervaz, dış pervaz*) (Derman 1998b, 47).

With his panel, Master Osman provided a paradigm for artistic emulation as well as creative variation. While *hilye-i şerif* calligraphies usually remained within his scheme during Ottoman times (Gruber 2019, 288), in late Ottoman panels the entire composition could succumb to a floral structure, with the *hilye* delicately inscribed on the rose petals. Coming across as an expression of "Ottoman Rococo", Muhammad here became "the roseate juncture between the white light of revelation and the red blood of humanity; as well as the sweet-smelling flower of paradise" with curative and mystic-talismanic qualities (Gruber 2019, 298). Other late-Ottoman panels analogised the rose in the abstract, remaining within Master Osman's scheme while moulding letters into rosary structures. Gruber reads such panels as reflections of a long (Arabic as well as Ottoman) poetic and pious tradition of Prophet-imagery/imagination, prioritising "abstract expression over literal iteration". Beyond representing Muhammad's corporeality, the rose could "activate the devotee's 'esoteric eye' (*al-bashar al-batina*) in an effort to transcend the limitations of optical sight" (Gruber 2017, 249).

If we turn to the presentation of the "Aşk-ı Nebi" expos of *hilye-i şerif* calligraphy during the past decade, the accompanying catalogue texts and information boards have tended to underscore the devotional aspects of the art, coupled with nationalist-historiographic motifs. Forewords emphasise (and construct) the uniqueness of the *hilye-i şerif* as an Islamic art form: its Ottoman origin as well as its Turkish context, in both the past and the present. After Quranic calligraphy, it is the best example of Turkish devotional art, claims Mehmet Lütfi Şen, curator of the 2011 "Aşk-ı Nebi" exhibition in the Vatican. Just as European icons are sacred images, he surmises, *hilye-i şerif* panels are "concrete representations of love towards the Prophet" (Hilye-i Şerif Catalogue 2011b, 14). The *hilye-i şerif* is represented as the pinnacle of Islamic devotional art, and Ottoman

Turkey as its hub. In his essay for the 2013 exhibition, İskender Pala (a bestselling novelist and historian of Ottoman literature) celebrates Prophet devotion not only as a pietistic ideal but as an aspect of the Turkish national character. In lyrical hyperbole, saturated with floral metaphors, Pala expounds on *hilye-i şerif* panels as

> the flowering of a love kindled in the soul of the Turk; they blossomed like roses in a sultan's garden. They were the flowers of a sacred love dedicated to the Master of the Masters. Flowers which proved that nowhere else among Muslim communities could the love of the Prophet be as great as in these lands. ... And thus did the lovers of the Rose who were to follow ... carve the Rose onto their hearts and write His face onto their consciousness. (Hilye-i Şerif Catalogue 2013, 17–21)

In the exhibitions, we have seen no examples of "Rococo" roses overtaking the entire composition. Most contemporary panels display a measure of graphic restraint. Yet references to the rosary theme (and other devotional symbols) recur in various forms. We find abundant examples of roses surrounding the *göbek* or al-Rashidun, decorating the inner and outer sills, and/or in the interpunction of the *hilye* and *âyet*. In a panel by Ferhat Kurlu (Fig. 3.5, left), roses embellish every element of Master Osman's scheme.

Others depart from the scheme entirely, and draw on the rose theme through stylised, floral structures composed of calligraphic letters, often coded red or pink. Again, sometimes the roseate structure succumbs altogether, abstracted into a chromatic theme. In a panel by İbrahim Halil İslam (Fig. 3.5, top right), the *göbek* is fashioned as a stylised, calligraphic rose dominating the panel. It is composed of petals in the seven-fold shape of the letter "w" (*waw*). The rose petals, in turn, contain the Prophet's description, finely scripted in pink. In Sufi tradition, the letter *waw* often abbreviates *hu* or *huwa*, referring to God (and the aspiration of mystical unity with the divine).[6] Similarly drawing on mystic traditions, a panel by Levent Karaduman (Fig. 3.5, bottom right) centres the *göbek* as a stylised, red/white rose of Muhammad, against a fond of Islamic green. Here the inner, red petals repeat "my people/nation" (*ummati*) twelve times, alternated with an eight-fold repetition of *shafaa* in white, referring to the

---

[6] Through the emphatic, rhythmic repetition of *Allah-hu* (where *hu* functions as an intensive, approximately meaning "him", or "just him"), or merely *hu*, a mystic-ecstatic state of consciousness is pursued in some Sufi *dhikr* ritual techniques.

Fig. 3.5 Variations of the rose of Muhammad in contemporary *hilye-i şerif*, by Ferhat Kurlu (*left*), İbrahim Halil İslam (*top right*), and Levent Karaduman detail (*bottom right*). (Photographs by author)

(theologically disputed) notion of the Prophet's eschatological intercession on behalf of the believers. Forming a square or a cross, the outer structure of the rose is composed of stylised "Allah" couplets (coded in white), visually recalling tulips.

Several panels represent the Prophet through sacred geography, either in realistic detail or in stylised form. A panel by Fatima Ali (the only female calligrapher represented in the "Aşk-ı Nebi" expositions and Hilye-i Şerif ve Tesbih Museum) symbolises Muhammad through the Prophet's Mosque of Medina, encircled by a *hilye* crafted in Persian Kufic script (Fig. 3.6, top left). A panel by Abdullah Güllüce remains closer to Master

3 LOVERS OF THE ROSE: ISLAMIC AFFECT AND THE POLITICS... 83

Fig. 3.6 Creative re-appropriations of the *Hilye-i şerif* tradition through references to sacred geography, nationalism, and cosmology. Panels by Fatima Ali (*top left*); Abdullah Güllüce (detail, *top right*); Gürkan Pehlivan (*mid left*); Ebubekir Altıok (*mid right*); Levent Karaduman (*bottom left*); Ömer Şen and Said Abuzeroğlu (*bottom right*). (Photographs by author)

Osman's scheme (Fig. 3.6, top right). Yet here the artist has chosen to omit the crescent and expanded the *göbek* into an arcane image of Mecca and the Kaba sanctuary. While such locational references may provide an element of concreteness to the panels, they also function symbolically, as geographical vestiges of prophethood, ritually interconnecting the (Turkish) "here and now" to sacred space and time. The most playful (and daring) example of such a nationalist-devotional, spatio-temporal, (re)anchoring we find in a panel by Ebubekir Altıok, crafted as a Turkish flag (Fig. 3.6, mid right). Here the *bismillah* is inserted in the star of the flag, while Muhammad's name, epithets, and description inscribe its crescent, ambiguously compounding Prophet, Turkish nation, and secular Republic.

The Kaba references also invite cosmological readings, drawing on Mecca as the cradle and omphalos of Islamic faith (and humankind). Such references are manifest in an inventive *Hilye-i şerif* design by Gürkan Pehlivan (Fig. 3.6, mid left). Here the belly/omphalos seems to open a loophole into starry space, where a free-floating Kaba structure hovers in the centre of the crescent, surrounded by the Prophet's *hilye*, and flanked by two additional crescents centring Allah.

Finally, several contemporary panels embrace abstraction completely, supplanting bodily, flowery, or locational references with calligraphic sign, abstract form, and geometric structure. Yet another panel by Levent Karaduman plays with a three-dimensional, architectural design, composing a structure, interiorly "tiled" with square, Kufic calligraphy (Fig. 3.6, bottom left) of the 99 Glorious Names of Allah (*al-asma al-husna*). The names guide the vision down the interior of a green structure—the interior of the Kaba?—towards the description of the Prophet at its bottom. Here Karaduman's graphic design draws on Mind Craft aesthetics rather than a classic calligraphic tradition.

Likewise, Ömer Şen and Said Abuzeroğlu employ square, Kufic script in their rich and playful elaboration of Master Osman's paradigm (Fig. 3.6, bottom right). Here, the visitor encounters Muhammad as a sigil (repeated 79 times in black, once in red), forming a path-like moulding which encapsulates the inner elements. Visually following this path, the viewer is invited to, as it were, walk with, along, and toward the Prophet. On the diagonal, the *hilye* sets out in red and gold (compounding body and revelation) and concludes in blue (chromatically harmonising with Ali and the other Rashidun, who are vertically piled in four blue, Kufic sigils). In the lower right register we find the verse (21:107) in green, while the *bismillah* is coded red, just like the square Muhammad-sigil in the centre of the second *hilye* section. And here, too, we find the 99 Divine Names, forming a miniature panel just below the red *bismillah*.

The panels illustrated in Fig. 3.6 amply illustrate the variety and inventiveness with which contemporary *hilye-i şerif* art re-appropriates an Ottoman calligraphic heritage and devotional traditions, sometimes in reference to Sufi mysticism. With Schick (2011), one may contemplate to what extent such innovative designs remain within the *hilye-i şerif* genre. In his catalogue text, Schick proposes we think of the innovative interpretations in terms of "free verse" in relation to a formal, poetic tradition (Schick 2011, 27f). It is perhaps of little surprise that the museum has refrained from exhibiting several of the most daring compositions, while early exhibitions displayed the full range of artistic creativity. As shall be clear from the following, however, innovation comes in many forms, and visual creativity may side with Sunni-theological orthodoxy.

Re-Scripting the Prophetic Body

Despite the many examples of innovative designs, the most cherished panels tend to remain comparatively close to Master Osman's scheme. Recent award-winning works (on permanent display in the museum and/or represented in national and international exhibits) are characterised by elaborate and meticulous calligraphic artistry, often resulting from a collaboration between calligrapher (*hattat*) and illuminator (*tezhipçi*). Notably, if we probe into textual and semiotic detail, they often emerge as rich in scriptural content and strict in orthodox emphasis. I shall conclude this section by analysing two such panels in some detail.

A panel crafted by Cevan Huran and Emel Türkmen (Fig. 3.7, left) contains three horizontal *âyets*. Above the *göbek*, we find the standard verse 21:107. Below it, two Quran quotations follow, rarely occurring in *hilye-i şerif* panels: "Indeed We have sent you as a witness and a bringer of good tidings and a warner" (33:45), and the almost identical verse 17 of *sura* 105. In addition, three more Quran verses are found in the vertical sidebars and around the belly (33:40, 33:56, 68:4), all lauding the Prophet as the Seal of the Prophets (*khatam an-nabiyyin*). As in Master Osman's format, the *hilye* text is subdivided into two sections, one within the *göbek* and one between the two lower *ayats*. Notably, however, Muhammad is also represented with abundant honorary names and epithets, eight of which are coded in red ink: four located in the corners; another four hovering around the *göbek*. In addition, in the very centre of the design, a

Fig. 3.7 Two award-winning panels. Cevan Huran and Emel Türkmen (*left*) provide a lexicon of Muhammad nomination, in fairly close compliance with Master Osman's scheme. The structurally more inventive design by Avni Nakkaş and Emel Selamet (*right*) invokes the Prophet as the defender of monotheism, through extensive Quran quotations and symbolic/textual cosmic references

quatrefoil repeats *nabi* (Prophet) four times, resembling a rose containing the symbol of eternity. The other epithets salute him (from top left) as *majid* (magnificent); *sadiq* (righteous); *ahmad, muhammad, mahmud, hamid* (all variations of praiseworthy); *ajwad* (generous); and *tahir* (pure). In addition to the epithets coded red, yet another series of 25 prophetic names surround the belly (e.g. *khalil, rasul, mujtaba, qasim, amin*). The panel hence provides a veritable lexicon of Prophetic nomination. While this indexical redundance departs from Master Osman's *hilye* template, it otherwise retains its compositional structure more or less faithfully.

A panel crafted by Avni Nakkaş and Emel Selamet (Fig. 3.7, right) goes further in compositional, textual, as well as chromatic innovation, contrasting Islamic green with deep blue; the latter strewn with delicate garlands of flowers recalling a starry night sky. Here Master Osman's single *göbek* has geminated, naming the Prophet (*Muhammad, Ahmad*) in parchment-coloured twin bellies, encapsulated by Quran verses forming the symbol of eternity. On either side, we find smaller roundels with two more prophetic epithets: to the right *mahi* (effacer [of polytheism]) and *hashir* (gatherer [of believers]) to the left. The panel hence recalls four of the five names Muhammad attributed to himself, according to hadith. The description surrounds the belly, and the *âyet* (64:4) is inserted into the bottom roundel.

The choice of Quran verses for this panel is noteworthy. From the top left and curving downwards to the right, we find two Quran verses (48:28–29) chastising disbelief. The same theme is carried through the extensive quotation (53:1–31) encapsulating the twin bellies and curving through the eternity symbol. This polemic and theologically important *sura* contains the famous rebuttal of the deities al-Lat, al-Uzza, and Manat (and denouncing of the notion of the "Satanic verses"). Striking a cosmic chord (harmonising with the starry sky of the panel), it emphasises Muhammad's immutable character and his relentless monotheism:

> By the star when it descends,
> Your companion [Muhammad] has not strayed, nor has he erred,
> Nor does he speak from [his own] inclination.
> It is not but a revelation revealed,
> Taught to him by one intense in strength—
> (Quran 53: 1–5)

In short, visually recalling a scroll rather than a human body, the panel expounds on Muhammad as the defender of creed and effacer of polytheism, establishing monotheism as the eternal order, with ample references to scripture and visual-cosmological codes.

The two panels are examples of how contemporary *hilye-i şerif* art may anchor an Ottoman affective-devotional legacy in orthodox mores, while disassociating from mystical motifs. Historically, Sufi devotion has cherished the prophet as "the idealized heart of Muslim piety as well as the pinnacle of love". More than representing prophesy and rulership, believers have "conjured his presence as lambent, boundless, and everlasting" (Schimmel 1985; Gruber 2019, 12). The paratextual presentations of the recent exhibitions to some extent draw on such motifs, and certain calligraphies refer to mystical traditions (often so in graphically innovative compositions). Several of the award-winning and most exhibited panels, however, affirm a more scriptural and less metaphoric Muhammad. As such, *hilye-i şerif* may purportedly serve as an Islamic "national art" under AKP patronage. It combines artistic brilliance with devotional themes, appealing to the ritual *mevlid* setting, yet safely situated within the confines of Sunni-orthodox imagination.

A Nation on Display under a Pious Gaze

"People from all over the world, from Africa to Siberia, come here to meet our Prophet. This is like a meeting point. They come with love (*aşkla*)" (Bariş Samir, interviewed in Haber Türk 2016). Every Ramadan, long queues wind outside the Mosque of the Noble Mantle (Hırka-i Şerif Camii) in the Fatih neighbourhood of Istanbul. According to tradition, the Prophet himself entrusted his cloak to Uwais al-Qarani (Veysel Karani, 594–656). Bariş Samir, 59th great-grandson of Uwais, today carries out the "noble and honourable duty" of its guardianship and display. It is a 400-year-long tradition, yearly attracting more than a million visitors during Ramadan.

The visiting of the Mantle/Prophet during the holy month illustrates the intimate connection of memory, display, and ritual performativity in contemporary Turkish-Islamic devotion. Quite literally, the devotees come by means of love (*aşkla*) to the Prophet. It is not the Mantle that brings forth the Prophet; it is the visitors' affect which conjures their proximity with him. The Mantle provides the material vehicle—and Ramadan the ritual juncture—for this performative transition of sense into sentiment.

Something similar may be said about the "Aşk-ı Nebi" exhibitions of recent years. Just like the Mantle, the *hilye-i şerif* has traditionally been perceived to engender a sense of proximity with the Prophet (Schick 2011; Gruber 2017). While the meeting-per-Mantle remains affective, however, the calligraphy also provides a descriptive image of Muhammad. It juxtaposes graphic, textual, and chromatic signs and symbols. Hence an iconic yet ambiguous image of a Prophetic "body" emerges. It remains more abstract than tangible. It is equally affective as it is visual. And its visual/affective emergence finds social form in a ritual context. Hence the "Aşk-ı Nebi" exhibitions resonate with Connerton's (1989) perspectives on social memory: they are inscribed, ceremonial, and bodily-performative vehicles for recollection.

We may discern three visual strategies at work in contemporary *hilye-i şerif* art, providing three ways of seeing/sensing the Prophet: (1) the calligraphic sign and its scriptural references (e.g. hadith, Quran, Prophetic epithets, *al-asma al-husna*); (2) the components of Hafız Osman's graphic-corporeal, calligraphic scheme (e.g. head, belly, skirt, and sleeves), sometimes exchanged or enrichened with other references (geographical, architectural, cosmological, temporal); and (3) variations of the rose theme, drawing on devotional and mystic motifs in iconic-realistic detail or symbolic-graphic abstraction, compounding Muhammad's human-prophetic nature. To the extent that the *hilye-i şerif* thereby functions as a "devotional object to be visited by believers, to occasion a nexus with the Prophet" (Schick 2011, 14), the visit remains abstract and imaginary, its nexus fleeting and affective. It is in this capacity the *hilye-i şerif* qualifies as a verbal icon: a symbolic representation of Muhammad as the (essentially unrepresentable) carrier of divine revelation (Gruber 2017). Representational restraint stimulates a pious-affective imagination of the Prophet, as lent to an "esoteric eye" (Gruber 2017, 249).

If the Prophet conjured through *hilye-i şerif* remains susceptible to the workings of individual imagination, one may expect its textual aspect to render the encounter more concrete. In panel after panel, in row after row, the visitor encounters the same textual description of Muhammad's physical body, as recalled by Ali and recorded in hadith. Yet this homogeneity is deceptive. The script is no less open to interpretation and imagination than the symbolic head, belly, or sleeves. The viewer may read Muhammad as an aesthetic ideal and object for devotional affect to emulate. He may be sought as a practical, moral ideal, and upholder of social order (again to be emulated). He may appear as the enigmatic, esoteric manifestation of sanctity beyond comprehension. Or he may come across as any combination thereof.

Whether envisaged as mysterious enigma or stern moral precedent, the object of depiction and description remains an idealised masculine—if Prophetic—body. Centuries of devotional-gendered imaginaries contribute to animate the Prophetic body under the visitor's gaze. This gaze, in turn, is staged within the ritual context of *mevlid* and memory spaces of Hagia Sophia and Topkapı Palace, recast into a cultural-educational celebration of Turkish-Islamic nationalism. As we have seen, current Turkish museal practices are part of a broader political venture, one aspiring to strengthen Islamic signifiers and socio-conservative gender norms in contemporary Turkish society. Indeed, the fixation of the *one* (idealised, male) individual and *one* singular historic moment recurs in the (museal and ritual) representations of Ottoman and Islamic history discussed in this chapter. Concomitantly, museums and public spectacles are more or less devoid of women's experiences or contesting historical narratives.

The nexus between visitor and exhibited/ritualised object therefore carries multiple social, normative, and political aspects. The exhibitions (aspire to) posit the visiting subject as a member of a faith community, within which the image/script gains its socially constructed, objectified meaning. Hence the non-representational character of the *hilye-i şerif* not only facilitates individual-affective imagination; the "blanks" are also filled with group affiliation. "Aşk-ı Nebi" exhibitions (just like the Sacred Trusts, the Panorama 1453, the reverted Hagia Sophia) invite the exercise of a social-affective community. They are memory-cultural vehicles for the crafting of Islamic-political imaginations.

To this end, Turkish museums claiming, commemorating, and constructing the Islamic-Ottoman heritage have successfully embraced aspects of a new museology. Exhibitions appeal to multi-sensory experience, religious-political affect, and communitarian as well as entertainment values. They do so by narrating parochial, Sunni-centric historiography, in a distinctly monological, mono-gendered, authoritarian, and social-conservative voice. Such observations provide critical perspectives onto the "rediscovery" of religion in contemporary curatorial practices and museum studies.

Concluding Note: A Valentinisation of Islamic-Ottoman Memory

In her ground-breaking analysis of gender representation in cinema, Laura Mulvey (1975, 8) committed to annihilating pleasure and beauty, insofar as it contributes to the narrative marginalisation and visual objectification of women. I have attempted something similar—if transposed to a venture of scrutinising the representation of history and religion in recent Turkish museal display. The aesthetic pleasure and devotional beauty traversing the "Aşk-ı Nebi" expositions, I have argued, are part and parcel of an authoritarian, memory-political dynamic. Museums under the auspices of the AKP government have become targets as well as mechanisms for a politics of memory-cultural Islamisation. The purpose of this chapter has been to expose and analyse how aesthetics, devotion, memory, ritual, and politics intersect in contemporary Turkish museal display.

The "Aşk-ı Nebi" exhibitions (now permanent in the Hilye-i Şerif ve Tesbih Museum) have established a cultural scene for gazing at objects crafted to inspire aesthetic pleasure and devotion. Ambiguously they intertwine detachment and affect, text and body, devotional imagination and Quranic injunction, inscription and performativity. If organised in seemingly dry art shows, the ritual *mevlid* setting as well as the choice of exhibit venues underscore their affective-political vibrancy. So do the Quran recitations and political speeches (performed by male dignitaries for overwhelmingly male audiences) in opening ceremonies and catalogue texts. All such factors contribute to animate the shows as devotional-commemorative, as well as nationalist-historiographical, public events. They invite visitors to claim the heritage and commemorate the past under a restorative and pious gaze.

Contemporary *hilye-i şerif* panels display a striking variety. While many follow Hafız Osman's classic scheme, expositions also testify to an inventive and playful relation to the artistic heritage. Yet, if several award-winning panels break ground in formal inventiveness, they also are rich in Quranic content. To be bluntly quantitative: gazing at numerous contemporary *hilye-i şerif* panels means gazing at considerably more scripture than Prophet. If the devotional, mystic, and curative relationship with the Prophet has traditionally been the object of this gaze, contemporary *hilye-i şerif* art exhibitions also forge other relationships: scriptural, ethical, gendered, and socio-political. This is not to suggest that devotional-affective aspects perish in contemporary *hilye-i şerif*-gazing. Yet the revival of the genre takes place in a context of state-organised, conservative Sunni orthodoxy, hardly encouraging mystical experience and affective intoxication.

The "Aşk-ı Nebi" exhibitions have taken place as "high cultural" events in a broader memory market of Ottoman/Islamic nostalgia and aesthetics, produced in commercial ventures and state-run memory institutions. This conspicuously establishes religious signifiers in Turkish public space. It not only sacralises and subverts (purportedly) secular public space and memory institutions. Accommodated to globalised cultural and aesthetic codes, it also commodifies history and religion. *Mevlid* films appropriate the glossy aesthetic of Discovery Channel documentaries. The iconisation of the red (not pink) rose of Muhammad draws on ancient symbolism as much as Valentine's Day aesthetics. Sacred history and geography are recreated in family infotainment theme parks. Such innovations and incursions into Turkish public space indeed spur pious enthusiasm, but also polemic, ironic riposte, and ridicule among those discontented with Islamisation.

The revitalisation of *hilye-i şerif* art thus surfaces in a memory-political context defined by contestation over the very definition of the Turkish public sphere, its institutions, and spaces. Heritage politics under the auspices of the AKP is organised in tandem with a construction of a matrix of nationalist virtues: a pious-affective ethics of citizenship. Or to draw on Carol Duncan: "Aşk-ı Nebi" exhibitions make the Turkish-Islamic state *look good*. On display is not only love (*aşk*) for the Prophet, but love for an Islamic Turkey. In a context of commodified Valentinisation, the mystical rose of Muhammad readily lends itself to such memory-political re-signification.[7]

References

Ames, Michael M. 1992. Biculturalism in Exhibitions. *Museum Anthropology* 15 (2): 7–15.

Anderson, Benedict. 1983. *Imagined Communities: Reflections on the Origin and Spread of Nationalism*. London: Verso.

Appadurai, Arjun. 1986. Introduction: Commodities and the Politics of Value. In *The Social Life of Things*, ed. Arjun Appadurai, 3–63. Cambridge: Cambridge University Press.

Ayşe-Kemal İnanç School: 12 November 2019. Mevlid-i Nebî Sergisi. http://akinancaihl.meb.k12.tr/icerikler/mevlid-i-neb-sergisi_8167929.html. Accessed 27 May 2021.

Barrett, Jennifer. 2012. *Museums and the Public Sphere*. Chichester: Wiley-Blackwell.

Bennett, Tony. 1988. The Exhibitionary Complex. *New Formations* 4 (Spring): 73–102.

———. 2018 [2015]. Museums, Nations, Empires, Religions. Reprinted in Tony Bennett, *Museums, Power, Knowledge: Selected Essays*, 78–98. London: Routledge.

Berger, John. 1972/2008. *Ways of Seeing*. London: Penguin.

Bozoğlu, Gönül. 2020. *Museums, Emotion, and Memory Culture: The Politics of the Past in Turkey*. London: Routledge.

---

[7] The research for this chapter has been generously supported by the Center for Advanced Middle Eastern Studies (CMES), Lund University, within the framework of the research project The Middle East in the Contemporary World (MECW).

Britton, Karla. 2017. Toward a Theology of the Art Museum. In *Religion in Museums: Global and Multicultural Perspectives*, ed. Gretchen Buggeln, Crispin Paine and S. Brent Plate, 21–27. London: Bloomsbury.

Buggeln, Gretchen. 2017. Museum Architecture and the Sacred: Modes of Engagement. In *Religion in Museums: Global and Multicultural Perspectives*, ed. Gretchen Buggeln, Crispin Paine and S. Brent Plate, 11–20. London: Bloomsbury.

Buggeln, Gretchen, Crispin Paine and S. Brent Plate. 2017. Introduction: Religion in Museums, Museums as Religion. In *Religion in Museums: Global and Multicultural Perspectives*, ed. Buggeln Gretchen, Crispin Paine and S. Brent Plate, 1–7. London: Bloomsbury.

Byrne, Denis. 2017. Museums, Religious Objects, and the Flourishing Realm of the Supernatural in Modern Asia. In *Religion in Museums: Global and Multicultural Perspectives*, ed. Gretchen Buggeln, Crispin Paine and S. Brent Plate, 71–79. London: Bloomsbury.

Chelkowski, Peter J. and Hamid Dabashi. 1999. *Staging a Revolution: Art of Persuasion in the Islamic Republic of Iran*. London: Booth-Clibborn Editions.

Çınar, Alev. 2005. *Modernity, Islam and Secularism in Turkey: Bodies, Places and Time*. Minneapolis: University of Minnesota Press.

Classen, Constance. 2016. *The Museum of the Senses: Experiencing Art and Collections*. London: Bloomsbury.

Connerton, Paul. 1989. *How Societies Remember*. Cambridge: Cambridge University Press.

Daily Sabah 11 April 2015. Turkey: Historic Istanbul Museum Hagia Sophia Witnesses its First Quran Recitation in 85 Years. https://www.dailysabah.com/istanbul/2015/04/11/turkey-historic-istanbul-museum-hagia-sophia-witnesses-its-first-quran-recitation-in-85-years. Accessed 27 May 2021.

Deringil, Selim. 1993. The Invention of Tradition as Public Image in the Late Ottoman Empire, 1808 to 1908. *Comparative Studies in Societies and History* 35 (1): 3–29.

Derman, Uğur M. 1998a. *Letters in Gold: Ottoman Calligraphy from the Sakıp Sabancı Collection, Istanbul*. New York: Metropolitan Museum of Art.

———. 1998b. Hat. In *Türkiye Diyanet Vakfı İslâm Ansiklopedisi*, vol. 18, 47–51. Istanbul: Türkiye Diyanet Vakfı. https://islamansiklopedisi.org.tr/hilye#2-hat. Accessed 27 May 2021.

Drago, Alex. 2014. The Emotional Museum. In *Challenging History in the Museum: International Perspectives*, ed. Jenny Kidd et al., 19–22. Farnham: Ashgate.

Duncan, Carol. 1991. Art Museums and the Ritual of Citizenship. In *Exhibiting Cultures: The Poetics and Politics of Museum Display*, ed. Ivan Karp and Steven D. Lavine, 88–103. Washington: Smithsonian Institution Press.

Eickelman, Dale F. and James Piscatori. 1996. *Muslim Politics*. Princeton: Princeton University Press.
Eldem, Edhem. 2010. Ottoman and Turkish Orientalism. *Architectural Design* 80 (1): 26–31.
———. 2013a. Cultural Heritage in Turkey: An Eminently Political Matter. In *Essays on Heritage, Tourism and Society in the MENA Region*, ed. Dietrich Haller, Achim Lichtenberger and Meike Meerpohl, 67–91. Leiden: Brill.
———. 2013b. Writing Less, Saying More: Calligraphy and Modernisation in the Last Ottoman Century. In *Calligraphy and Architecture in the Muslim World*, ed. Muhammad Gharipour and İrvin Cemil Schick, 465–483. Edinburgh: Edinburgh University Press.
Ersoy, Ahmet. 2016. *Architecture and Late Ottoman Historical Imaginary: Reconfiguring the Architectural Past in a Modernizing Europe*. Abingdon: Routledge.
Fraser, Nancy. 1992. Rethinking the Public Sphere: A Contribution to the Critique of Actually Existing Democracy. In *Habermas and the Public Sphere*, ed. Craig Calhoun, 109–142. Cambridge, Mass: MIT Press.
Gelvin, James L. 2002. Secularism and Religion in the Arab Middle East: Reinventing Islam in a World of Nation States. In *The Invention of Religion: Rethinking Belief in Politics and History*, ed. Derek R. Peterson and Darren R. Walhof, 115–132. New Brunswick, NJ: Rutgers University Press.
Gruber, Christiane. 2017. The Rose of the Prophet: Floral Metaphors in Late Ottoman Devotional Art. In *Envisioning Islamic Art and Architecture: Essays in Honor of Renata Holod*, ed. David J. Roxburgh, 223–249. Leiden: Brill.
———. 2019. *The Praiseworthy One: The Prophet Muhammed in Islamic Texts and Images*. Bloomington: Indiana University Press.
———. 2020. Bereket Bargains: Islamic Amulets in Today's 'New Turkey'. In *Islamicate Occult Sciences in Theory and Practice*, ed. Liana Saif et al., 572–606. Leiden: Brill.
Guidi, Dilletta Virginia. 2019. *"L'islam des Musées": Sociohistoire de la (re) Présentation de l'Islam dans les Politiques Culturelles Françaises. Les Cas du Louvre et de l'Institut du Monde Arabe. Thèse en Preparation à Paris Sciences et Lettres*. Paris: École doctorale de l'École pratique des hautes études.
Haber Türk. 2016. Barış Samir: Hırka-i Şerif için Yalı Teklif Edildi. June 11. https://www.haberturk.com/ramazan/haber/1252334-baris-samir-hirka-i-serif-icin-yali-teklif-edildi. Accessed 27 May 2021.
Halperin, Julia and Charlotte Burns. 19 September 2019. Museums Claim They're Paying More Attention to Female Artists. That's an Illusion. *Artnet News*. https://news.artnet.com/womens-place-in-the-art-world/womens-place-art-world-museums-1654714. Accessed 27 May 2021.

Harrison, Julia. 2005. Ideas of Museums in the 1990s. In *Heritage, Museums and Galleries: An Introductory Reader*, ed. Gerard Corsane, 38–53. London: Routledge.
Hetherington, Kevin. 2011. Foucault, the Museum and the Diagram. *The Sociological Review* 59: 457–475.
Hilye-i Şerif Catalogue. 2011a. *Mehmet Çebi Koleksiyonu'ndan Hilye-i Serif ve Tesbihler.* Istanbul: İstanbul Büyükşehir Belediyesi.
———. 2011b. *Aşk-ı Nebi Sanat Olunca.* Istanbul: İstanbul Büyükşehir Belediyesi.
———. 2013. *Aşk-ı Nebi Sanat Olunca. Mehmet Cebi Koleksiyonu'ndan.* Istanbul: İstanbul Büyükşehir Belediyesi.
Hobsbawm, Eric. 1983. Introduction: Inventing Traditions. In *The Invention of Tradition*, ed. Eric Hobsbawm and Terence Ranger, 1–14. Cambridge: Cambridge University Press.
Hürriyet. 5 June 2020. Son Dakika Haberler: Ayasofya'ya Formül Aranıyor! Cumhurbaşkanı Erdoğan: Çok Hassas Olun, İyi Araştırın. https://www.hurriyet.com.tr/gundem/son-dakika-haberler-ayasofyaya-formul-araniyor-cumhurbaskani-erdogan-talimat-verdi-41534302. Accessed 27 May 2021.
Hürriyet Daily News. 21 April 2015. 'Replica Mecca' in Istanbul Raises Eyebrows. https://www.hurriyetdailynews.com/replica-mecca-in-istanbul-raises-eyebrows-81375. Accessed 27 May 2021.
———. 2016, July 2. First Call to Prayer inside Istanbul's Hagia Sophia in 85 Years. https://www.hurriyetdailynews.com/first-call-to-prayer-inside-istanbuls-hagia-sophia-in-85-years-101161. Accessed 27 May 2021.
———. 2019, March 25. Hagia Sophia Can be Reverted to a Mosque: Erdoğan. https://www.hurriyetdailynews.com/hagia-sophia-can-be-reverted-to-a-mosque-erdogan-142153. Accessed 27 May 2021.
Janson, Torsten. 2012. Imaging Islamic Identity: Negotiated Norms of Representation in British Muslim Picture Books. *Comparative Studies of South Asia, Africa and the Middle East* 32 (2): 323–338.
Janson, Torsten and Neşe Kınıkoğlu. 2021. Sacred (re)Collections: Culture, Space and Boundary Negotiation in Turkish-Islamic Memory Politics. *Middle East Journal of Culture and Communication.* October 6. https://brill.com/view/journals/mjcc/aop/article-10.1163-18739865-20219105/article-10.1163-18739865-20219105.xml
Karahasan, Neşe. 2015. *Exhibiting 'Turkishness' at a Time of Flux in Turkey: An Ethnography of the State.* Edinburgh: University of Edinburgh.
Karp, Ivan and Steven Lavine, ed. 1990. *Exhibiting Culture: The Poetics and Politics of Museum.* Washington: Smithsonian Institution Press.
———, ed. 1992. *Communities: The Politics of Public Culture.* Washington: Smithsonian Institution Press.

Kidd, Jenny. 2014. Introduction: Challenging History in the Museum. In *Challenging History in the Museum*, ed. Jenny Kidd et al., 1–22. London: Routledge.

Kınıkoğlu, Neşe. 2021. Displaying the Ottoman Past in an 'Old' Museum of a 'New' Turkey: The Topkapı Palace Museum. *Southeast European and Black Sea Studies*. 21 (4): 549–569.

Koyuncu, Büke. 2014. *'Benim Milletim...': AK Parti İktidarı, Din ve Ulusal Kimlik*. Istanbul: İletişim.

McClellan, Andrew. 2008. *The Art Museum from Boulee to Bilbao*. Berkeley: University of California Press.

Mills, Robert. 2008. Theorizing the Queer Museum. *Museums and Social Issues* 3 (1): 41–52.

Mulvey, Laura. 1975. Visual Pleasure and Narrative Cinema. *Screen* 16 (3): 6–18.

Paine, Crispin. 2013. *Religious Objects in Museums: Private Lives and Public Duties*. London: Bloomsbury.

Petersen, Derek and Darren Walhof. 2002. 'Rethinking Religion'. In *The Invention of Religion: Rethinking Belief in Politics and History*, ed. Derek R. Peterson and Darren R. Walhof, 1–16. New Brunswick, N.J.: Rutgers University Press.

Pinterest. 26 October 2017a. Kutlu Doğum Haftası. https://www.pinterest.ca/pin/390054017707934622/. Accessed 27 May 2021.

———. 26 October 2017b. Kutlu Doğum Haftası. https://www.pinterest.ca/pin/389279961529798232/. Accessed 27 May 2021.

Public Library of Science. 2019. *Diversity of Artists in Major U.S. Museums*. Submission, February 11. https://arxiv.org/pdf/1812.03899.pdf. Accessed 27 May 2021.

Roberts, Mary Nooter. 2017. Altar as Museum, Museum as Altar: Ethnography, Devotion, and Display. In *Religion in Museums: Global and Multicultural Perspectives*, ed. Gretchen Buggeln, Crispin Paine and S. Brent Plate, 49–56. London: Bloomsbury.

Schick, İrvin Cemil. 2008. The Iconicity of Islamic Calligraphy in Turkey. *RES: Anthropology and Aesthetics* 53 (1): 211–224.

———. 2011. The Noble *Hilye* or Felicious *Hilye*. In *Aşk-ı Nebi Sanat Olunca*, ed. Tuğrul Tuna, 16–29. Istanbul: İstanbul Büyükşehir Belediyesi.

Schimmel, Annemarie. 1985. *And Muhammad is His Messenger: The Veneration of the Prophet in Islamic Piety*. Chapel Hill, NC: University of North Carolina Press.

Shaw, Wendy. 2002. Trav(ei)ls of Secularism: Islam in Museums from the Ottoman Empire to the Turkish Republic. In *The Invention of Religion: Rethinking Belief in Politics and History*, ed. Derek R. Peterson and Darren R. Walhof, 133–155. New Brunswick, NJ: Rutgers University Press.

———. 2010. Between the Secular and the Sacred: A New Face for the Department of the Holy Relics at the Topkapı Palace Museum. *Material Religion* 6 (1): 129–131.

Stam, Deidre C. 2005. The Informed Muse: The Implications of 'The New Museology' for Museum Practice. In *Heritage, Museums and Galleries: An Introductory Reader*, ed. Gerard Corsane, 54–70. London: Routledge.
Stern Hein, Hilde. 2007. Redressing the Museum in Feminist Theory. *Museum Management and Curatorship* 27 (1): 29–42.
Tokdoğan, Nagehan. 2018. *Yeni Osmanlıcılık: Hınç, Nostalji, Narsisizm*. Istanbul: İletişim.
Turek, Lauren F. 2017. Religious History Objects in Museums. In *Religion in Museums: Global and Multicultural Perspectives*, ed. Gretchen Buggeln, Crispin Paine and S. Brent Plate, 57–62. London: Bloomsbury.
Üsküdar Municipality Website. 2015, October 8. Üsküdar'da Asr-ı Saadet Coşkusu. [Author's archived material].
Uzun, Mustafa İsmet. 1998. Hilye. In Türkiye Diyanet Vakfı İslâm Ansiklopedisi, vol. 18, 44–47. Istanbul: Türkiye Diyanet Vakfı. https://islamansiklopedisi.org.tr/hilye#1
Van der Veer, Peter and Hartmut Lehmann. 1999. Introduction. In *Nation and Religion: Perspectives from Europe and Asia*, ed. Peter Van der Veer and Hartmut Lehmann, 3–14. Princeton: Princeton University Press.
Wedeen, Lisa. 1999. *Ambiguities of Domination: Politics, Rhetoric, and Symbols in Contemporary Syria*. Chicago: University of Chicago Press.
Weil, Stephen E. 1990. Rethinking the Museum: An Emerging New Paradigm of Essential Museum Functions Reduces the Number to Three: Preserve, Study, and Communicate. *Museum News* 69 (2): 56–61.
Yeni Akit. 29 May 2020. Müthiş Mesaj: Ayasofya Camii'nde Tüm Dünyaya İlan Edeceğiz. https://www.yeniakit.com.tr/foto-galeri/muthis-mesaj-ayasofya-camiinde-tum-dunyaya-ilan-edecegiz-22199. Accessed 27 May 2021.
Yilmaz, Secil and V. Safak Uysal. 2007. MinaTurk: Culture, History and Memory in Turkey in Post-1980s. In *Making National Museums*, ed. Peter Aronson and Magdalena Hillström, 115–125. Linköping: Linköping [University] Electronic Conference Proceedings. https://ep.liu.se/ecp/022/ecp07022.pdf. Accessed 27 May 2021.
Zakariya, Muhammed. 2004. The Hilye of the Prophet Muhammad. *Seasons*, Autumn–Winter 2003/2004: 13–22.
Zuanni, Chiara. 2017. Archaeological Displays: Ancient Objects, Current Beliefs. In *Religion in Museums: Global and Multicultural Perspectives*, ed. Gretchen Buggeln, Crispin Paine and S. Brent Plate, 63–70. London: Bloomsbury.
Zubaida, Sami. 2011. *Beyond Islam: A New Understanding of the Middle East*. London: I.B. Tauris.

CHAPTER 4

Between Memory and Forgetting and Purity and Danger: The Case of the Ulucanlar Prison Museum

Courtney Dorroll

SITUATING THE ULUCANLAR PRISON MUSEUM CASE STUDY

The national Turkish capital of Ankara is not only the seat of government of the Turkish Republic, but is also central to the development of Turkish national identity. Built up from a small town into a national capital over the twentieth century, the changes in urban space in Ankara often epitomise larger social shifts and dynamics in contemporary Turkey. The history and transformation of the Ulucanlar Prison complex is one such case. Originally constructed in 1925, just a few years after the founding of the Turkish Republic, to house political opponents of the secular nationalist Kemalist regime, it was reopened in 2011 as a museum. As this chapter demonstrates, this particular change in Ankara's urban and architectural

C. Dorroll (✉)
Wofford College, Spartanburg, SC, USA
e-mail: dorrollcm@wofford.edu

© The Author(s), under exclusive license to Springer Nature Switzerland AG 2023
C. Raudvere, P. Onur (eds.), *Neo-Ottoman Imaginaries in Contemporary Turkey*, Modernity, Memory and Identity in South-East Europe,
https://doi.org/10.1007/978-3-031-08023-4_4

history epitomises crucial shifts in collective memory and public space under the AKP.

In 2006 the Greater Ankara Municipality condemned the Ulucanlar Prison complex, located in the Ulus neighbourhood of Ankara in the Altındağ Municipality, planning to demolish it and build a mall.[1] The Chamber of Architects and Engineers in Ankara (Türk Mühendis ve Mimar Odaları Birliği or TMMOB) strongly objected to the project and, along with a number of art historians, staged festivals in the grounds to garner support for making the prison complex a historic monument. Their efforts to secure structure protection from the Ministry of Culture and Tourism were successful; Ulucanlar Prison was awarded the designation of historic landmark and has been restored by the Altındağ Municipality as a museum that alludes to the secular Kemalist persecution of political dissidents during the early years of the republic. This transformed the prison from a space of active forgetting into a space of memory that publicly commemorates persons previously deemed unworthy of remembrance. The Ulucanlar Prison Museum is thus a clear example of the dynamics of memory and forgetting under AKP neo-Ottomanism.

Between 2009 and 2011, the Altındağ Municipality oversaw and completed the project to restore and convert the working prison into a prison museum combined with a small arts district consisting of a street devoted to artists' shops. Looking at photos of the area taken in 2006, it is clear that the prison had fallen into extreme disarray and dilapidation. Today, however, it seems that the gates that were once meant to keep the public safe from the prison have the reverse function of separating the now touristy space from the poverty of its surrounding neighbourhood.

Focusing on the local AKP municipality's transformation of the space from a prison into a museum, this chapter argues that the Ulucanlar Prison Museum can be read as an attempt by the AKP to purify the memory of political dissidents that the secularist Kemalist state originally deemed "dirty" and "dangerous". This chapter applies theoretical categories from Mary Douglas' *Purity and Danger* to understand how the Ulucanlar Prison Museum can be understood as a hybrid of the basic functions of a prison and a museum. In general, a prison serves as a space where the state isolates persons that it designates as socially dangerous. By contrast, a museum

---

[1] For other research on recent urban renewal in the area, see Dorroll (2016) and Onur (2018).

serves as a space for official remembering of what is deemed socially desirable, while objects that have been curated and presented to the public in the museum become "official" memories. The former is an institution of forgetting and exclusion, the latter of remembering and inclusion.

As a hybrid of these contrasting institutions, the Ulucanlar Prison Museum reveals how shifting concepts of what the Turkish state considers dirty or dangerous are reflected in the curation of the prison space, revealing who is remembered and who is forgotten in the contemporary social and political imaginaries of the AKP. By focusing in particular on the imprisoned political dissident as a category that blurs, transforms, and hybridises the distinction between socially pure and impure, this analysis will therefore complicate the space of the prison as a place where persons are generally categorised as impure or dangerous. In the Ulucanlar Prison Museum, however, instead of being a space where the Kemalist state attempted to isolate and forget the pious or dissident person, it has now become under the AKP a space to commemorate those persecuted by the Kemalist state, transforming it from an instrument of forgetting into an instrument of remembrance. This chapter will therefore use the Ulucanlar Prison Museum as an example of the broader process by which those persons considered "dirty" or dangerous by the Kemalist state were considered by the AKP and its political imaginary to be instead "pure" and virtuous.

This analysis also further builds on my earlier research into Erdoğanian neo-Ottomanism, which I define as the transformation and recreation of public space to fit AKP social values and political hegemony (Dorroll 2016).[2] In its theoretical framework, this chapter aims to accord with recent re-readings of Mary Douglas that go beyond dichotomies and structural thinking, such as the work included in the edited volume, *Purity and Danger Now: New Perspectives* (Duschinsky et al. 2017). It also draws on work done in the third part of Paul Connerton's trilogy, *The Spirit of Mourning, History, Memory and the Body* (2011) that helped conceptually align the case study of Ulucanlar Prison Museum with other sites of memory and mourning.

---

[2] This chapter has been adapted and revised significantly from Courtney Dorroll's dissertation, The Spatial Politics of Turkey's Justice and Development Party (AK Party): On Erdoğanian Neo-Ottomanism (University of Arizona, 2015). For more on Erdoğanian neo-Ottomanism, please see the forthcoming book with Edinburgh University Press by C. Dorroll and P. Dorroll, *Spatial Politics in Istanbul: Turning Points in Contemporary Turkey*.

ON PUBLIC SPACE, MUSEUMS, AND COLLECTIVE MEMORY IN TURKEY

As Steven Conn writes, museums face the issue of the historical narrative itself: "What—or—whose story to tell?" (2010, 40). As public spaces dedicated to public remembrance, museums have become central to the politics of memory. Esra Özyürek, drawing on Arjun Appadurai and Carol Breckenridge's concept of "public culture", identifies a realm of "public memory" as denoting the space within which national contestations have taken place throughout modern Turkish history (Özyürek 2007, 8–9). Özyürek points out that denoting this arena as *public* memory highlights the conflicted nature of these constructions. This concept is therefore particularly suited to our purposes because it identifies cultural memory as a space of conflict and contestation, a dynamic that plays out in the construction of public memory in modern Turkey, revealing museums as spaces of ideological contention. Ayşe Öncü's and Zeynep Çelik's prolific work on city culture and spaces greatly informed this chapter; Michael Meeker provides an early reading Ankara's cityscape and Amy Mills' reading of Istanbul's cityscape also helped me contextualise and map Ulucanlar within Ankara and other urban areas within Turkey.

As Hart and Keser note, the objectification and re-organisation of a complex historical reality is a crucial constitutive process of cultural modernisation and nationalisation (Hart 2007, 37; Keser 2000, 108). Turkish museums have served this function since the founding of the Republic. Nearly every major Turkish city has its own local archaeological museum and over fifty state-funded archaeological museums have appeared since the 1940s (Gür 2007, 42). "Nationalist archaeologies", such as that practiced by Turkish archaeologists and academics during the period of nation building, "draw attention to the political and cultural achievements of ancient civilisations or other forms of complex societies" (Trigger 1984, 360). Perhaps the most notable example of this is the nine-thousand-year-old archaeological site of Çatalhöyük, located in central Anatolia (Bartu-Candan 2007, 72–73). Artefacts found at the site form an important component of the Anatolian Civilizations Museum in Ankara and are considered some of the most ancient examples of human civilisation in the homeland of the Turkish nation.

The Ethnography Museum, opened in 1930, contributed to the objectification of marginalised pasts in service to the nationalist narrative. Much of the museum's collection was in fact composed of Ottoman-era religious objects, such as dervish prayer beads, plundered from the thousands of holy sites and shrines that the Turkish state systematically closed down, beginning in 1925 (Keser 2000, 110). Moreover, the museum was built on top of Namazgâh (Prayer-place) Hill, an area littered with the kind of sacred sites suppressed by the Turkish state only a few years previously. As Keser points out, the most poignant irony in the site's placement is the fact that Atatürk's body was laid to rest in the hall of the museum for fifteen years after his death until the now famous mausoleum was constructed to serve as his permanent resting place (2000,114). Thus, a place of Ottoman religious pilgrimage was elided and replaced by a place of nationalist pilgrimage. As the analysis below demonstrates, the AKP has utilised museums and public memory in similarly politicised ways. As with the early Kemalist state and its secularist and anti-Ottoman politics, the contemporary AKP has used museum space to shape and re-present historical memory in ways that underpin their devout Muslim, neo-Ottoman values and political identity.

On Neo-Ottomanism

The emergence of the modern secularist Turkish state was enabled by politicised acts of memory. As political change occurred in Turkey from the end of the Ottoman Empire to the nascent nation-state, the forgetting of the Ottoman past allowed nationalist leaders to forge a new memory and national identity: secular, West-facing, and Turkish. The central political dimension of memory and forgetting in modern Turkey has therefore been the issue of the Ottoman past. In recent years, attempts to reclaim the Ottoman, Islamic past have become increasingly frequent alongside critiques of the Kemalist marginalisation of pious Muslim identity. As Thelen points out, "people construct memories in response to changing circumstances [...] individuals, ethnic groups, political parties, and cultures shape and reshape their identities—as known to themselves and to others" (1989, 1118). This phenomenon, referred to as "neo-Ottomanism" in the Turkish context, employs cultural heritage that focuses on remembering and commemorating the Ottoman past. The specifics of how the Ottoman past is constructed by neo-Ottomanism matters a great deal: the who and what, and how it is being remembered, can bring up issues of varying complexity, including race, religion, class status, political leanings, and economic markets. Memory and forgetting, therefore, become key lenses through which to view neo-Ottomanism.

Pious and conservative Turkish Muslim political activists and leaders developed neo-Ottomanism in the 1980s and 1990s as a reclamation of Ottoman cultural memory, which had been denigrated and deliberately forgotten by the Kemalist regime. Yet, as Yılmaz Çolak pointed out, although the Ottoman past was forgotten in the official narrative voice of the new Turkish Republic, it remained alive in Turkish popular culture (2006, 591; also see Yavuz 2016, Walton 2017). This made neo-Ottomanism widely appealing to a broad section of the Turkish populace. As Çolak also demonstrates, it was Prime Minister Turgut Özal who reintroduced Ottoman memory into the political arena in 1980s and 1990s in Turkey. His conception of neo-Ottomanism utilised the rhetoric of the melting pot and cultural pluralism, and was publicised as an "imperial vision" of an Ottoman pluralist system (Çolak 2006, 592).

Esra Özyürek, examining the popular trend in Turkey since the 1990s to research family history for links to the Ottoman past, describes neo-Ottomanism in today's Turkey as a tool with which to search for the past, employing historical genealogy to understand and control the present (2007, 2–10). While officially the Ottoman past was forgotten by means of the governmentality of culture, public memory allowed the memory to live on. Özyürek cites the Kemalist reforms of the 1920s and 1930s as examples of "administered forgetting": ways of controlling memory to forget the Ottoman and Islamic past. If the twentieth century was termed a time of amnesia, then Özyürek states that the twenty-first century was a time of nostalgia following the 1990s period of commodifying memory for global service industries and international tourists. Neo-Ottomanism was thus a product of new economic structures in Turkey which allowed Ottoman cultural memory to be commodified and distributed.

In contrast with the pluralist neo-Ottomanism described above, Recep Tayyip Erdoğan developed a form that emphasises hierarchy, homogeneity, and the power of the state. I call this Erdoğanian neo-Ottomanism, and it is the specific way in which the AKP, under Erdoğan's leadership, frames the Ottoman past, particularly when reshaping the urban landscape and the public sphere (Dorroll 2016, 2). Erdoğanian neo-Ottomanism is characterised by the top-down transformation of public space to create architectural space that reflects the homogenising social vision of the AKP and its neoliberal economic policies. I argue that Erdoğanian neo-Ottomanism is characterised by the use of multiculturalist and pluralist rhetoric and the simultaneous application of homogenising social and spatial politics. Its rhetoric is multicultural, but its tactics are homogenising. These tactics and forms of spatial politics include expropriation, the "clean up" of poor neighbourhoods, attempts to whitewash the complex heritages of public spaces in order to enact a homogenised neo-Ottoman architectural space, and the use of arts and culture programming to accomplish these goals. In this chapter, I examine this cleaning up in terms of the memory of a prison.

THE SPACE OF THE PRISON MUSEUM

Ulucanlar Prison, established in 1925, was built in the First National Style and is reminiscent of nationalist architecture from that time period (Çaylı 2011, 370) (see Fig. 4.1). The prison had a series of name changes, first being called the Cebeci General Penitentiary, then Ankara Prison, then Ankara Cebeci Civil Prison, Ankara Central Closed Prison, and then finally Ulucanlar Prison (*Ulucanlar* 2012, 8). After it was closed in 2006, the inmates were taken to a newly constructed prison in the Sincan neighbourhood on the outskirts of Ankara. My guide, Merve Bayıksel, who works for the museum and has a degree in political science, noted that the new prison is more comfortable. Where Ulucanlar housed twenty to fifty prisoners per room, the new prison was constructed to house two to three prisoners per cell.

My guide confirmed that the Greater Ankara Municipality originally planned to demolish the prison and build a shopping centre. When word of this circulated, the Ankara Chamber of Architects and Engineers applied to the Cultural and Natural Assets Protection Council (Kültür ve Tabiat Varlıklarını Koruma Müdürlüğü) to certify the area with historic protected status (Çaylı 2011, 371). Prior to applying for the historical status, the Chamber housed a festival in 2007 in the grounds of the abandoned prison (Çaylı 2011, 373) which was meant to bolster public use of the prison, but in fact the majority of the festivalgoers were former prisoners. The event generated ideas on how the restored space would be used now that it had acquired protected status, and the ex-prisoners were welcomed and encouraged to share their past experiences at the festival (Çaylı 2011, 373–374). It was at the event that the idea of turning it into a museum emerged. A former lawyer to three students who were executed in Ulucanlar in 1972 was documented in the Chamber of Architects oral history publication from the festival as saying:

Fig. 4.1 Ulucanlar courtyard. (Photograph by author)

This is a place that has born witness to so much torture, so many arrests, and executions. Turning this place into a mall or using it for any other purpose will mean the destruction of memories. In turn, people will not be able to see, hear about, and study these memories. That is why this place has to be defined as a culture centre. (Ünalın 2010. 24–25, cited in Çaylı 2011, 374)

The Chamber also held other events at the site to which journalists and writers were invited. One such journalist was Can Dündar, who wrote as follows:

> I walked through the tiny dark visitors' chambers, solitary cells that both intimidate and enrage, cramped wards, torture rooms, filthy toilets, deteriorated bathrooms, dank hallways now ruled by rats. Then I imagined the days when torture tools would be exhibited in torture rooms, gallows in courtyards, execution records in wards—days when new generations would see all these in an "Ulucanlar Museum". They would say thankfully, "Now all this is in the past", and walk freely out the heavy iron gates. (Çaylı 2011, 376; Dündar 2 July 2007)

Due to the immense historical significance of the site and the great amount of interest and press coverage that it generated, Altındağ Municipality successfully applied for the prison to be considered a historic landmark, and it was handed over to them by the Greater Ankara Municipality with authorisation to implement and manage the restoration project and turn it into a museum and art and culture centre (*Ulucanlar* 2012, 10). Ulucanlar Prison Museum became the first and only prison museum in Turkey.

Bayıksel informed me that usually three to four hundred people visit the museum each day, rising, during the Ramadan holiday season, to a record twelve hundred people in one day; in the prison museum's first year, 120,000 visitors toured it (*Ulucanlar* n.d., 8). Bayıksel stressed that the purpose of the museum was to tell the stories of the political, religious, and literary prisoners, not those of the common prisoner, and serves today as a symbol of how Turkey has become more democratic, observing, "In the past people in Turkey were imprisoned for their ideas, this does not happen in Turkey today." The irony of that summer's Gezi Park arrests seemed to elude her; nor did she acknowledge the increasing number of such imprisonments among journalists in Turkey. There is, therefore, a clear disconnect in the museum's mission and the political reality in which it is situated. In 2010, before the museum was opened to the public, Eray Çaylı (a graduate student at University College London) was allowed to visit it. His fieldnotes demonstrate that the museum was marketed to the public as "being true to the original" and "an opportunity for experiencing prison life" (Çaylı 2011, 369).

By touring the museum with Bayıksel, I experienced the museum from the "official" curatorial point of view, while the Ulucanlar literature produced by the Altındağ Municipality expanded on the "official narrative". The Ulucanlar complex is titled "Ulucanlar Prison Museum and Culture-Art Center", and the semi-open prison in the complex's grounds is titled "Ulucanlar Semi-Open Prison Congress Center"; these designations very deliberately highlight the importance of the space as a culture and arts venue, a theme that Altındağ also heavily promoted in the urban renewal of the Hamamönü district.

One of the books provided by the prison museum describes the museum and culture-art centre with the sentence, "If someday you happen to visit the jail, after you rub your hands over the dusty walls and inhale the smell of humidity, where rats share your bread ... freedom and time stops ..." (*Ulucanlar* 2012, 1). Despite the attempt at authenticity, this description did not match my own experience. The space smelled fresh and was not dusty, while the only rat was made of wax. It made me question the "restoration" of the prison as a project with any kind of authenticity. The building was remodelled and freshly painted. When I saw pictures of the prison shortly after it had ceased being a working prison in 2006, I immediately began to question the quality and the goals of the renovation. The photos certainly fitted the above description: the walls were crumbling, the floors seemed to be of dirt; everything was old and run down. It was hard to imagine that humans lived there. Yet this is not the case when one walks into the newly remodelled Ulucanlar Prison Museum. The floors are new, the outside is paved with brick, and the exterior walls have a fresh coat of light pink. It feels more as if the prison was remodelled as upscale condominiums than restored to reflect reality. Despite its marketing as an authentic representation of the hardship of prison life, I walked about feeling like this space projected, in fact, an idealised version of prison life in Turkey.

At one point I was taken to a corridor of solitary confinement cells in which a horrid audioscape of male voices screaming and yelling supposedly amplified the experience. The voices being projected were entirely male, eliding the experience of female prisoners in that space. It was as if the museum space was supposed to be distressing only in this single corridor, but the exposure felt very forced and contrived. Had the dank colouring or crumbling bathing facilities been kept one might have felt the real-life dread of the prison; instead, those items were eliminated and whitewashed and an artificial "horror house" type soundtrack was piped in to elicit some sort of emotion. It is as if the prison museum had always been an afterthought, and the conference centre and the street of the arts constituted the main goals of the complex. This was likely due to the fact that ultimately the Greater Ankara Municipality had intended to transform the complex into a mall, a commercial entity. Because of the activism of the Chamber of Architects, the prison was designated a historic landmark, thus not liable to demolition. My guide's own information confirmed this suspicion; she told me that the museum planners simply looked online to research other prison museums and that no money was invested in visiting them. This also helps to explain the odd combination of prison museum and arts centre: the prison restoration was necessary for the Altındağ Municipality due to the site's historic status, and they kept it out of necessity, but did what they could to monetise the remaining spaces.

The Ulucanlar Prison book states that "visitors will make a sentimental journey to the past, after entering the main door, passing through to the dark, cold, and damp-smelling corridor and […] the nine and ten wards" (2012, 16). I walked in this very space and did not smell any dampness nor feel cold. When I entered the prison courtyard it looked more like the grounds of an art museum rather than an area supposed to conjure up the feeling of a dark and damp prison. The wards themselves are supposed to be "created as appropriate in the circumstances of the past" (*Ulucanlar* 2012, 24). In this scenario I felt that, again, the space was idealised. There were only seven wax figures in the room, and the beds had considerable space between them. Therefore, the true, cramped conditions of prison life are not felt in the actual experience of the museum. The room is clean and newly repainted; it does not resemble the picture from the operating prison nor does it "remind [one of] the images of prison in the old Turkish movies" as suggested (*Ulucanlar* 2012, 24). In one area, a grouping of three wax figures sits at a small table drinking tea while one wax figure plays the *saz*. Displays such as these focus heavily on male prisoners. The setting recalls one of friends sitting around a normal table and the atmosphere seems almost festive. This does not seem to fit the idea of prison life in Turkey, or anywhere else for that matter (*Ulucanlar* 2012, 31). When one steps into the *hamam*, or bath, it looks very newly renovated and, in fact, "the *hamam* was renovated according to its original design" (*Ulucanlar* 2012, 38). This room is, once again, an idealised space that does not even visually reflect its original condition. The reality has been painted away.

The former semi-open penitentiary is located in the same grounds as the closed prison. The former building has been transformed into a culture and arts centre and conference hall. This area was not considered part of the "protected structure" as declared by the Cultural and Natural Assets Protection Council. Therefore, it was not treated in an historically sensitive way and instead was subjected to the more familiar urban renewal strategy of the Altındağ Municipality, which is one of replacing vulnerable, subaltern spaces with arts and culture centres. "Designed as a culture, art and conference center this ex-semi-open facility began hosting important events of Ankara ... Ulucanlar Penitentiary now provides a different journey to all visitors" (*Ulucanlar* n.d., 2). This particular usage of the space is clearly meant to resist any experience of it as a historic location or encounter. Moreover, the arts and culture district is clearly of greater importance to the municipality, mirroring the attention that it has lavished on Hamamönü. The *Ulucanlar Semi-Open Prison* book states that there are now "prayer areas and toilets [that] resemble luxurious hotels" (n.d., 53). The restrooms are in fact floor to ceiling marble, while the grounds are beautifully landscaped, affirming this area as the centrepiece of the whole complex.

Remembering Political Dissidents in the Prison Museum

During the years of the new Turkish Republic, the number of political prisoners rose drastically as the Kemalist state sought to suppress dissent, and the Ulucanlar Prison held many of them. One of the key reasons the prison museum was funded and created by AKP politicians from the Altındağ Municipality was to showcase the abuses of the past and, in particular, to highlight the early Kemalist oppression of political opposition. For instance, devout Muslims and intellectuals such as Necip Fazıl Kısakürek (1904–1983) and İskilipli Mehmed Atıf Hoca (1875–1926) featured prominently among the lists of the prisoners in the museum. Kısakürek was one of the most significant dissidents of the early Republican period, known for his principled and intellectual stance against Kemalist reform projects. He was the owner of the highly influential magazine, *The Great East* (*Büyük Doğu*), whose first issue was published on 1 September 1943. The magazine became a major vehicle of protest against the Kemalist regime and its Westernising policies, all of which Kısakürek stridently opposed (Yılmaz 584). Although the magazine ceased publication in 1951, its wide influence in anti-Kemalist circles certainly helped earn

Kısakürek a place in Ulucanlar Prison. İskilipli Mehmed's crime was even more intangible. The author of tracts opposed to Westernisation published in the 1920s was hanged in Ulucanlar Prison on 4 February 1926 for violating the infamous Republican legislation regulating Muslim headgear in the new Turkish Republic.

The prisoners featured in the museum also included leftist dissidents, highlighting the breadth of the ideological spectrum that was suppressed and criminalised by the Kemalist regime. The commemoration of leftist dissidents is particularly noteworthy given the continuing brutal suppression of leftist politics by successive military coups and governments in Turkey over the latter decades of the twentieth century: for instance, the prominent late-1960s leftist activists—Deniz Gezmiş, Yusuf Aslan, and Hüseyin İnan—are commemorated in the museum's displays. Most heavily emphasised, however, is the heroism of the devout Muslim prisoners (such as Kısakürek). By including such a broad range of ideological dissidents, the museum displays associate the AKP period with openness and democratisation, yet the stronger focus on devout Muslim prisoners emphasises the AKP's particular solidarity with the previously suppressed devout Muslim identity in Turkey. It is also important to note that, as mentioned above, the experiences of male prisoners are strongly privileged in the museum's displays and discussions of torture and suffering, therefore silencing the voices of female inmates in the museum's most important ideological narratives.

The museum's focus on political prisoners, especially devout, male, political prisoners, is central to the museum's political narrative and construction of historical memory. Artefacts associated with political prisoners—including personal effects, such as prayer beads and copies of the Quran—make up the bulk of what is displayed to the public. By focusing on political prisoners, the museum draws attention to the pattern of political oppression under previous Kemalist regimes in Turkey. As part of the AKP's spatial politics, it participates in the simplified and idealised AKP narrative of the party as an engine of human rights reform whose election to public office ended years of Kemalist oppression; the political prisoners who were imprisoned in the facility receive sympathetic attention but the museum does little to engage with the context of contemporary political prisoners in Turkey. Indeed, the only reference to them is found in the museum's gift shop, which sells handicrafts which prisoners have produced while incarcerated.

The AKP municipality's idealisation of the space, and its employment of the prison museum in a historical narrative of the oppression of dissidents under secular Kemalists, necessitated the elimination of certain key components of the actual experience of the prison itself that did not fit this narrative. For example, the living conditions of the prisoners, as has been described, were whitewashed by the restoration. Furthermore, the fact that the prison continued to operate in its former dilapidated condition until 2006 (under the AKP government) was conspicuously absent from my guided tour and did not feature in museum signage or brochures. This important point is hidden because it blurs the clarity of the accusation of Kemalist oppression on behalf of pious Turks which the restoration represents.

Çaylı mentions the documentary film, *Ölücanlar* ("Dead Souls"—a play on the name "Ulucanlar", which means "Sublime Souls") by Murat Özçelik as actual evidence of the conditions of the prison until 2006, writing,

> [...] it portrays how different Ulucanlar actually used to look before renovation. The barbed wire surrounding the prison grounds and the iron mesh over the courtyards are now absent in the museumified Ulucanlar. Also gone are the sort of wall writings Özçelik encounters as he walks through the abandoned wards: *I was tortured until 10.11.2000*. (Çaylı 2011, 385)

The documentary shares the darker side of the prison which Özçelik had experienced as an inmate, a side that I failed to see during my visit. As he describes, "The bathroom evokes very different sentiments in me. Here they beat us with iron planks. That's how a friend died. My own thumb and head were also smashed" (Çaylı 2011, 385). *Ölücanlar* also features a former female inmate who noted of her prison experience, "The clothes of our friends who were killed and whose bodies were taken away were stored here. All the way from the infirmary up to here the hallway was covered with bloody clothes, shirts and jackets" (Çaylı 2011, 385).

Like the conditions of the original prison, the current prison population is also forgotten and hidden from view in the museum restoration. Little or no information is related about the current whereabouts of the prisoners who inhabited the run-down prison until 2006. This constitutes an attempt by the municipality to hide from view the subaltern inhabitants of the neighbourhood.

It surprises Bayıksel, the curator, and other staff members of the Ulucanlar Prison Museum that the highest number of visitors are former prison inmates, who come back again and again, and describe the prison as a type of school for them. Every week their names fill the visitor's book. Bayıksel said that the museum staff was not expecting this. Here, in fact, these invisible populations are making themselves visible: visiting the space and interacting with the place where they were once incarcerated. Bayıksel also described a common occurrence at the museum: ex-prisoners taking their family members on tours of the museum. She told me that they often point out the room in which they were imprisoned, and that many people weep. A follow-up study would be to ask the ex-prisoners what they think of the renovations, what significance this museum has for them and their family and have their voices represented in the official narrative of the prison museum, rendering and displaying their humanity instead of using them as empty signifiers, or wax figurines. This is an example of the power and privilege of the museum in who is remembered, how they are remembered, and what voices get to tell the story and curate and frame the prison-turned-museum. An ethnographic accounting of the ex-prisoner would add complexity to this museum, a sense of shared humanity, and allow perhaps a more authentic framing to emerge. If this doesn't occur officially by the museum itself, perhaps an ethnographer can go in and do this second step and publish the findings in an academic narrative.

Reading the Ulucanlar Prison Museum

The concepts of memory and forgetting help interpret the hybridity of the Ulucanlar Prison Museum. Through this particular example, one can read a history of the new Turkish nation state mapped onto the crime and punishment structure of the prison and the curated memories of the prison-turned-museum. As Kundera writes, "The struggle of man against power is the struggle of memory against forgetting" (1999 [1978], 4). At Ulucanlar, pious political prisoners were housed inside the walls of the prison complex, to be forgotten and no longer seen. With the transformation of the prison into a museum, however, the curating of political prisoners and their pasts involves their being reclaimed and officially remembered. Through this practical application of neo-Ottomanism, the traumatic pasts of those who did not benefit from the Kemalist state project can be remembered, restored, and reclaimed.

The Ulucanlar Prison Museum features a hybrid structure and history, composed of both prison and museum. These two types of spaces stand in stark contrast to one another. Prisons in general are buildings used to punish those who are considered by the state to be socially dangerous, who do not have the right politics or the social capital to oppose the justice system. Simply put, the unwanted are stored (so to speak) in prison. They are taken from the public sphere and erased from the public eye. Typically, the prisoner is viewed as shameful and considered deviant: a subjective category determined by those in power and conditioned by how those in power categorise right and wrong. All of these concepts are therefore ideals that are not fixed but, rather, fluid and contextual. The confines of the prison walls produce forgetting and provide the active and official space for forgetting. The mechanisms in place in the prison have routinised forgetting and erasure, a politicised act because, as Paul Connerton notes, "What is allowed to be forgotten provides living space for present projects" (1989, 63).

Mary Douglas's concepts of purity and danger can be used here to understand precisely how the prison in general accomplishes this act of forgetting. Douglas's work discusses the ways in which religions and, by extension, culture in general, create designations of "danger" and "purity" for items that are deemed socially acceptable or unacceptable. Items or persons that are considered socially "dangerous" are interpreted as "dirty", thus necessitating the cleansing of society of these dangerous elements. As Douglas puts it, "dirt is essentially disorder. There is no such thing as absolute dirt: it exists in the eye of the beholder [...] Dirt offends against order. Eliminating it is not a negative movement, but a positive effort to organise the environment" (Douglas 2006 [1966], 2). Prisons can be understood as spaces used by the state to isolate persons they consider "dirty" and socially dangerous, thus, in the eyes of the state, cleansing society of their threatening presence. The forgetting engendered by the prison is an act of removing danger from social view, and thus from social consciousness and memory.

As Douglas writes,
The whole universe is harnessed to men's attempts to force one another into good citizenship. Thus we find that certain moral values are upheld and certain social rules defined by beliefs in dangerous contagion, as when the glance or touch of an adulterer is held to bring illness to his neighbours or his children. (Douglas 2006 [1966], 4)

In other words, concepts of dirtiness and cleanness indicate the presence of a system. "Where there is dirt there is system. Dirt is the by-product of a systematic ordering and classification of matter, in so far as ordering involves rejecting inappropriate elements" (Douglas 2006 [1966], 44). This is why the concepts of purity and danger can be mapped onto the politics of memory and forgetting: the politicised nature of memory classifies experiences and persons in the same way that notions of dirtiness and cleanness, danger and safety operate in cultural systems.

For decades, Turkish political parties and government structures have dictated and decided who is to be deemed a good citizen. Secular Kemalist political elites interpreted the secular citizen as good, and groups such as pious Muslims and ethnic minorities as dangerous to the formation of the new Turkish nation state, the period in which Ulucanlar Prison was built. Thus, when it was constructed, it was designed to support the values of the new Kemalist nation state by isolating persons it considered dangerous, and rendering the new nation "safe" from their potential political "danger".

The nature of a museum stands in diametric opposition to that of the prison. In general, a museum's purpose places it squarely in the realm of the public sphere. Museums are revered structures that house the items deemed worth remembering, showcasing, and preserving. Indeed, the act of preserving something is by its very nature a part of memory. People enter museums for a minimal fee, if not for free, and they are clean, organised, and well-maintained public spaces. The power and privilege of a society adorn the walls. People, perhaps including the state, wealthy donors, a large grass-roots collective, must come together to fund and maintain the museum space. The educated elite can become curators and the museum is marketed to the public and sometimes even to international audiences. Museums are memory on official display. Yet they are fluid; as directors change, and as political and social issues shift, so do the curated walls of museums. They act as the medium through which a collective, public memory has created public history and documented how it has changed over time. The museum displays public historical representations that interpret history. Museums possess both tangible and intangible worth, giving them authority and power over collective memory.

The transition from Ulucanlar Prison to Ulucanlar Prison *Museum* can be read as a process of "cleansing" the memories it stores in order to render it suitable for the AKP's political imaginary. Just as the secularist Kemalist state used the original prison as a way to "cleanse" society of political threats, the contemporary Turkish state under the pious values of

Fig. 4.2 Mugs for sale in the prison museum giftshop. Pictured on the mug is Nazım Hikmet, modern Turkey's most famous poet who was a political prisoner in Turkey during his lifetime. (Photograph by author)

the AKP has transformed the prison into a museum by "cleansing" the prison itself of its associations with Kemalist secularism. Instead of being a space of forgetting the pious or dissident person, it has become a space to commemorate those persecuted by the Kemalist state, transforming it from an instrument of forgetting into an instrument of remembrance (see Fig. 4.2).

As Douglas writes, "uncleanness is matter out of place, we must approach it through order. Uncleanness or dirt is that which must not be included if a pattern is to be maintained" (2006 [1966], 50). In the case of the prison, prisoners stand for dirt and danger, and thus must be isolated from society in order to cleanse society of their threatening presence. The museum, however, is a space of cleansing and remembrance. If danger is linked with forgetting via the prison, then purity is linked with memory via the museum. The museum can purify the danger of the prisoner by turning them into an official memory when they become subject to museumification. This is what occurred when the AKP-run Altındağ Municipality in Ankara transformed the Ulucanlar Prison into the hybrid space of the prison museum. The museumification of the memory of the political prisoners that were housed in Ulucanlar during the Kemalist period classified and organised the memory in the new moral terms of the values of the AKP, thus rendering it pure and safe for interaction in the space of the museum. The new moral terms and values of the AKP include solidarity with the previously suppressed devout Muslim identity, and also emphasise the masculine heroism of these particular inmates due to the museum's much weaker emphasis on the experiences of female prisoners.

Political prisoners exemplify these dynamics particularly well. This is because the political prisoner is an anomaly. The category of the political prisoner, someone categorised as dangerous yet someone who is also morally virtuous, blurs the distinctions between dirty and clean, dangerous and virtuous. Public and official commemoration of the political prisoner transforms the boundary between purity and danger, redefining what these categories mean in accordance with the prevailing political categories and commitments of those who have designated the political prisoner appropriate for commemoration and remembrance, rather than consigning them to forgetting and isolation.

Douglas asks, "Can there be any people who confound sacredness with uncleanness?" (2006 [1966], 196). This is the case with the political prisoner. Being designated an "unclean" person by the state raises the political prisoner to the status of a virtuous hero in the eyes of those who share their political and moral commitments. When the state that the dissidents oppose classifies the political prisoner as "dirt" and defilement, it becomes an occasion of celebration and honour. The political prisoner, the person imprisoned for their political dissent, embodies the potential of the categories of "dirty" and "pure", honourable and dishonourable, to shift in meaning and even trade places in accordance with political shifts in public memory. This is why political prisoners are so threatening to prevailing power structures: they unsettle the categories that hold the moral imaginary of political power together. As Douglas writes,

> Order implies restriction; and from all possible relations a limited selection has been made and from all possible relations a limited set has been used. So disorder by implication is unlimited, no pattern has been realized in it, but its potential for patterning is indefinite. This is why, though we seek to create order, we do not simply condemn disorder. We recognize that it is destructive to existing patterns; also that it has potentiality. It symbolizes bother danger and power (2006 [1966], 117)

This is the power and the danger that the political prisoner poses to the established order, and this is why shifts in how the political prisoner is remembered or forgotten signify shifts in conceptions of group identity and belonging.

By transforming a prison used to isolate and actively forget Kemalist dissidents into a museum that actively commemorates these very same political prisoners, the AKP has purified and cleansed the originally secularist meaning and the reading of the text of Ulucanlar Prison, thereby purifying the memory of the prison. As described above, this is evident not only in texts about and produced by the museum, but also in its physical presentation. The modern museum structure symbolises and demands order and cleanliness for its visitors because it represents the pure moral categories of its curator. This is exactly how the AKP transformed Ulucanlar, by literally cleaning and whitewashing away the originally harsh physical conditions of the space itself. As my description of the museum itself demonstrates, the transformation of the prison into a museum was physical accomplished by visually sanitising and whitewashing it, thereby accomplishing its transition from a place of dirt, moral danger, and impurity into a place of purity and moral virtue.

Douglas insightfully notes that "[religions] sacralize the very unclean things which have been rejected with abhorrence. We must, therefore, ask how dirt, which is normally destructive, sometimes becomes creative" (2006 [1966], 196). This is exactly what the AKP's transformation of Ulucanlar Prison into a museum achieved: through a shift in the politics of memory and forgetting, the AKP transformed the despised and forgotten "dirt" of secularist Kemalism into commemorated museum treasures of neo-Ottoman public memory. The real, physical dirtiness experienced by the actual prisoners is also cleaned away in this process, replaced with lifeless, wax figurines who are fictive, nameless stand-ins: purified placeholders for the realities the prisoners themselves would have faced (see Fig. 4.3).

Neo-Ottomanism and the Prison Museum

The particular political and cultural narrative of neo-Ottomanism makes the dissidents of the Kemalist state worthy of memory, including memory in the public sphere. It opens up and rewrites the categories of who can be remembered and who should be forgotten. This is a major reason why neo-Ottomanism has such popular appeal, particularly among the AKP's pious voter base. It dignifies the identity of former dissident groups, such

Fig. 4.3 Wax figure display of prisoners in a communal cell inside the museum. (Photograph by author)

as devout Muslims, in a way that was never possible under secular Kemalism, which condemned the pious Turkish identity to being forgotten; now, however, it can be publicly honoured and remembered. Neo-Ottomanism is, therefore, also a critique of the exclusive nature of secular Kemalism.

At the same time, the transformation of the Ulucanlar Prison into a museum demonstrates the importance of state control under neo-Ottomanism. The museum was only possible because of state control: the AKP Altındağ Municipality government led and took over the project. It is ultimately the state that gets to decide who can be remembered in the public sphere and who will be actively forgotten and hidden away behind the walls of a prison. In the case of the Ulucanlar Prison Museum, there was significant popular desire to honour the memory of the pious dissidents of the Kemalist period. The neo-Ottoman reframing of who can be remembered in Turkish society made it possible for this remembrance to take place in the Turkish public sphere. It was, then, the Turkish state that made the remembrance a reality, by officially adopting the ideology of neo-Ottomanism and by financially and administratively directing the transformation of Ulucanlar Prison into a museum.

Having established that the municipality deliberately transformed the prison museum into an idealised space that is fundamentally unconcerned with accurate historic preservation (against the wishes of the Ankara Chamber of Architects and others), it is important to ask why this took place: what were the ideological motivations for this policy? I argue that the answer can be found in the utilisation of the space as a component of the AKP's neo-Ottomanism. The Ulucanlar complex was constructed in order to remember select aspects of Turkish national history and thereby promote the AKP's own vision of the Turkish moral subject. In order to accomplish this project, the prison had to be restored in such a way as to serve a historical narrative. Its original condition was whitewashed in order to contribute to the spatially politicised AKP moralising project. Furthermore, the patriarchal dimensions of the neo-Ottoman political identity are also evident in the emphasis on the experiences of male prisoners in the museum. The maleness of the prison museum space reinforces just how important neo-Ottomanism was to its construction and its particular narrative of historical memory.

The shift from prison to museum at Ulucanlar exemplifies how the state determines who is worthy of memory and who is to be forgotten. In the case of contemporary Turkey under the AKP, it is the ideology of neo-Ottomanism that enables the Turkish state to rewrite the categories of memory and forgetting. Because neo-Ottomanism highlights the pious Muslim identity, the Turkish state now renders people who fit that category of identity worthy of remembrance. And because neo-Ottomanism is now supported by the power of the state, AKP voters can construct and celebrate the memory of the pious Muslim Turk in the public sphere. The Turkish state, using the ideology of neo-Ottomanism, has been able to transform the prison into the museum: forgetting into remembering.

Concluding Remarks

As this chapter has demonstrated, the transformation of Ulucanlar Prison into a museum exemplifies the politicised dimensions of memory and forgetting in contemporary Turkey. In this specific case, the AKP municipality in charge of the project attempted to "purify" public memory of the

Kemalist state by reframing the prison space as a space of remembrance rather than one of forgetting. Persons categorised as impure, dangerous, and meant to be forgotten by Kemalism were re-categorised as morally pure and worthy of commemoration by the AKP. This is demonstrated particularly clearly in the museum's emphasis on the political prisoner, as such dissidents occupy an anomalous position within these categories: they were deemed impure and dangerous by the state for actions deemed morally pure and virtuous by their followers. Thus, reframing the memory of political dissidents by the museum was a particularly effective method of "purifying" and reframing the public memory of the early Kemalist period.

Yet, as Douglas points out, the attempt to create order and safety that this process of categorisation represents is inherently contradictory. "The final paradox of the search for purity is that it is an attempt to force experience into logical categories of noncontradiction. But experience is not amenable and those who make the attempt find themselves led into contradiction" (2006 [1966], 200). The AKP's curation of this prison museum in 2013, while police were imprisoning Gezi Park political protestors, represents this paradox. Moreover, the museum continued to commemorate the experiences of Ulucanlar prisoners during the massive crackdown on civil society that the Turkish state launched after the coup attempt in July of 2016.

Consideration of the case of Ulucanlar raises a number of questions: Which political prisoners are remembered? Why? Who is now being imprisoned by the AKP because of their politics? How are the categories of pure and impure, virtuous and dangerous, shifting in the post-coup-attempt political landscape in Turkey? As Douglas notes, the contrast between these dichotomous concepts is a necessary component of social order.

If anyone held the idea that death and suffering are not an integral part of nature, the delusion is corrected [...] In painting such dark themes, pollution symbols are as necessary as the use of black in any depiction whatsoever. Therefore we find corruption enshrined in sacred places and times. (Douglas 2006 [1966], 220)

The tension between the commemoration of the political prisoners at Ulucanlar and the active forgetting of imprisoned political dissidents after the coup attempt is yet a further reminder that the politics of memory remain as important in today's Turkey as they did at the founding of the Republic.

References

Çaylı, Eray. 2011. Architecture, Politics and Memory Work: Fieldnotes from the Ulucanlar Prison Museum. In *Museums of Ideas: Commitment and Conflict.* Edinburgh: Museums Etc.

Çolak, Yilmaz. 2006. Ottomanism vs. Kemalism: Collective Memory and Cultural Pluralism in 1990's Turkey. *Middle Eastern Studies* 42 (4): 581–602.

Bartu-Candan, Ayfer. 2007. Remembering a 9000 Years Old Site: Present-ing Çatalhöyük. In *Politics of Public Memory: Production and Consumption of the Past in Turkey*, ed. Esra Özyürek. Syracuse: Syracuse University Press.

Conn, Steven. 2010. *Do Museums Still Need Objects?* Philadelphia: University of Pennsylvania Press.

Connerton, Paul. 1989. *How Societies Remember.* Cambridge: Cambridge University Press.

Dorroll, Courtney. 2016. Hamamönü: Reconfiguring an Ankara Neighborhood. *Journal of Ethnography and Folklore* 1 (2): 55–86.

Douglas, Mary. 2006 [1966]. *Purity and Danger.* New York: Routledge.

Duschinsky, Robbie, Simon Schnall and Daniel H. Weiss eds. 2017. *Purity and Danger Now: New Perspectives.* New York, NY: Routledge.

Dündar, Can. 2007. Ulucanlar Müze Olmalı! *Milliyet*, July 2.

Gür, Aslı. 2007. Stories in Three Dimensions: Narratives of Nation and the Anatolian Civilizations Museum. In *The Politics of Public Memory in Turkey*, ed. Esra Özyürek. Syracuse: Syracuse University Press.

Hart, Kimberly. 2007. Weaving Modernity, Commercializing Carpets: Collective Memory and Contested Tradition in Örselli Village. In *The Politics of Public Memory in Turkey*, ed. Esra Özyürek, 16–39. Syracuse, NY: Syracuse University Press.

Keser, Zeynep. 2000. Familiar Things in Strange Places: Ankara's Ethnography Museum and the Legacy of Islam in Republican Turkey. *Perspectives in Vernacular Architecture* 8: 101–116.

Kundera, Milan. 1999 [1978]. *The Book of Laughter and Forgetting.* New York: HarperPerennial.

Onur, Petek. 2018. Re-creating Nostalgia: Urban Culture in the Citadel, Hamamönü and Hamamarkasi Neighborhoods of Ankara. *Journal of Ankara Studies* 6 (2): 145–166.

Özyürek, Esra. 2007. Introduction: The Politics of Public Memory in Turkey. In *The Politics of Public Memory in Turkey*, ed. Esra Özyürek, 1–15. Syracuse, NY: Syracuse University Press.

Thelen, David. 1989. Memory and American History. *The Journal of American History* 75 (4): 1117–1129.

Trigger, Bruce. 1984. Alternative Archaeologies: Nationalist, Colonialist, Imperialist. *Man* 19: 355–370.

Ulucanlar Prison Museum and Culture—Art Center. 2012. Ankara: Altındağ Municipality Publication.
Ulucanlar Semi-Open Prison Congress Center. n.d. Ankara: Altındağ Municipality Publication.
Ünalın, Çetin. 2010. *Tanıkların Ulucanlar'ı: Sözlü Tarih,* 86–87. Ankara: TMMOB Mimarlar Odası Ankara Şubesi.
Walton, Jeremy. 2017. *Muslim Civil Society and the Politics of Religious Freedom in Turkey.* Oxford: Oxford University Press.
Yavuz, M. Hakan. 2016. Social and Intellectual Origins of Neo-Ottomanism: Searching for a Post-National Vision. *Die Welt des Islams* 56: 438–465.

CHAPTER 5

Architectures of Domination? The Sacralisation of Modernity and the Limits of Ottoman Islamism

Kerem Öktem

Debates on Neo-Ottomanism and the "new Turkey" of the AKP (Adalet ve Kalkınma Partisi, Justice and Development Party) have mostly focused on social, cultural, and political transformations and on the country's changing place in the world. The transformation of Turkey's representative architecture and its political implications, however, have been less examined and mostly limited to architectural history and critical architectural and memory studies (cf. Batuman 2013, 2016, 2018; Çeler 2019; Çınar 2020). Yet representative architecture is a field wherein politics, ideology, and society intersect in variegated and insightful ways that merit closer study. In this chapter, I engage with how the AKP has sought to dominate and "Islamicise" the urban landscapes of Turkey through major "grand projects"—that is, large, government-funded or supported

K. Öktem (✉)
Ca' Foscari University of Venice, Venice, Italy
e-mail: kerem.oktem@unive.it

© The Author(s), under exclusive license to Springer Nature Switzerland AG 2023
C. Raudvere, P. Onur (eds.), *Neo-Ottoman Imaginaries in Contemporary Turkey*, Modernity, Memory and Identity in South-East Europe,
https://doi.org/10.1007/978-3-031-08023-4_5

structures—the changes these projects have brought about, and the constraints and challenges they have faced. I also examine the conflict-laden relationship between neoliberal urban development and state- and municipality-led "grand projects"—such as mosques, government buildings, and infrastructure projects—which stand at the core of the attempt by AKP elites to leave their mark in space and time. I further argue that the space within which these elites have sought to project their power is not only curtailed, but in most cases structured by the purposes of rent-creation. While I trace attempts to destroy, belittle, or discursively redraw the heritage of the early republic and to attach an Islamic aura to the bland visual repertoire of modern Turkish cities with "Ottoman-Seljuk"-style buildings, I also discuss notions of an understated "republicanism"—or, rather, a notion of the "common good"—present in some of the grand projects, where one would not necessarily expect them.

The empirical basis of this chapter comprises photographic evidence, interviews, and observations collected during several fieldwork trips in the winter of 2017 and the summer and autumn of 2020 in Ankara and Istanbul, accompanied by a critical reading of speeches by President Erdoğan at the opening ceremonies of a number of structures. Most of the projects discussed here—and, thanks to neoliberal preferences to turn complex processes of transformation into easily recognisable and marketable products, all of these are indeed projects—are based in Ankara. Unlike Istanbul, where a more enduring cosmopolitanism seems to persevere (Fisher Onar et al. 2018), Ankara was the showcase of the modern republic, with several iconic buildings and urban ensembles manifesting the early republic's values of secular modernity (Bozdoğan 2001; Kezer 2010, 2015; Batuman 2008, 2018). Much of Ankara, extra muros, was built from the 1920s to the 1940s and, until recently, parts of the city centre were dominated by architecture of the late Ottoman and early republican eras. Under the leadership of AKP mayor, Melih Gökçek, from the late 1990s to 2019, the city turned into a battle ground over which symbols should stand for the Turkish nation, and once again attained prominence as the showcase for a "new Turkey", this time represented by the Ottoman Islamist nation-building project. Attempts at spatial domination and transformation through architecture are, hence, most legible in the urban space of Ankara.

The analysis of this chapter is driven by individual architectural projects and megastructures which have larger political significance, and which have been discussed controversially in public. I engage with them in two distinct but overlapping analytical exercises, discussing the specific details of each project and exploring its functions in the larger context of the AKP's identity politics.

The case under examination, the architectures of "Neo-Ottomanism", is a complex one, as there is no unitary blueprint or officially promoted government building programme, although there is a diffuse but widespread preference for an "Ottoman-Seljuk" canon (Batuman 2016). This is indeed different from other societal and political fields; political Islam in the Milli Görüş (National View) tradition (Fisher Onar 2009, 234) has, for instance, relatively clearly defined goals in the fields of education, foreign policy, and institutional reform. Representative architecture, however, has developed in different parts of the state, and has become more streamlined only since the consolidation of power in the hands of President Erdoğan and after Turkey's "exit from democracy" with the coup attempt of 15 July 2016 (Öktem and Akkoyunlu 2018). It has also changed styles from diffuse notions of the "Ottoman-Seljuk" architecture of the sixteenth century to generic eclectic historicism in the most important and representative structures of the AKP era, including the Library and Mosque of the Nation in the Presidential Complex in Ankara (Cumhurbaşkanlığı Külliyesi) and the Taksim Mosque in Istanbul.

SACRALISATION AND RESTORATION: ISLAM, THE OTTOMAN EMPIRE, AND THE AKP

Neo-Ottomanism is a highly contested and fuzzy term that owes as much to think-tank reports as to scholarly erudition. As an analytical concept, it is both too narrow and too wide, and above all confusing. It revives the term "Ottomanism" which, as a historical precedent, connotes the elements of cosmopolitanism (Fisher Onar 2009), ethnic and religious inclusion, civic citizenship, and non-religious notions of membership in an Ottoman "nation", but turns it into its very opposite. For many of its authors, Neo-Ottomanism, therefore, stands for a neo-imperial project that actively seeks to reconnect to notions of Ottoman grandeur and dominance over a vast geography (Yavuz 1998) with a prominent Islamist content (Benhaim and Öktem 2015). Practitioners of Turkish domestic and foreign policy, however, do not identify as "Neo-Ottoman", even if they follow the aforementioned neo-imperial agenda.

For the purpose of this inquiry, I find the concept of "identity proposals", which Lisel Hintz (2018) develops based on the Turkish case, particularly useful. She operationalises the debate on Neo-Ottomanism and defines the AKP's identity proposal as "Ottoman Islamism", contrasting it with the competing proposals of Republican Nationalism, Pan-Turkic Nationalism, and Western Liberalism. This proposal is defined by norms of membership, social purpose, relational meaning, and cognitive worldview. In terms of membership, Ottoman Islamism, in this reading, is based on Sunni Muslim piety, a politics of gender that clearly positions women in a position subservient to men, and the absolute authority and understanding of Ottoman rule as the greatest era in Turkish history. The social purposes of this identity project include the spread of Islam in the public sphere—this includes the imposition of rigid gender roles and the eventual repeal of secular civil law—the aim to deepen ties with Muslim people globally, and regain some form of Ottoman glory. The relational meanings—views vis-à-vis various outgroups—are based on the perspective of natural kinship with other Muslim peoples, good relations with former Ottoman territories, hostility towards the West, and enmity towards Israel (Hintz 2018, Table 3.1). This identity proposal is further consolidated by a historical worldview that portrays "the transition to modernity and the nation-state in terms of almost transcendental bereavement, a trauma in which subjecthood was shattered" (Fisher Onar 2009, 235).

By framing the Islamist political project as, above all, a politics of identity, and dividing it into the four functional components presented above, Hintz both demystifies the contested and fuzzy notion of "identity" (Brubaker and Cooper 2000) and further develops Jenny White's preceding analysis of "Muslim Nationalism" (2013), which also emphasises the identity component of the AKP's policies and their enactment in everyday life. And indeed, one of the key insights from the projects discussed here is that they are not rooted in an understanding of history as a continuous flow of events, but rather share a Huntingtonian worldview of a clash between immutable and essentially unchangeable identities (Huntington 1993). To this, we can add the notion of "restorative nostalgia", which Svetlana Boym (2007) defines as the goal of "transhistorical reconstruction of the lost home", referring to the notion of nostalgia as longing not only for a lost time, but also for a lost home. In *Nostalgia and Its Discontents* (2007), she argues that the danger of nostalgia lies in confusing actually existing and imaginary homes:

In extreme cases it can create a phantom homeland, for the sake of which one is ready to die or kill. Unreflective nostalgia can breed monsters. Yet the sentiment itself, the mourning of displacement and temporal irreversibility, is at the very core of the modern condition. While claiming a pure and clean homeland, nostalgic politics often produces a "glocal" hybrid of capitalism and religious fundamentalism, or of corporate state and Eurasian patriotism. The mix of nostalgia and politics can be explosive. (Boym 2007)

The AKP's grand projects, as well as the Ottoman-Islamist identity proposal, can be read through the lenses of restorative (at least in the eyes of the followers of the Islamist identity proposal) and unreflective nostalgia, as these are indeed the created hybrids of capitalism and religious fundamentalism.

This notion of nostalgia helps to explain the preference in almost all recent grand mosque projects for what Batuman (2016) calls the "mimicry" of sixteenth-century mosque architecture, which arguably represents both the pinnacle of Ottoman mosque architecture and the highpoint of the empire's territorial expansion. In line with Lisel Hintz's argument that the AKP government has extended Turkey's internal nation-building project into the realm of the country's foreign policy engagements, the same Ottoman sultans' mosques (*selatin camii*)[1] are not only constructed in Istanbul and in Turkey's provincial centres, but also in cities worldwide, and particularly in the Balkans (Beck 2019).

We can, therefore, argue that the actors engaging in the building of a "new Turkey"—state agencies like the Presidency for Religious Affairs (Diyanet), religious foundations, municipal mayors, and construction companies close to the government and private persons—are guided by the social purpose of spreading Islam in the public sphere through the creation of an "Islamic public space" (Batuman 2018). This reflects the aim of reconnecting with imagined notions of Ottoman glory, a strategy we can also refer to as "re-sacralisation" (Zaidi 2006; Gao 2020), or "re-enchantment" (Yang 2020). Yang's work is particularly insightful in this context, as she understands, in the context of China, the re-emergence of religion "not as a stubborn 'cultural remnant' but as an active

---

[1] Sultan's mosques (*selatin camii*) are large mosques built and financed with the private funds of a sultan (Özdemir 2012). Istanbul's classic sixteenth-century mosques (Sultanahmet, Süleymaniye, Fatih, Valide) are sultan's mosques. Many of the new representative mosques of the AKP era copy the style of these mosques and pose as if they were sultan's mosques, even though they are built either with state or private funds.

engagement with modernity, a willed re-enchantment" (9), which operates in a "ritual economy... where religion and economy are inseparable" (318). These strategies are, indeed, constrained by the political-economic arrangements of the AKP era, which have morphed from a neoliberal configuration with authoritarian elements (Özbay et al. 2016) into neoliberal authoritarianism with an increasingly state-capitalist outlook (Öniş 2019; Kutlay 2020). Neoliberalism here is understood as a governing rationality "through which everything is 'economized' ... human beings become market actors and nothing but, every field of activity is seen as a market, and every entity ... is governed as a firm" (Wendy Brown in Shenk 2015). In the Turkish case, Göçek reminds us, "not only the market and the state, but history also structure current neoliberal practices" (2017, 2). If in liberal European states, neoliberalism gradually replaces the underpinnings of democracy, in peripheral countries like Turkey, neoliberal rationality becomes particularly toxic and creates a situation where "capitalism finally swallows humanity" (Brown 2015, 44). This dehumanising aspect of neoliberalism is further aggravated when articulated with the unchecked state power of the current hyper-presidential arrangements in Turkey (Esen and Gumuscu 2018; Öktem 2019).

Capitalism, here, does not only swallow humanity, but also the ideological content of political projects that are not primarily rent-generating—hence the extremely narrow confines in which modernity can be re-sacralised or re-enchanted, an Islamic public space can be created, urban space can be Islamicised, and meaning can be inserted into modern cityscapes. It appears that every attempt to project Ottoman grandeur, Islamic meaning, and Islamist social norms is undermined by the logic of rent-generation, urban transformation, high-rise office and residential developments, major infrastructure projects, and the inherent functions of dispossession and redistribution. Attempts to create Muslim cityscapes seem to falter in the face of neoliberal capital accumulation and, if anything, appear merely to add another layer of ideologically imbued buildings and behavioural practices to what, in most cases, are historically complex cities.

This does not mean, however, that under the successive AKP governments since 2002, and the Welfare Party (Refah Partisi) municipalities since 1994, cities in Turkey have not visibly changed or become more religiously connotated in appearance and atmosphere. In fact, the skylines of cities in Turkey are now dominated by minarets, which are in constant competition with the high-rise buildings that surround them, and almost every provincial city in Turkey is now home to a major grand mosque built in the last decade. Many lower-middle class and poor neighbourhoods in Ankara and Istanbul have been shaped by almost three decades of Islamist municipal politics and their social programmes. And even without architecture, urban space can be imbued with Islamic symbols and Islamist content, as Basdurak shows in her work on the effects of the strategic use of the call to prayer and the resulting "soundscapes of Islamic populism" (2020, cf. Koymen 2017). Ankara's central Kızılay Square[2] is a case in point. As one of the iconic squares of republican Ankara thanks to the "Security Monument" (Güven Anıtı), the square lacks a visible mosque structure. During the rule of the AKP mayor, Melih Gökçek, a prayer room was built in the metro station under the square, and there are several smaller prayer rooms in the adjacent streets. Yet, before prayer times, the call to prayer, or *ezan* (*adhan*) is so overpowering that one intuitively assumes that a physical mosque must be nearby. With an overpowering sound system, Kızılay Square is transformed into the imagined forecourt of a grand mosque five times a day.

The Representative Architecture of the AKP Era

Some of the most consequential representative building projects of the AKP governments under President Recep Tayyip Eroğan were built since 2010. I divide them into three loosely defined heuristic categories emanating from the field and based on their perceived effect in urban space (in the author's view, and in terms of how they relate to republican history and give rise to contestation). These are projects that primarily aim to sacralise public space (the Hacıbayram Mosque and neighbourhood); projects that are geared towards diminishing or effacing the republican past (Ulus and Taksim Squares); and projects that, above all, seek to demonstrate power and domination (the North Ankara Mosque Complex, the Çamlıca Mosque, the Presidential Complex).

Re-enchanting Modern Cityscapes: The Hacıbayram Mosque and Neighbourhood

The attempt to re-enchant modernity is not limited to Islamism, but it is particularly prominent in Islamist political projects that reject the "Godlessness" of secular modernity. Turkey's modern cities, and especially

---

[2] The square was renamed after the coup attempt in 2016 as the impossibly worded "15 Temmuz Kızılay Milli İrade Meydanı" (15 July Red Crescent National Will Square).

Ankara, had few large mosques well into the 1980s, when mosque-building accelerated as a function of the Turkish-Islamic synthesis (*Türk Islam sentezi*) mandated by the military government of the 1980 coup and subsequent centre-right governments. One of the first large mosque projects to be inaugurated in the republic was the Kocatepe Mosque in Ankara, opened under the auspices of Prime Minister Turgut Özal in 1987 as a prototype of "Ottoman-Seljuk" revivalist architecture. Ever since, large mosque projects undertaken by Diyanet and its Foundation (Diyanet Vakfı), or by private persons and companies, have mostly followed the blueprint of combining the architectural language of sixteenth-century Ottoman sultan's mosques built by Mimar Sinan, coupled with more modern amenities and infrastructures such as car parks, elevators, super markets, libraries, and cultural centres.

A prime example of the effort to sacralise an urban square, while creating an alternative to the most established symbol of republican Ankara, the mausoleum of Atatürk (Anıtkabir;), is the Hacıbayram Mosque and urban renovation project, realised by the Ankara municipality under its conservative mayor Melih Gökçek (Fig. 5.1). The Hacıbayram Mosque is one of the oldest in Ankara, although its architecture and proportions are rather humble. Yet, located in a part of the city's old town that is within walking distance of Ulus (Nation) Square—one of the most revered and ideologically laden ensembles of the early republic—it is a perfect place to create the image of a historic city that predates the republican project of nation building and takes pride in its deeply rooted Islamic history (Fig. 5.2). With this aim in mind, the urban planners and architects under the leadership of Öner Tokcan[3] demolished the entire neighbourhood and replaced it with prototypes of white-washed "Ankara houses"—simplified and typified versions of the local vernacular architecture—shopping arcades, and a pedestrianised square around the mosque, which also incorporates the ruins of the Roman temple of Augustus.

The intention to create a symbolic new centre for Ankara defined by the Seljuk-Ottoman heritage and Islamic piety seems to have worked: while few people live in the Ankara houses, most are occupied by Islamic foundations, religious institutions, cultural centres, cafes, and teetotal restaurants. Most units in the shopping arcade cater to the needs of pilgrims and

---

[3] Öner Tokcan was one of the star architects of the Ankara municipality under Melih Gökçek, also responsible for the North Ankara Mosque Complex discussed later. Cf. http://www.gelisimmimarlik.com.tr/hakkimizda/. Accessed on 12 May 2021.

5 ARCHITECTURES OF DOMINATION? THE SACRALISATION...

Fig. 5.1 *Top left*: The Mausoleum of the state founder Atatürk (Anıtkabir), *Top right*: Hacıbayram Mosque and plateau, *Bottom left*: Streets in the Hacıbayram neighbourhood, *Bottom right*: View from Hacıbayram to lower-middle-class neighbourhoods. (The source of all figures is the author)

pious folk, selling religious paraphernalia, prayer rugs, hijabs, and religious literature. Many men here wear long beards and skullcaps, while many women are veiled. The atmosphere in the arcade may feel unwelcoming to non-religious people, but due to the large number of visitors—pious and non-religious, foreigners and locals—there appears to be little conflict, as Metin, a local shopkeeper, remarks:

> Sure, there are many men here with beards and robes. But this is Ankara. They are conservative, but they would never cause a problem, they mind their own business. That's why you can have a woman sitting here wearing a miniskirt, and no one takes notice. There were times when it could be scary here, when the demolition continued and the project was not yet com-

Fig. 5.2 *Top left*: Ulus Square, *Top right*: Melike Hatun Mosque, *Bottom left*: Gençlik Park Entrance, *Bottom right*: Melike Hatun Mosque seen from the north

pleted, but now it is all good. You see it yourself, it has become a touristic place, and people like it.[4]

The scary times refer to the period of urban renovation, when houses and shops were demolished, schools were closed, and jobless youth took to drugs and violence. Jihadist organisations close to the Islamic State became active in the area under the eyes of the security services, with the effect that probably more than a hundred local teenagers joined Jihadist groups in Syria (Yeginsu 2014).

Despite the brutal destruction of the old neighbourhood, the Hacıbayram plateau and its adjacent streets and arcades feel almost like the historic heart of a minor Ottoman city, even though, apart from the mosque and the temple ruins, few structures are is older than ten years. In terms of the ideological components of Ottoman Islamism, the project indeed succeeds in connecting to the Ottoman past and in elevating Islam

[4] All direct quotes, whether citations or interview transcripts, were translated by the author.

to become the core element of Turkish identity and Ankara history. It also draws attention away from the neighbourhood's proximity to the city's largest brothel complex, Bentderesi, which was only dismantled in 2011 (Cantek 2018).

The ensemble of whitewashed houses, somewhat generic but evocative of vernacular architecture of central Anatolian cities as well as the Baščaršija in the centre of Sarajevo, together with the historical ensemble of the mosque and the temple ruins, do amount to a place with some historical significance that attracts both visitors and locals. Yet the Hacıbayram plateau also demonstrates the limits of the effort to create meaning and Ottoman connections, as the area is encircled by high-rise buildings that are impossible to ignore.[5] With their size and brutal uniformity, they seem to demonstrate that the structures on the plateau belong to an albeit cherished past, while the lived present, particularly for the lower-middle classes, is one of steel, concrete, dehumanizing scale and extremely high population density.

Diminishing the Republican Past in Ankara and Istanbul: Ulus and Taksim

Two urban ensembles represent late Ottoman and republican architectural heritage in highly symbolic ways: Ulus (Nation) Square in Ankara and Taksim Square in Istanbul. Ulus Square and its adjacent quarters form the heart of pre- and early republican Ankara and host a large number of iconic buildings and monuments: the building used by the first parliament of the republic and the city's largest Atatürk monument—structures in different architectural styles that represent the economic and political tenets of independence and self-sufficiency of the early republic—as well as modernist buildings from the 1950s, all dominated by the citadel. The symbolism of the Atatürk statue and its location cannot be overestimated: it is at the centre of "Nation Square", and therefore at the imagined heart of modern Turkey. In close proximity are further structures that are intricately linked to early republican nation-building: the Gençlik (Youth) Park designed by German architect Herman Jansen, who also prepared the

---

[5] The block of flats under construction in the background is located in the lower-middle class neighbourhoods of Demetevler and Yenimahalle. From the vantage point of Hacıbayram, these neighbourhoods look actually even more dense and dominated by concrete than they are in reality.

city's first zoning plan, the train station, and cultural buildings in the late imperial and the so-called first national architecture styles (1. Ulusal Mimarlik) of the late Ottoman empire, as well as government buildings in the radical modern architectural forms of the 1930s and 1940s (Fig. 5.2).

In September 2018, the Ankara municipality published an urban transformation project for the Ulus area, which would have largely effaced its late Ottoman and early Republican heritage.[6] The project provided for the square's pedestrianisation and the demolition of a significant number of modern buildings and their replacement with historicising structures in the "Ottoman-Seljuk" style. While the Atatürk Monument itself was not touched, its prominence was diminished by the planting of trees, obscuring the monument's centrality, thereby insinuating that Atatürk was only one of many great men in Turkey's recent history, and not the most important one. The project was opposed by civil society organisations like the Ankara Chamber of Architecture (Karakoç 2018), and was ultimately shelved with the election victory of the opposition mayor, Mansur Yavaş, in 2019.

While the destruction and rebuilding of Ulus Square has been avoided, the more subtle strategy of obscuring the republican heritage continued with the transformation of the iconic Sümerbank Building, built in 1937 by Martin Elsaesser, into the Ankara Social Sciences University (Ankara Sosyal Bilimler Üniversitesi). While Sümerbank, as a state-owned, textile production enterprise established in 1933, was a symbol of Turkey's early industrialisation efforts and economic independence, the new tenant is a newly founded state university that is supposed to become an intellectual centre for Islamist thinkers and aims to create a national conservative alternative to Turkey's secular elite universities.

A more robust intervention into the urban fabric is the nearby Melike Hatun Mosque, opened in 2017 as Ankara's third grand mosque (Fig. 5.2).[7] It was apparently financed by a private donor, but was made possible due to massive state support. It is located on what used to be the "Opera Square" (Opera Meydanı) and was renamed in 2013 after Turkey's

---

[6] An animation of the project can be found here: https://www.youtube.com/watch?v=kzXZpU0X4Sc (Accessed on 12 May 2021). Note the juxtaposed layers of the musical backdrop, which combine a "sufi"-style instrumental introduction with a more Western melodical structure.

[7] The first two largest mosques are the Kocatepe Mosque completed in the 1980s and the more recent Ahmet Hamdi Akseki Mosque on the campus of the Presidency of Religious Affairs, Diyanet.

first Islamist prime minister, Necmettin Erbakan, just across from the Youth Park in the immediate neighbourhood of Ulus Square, and next to the city's main Atatürk Boulevard. Below the square in front of the mosque, there is a shopping centre and the entrances to washrooms for ablution, which are separated according to gender. Signs on the square indicating dedicated entrances to the women's and men's sections of the mosque carry the religiously connotated separation of men and women into what should be an ostensibly secular space, thereby creating a grey zone between secular and religious space, or more accurately, a space in which the gender norms of the mosque are projected onto secular space.

Thanks to its centrality, to its large size, and its symbolic location, the mosque's opening ceremony in October 2017 attracted a large crowd of members of the government as well as of heads of states from Muslim countries. In his speech, after introducing the mosque's eponym, Melike Hatun, as a woman of Islamic learning and piety of the fourteenth century, President Erdoğan delivered a major programmatic speech, contrasting secular modernity with a societal and urban vision for a more religious Turkey:

> Ankara is not only the capital of the republic, but also a central city of the Seljuks and the Ottomans. I believe that with its Ottoman, Seljuk, and modern architectural characteristics this work will be one of the symbols of Ankara... With the Melike Hatun Mosque, we bring together the Ankara of the republic and the Ankara of the Ottomans and the Seljuks....
>
> It is an undeniable fact that, especially during the one-party era, efforts were made to detach Ankara from its ancient identity and to render it devoid of mosques. The mindset that turned older mosques into stables condemned the masjids to cellars, basements, and to the darkest spots of buildings. Those who prevented people from entering the city centre based on the way they dressed planned their newly constructed cities without mosques, without adhan, without spirit. Underground mosques, which do not befit a capital were, for a long time, the destiny of Ankara. ... My Lord, may you not leave our country without adhan, our mosques without the pious and without a community. (Diyanet 2017)

Erdoğan posits that Ankara is more than the capital of the republic, criticises the republican elites for having cut the city's ties with its "ancient identity"—depicted here as exclusively Muslim[8]—and holds secular modernity responsible for cities "without mosques, without adhan, without spirit". Hence, the counter proposal is to build cities with mosques, with adhan, and with spirit. From this perspective, the building of the Melike Hatun and other grand mosques is a restorative action to heal the wounds caused by republican disrespect towards religion, to bring Islam back into the public space, and to reconnect to the "ancient" and Muslim identity of the city. Understood in this vein, Erdoğan's speech here could be seen as a case for "restorative nostalgia", a term which Svetlana Boym (2007) applies to what she calls "transhistorical reconstruction of the lost home".

This restoration, however, seems to require not only the construction of a new structure, but also the obfuscation, or at least the diminishment, of the republican heritage just around the corner. With its massive size—it can hold up to 7000 people in the main prayer room and another 1000 in its conference centre—the mosque singlehandedly interrupts the continuum of late Ottoman, early republican, and modern architecture and dominates the major visual connections of the area. The Youth Park in particular, a prime example of the modern architecture of the 1930s and a showcase for secular forms of socialisation, is now overtopped by the minarets of the mosque. Yet, rather than establishing an incontrovertible spatial hegemony here, the Melike Hatun Mosque, above all, seems to add yet another layer of identity to the palimpsest of the city, and to a public space oversaturated with the symbols and references of different identities. This is particularly the case at the park's eastern entrance, which faces the mosque, where the modern architecture of the 1930s coincides with an allegedly "Seljuk" portico added by Mayor Gökçek, a poster of Atatürk, a display case with photographs of the "martyrs of 15 July"—people killed during the coup attempt in 2016—and the mosque itself.

The Atatürk Cultural Centre and the Taksim Mosque
Another prominent urban ensemble with a republican heritage, if of a more variegated kind than Ankara's Ulus, is Istanbul's Taksim Square (Fig. 5.3). The square hosts the Orthodox Church of the Holy Trinity (Haghia Triada), a late nineteenth-century water cistern and fountain, and the city's main Atatürk monument of 1928. To the north, the square is flanked by the municipal gardens, another modernist structure of the late

---

[8] Ironically, like the republican nationalist historiography of Ankara, the Islamists also efface non-Muslim communities from the city's memory (Kezer 2017).

Fig. 5.3 *Top*: Taksim Mosque, *Bottom*: Taksim Mosque and commemoration of Atatürk's death

1930s, apartment buildings of the 1930s and 40s, and the city's opera, the Atatürk Cultural Centre. Modernist hotel structures of the 1970s and some historicising reconstructions sit in the north-eastern part. As Istanbul's most iconic square, and unlike Ulus, Taksim never felt like a *mise-en-scène* of Kemalist urbanism, but it was nevertheless shaped by different phases of modernist urbanity. From the 1970s, it became the central square for demonstrations, and a place symbolising the struggles of the labour movement and the socialist left (Öktem 2013). It was also the venue for major public protests when the Istanbul municipality, in June 2013, attempted to uproot trees in the nearby Gezi Park to re-build a long-demolished Ottoman barracks as a shopping centre (Erensü and Karaman 2016).

Following the Gezi protests, the demolition of the park and the construction of the shopping centre were halted, but two other major projects were begun by state agencies, with the intention of establishing symbolic domination over the square where President Erdoğan had been booed and ridiculed. The first was the demolition and rebuilding of the Atatürk Culture Centre (Atatürk Kültür Merkezi, AKM). After contemplating a "magnificent opera building in baroque style" suggested by Erdoğan during the Gezi protests, a compromise solution was chosen instead. The new structure stays largely true to the original building's 1970s modern form, while significantly expanding its size and adding some playful architectural elements, like the exposed shell of the main hall.[9]

The second, and more consequential project, was the construction of a grand mosque, a project that had been on the books since 1977 when a zoning plan revision to allow for mosque construction was granted. But the project remained deeply contested. It was only the state of exception following the military coup attempt of 15 July 2016 and the subsequent suspension of the rule of law that allowed mosque construction to begin in 2017. While clearly a pet project of President Erdoğan, the mosque was financed and built by Sur Yapı, a leading construction company whose owners are close associates of the president. Unlike other new grand mosques, the Taksim Mosque holds only about 1000 worshippers and its dimensions are less intimidating than, for instance, those of the Melike

---

[9] The new Atatürk Culture Centre was planned by Murat Tabanlıoğlu, the son of the original architect Hayati Tabanlıoğlu. This compromise solution is indeed surprising, as the contestations around the AKM were particularly polarised and a visible compromise is usually not part of the AKP's mode of politics.

Hatun Mosque. It nevertheless successfully revises the square's largely non-Islamic content, defined by secular and non-Muslim religious structures which it by far overtowers. Built and financed by a construction company with very close links to the government, the mosque also stands out with its deviation from the official Seljuk-Ottoman-style cannon and its slightly generic, even orientalising architecture.[10]

In a similar fashion to its approach to Ulus Square, the original intent of the AKP government, both on a national and on municipal level, had been to completely change the square's composition and efface its early republican and modern heritage by rebuilding a former Ottoman barracks structure as a shopping centre, replacing the AKM with a historicising hall, and adding a mosque to this once most iconic square of Istanbul. Due to the pronounced resistance to these projects and the subsequent change in municipal governments in 2019, only the mosque was built, while the AKM was rebuilt with minor changes. Taksim Square is now dominated by a mosque. Once the culture centre opens for concertgoers, the view from the main lounge will be of the new mosque, while the Atatürk Monument will be barely visible. The square has indeed been "sacralised". But the mosque is now also the locale of contestation between the Ottoman Islamist project it represents, and the Republican People's Party, which holds the municipality and frames the mosque by emphasising Atatürk as founder of the Turkish nation.

Dominating the Present: Power and the Common Good

The aforementioned projects constituted interventions into the existing urban fabric, by which they were constrained spatially and functionally. In this final section, I focus on three "grand projects", the North Ankara Mosque Complex, the Çamlıca Mosque in Istanbul, and the Presidential Complex, which were built on empty spaces with few physical limitations. They are massive in their dimensions, but they are also relatively distant from the city centres, and therefore not easily accessible and viewable. This is particularly true of the North Ankara Mosque Complex (Kuzey Ankara Külliyesi), which is located on a promontory on the northern outskirts of the town and can only be reached by a single access road (Fig. 5.4). It is, however, the first representative structure travellers coming from the

---

[10] The mosque's planner, Şefik Birikiye, is a Brussels-based architect and real estate developer who also designed the Presidential Complex in Ankara.

Fig. 5.4 *Top left*: North Ankara Mosque Complex, general view, *Top right*: North Ankara Mosque Complex park, *Bottom*: North Ankara Mosque Complex Hacıbayram University

airport encounter on their way to the city centre, and it dominates the views of what is one of the foremost urban transformation projects of former Ankara mayor, Melih Gökçek. The complex hosts a mosque for 15,000 worshippers, a conference centre for 5000 guests, and a museum (Diyanet 2019a), as well as the theology faculty and administrative buildings of a new state university.

The complex subscribes to the official Ottoman-Seljuk blueprint, but with a few unexpected twists that are reminiscent of the eclectic architecture of themed hotels on Turkey's Mediterranean shores, such as the Topkapı Palace Hotel in Antalya (Salah 2006). Its architectural forms have been chosen indiscriminately from sixteenth-century Ottoman sultans' mosques and the Topkapı Palace, with a nod to the kinship with Muslim people and traditions elsewhere; it even sports a replica of the minaret of the Mosque of Samarra. Like many of the new grand mosques, however, it does not have a congregation of its own. When I first visited on a Sunday morning, the only open facility was a tea shop managed by a man in his sixties, who was anxious to explain why he bought a shop there:

> Look, this is the perfect location for a grand mosque. The Kocatepe Mosque is right in the city centre. When you have a state funeral, the traffic in all of Ankara comes to a standstill. And even the Diyanet Mosque is not sufficient anymore. They were saying that this would become the main "protocol" mosque.[11] ...
> You know, when we have the martyrs who are killed in the war against terrorists, then we have 10,000–20,000 people in a funeral service. When that happens in Ankara, it ruins the traffic of the entire city. This is why they will move here. People can come here, leave their cars in the car park, do their prayers, and off they are again on the motorway. Without causing any traffic problems. It makes much more sense. ...
> This was Melih Gökçek's project. It is so big, and it will hopefully be a big success. But people have to come from the outside; there is no congregation here. We thought this would be a good investment for our retirement. But they never fully opened it. And now, it is all unclear. It's all about politics.

The mosque, a pet project of Mayor Melih Gökçek, was opened just after he lost the city to the Republican People's Party in the municipal elections of March 2019. The project was left half-finished, and the mosque had not yet been declared a "protocol mosque" for state funerals at the time of writing.[12] The nonchalance with which my interlocutor was making his calculations involving martyrs, worshippers, and tea sales was therefore understandable, as he had invested his retirement money into what looked like a bad business idea. It also comes as a reminder that these mosque complexes are very much part of a "ritual economy", where religion and economy, as well as politics, "support and stimulate each other" (Yang 2020, 318).

---

[11] Mosques which are used for state functions (i.e. state funerals) are often referred to as 'protokol cami', i.e. "mosques for state protocol".

[12] While the building materials are of a high quality, the execution of details seems to be lacking craftsmanship. After I told a security guard that I had studied architecture, he asked me, "Is it normal that such a new building starts leaking everywhere? You just need a gentle rain, and nothing stays dry. They have spent so much money on this, I don't understand why this happens."

Empty as it is, the North Ankara Complex is, above all, a new landmark which no traveller arriving by plane can miss, and a grand mosque, which overlooks many smaller mosques, reminders of the poor neighbourhoods that once occupied the valley and the adjacent hills stretching in front of it.

The Çamlıca Mosque

The Çamlıca Mosque is Turkey's largest religious structure, designed to hold more than 60,000 worshippers at the same time (Diyanet 2019b), financed by a mosque-building association with the donations mostly of businessmen close to the government (Fig. 5.5). Like the North Ankara Complex, it sits in splendid isolation—accessible via road tunnels and escalators—on a high plateau, overlooking a substantial part of the Istanbul metropolitan region, and hence visible from much of central Istanbul. The gesture of domination, of transforming nature for religion's sake, and the aim of "transhistorical reconstruction of the lost home" (Boym 2007) is nowhere more obvious than in this overwhelmingly colossal structure of concrete and marble. In his opening speech in May 2019, President Erdoğan touched on these issues almost apologetically:

> Our places of worship were constructed in grandeur and magnificence, because [in this way] they add meaning to the cities in which they rise. Wherever there is a dome, a minaret, wherever our adhans blend into the firmament, without doubt that place is a Muslim home. (Diyanet 2019b)

The admonition that Turkey's cities, until recently, were lacking representative mosques as centres of spiritual meaning may be justified for Ankara, but it cannot possibly be made with reference to Istanbul, which is home to some of the most splendid Ottoman houses of worship anywhere. This may partly explain the apologetic turn in the President's speech. The new mosque not only seeks to dominate the entire Istanbul skyline, it also establishes a visual connection with the sultans' mosques on the historical peninsula and seeks to outshine them both in size and importance.[13]

Some complications, however, compromise the project's inherent gesture of domination. The structure is no doubt massive but, with the exception of the northern districts on the Bosporus, it is always too far away to allow a full appreciation of its dimensions. Unlike the sultans' mosques of

---

[13] Considering that the mosque's inauguration was an international event attended by political and religious leaders from Muslim majority countries, the Çamlıca Mosque can also be read as a claim to dominance in the Muslim world.

Fig. 5.5 *Top*: Çamlıca Mosque, general view, *Bottom*: View to central Istanbul from the plateau

Istanbul's historical peninsula, which can be contemplated from their immediate surroundings, as well as from Galata, the Anatolian side, and during boat trips, the Çamlıca Mosque cannot be seen from close by unless one climbs up to the plateau on which it sits. On rainy days, it disappears from sight completely. The mosque's spatial isolation means that it has no congregation. Despite the many additional facilities—a library, a museum of Islamic arts, a conference centre—the whole complex is eerily quiet, even during Friday prayers, as a member of staff pointed out:

> During Friday prayers, it gets more lively. Of course, there is the pandemic at the moment. There are hardly any tourists. We used to get many Arabs and tourists from all over the world. They see the mosque from afar and want to visit. And we have a great view here. The problem is that we are simply too far away. People cannot just come here and pray; they have to make an effort. Thank God there is a good bus connection. But there is always a mosque closer to them, even on Fridays. To fill this [the mosque], we need bigger events, like a visit from the President. Otherwise, without a congregation, it is impossible. İnşallah, once all the other facilities are fully operational, after COVID, there will be more life here.

Due to its size, visibility, and sweeping views over Istanbul, the Bosporus, and the Marmara Sea, the complex could eventually become a destination for tourists, especially if its accessibility can be improved. Yet it looks very unlikely that it will become the lively cultural and religious centre that the President of the Diyanet, Dr Ali Erbaş, conjured up in his prayer at the opening ceremony, "Do not leave this mosque without a congregation, my Lord, do not leave this mosque without children, my Lord, do not leave this mosque without young people, my Lord" (Diyanet 2019b).

The Presidential Complex
The Presidential Complex (Cumhurbaşkanlığı Külliyesi) is, without doubt, the most contested and most opposed structure built under the AKP and President Erdoğan (Fig. 5.6). For a long time, the republican opposition referred to it as the "Illegal Palace" (Kaçaksaray), referring to the lack of planning oversight, the development of parts of the urban forest bequeathed to the city by Atatürk (Atatürk Orman Çiftliği), and the inflated building costs (Gür and Altan 2015; Karakuş Candan 2015). But with the sheer power of facticity, the "Külliye" has become the power centre of Erdoğan's new Turkey. It is a massive complex containing the Presidential Residence, an office block with more than a thousand rooms,

Fig. 5.6 *Top left*: General view of the Presidential Complex, *Top right*: Mosque of the Nation (Millet Camii), *Bottom left*: Forecourt of the Library of the Nation (Millet Kütüphanesi), *Bottom right*: Main reading hall of the library

a mosque, a conference centre, a concert hall, and a library.[14] Initially, the whole complex was open to the public. Since the coup attempt of June 2016, however, the residence and office areas are cordoned off, while the "Mosque of the Nation" (Millet Camii) and "Library of the Nation" (Millet Kütüphanesi) remain open for visits amid strict security controls under the presence of armed personnel (Fig. 5.6).

The Presidential Complex is, by far, the largest and most symbolic project of the AKP era, as it seeks to replace the established republican institutions of the parliamentary regime (and their buildings dating mostly from the early republican era) with a new set of institutions (and buildings) of

---

[14] Due to its size, and the distance between its components, none of which are very monumental taken by themselves, the complex does not feel overwhelming. In fact, it cannot be grasped in its full dimensions except from a sizeable distance, whereupon it merely appears like a collection of random buildings.

the presidential regime inaugurated with the elections in June 2018. More importantly, the Presidential Complex is also distinct thanks to its hyper-eclectic architectural language. Rather than following the Ottoman-Seljuk blueprint of mosque architecture, the Külliye contains a range of different styles: the mosque presents a more generic, universal style of architecture while the residence resembles a pavilion structure with alcoves. The library, with its more than two million books, is the most eclectic building, with Egyptian columns in the forecourt, and a circular main reading hall, clearly inspired by the Library of Congress.

As a whole, the complex is unreservedly historicising and eclectic. The longing for a "lost home" that never was, and for historical grandeur, are the most pronounced elements, even in the absence of legible references to the Ottoman Empire. With this quality, it most clearly manifests the general constitution of Turkey's Islamist movement—or the version thereof it has become under the conditions of neoliberal authoritiarianism of the late AKP era—as a political project rooted in a past that never existed, longing for a "phantom homeland" (Boym 2007). At the same time, the Külliye's facilities are of such high quality that its users can only feel pampered. Whether in the mosque or the library, all the facilities resemble those of a five-star hotel,[15] while the library's circular reading room is indeed quite an architectural feat; all of this is received positively by the general public. Despite the intrusive security controls, the library is full of students at all times, and the complex attracts a steady flow of visitors. Visitors are allowed to enter the library without prior registration and many do, to sit in the comfortable lounges or promenade the lavish corridors, albeit in respectful silence. A member of a family who was visiting the library and mosque juxtaposed the two most prominent symbols of power in Ankara, when she saw me taking photos:

> Look, today we have also been to the Anıtkabir, we have seen everything there. It is nice of course, and it is the resting place of our ancestor/Atatürk [Atamız]. But it is a bit cold there. You can't really do anything. Now, look at all this here, there is a library, a mosque, a concert hall. When you compare, it is so much nicer here. Everything is of the highest quality. They have made a real effort here.

---

[15] This is no coincidence. The architect, Şefik Birikiye, often referred to as the "Architect of New Turkey", first became known in Turkey in the 1990s with the Klassis Hotel in Istanbul Silivri. With its "neo-classical" fantasy architecture, it was a major departure from the overwhelmingly modernist architectiural language of hotels prevalent in Turkey until then (Yilmaz 2015).

Indeed, despite the clear intention to replace the republican symbols of power in Turkey with the autocratic institutions of "Hyper-Presidentialism", and despite the will to dominate space and time, the public areas of the Presidential Complex seem to contain the residues of a republican notion of the common good that is at the disposal of every citizen.[16]

CONCLUSION

The structures examined in this chapter are meaningfully connected to what Lisel Hintz calls the "Ottoman-Islamist" identity proposal of President Erdoğan and the AKP. They all are manifestations of a form of Sunni Muslim piety, geared towards sacralising and re-enchanting secular public space. They aim at creating a perfect Muslim homeland of the past and at reconnecting to what is understood as Ottoman glory. On a deeper level, this sacralisation is connected to attempts to restore the "shattered subjecthood" (Fisher Onar 2009, 235) which Islamists associate with the trauma of secular modernity and the early republic. Yet all the projects are also part of an attempt to attain hegemony by building cities "with mosques, with adhan, and with spirit" that, by default, symbolically exclude all those who do not subscribe to the Ottoman Islamist identity proposal.

While overwhelming in their size and number, the new grand mosques and palaces, as well as the identity proposal underlying them, face several challenges and internal contradictions. The challenge of neoliberal capitalism is probably the most unsurmountable. The logic of rent generation and construction is at the heart of Turkey's vulnerable economy. Since the coup attempt of 2016, the Erdoğan government has been advancing the idea of cities with ever larger mosques, taller minarets, and louder adhans. At the same time, the construction of large infrastructure projects, motorways, high-speed train lines, and upscale residentials has increased beyond compare. More often than not, the grand mosques are financed by those very construction companies that build the faceless residential and office high rises and motorways that constitute the backdrop to all these projects and thereby effectively render void any "restorative purpose" that its authors might have had. The limits of this "ritual economy" (Yang 2020)

---

[16] Alternatively, the pomp and circumstance of the Külliye could also be understood as the magnanimous invitation of a sultanic ruler to his subjects to partake of the treasures of his own property, although this is not the ethos I felt.

are further demonstrated by the massive corruption, which underlies many "grand projects" of the AKP era.

No matter how big and uncompromising these structures are, when they are built into existing urban patterns, they usually fail to dominate a place. Instead, they constitute yet another addition to what already is a historically and ideologically complex and contested setting. The Melike Hatun Mosque indeed dominates its surroundings and projects Islamic gender norms into public space, but it is still surrounded by a multi-layered early republican heritage, as well as by modernist architecture of the post-war years. The Taksim Mosque adds an "Islamic" element to what continues to be a diverse urban situation which harbours the possibility of renewed contestation. In the cases of the North Ankara Mosque Complex, the Presidential Complex, and the Çamlıca Mosque, built on the (almost) empty slates of suburban peripheries, the structures are so far away from the city centre that they fail to serve as poles of visual attraction. Particularly with regard to the mosques in those distant locations, their function as centres of social and religious gathering—that is their main function—is heavily compromised. They might well become empty shells whose upkeep will be a major financial burden for future governments.

Acknowledgement I express my gratitude to our editors Catharina Raudvere and Petek Onur, Ipek Yosmaoğlu (Northwestern University), and Ebru Soytemel (Aston University) for their comments and contributions.

References

Basdurak, Nil. 2020. The Soundscape of Islamic Populism. *SoundEffects—An Interdisciplinary Journal of Sound and Sound Experience* 9 (1): 132–148.

Batuman, Bülent. 2008. Photography at Arms: 'Early Republican Ankara' from Nation-Building to Politics of Nostalgia. *Orta Doğu Teknik Üniversitesi Mimarlık Fakültesi Dergisi* 25 (2): 99–117.

———. 2013. Minarets without Mosques: Limits to the Urban Politics of Neo-Liberal Islamism. *Urban Studies* 50 (6): 1097–1113.

———. 2016. Architectural Mimicry and the Politics of Mosque Building: Negotiating Islam and Nation in Turkey. *The Journal of Architecture* 21 (3): 321–347.

———. 2018. *New Islamist Architecture and Urbanism: Negotiating Nation and Islam through Built Environment in Turkey*. London: Routledge.

Beck, John M. 2019. Turkey's Global Soft-Power Push Is Built on Mosques. *The Atlantic*. Accessed 12 May 2021. https://www.theatlantic.com/interna-

tional/archive/2019/06/turkey-builds-mosques-abroad-global-soft-power/590449/.
Benhaim, Yohanan and Kerem Öktem. 2015. The Rise and Fall of Turkey's Soft Power Discourse. *European Journal of Turkish Studies* No. 21. Accessed 12 May 2021. https://ejts.revues.org/5275.
Boym, Svetlana. 2007. Nostalgia and Its Discontents. *The Hedgehog Review* 9 (2). Accessed 12 May 2021. https://hedgehogreview.com/issues/the-uses-of-the-past/articles/nostalgia-and-its-discontents.
Bozdoğan, Sibel. 2001. *Modernism and Nation Building: Turkish Architectural Culture in the Early Republic*. Seattle, WA: University of Washington Press.
Brown, Wendy. 2015. *Undoing the Demos. Neoliberalism's Stealth Revolution*. New York: Zone Books.
Brubaker, Rogers, and Frederick Cooper. 2000. Beyond 'Identity'. *Theory and Society* 29 (1): 1–47.
Cantek, Funda. 2018. Genelevin enkazında kimler kaldı? *Gazete Duvar*. Accessed 12 May 2021. https://www.gazeteduvar.com.tr/yazarlar/2018/03/16/genelevin-enkazinda-kimler-kaldi.
Çeler, Zafer. 2019. Pseudo-Historicism and Architecture: The New Ottomanism in Turkey. *Journal of Balkan and Near Eastern Studies* 21 (5): 493–514.
Çınar, Reyhan Ünal. 2020. *Ecdadın İcadı. AKP İktidarında Bellek Mücadelesi*. Istanbul: İletişim Yayınları.
Diyanet İşleri Başkanlığı. 2017. Melike Hatun Camii Dualarla İbadete Açıldı. *Diyanet İşleri Başkanlığı Haberler*. Accessed 12 May 2021. https://www.diyanet.gov.tr/ru-RU/организационная/деталь/10974/melike-hatun-camii-dualarla-ibadete-acildi.
———. 2019a. Diyanet Bilim ve Kültür Merkezi Dualarla Açıldı. *Diyanet İşleri Başkanlığı Haberler*. Accessed 12 May 2021. https://diyanet.gov.tr/tr-TR/Kurumsal/Detay/25607/diyanet-bilim-ve-kultur-merkezi-dualarla-acildi.
———. 2019b. Büyük Çamlıca Camii Dualarla Açıldı'. *Diyanet İşleri Başkanlığı Haberler*. Accessed 12 May 2021. https://diyanet.gov.tr/tr-TR/Kurumsal/Detay/25585/buyuk-camlica-camii-dualarla-acildi.
Erensü, Sinan, and Ozan Karaman. 2016. The Work of a Few Trees: Gezi, Politics and Space. *International Journal of Urban and Regional Research*: 1–18. https://doi.org/10.1111/1468-2427.12387.
Esen, Berk and Sebnem Gumuscu. 2018. The Perils of 'Turkish Presidentialism'. *Review of Middle East Studies* 52 (1): 43–53.
Fisher-Onar, Nora. 2009. Echoes of a Universalism Lost: Rival Representations of the Ottomans in Today's Turkey. *Middle Eastern Studies* 45 (2): 229–241.
Fisher-Onar, Nora, E. Fuat Keyman and Susan C. Pearce, ed. 2018. *Istanbul: Living with Difference in a Global City*. New Brunswick, NJ: Rutgers University Press.

Gao, Quan. 2020. Resacralization. In *The Sage Encyclopedia of the Sociology of Religion*, ed. Adam Possamai and Anthony J. Blasi. London: Sage Publications.

Göçek, Fatma Müge. 2017. Introduction Contested Spaces in Contemporary Turkey. In *Contested Spaces in Contemporary Turkey. Environmental, Urban and Secular Politics*, ed. Fatma Müge Göçek, 1–30. London: I.B. Tauris.

Gür, Berin F., and T. Elvan Altan. 2015. 'İktidarin Gösteri(Ş) Mekâni: Cumhurbaşkanlığı Kompleksi' TMMOB Mimarlar Odası Ankara Şubesi. *Dosya* 34 (1): 1–7.

Hintz, Lisel. 2018. *Identity Politics Inside Out: National Identity Contestation and Foreign Policy in Turkey*. New York, NY: Oxford University Press.

Huntington, Samuel. 1993. The Clash of Civilizations? *Foreign Affairs* 72 (3): 22–49.

Karakoç, Nilüfer. 2018. TMMOB'dan 'Yeni Ulus Meydanı Projesi' Açıklaması. *arkitera.com*. Accessed 12 May 2021. https://www.arkitera.com/haber/tmmobdan-yeni-ulus-meydani-projesi-aciklamasi/.

Karakuş Candan, Tezcan. 2015. Cumhuriyetle Hesaplaşmanın Zirve Mekânı Atatürk Orman Çiftliği ve KaÇak Saray. *Dosya* 34 (1): 8–19.

Kezer, Zeynep. 2010. The Making of Early Republican Ankara. *Architectural Design* 80 (1): 40–45.

———. 2015. *Building Modern Turkey: State, Space, and Ideology in the Early Republic*. Pittsburgh, PA: University of Pittsburgh Press.

———. 2017. Ankara's Forgotten Mental Maps, Changing Demography, and Missing Minorities. In *Contested Spaces in Contemporary Turkey. Environmental, Urban and Secular Politics*, ed. Fatma Müge Göçek, 76–106. London: I.B. Tauris.

Koymen, Erol. 2017. From Coups that Silence Ezan-s to Ezan-s that Silence Coups!: Sonic Resistance to the 2016 Turkish Military Coup. *Current Musicology* 101: 99–124.

Kutlay, Mustafa. 2020. The Politics of State Capitalism in a Post-Liberal International Order: The Case of Turkey. *Third World Quarterly* 41 (4): 683–706.

Öktem, Kerem. 2013. Contours of a New Republic and Signals from the Past: How to Understand Taksim Square. *Jadaliyya*. Accessed 12 May 2021. http://www.jadaliyya.com/pages/index/12088/contours-of-a-new-republic-and-signals-from-the-pa.

———. 2019. Erasing Palimpsest City: Boom, Bust and Urbicide in Turkey. In *Routledge Handbook on Cities in the Middle East*, ed. Haim Yacobi and Mansour Nasasra, 295–318. Abingdon: Routledge.

Öktem, Kerem and Karabekir Akkoyunlu. 2018. *Exit from Democracy: Illiberal Governance in Turkey and Beyond*. Abingdon: Routledge.

Öniş, Ziya. 2019. Turkey under the challenge of State Capitalism: The Political Economy of the Late AKP Era. *Southeast European and Black Sea Studies* 19 (2): 201–225.

Özbay, Cenk, Maral Erol, Ayşecan Terzioğlu and Umut Türem, ed. 2016. *The Making of Neoliberal Turkey*. Abingdon: Routledge.
Özdemir, Cengiz. 2012. Çamlıca: Son Selatin Cami. *T24*. Accessed 12 May 2021. https://t24.com.tr/yazarlar/cengiz-ozdemir/camlica-son-selatin-cami,5918.
Salah, Ebru. 2006. Hyper-Tourism in the Mediterranean Riviera of Turkey. Conference proceedings Tenth International Association for the Study of Traditional Environments-Hyper Traditions, Volume XVIII. Eugene, OR: IASTE.
Shenk, Timothy. 2015. Booked #3: What Exactly Is Neoliberalism? Wendy Brown: Undoing the Demos. *Dissent Magazine*. Accessed 12 May 2021. https://www.dissentmagazine.org/blog/booked-3-what-exactly-is-neoliberalism-wendy-brown-undoing-the-demos.
White, Jenny. 2013. *Muslim Nationalism and the New Turks*. Princeton: Princeton University Press.
Yang, Mayfair. 2020. *Re-enchanting Modernity Ritual Economy and Society in Wenzhou, China*. Durham, NC: Duke University Press.
Yavuz, M. Hakan. 1998. Turkish Identity and Foreign Policy in Flux: The Rise of Neo-Ottomanism. *Critique: Critical Middle Eastern Studies* 7 (12): 19–41.
Yeginsu, Ceylan. 2014. ISIS Draws a Steady Stream of Recruits from Turkey. *New York Times*. Accessed 12 May 2021. https://www.nytimes.com/2014/09/16/world/europe/turkey-is-a-steady-source-of-isis-recruits.html.
Yilmaz, Ömer. 2015. Ak Saray'ın Mimarı. arkitera.com. Accessed 12 May 2021. https://www.arkitera.com/gorus/ak-sarayin-mimari/.
Zaidi, Ali Hassan. 2006. Muslim Reconstructions of Knowledge and the Re-Enchantment of Modernity. *Theory, Culture & Society* 23 (5): 69–91.

CHAPTER 6

Claiming the Neo-Ottoman Mosque: Islamism, Gender, Architecture

Bülent Batuman

This chapter focuses on the politics of mosque architecture in contemporary Turkey in a context in which the ruling AKP (Adalet ve Kalkınma Partisi, Justice and Development Party) has encouraged the neo-Ottoman idiom.[1] For a good part of the twentieth century, the major architectural strategy employed to ease the tension between the nation-state and Islam, which were struggling to absorb each other, was mimicry in the form of the neo-Ottoman mosque. This particular idiom produced distinct ideological meanings within different political contexts. While it served the goal of absorption of Islam(ism) by the nation-state throughout the twen-

---

[1] This chapter is drawn from my earlier research on politics of mosque architecture in Turkey, published in Batuman (2018a, b, Chap. 2).

B. Batuman (✉)
Bilkent University, Ankara, Turkey
e-mail: batuman@bilkent.edu.tr

© The Author(s), under exclusive license to Springer Nature Switzerland AG 2023
C. Raudvere, P. Onur (eds.), *Neo-Ottoman Imaginaries in Contemporary Turkey*, Modernity, Memory and Identity in South-East Europe,
https://doi.org/10.1007/978-3-031-08023-4_6

155

tieth century, it has recently begun to serve a purpose which is the exact opposite: the absorption of nationalism and the remoulding of the nation-state by the AKP's Islamism and the making of the Islamic nation, or *millet*.[2]

The shift in meaning of the neo-Ottoman mosque was neither spontaneous nor smooth; on the contrary, mosque building has been an ideological enterprise for the AKP that has required various legitimising strategies. The promotion of the mosque as a social space by the AKP's conservative policies has resulted in a gradual increase in women's involvement as mosque users, accompanied by demands to have a say in the spatial organisation of their sections. While women's demand for equal space inside the mosque is striking, another interesting point is the emergence of women as designers of mosques for the first time. The overlap between women's demands and the government's agenda to endorse mosques also played a role in the promotion of neo-Ottoman mosque architecture. Indeed, new neo-Ottoman mosques have been praised as "women-friendly" and have derived legitimacy from female architects.

I begin with a historical account of the emergence of neo-Ottoman mosque architecture. I then discuss the AKP's approach to mosque design in two stages: first, I examine the government's aims to build a monumental mosque and the secularist establishment's attempts to block the endeavour, and, second, the AKP's reproduction of the neo-Ottoman idiom as a signifier of Islamist hegemony. As the discussion underlines, in both stages gender politics were instrumentalised to legitimise the government's approach to mosque architecture.

---

[2] The AKP's definition of "nation" departs equally from the rejection of nation(alism) by traditional Islamists in favour of a global *ummah*, and its secular conception by the Turkish nation-state. It presents Turkishness and Islam as qualities of the same entity, which differs significantly from the republican definition's reference to a secular and ethnically homogeneous body. While the Kemalist state invented the term *ulus* in the 1930s to define the secular nation, the ideologues of the AKP use *millet*, a term of Arabic origin which denoted religious communities in the Ottoman Empire. The Ottoman *millet* system allowed limited autonomy to non-Muslim communities to conduct their internal affairs. The term took on the meaning of "nation" in the nineteenth century; emergent nationalisms of ethnic groups within the Empire drew essence from their religious-communal experience in the *millet* system (Karpat 2002, 611). It has been used in the twentieth century, especially by conservative intellectuals, as a reaction to linguistic Turkification; yet, as I discuss below, the reference to *millet* by the AKP is significantly different.

The Birth of Neo-Ottoman Mosque

The radical secularism of the Turkish nation-state resulted in the mosque being renounced as a national symbol. This made Turkey an exception among countries with Islamic populations as even secular states did not hesitate to use the mosque as a cultural manifestation of nation-building (Batuman 2018b, 15–19). Thus, in early republican Turkey, mosque building was only a response to communal needs; those built were relatively small and they followed local traditions. In this respect, the iconography of the mosque was not debated in Turkey, and Ottoman examples were followed merely due to the continuity of building traditions. That is, these examples cannot be labelled "neo-Ottoman" since they do not express a choice to revert to Ottoman forms, a choice requiring an encounter with modernist mosque design.

The public's encounter with the modernist mosque occurred through an undertaking of the Democrat Party, which came to power in 1950 with the end of the single-party regime. Although the party followed a path of republican secularism, it embraced the mosque as a national symbol—in parallel with the newly born nation-states of the post-war years[3]—initiating the construction of a mosque (Kocatepe) on high ground overlooking the capital's new city centre (Meeker 1997). Its design was determined by the outcome of a competition in 1957 won by Vedat Dalokay and Nejat Tekelioğlu. The architects proposed a modernist scheme which made use of a thin shell dome to define the main prayer hall as a unified space flooded with light from all sides. The corners where the shell touched the ground were marked by four slender minarets, whose abstract, rocket-like forms were perceived by the public as rather alien (İltuş and Topçuoğlu 1976) (Fig. 6.1, left).

The mosque quickly became the topic of a clash—initially a mild one—between religious traditionalists and secular modernists. While conservative circles voiced their criticism, the government proudly presented the modernist design as a symbol unifying modernist will and cultural identity. However, in the wake of the military coup that toppled the Democrat Party in 1960, the modernist architecture of the mosque (which was still under construction) came to be identified with the military intervention. Increasing conservative pressure resulted in the cancellation of the project and destruction of its foundations in 1966, and it was finally realised as a

---

[3] For a discussion of the politics of mosque architecture, see Rizvi (2015).

Fig. 6.1 *Left*: The original proposal for Kocatepe Mosque designed by Vedat Dalokay and Nejat Tekelioğlu. (Source: Vedat Dalokay Archive). *Right*: Kocatepe Mosque dominating the skyline of Ankara. (Photograph by author. The reversion to classical Ottoman mosque architecture represented by this project involved not only the reproduction of the external image. The interior organisation, as well as traditional decorations, also strictly followed classical examples, and this approach henceforth defined the mainstream in mosque architecture endorsed by the Presidency of Religious Affairs)

much larger edifice that closely resembled the Şehzade Mosque from the sixteenth century (Fig. 6.1, right). The termination of the original modernist project represented a breaking point that gave birth to neo-Ottomanism: that is, the mimicry of classical Ottoman mosque architecture, which emerges here as an architectural idiom in tune with right-wing imaginaries.[4] The imperial era of the sixteenth century presented the perfect combination of nation and Islam, yet this image was nostalgic: it

---

[4] The dominant right-wing ideological current that contained Islamism was labelled "nationalist conservatism" (Bora 2009). With the end of single-party rule and the rise of Cold War geopolitics, the nationalist-conservative current successfully blended nationalist and Islamist streams on the common ground of anti-communism. This ideological amalgam merged opposition to radical modernism and secularism (as well as any strands of leftism) while emphasising the need for a powerful state to defend national unity. The origins of this current mainly lay in a circle of intellectuals representing conservative thought in opposition to the radical modernisation efforts of the early republican years (Taşkın 2007).

longed for the golden age of the nation but with an awareness that the moment had long gone.

Homi Bhabha (1994) defines mimicry as an attempt by the colonised to imitate the colonisers, with a result that is "almost the same but not quite": mimicry constantly troubles the colonisers' authority by minimising difference and simultaneously fails the colonised to fully assume the identity of the coloniser. This definition of the concept may be usefully applied to the case of neo-Ottoman mosque architecture in Turkey, although what is at stake is not the relationship between a subject position and the colonial Other that defines it, but one between a subject position and a constitutive referent, which itself is a representation: that of the sixteenth-century Ottoman Empire. The mimicking of classical Ottoman mosque architecture reflects the desire to imitate the glory of the imperial image. Yet, while replication is achieved visually, there is an essential failure here. What makes classical Ottoman mosques historically monumental is not their size but their innovative achievements in terms of construction techniques. Contemporary reinforced concrete structures, imitating the forms of the stone architecture of the sixteenth century, silently confirm their inferiority in relation to the originals they are imitating.

After the modernist design for Kocatepe Mosque was abandoned, neo-Ottoman mosque architecture, with few exceptions, became the paradigm for the following decades. The professional community continued to protest against the sixteenth-century imitations that cropped up, while a series of right-wing governments continued to build monumental examples in various cities throughout the 1980s and 1990s, with the mosques receiving approval from the majority of the public. The mimicry of the classical Ottoman mosque was a trademark of a state ideology internalising Islam within nationalism, which would even be used as an instrument of foreign policy, particularly in the post-Soviet Turkic world.[5]

An Ambiguous Start: Islamism and Mosque Design

The AKP came to power in 2002, after a decade of Islamist rule in the local administrations of major Turkish cities (Batuman 2013). Throughout the 1990s, a pious bourgeoisie emerged that played an important role in the AKP's rise to power. The freedom enjoyed by religious groups in the 2000s also resulted in the recognition of the mosque as a signifier of

[5] For details, see Batuman (2018b, 24–26).

distinction. The emergent devout patrons freely chose from diverse typologies for the mosques they sponsored, and mosque design outside architectural mimicry began to receive popular approval for the first time. Within such plurality, the AKP had ambitions to build a monumental mosque with ideological aspirations. The opportunity presented itself in the form of the new Presidency of Religious Affairs (Diyanet İşleri Başkanlığı, Diyanet) campus outside the city centre of Ankara. An invited competition was organised but not publicly announced early in 2007.

This was a time of turmoil when the AKP was struggling with the pressure of the armed forces which would block the election of an Islamist president with a memorandum in 2007. Although the AKP responded to the military memorandum with early elections and derived another landslide victory, the mosque became the subject of dispute between the Islamist government and the secularist establishment. Construction work only started late in 2008 and even the name of the mosque reflected conflict: it was cynically referred to as the "VIP mosque" in secular media and later named after Ahmet Hamdi Akseki, one of the prominent directors of the Diyanet.

The Ahmet Hamdi Akseki Mosque, which is among the largest in Turkey with its 33-metre-wide dome, displays a modernist outlook (Fig. 6.2). Similar to the unbuilt proposal for Kocatepe, it presents an austere interpretation of the traditional Ottoman mosque, characterised by the central dome, here structurally resting on four arches standing on four pillars. Yet the massing creates an image wherein the dome is sitting on top of another, rather flat, domical surface defining side galleries on four sides. This symmetrical organisation is further emphasised by the four corner minarets, as well as the elimination of the traditional Ottoman courtyard.[6]

The fact that the mosque's design was determined through a restricted competition shrouded in secrecy resulted in public uproar as construction of the mosque began in 2008, most of which was ideologically based, denouncing the building as an Islamic symbol that countered decades of secular rule. Yet there were also internal tensions between the architect and the client over the architectural features of the mosque. The designer of the mosque, Salim Alp, was an experienced professional with 35 years of practice. Although they accepted his modernist interpretation, Diyanet

---

[6] For an historically contextualised assessment of the mosque's architecture, see Özaloğlu (2017).

Fig. 6.2 The Ahmet Hamdi Akseki Mosque inside the Diyanet compound, designed by Salim Alp. (Photograph by author. Located along the main road tying Ankara to Eskişehir, the mosque rises as a landmark visible to everyone approaching the city from the western suburbs)

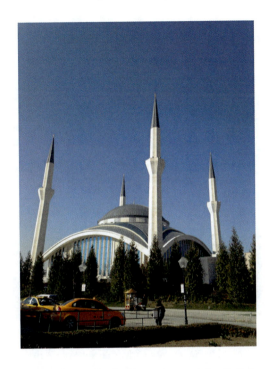

officials demanded that the mosque also embody Ottoman and/or Seljuk elements that would link it to traditional Turkish Islamic architecture. The most radical dispute involved the façade design. Using the problem of extensive daylighting due to the transparency of the facades as an excuse, the Diyanet officials asked the designer to produce different proposals for the portal, which he did.

To the architect's dismay, however, the Diyanet officials had also asked the Diyanet's construction office to design a radically different portal, with a block that imitated historical Seljuk portals (Fig. 6.3). Both the surface of this block and larger vertical strips added to the eastern and western facades were decorated with Seljuk patterns. This addition was made during the construction phase and the architect only learned about it by observing the construction of the bulky concrete mass. Although he demanded the elimination of this addition and threatened to take the officials to court, he was finally persuaded to accept the *fait accompli*.[7] With

[7] Interview with Salim Alp, 25 July 2017.

Fig. 6.3 The Ahmet Hamdi Akseki Mosque inside the Diyanet compound, designed by Salim Alp: early stage and the actual building. Note the change in the main entrance to the mosque. (Source: Salim Alp Mimarlık and author)

these additions, the modernist look of the mosque was hybridised, and the design was presented to the public as "neoclassical".

By 2010, preliminary construction of the Ahmet Hamdi Akseki Mosque was coming to an end, but the tension between the client and the architect was intensifying as the architect witnessed continued interventions in his design. As the time arrived to plan the interior design and detailing, this tension reached the point of rupture. After Alp had already begun working on it, the client suddenly decided to postpone the design process. Soon after, Diyanet removed the architect entirely from the project.

At this point, Diyanet (and the government by extension) had three problems. The first two concerned the ongoing construction: it was necessary to block the architect's claims to its design and also find a new professional whose work could be tightly controlled by Diyanet. The third problem was external to the construction and political in nature: the legitimacy of the monumental mosque in the public eye was still at a very low level. This was a serious problem due to the political situation in the country. The AKP was working hard to end the threat from the military by a referendum, and was thus seeking to find allies among various political agents ranging from liberals to Kurdish parties and Alevi organisations. An important dimension of this tolerant attitude was respect for women's rights.[8]

A noteworthy outcome of hearing women's voices was the recognition of their demand to be involved in mosque organisation and the rituals they sheltered, and their critique of the spatial organisation of women's sections in the mosques, since the segregated spatial organisation of the mosques has always been controlled by men. While women were welcome, women's sections had generally been organised poorly and located in basements or behind curtains, while neglect of women's ablution spaces was a particular discouragement to their mosque attendance. Yet the 1990s saw the rise of activism and scholarship agitating for gender equality in Islam globally (Wadud 1992, 2006); in many countries the demand for men and women to be able to perform prayer together and the possibility of woman-led prayers came to the fore (Elewa and Silvers 2011; Bano and Kalmbach 2011). Although there were parallel endeavours in Turkey in the 1990s, female-led prayer, unlike in other parts of the Islamic world, has never even been discussed. Nevertheless, women's demands for equal space inside the mosque gradually gained ground due, on the one hand, to the increased social mobility of pious women, and, on the other, the perception of women's exclusion from the mosque space as discrimination for the first time (Yılmaz 2015, 207–220).[9]

Here, there is an interesting overlap between women's demands to participate in the mosque as public space and Diyanet's positive response to it. The demand for transformation of mosques to welcome women's participation readily found an echo in Diyanet's work to popularise mosque

---

[8] Despite the optimism of this period and the establishment of a Ministry of Women's Rights to adapt EU regulations, the AKP soon reverted to conservative defence of patriarchy (Acar and Altunok 2013).

[9] In response to criticisms from female Islamic intellectuals on the inadequacy of proper spaces for women and the miserable conditions of the existing women's sections, the Mufti Office (a branch of Diyanet) in Istanbul launched a project to assess the state of the mosques in Istanbul in terms of women-friendliness, which concluded that half of the approximately 3000 mosques in Istanbul were not suitable for the performance of women's prayers (Erdemli 2013, 127).

attendance, which, in turn, enabled women to step in as designers of mosque space for the first time.

After a lengthy period, Diyanet awarded the interior design project of the Ahmet Hamdi Akseki Mosque to architect Sonay İlbay. Although the choice could not be reduced to the designer's gender, it is plausible to say that the Diyanet officials were pleased to be working with a female designer despite her lack of expertise in mosque design.[10] A female designer was in tune with their ongoing projects promoting women's participation in the mosques. The job was to be supervised by the construction company, which appointed art historians and acoustics experts as consultants, in addition to artisans who were masters of traditional techniques of murals, calligraphy, inlay, stained glass, and woodwork. Thus, the lack of expertise on the part of the designer was offset by the involvement of the construction company in overseeing the process. This was also a mechanism to guarantee both the quality and the dominance of traditional decorations.

Upon its inauguration, the mosque was widely publicised, and praised as a synthesis of tradition and contemporary technology. Curiously, the architecture of the building was almost always presented through its decorations and interior design, to the extent that Alp's name was virtually never mentioned in the press coverages. Even the lengthy description of the building on the website of the construction company mentions the names of nine designers (and artisans) and eight consultants, but not the architect.[11] When President Abdullah Gül visited the mosque, it was a female architect from the staff of the construction company who accompanied and briefed him on its architecture (*Habertürk*, 26 April 2013). The interior designer, on the other hand, was named and praised for her work. In mainstream media, it was İlbay who was interviewed about the mosque, with emphasis placed on her gender (*Akşam*, 24 April 2013). That is, although a non-traditional outlook was approved to realise such a large mosque, the mosque itself was recognised only by its interior architecture, which displayed traditional decorative arts; the political dismissal of the modernist outlook was concealed behind praise for the interior. The

---

[10] İlbay had twenty years of experience in the construction unit of a public bank before starting her own office. Her work in Ahmet Hamdi Akseki Mosque led to new commissions on mosque interiors in Turkey and abroad. Interview with Sonay İlbay, 21 March 2017.

[11] "Ahmet Hamdi Akseki Camii", available online: http://enderinsaat.com/Icerik.ASP?ID=1316 (accessed on 02 August 2016).

gender of the architect was successfully instrumentalised both to side-line Alp and to present the mosque in a sympathetic light to the secular public.

Representing Islamist Hegemony: (Re)producing Neo-Ottomanism

In the wake of the 2011 elections, the AKP was confident enough to pursue its own political agenda without the need for reluctant alliances. Although I will not go into the details of the political process, what is significant for my discussion is that this confidence was illustrated in the monumental mosque projects following one after another that ensued. Here I discuss two particular examples built in Istanbul: the Mimar Sinan Mosque in Ataşehir and the Çamlıca Mosque. I use the former to illustrate the shifting meaning of architectural mimicry under the Islamist government and the latter to demonstrate the instrumentalisation of gender in order to derive legitimacy for a controversial enterprise.

Designed by Hilmi Şenalp, the Mimar Sinan Mosque in Ataşehir was the first grandiose neo-Ottoman example of the AKP era. With a 42-metre-high dome and four 72-metre minarets, it was large enough to welcome 12,500 people to prayer (Fig. 6.4). While the structure reproduces the image of an Ottoman mosque, its program follows a strategic incorporation of commerce into the complex, which contains conference and exhibition halls, classrooms, shops, a library, and a two-storey car park. Strikingly, all of these facilities are located underground, although there is no shortage of land for construction. That is, although the mosque is attached to shopping as the central function defining public space, it was considered inappropriate to exhibit any sign of this, so as not to harm the Ottoman look of the mosque. The underground floors are designed in stark contrast to the mosque's traditional image, fashioned as typical shopping mall interiors. The complex also contains a VIP lounge, which stirred debate at the time of the inauguration since a mosque, by definition, implies the equality of congregating worshippers.

The mosque was built in twenty-two months for an estimated cost of $US20 million (*Haberturk* 21 July 2012). Although the intention had been to name it the "Anatolian Great Mosque", this was changed on the Prime Minister's instruction to honour the sixteenth-century master. This choice is not surprising since Sinan has had a mythical cultural status in the political power of architecture: nationalistic nostalgia for a glorious

Fig. 6.4 The Mimar Sinan Mosque designed by Hilmi Şenalp. (Photograph by Gülse Eraydın. Located in Ataşehir, a rapidly growing district in the Anatolian part of Istanbul, the mosque is situated at the north-western corner of a large park surrounded by two highways and a busy street. To the west of the park lies an upper-class mixed-use compound of high-rise blocks. Thus, although it is huge in size, the mosque is unavoidably dwarfed by the blocks towering over it)

imperial past represented by classical Ottoman architecture comprises one of the origins of national(ist) architecture. Indeed, the dedicatory inscription signed by the Prime Minister himself explained the significance of "Sinan the master" as lying in his having demonstrated "the glorious face of a nation and civilisation" with his works. Here, the curious expression of "a nation and civilisation" is not a case of awkward translation; the Turkish phrase itself refers not to the Turkish nation and Islamic civilisation as two separate entities but rather implies two qualities of one and the same entity.

Putting this odd point aside to return to later and turning to the mosque itself: according to Erdoğan, it fulfilled a crucial need in the Anatolian part of the city which lacked a "*selatin* mosque" (*CNNTurk* 20 July 2012). The choice of the word "*selatin*" was significant and very conscious as it is literally the plural form of "Sultan" and is used to define mosques built by royal family members in the Ottoman era. Considering that the Maltepe Mosque, built between 1988 and 2001, dominated the skyline of the Anatolian side, it was clear that the Prime Minister was not referring to the size of the mosque, but to its political symbolism signifying Ottoman power.

Finally, among those who attended the inauguration ceremony, as well as a group of ministers, the Prime Minister was accompanied by the President of Gabon and the President of the Iraqi National Assembly. While the former represented Turkey's growing involvement in Africa under the AKP, the latter embodied significance in terms of the ethnoreligious divisions within Middle Eastern politics. As the Sunni representative occupying the third most powerful position (after the Kurdish President and the Shiite Prime Minister) within the delicate and at times tense power relations in Iraq, the Speaker of the Parliament was a close ally of Turkey. Thus the attendance of the foreign visitors was a political gesture in tune with Erdoğan's victory speech on the night of the elections in June 2011, when he hailed "all those in Baghdad, Cairo, Sarajevo, Baku, Nicosia and all other friendly and brotherly peoples who turned their eyes to Turkey" and stated that their victory was the victory of "the oppressed and the aggrieved" across the Muslim world (*Hürriyet* 13 June 2011).

These three issues present at the inauguration of the Mimar Sinan Mosque—namely, the metonymic use of the (Turkish) nation and (Islamic) civilisation; the reference to Ottoman rule symbolised by *selatin* mosques; and Prime Minister Erdoğan's political ambitions to be influential across the Muslim world—define the operation of mimicry in the reversal by neo-Ottoman mosques of the relation between the state and Islam. As illustrated by Erdoğan's dedicatory inscription, the presentation of Turkishness and Islam as qualities of the same entity is significantly different from the republican definition of the nation which references a secular and ethnically homogeneous body. The *millet* is now envisaged through self-othering: it is conceived as a majority which had been oppressed by the elite minority throughout republican history. The AKP, thus, represented the *millet* and brought an end to their oppression. Within this context, the neo-Ottoman mosque comes to represent, rather than Islam (as a part) in the nation, the nation (as privileged representative) in Islam.

Here it is also worth considering the discourse of neo-Ottomanism within architecture. Hilmi Şenalp, the architect of the Mimar Sinan Mosque, had already designed a number of neo-Ottoman mosques funded by the Turkish government in Tokyo (1993–2000), Ashgabat (1992–1998), Yekaterinburg (2002), and Berlin (2004). He would continue to be the favoured designer for state-sponsored mosques under the AKP. Therefore, Şenalp's views on mosque architecture are illustrative in terms of neo-Ottomanism. Rejecting categories of "modern" and "contemporary" in mosque architecture, Şenalp suggests that one cannot speak of a "modern" mosque as it is not possible to speak of a "modern Islam", arguing, "What we call modern is the continuation of someone else's tradition" (Şenalp 2013, 180). According to him, the West, looking through Orientalist lenses, has never accepted Islam as a "civilisation". Hence, Turkish-Islamic art and culture, in particular, have been viewed merely as a local flavour in the Arabic-Persian context. According to him, "*our* civilisation, based on the Slejuk-Ottoman lineage" (emphasis added) was particularly regarded with hostility due to its "welcoming quality [of] embracing other religions and civilisations without creating 'others' and its essentially anti-colonial characteristics" (Şenalp 2007, 76). Within this context, the Turkish nation, which is "not a Hotanto or Zulu tribe" but a nation that "produced awe-inspiring cultural examples for over 1000 years", had a privileged position (Şenalp 2007, 78). For Şenalp, the Ottoman architectural heritage "showed whom this land belonged to" and thus contributed to the making of *millet* by generating "belonging" in the present. Thus, the neo-Ottoman mosque is simultaneously a representation of *millet*, while excluding those who fail to identify with it, and a tool for the promotion of the privileged strand of Turkish Islam across the globe.

On 29 May 2012, the 559th anniversary of the conquest of Istanbul, Erdoğan announced that a monumental mosque was to be built on Çamlıca Hill, that would be "among the largest in the world and [...] visible from everywhere in the city" (*Radikal* 30 May 2012). This district is closely associated with Erdoğan himself, since his residence is located there. Within two months an architectural competition was announced for the design of the mosque and participants were given only forty days to submit their proposals. The brief explicitly asked entrants to come up with proposals "reflecting Ottoman-Turkish architectural style, connecting tradition to the future and adding an original link to *our* culture's chain of tradition" (emphasis added) (*Arkitera.com* 23 July 2012). The competition was boycotted by the Chamber of Architects and prominent professionals, who questioned both the legitimacy of such a colossal mosque and the reliability of the competition, whilst leading scholars declined to join the jury. The results of the competition further fuelled debate, since no first prize was awarded while two projects were awarded the second prize. One of the second-prize winners featured an Ottoman replica while the other was a modernist scheme; the Prime Minister himself decided that the former was to be executed.

The project was presented to the public as a competition won by two young women. Moreover, the photographs accompanying the news articles showed the two women in their headscarves, which implicitly claimed a success on the part of the pious Muslim women. Designed by Hayriye Gül Totu and Bahar Mızrak, the chosen proposal is almost a copy of the Sultan Ahmet Mosque (Fig. 6.5). To counter criticisms of copying an existing mosque, the designers responded that this was not an issue of imitation but of style, and style was a matter of choice. As they asserted, "Some prefer a contemporary modern style and what we embrace is the Turkish-Islamic style... You cannot question the style of a poet and ask, 'why do you write epic poems?'" (*Milliyet* 16 November 2012). Defining the dome, half-domes, minarets, and courtyard as essential elements in the Turkish-Islamic tradition, the designers argued that every mosque is inspired by another one. Thus, they claimed that their use of existing

Fig. 6.5 The Çamlıca Mosque, designed by Hayriye Gül Totu and Bahar Mızrak: (*left*) under construction with Erdoğan's posters surrounding the site in August 2016; (*right*) view from across the Bosphorus in January 2017. (Photographs by author. The billboards, part of mobilisation efforts following the failed coup, read, "Whatever they do, it is futile/There is [This is] a divine judgement coming from heaven")

mosques as a source was "not imitation or replication but inspiration through the continuity of tradition". Criticism of the size and unimaginativeness of the mosque was also raised by Islamic intellectuals (Cündioğlu 2012, 3–12; Eygi 2012).

Interestingly, the designers sought to include original elements to differentiate their work. In addition to the six minarets, resembling those of the Sultan Ahmet Mosque, they proposed a seventh octagonal "time minaret" on top of the *şadırvan* (ablution fountain) in the centre of the courtyard, which essentially was a clock tower. Furthermore, the central dome in their proposal was unusually high, almost a full hemisphere above the drum, which was a departure from the rather flat Ottoman mosque domes.

Erdoğan asked for certain modifications to the project, in consultation with a group of experts from Istanbul Technical University and Mimar Sinan University, supervised by the Ministry of Environment and Urbanism, and the outcome was proudly announced by the minister. The revisions removed the seventh minaret, flattened the central dome to resemble Ottoman domes, emphasised the entrance to the courtyard with a Seljuk-style portal, and replaced the proposed canopies shaped like reverse umbrellas bordering the terrace outside the courtyard with a traditional Ottoman portico (*Arkitera.com* 20 February 2013). That is, the revisions made by "expert" *men*, following the suggestions of the Prime Minister, mainly aimed to make the mosque look more like classical Ottoman examples. In its final version the mosque has a 72-metre-high dome with a diameter of 34 metres and can accommodate 63,000 worshippers. The whole complex covers a site of 57,500 square metres and includes workshops, classrooms, a 1000-person conference hall, a 250-person meeting hall, a library, a museum, a 3500 square meter exhibition hall and a car park accommodating 3500 vehicles. The museum is appropriately assigned to be a "Museum of Turkish-Islamic Art". At this size, the mosque is one of the largest in the world.

Once the competition and PR stage of the project was over and construction had begun, the two female architects were removed from the process and even their names were suppressed. Neither the web site designed to provide information on the ongoing construction (www.istanbulcami.com) nor occasional media coverage mentions either of them.

Nevertheless, the design process of the Çamlıca Mosque provided an example to follow when the construction of large-scale mosques stirred controversy. In several other cases female designers were similarly employed to fend off criticism. For instance, the Ramazanoğlu Mosque (2006–2014), another neo-Ottoman mosque built in Adana, was designed by four female architects and advertised as "women-friendly", claiming to respond to the needs of women in its design (*AljazeeraTurk*, 9 August 2011).

Conclusion

The emergence of neo-Ottoman mosque architecture based on mimicry of sixteenth-century examples that represent the zenith of Ottoman imperial power was not an Islamist enterprise but rather one that aimed to subsume Islam within nationalist conservatism. With the AKP's rise to power, however, this particular idiom has become operative in precisely the opposite direction. Now it serves the absorption of nationalism, the remoulding of the nation-state by the AKP's Islamism, and the making of *millet*, the Islamic nation.

However, regardless of its architectural form, mosque building has always been perceived as an anti-secular enterprise in Turkey. While objections to large-scale mosques from the secularist public were readily nullified by the right-wing populisms of mainstream governments, they became a tougher challenge for the Islamist government. Beginning with the Ahmet Hamdi Akseki Mosque, both the AKP and its opponents saw the construction of such edifices as aggressive manoeuvres in an ongoing ideological battle. Within the complicated power networks defining mosque architecture, gender emerged as a suitable instrument with which to overwhelm opposing positions on grounds of political correctness. In cases of disputes between architects and their clients, as well as in order to suppress ideological opposition to mosque building, female designers were invited in to override professional conventions.

Although this chapter has only addressed the instrumentalisation of women's agency in Islamist politics, it is crucial to note that increasing attention to gender, even in the course of power struggles among men and their institutions, has also opened up possibilities for appropriation and empowerment on the part of women. The mosque as a space of worship embodies gender politics stemming from historically rooted traditions of patriarchy. Yet it is crucial to understand the mosque as a site of struggle over the use and meaning of religiosity in its relations to gender.

References

Acar, Feride and Gülbanu Altunok. 2013. The 'Politics of Intimate' at the Intersection of Neo-Liberalism and Neo-Conservatism in Contemporary Turkey. *Women's Studies International Forum* 41 (1): 14–23.
Akşam. Sonsuzlukta Kadın İmzası. 24 April 2013. Accessed 2 August 2015. http://www.aksam.com.tr/guncel/sonsuzlukta-kadin-imzasi/haber-198976.
AljazeeraTurk. Kadınlara Özel Cami. 9 August 2011. Accessed 11 August 2015. http://www.aljazeera.com.tr/haber/kadinlara-ozel-cami.
Arkitera.com. İstanbul Çamlıca Camii Mimari Proje Yarışması. 23 July 2012. Accessed 31 August 2015. www.arkitera.com/yarisma/239/istanbul-camlica-camii-mimari-proje-yarismasi.
———. Erdoğan'ın Çamlıca'sı. 20 Ferbruary 2013. Accessed 27 August 2015. www.arkitera.com/haber/12243/erdoganin-camlicasi.
Bano, Masooda and Hilary Kalmbach, ed. 2011. *Women, Leadership, and Mosques Changes in Contemporary Islamic Authority.* Leiden: Brill.
Batuman, Bülent. 2013. City Profile: Ankara. *Cities* 31: 578–590.
———. 2018a. Appropriating the Masculine Sacred: Islamism, Gender and Mosque Architecture in Contemporary Turkey. In *The Routledge Companion to Modernity, Space and Gender*, ed. Alexandra Staub, 270–287. Abingdon and New York: Routledge.
———. 2018b. *New Islamist Architecture and Urbanism: Negotiating Nation and Islam through Built Environment in Turkey.* Abingdon and New York: Routledge.
Bhabha, Homi K. 1994. Of Mimicry and Man: The Ambivalence of Colonial Discourse. In *The Location of Culture.* London and New York: Routledge.
Bora, Tanıl. 2009. *Türk Sağının Üç Hali: Milliyetçilik, Muhafazakarlık, İslamcılık.* Istanbul: Birikim.
CNNTurk. Erdoğan: 'Anadolu Yakasında Selatin Cami Yoktu'. 20 July 2012. Accessed 14 April 2017. www.cnnturk.com/2012/turkiye/07/20/erdogan. anadolu.yakasinda.selatin.cami.yoktu/669647.0/index.html.
Cündioğlu, Dücane. 2012. *Mimarlık ve Felsefe.* Istanbul: Kapı Yayınları.
Elewa, Ahmed and Laury Silvers. 2011. 'I Am one of the People': A Survey and Analysis of Legal Arguments on Woman-Led Prayer in Islam. *Journal of Law and Religion* 26: 141–171.
Erdemli, Kadriye A. 2013. Cami Mimarisinde Kadınların Yeri ve İstanbul Müftülüğü Camilerin Kadınlar Bölümünü Güzelleştirme Projesi (3T Projesi). In *1. Ulusal Cami Mimarisi Sempozyumu Bildiri Kitabı*, 113–128. Ankara: DİB Yayınları.
Eygi, Mehmet Şevki. 2012. Çamlıca Camii Güzel Olacak mı. *Milli Gazete*, 28 November 2012. Accessed 13 August 2016. www.milligazete.com.tr/camlica_camii_guzel_olacak_mi/mehmed_sevket_eygi/kose_yazisi/12466.

Haberturk. Bu Caminin Önemli Bir Özelliği Var!. 21 July 2012. Accessed 25 August 2014. www.haberturk.com/ramazan/haber/760529-bu-caminin-onemli-bir-ozelligi-var-.

———. Cumhurbaşkanı Gül Soruları Cevapsız Bıraktı. 26 April 2013. Accessed 2 August 2015. http://www.haberturk.com/gundem/haber/839315-cumhurbaskani-gul-sorulari-cevapsiz-birakti.

Hürriyet. Başbakan'dan Üçüncü Balkon Konuşması. 13 June 2011. Accessed 25 August 2014. www.hurriyet.com.tr/gundem/18015912.asp.

İltuş, Selim and Nazif Topçuoğlu. 1976. Kocatepe Camii Muamması. *Mimarlık* 135: 65–73.

Karpat, Kemal H. 2002. Millets and Nationality: The Roots of the Incongruity of Nation and State in the Post-Ottoman Era. In *Studies on Ottoman Social and Political History: Selected Articles and Essays*, 611–675. Leiden: Brill.

Meeker, Michael E. 1997. Once There Was, Once There Wasn't: National Monuments and Interpersonal Exchange. In *Rethinking Modernity and National Identity in Turkey*, ed. Sibel Bozdoğan and Resat Kasaba, 157–191. Seattle: University of Washington Press.

Milliyet. Çamlıca'ya Yapılacak Cami Taklit mi? 16 November 2012. Accessed 31 August 2015. www.milliyet.com.tr/camlica-ya-yapilacak-cami-taklit-mi-/gundem/gundemdetay/16.11.2012/1628040/default.htm.

Özaloğlu, Serpil. 2017. An Attempt to Transform Popular Religious Images into Contemporary Mosque Architecture: Ahmet Hamdi Akeski Mosque. *Journal of Architectural and Planning Research* 34 (2): 114–132.

Radikal. İstanbul'a Dev Cami Geliyor. 30 May 2012. Accessed 31 August 2015. www.radikal.com.tr/politika/istanbula_dev_cami_geliyor-1089547.

Rizvi, Kishwar. 2015. *The Transnational Mosque: Architecture and Historical Memory in the Contemporary Middle East.* Chapel Hill: University of North Carolina Press.

Şenalp, Hilmi. 2007. Hilmi Şenalp. In *Cami Projeleri İstişare Toplantısı*, ed. Aytekin Uzunoğlu, 75–88. Ankara: Diyanet İşleri Başkanlığı.

———. 2013. Muharrem Hilmi Şenalp. In *1. Ulusal Cami Mimarisi Sempozyumu Bildiri Kitabı*, ed. Hale Tokay et al., 172–183. Ankara: Diyanet İşleri Başkanlığı Yayınları.

Taşkın, Yüksel. 2007. *Anti-Komünizmden Küreselleşme Karşıtlığına Milliyetçi Muhafazakar Entelijansiya.* İstanbul: İletişim.

Wadud, Amina. 1992. *Qur'an and Woman.* Kuala Lumpur: Fajar Bakti Publications.

———. 2006. *Inside the Gender Jihad: Reform in Islam.* Oxford: One World Publishers.

Yılmaz, Zehra. 2015. *Dişil Dindarlık: İslamcı Kadın Hareketinin Dönüşümü.* İstanbul: İletişim.

CHAPTER 7

Commemorating the First World War and Its Aftermath: Neo-Ottomanism, Gender, and the Politics of History in Turkey

Nazan Maksudyan and Hilal Alkan

INTRODUCTION

In one of its earliest definitions, neo-Ottomanism referred to a revised understanding of Turkish nationalism that stressed political and cultural diversity and tolerance as it was supposedly "embodied in the Ottoman past", and in better economic, cross-border integration with neighbouring countries in the Balkans, Caucasus, and the Middle East (Yavuz 1998, 40). Turgut Özal (prime minister 1983–1989; president 1989–1993) was the first to refer to the country's Ottoman legacy in order to resolve the

N. Maksudyan (✉)
Freie Universität Berlin/Centre Marc Bloch, Berlin, Germany
e-mail: nazan.maksudyan@fu-berlin.de

H. Alkan
Leibniz Zentrum Moderner Orient, Berlin, Germany
e-mail: hilal.alkan.zeybek@zmo.de

© The Author(s), under exclusive license to Springer Nature Switzerland AG 2023
C. Raudvere, P. Onur (eds.), *Neo-Ottoman Imaginaries in Contemporary Turkey*, Modernity, Memory and Identity in South-East Europe,
https://doi.org/10.1007/978-3-031-08023-4_7

internal political tensions resulting from the long-term Kemalist denial of ethnic and cultural diversity, and to formulate a new Turkish foreign policy toward the Balkans (Çolak 2006, 587). The legacy of Özal's "Turkish-Islamic synthesis" had an impact on school curricula from the 1980s onwards, as well as popularising certain Ottoman cultural traits, such as classical Turkish music and literary forms. Throughout the second half of the 1990s, newly elected Welfare Party (Refah Partisi) mayors revived several genres of the Ottoman arts, including calligraphy, language courses, culinary culture, and architectural forms. During this period, Turkey faced the rise of an Islamist politics, which successfully Islamicised this already existing vein of neo-Ottomanism.

The late 1990s and early 2000s was a period in which Turkey underwent significant legal and institutional reforms in minority and cultural rights as part of an agenda to meet the criteria for EU membership (Ayata 2012, 5). Thorough legal reforms to achieve EU membership went hand in hand with the rise of a new image of Turkey as a tolerant nation embracing its cultural plurality, which was due to the positive light in which the re-discovery of its Ottoman imperial heritage was regarded. The commemoration of the 700th anniversary of the "birth" of the Ottoman state in 1999 emphasised the empire's "multicultural heritage" with its central message of "religious tolerance".[1] Thus, the image of a new tolerant Turkey was mostly based on an idealised picture of the country's multireligious Ottoman past. Initially voiced by leading liberal and conservative intellectuals in the early 1990s, the fascination and identification with an essentially pluralistic view of Turkish identity has also been embraced by larger and more critical segments of society in the 2000s. The research on the subject emphasises that neo-Ottomanism has emerged as a critique of the homogeneous Kemalist nation-building project, which has led to the production of glowing accounts of *Pax Ottomania*, as a "harmonious utopia" (Riexinger 2014). Other researchers have stressed that exaggerated references to multicultural citizenship, "cosmopolitan liberal values", and pluralism were also reproduced and circulated by liberal intellectuals and academics (Fisher-Onar 2009, 237–238) in literary (Göknar 2006; Furlanetto 2015; Konuk 2011), artistic, and cultural productions (Ergin and Karakaya 2017), and in urban politics (Mills 2011; Tokdoğan 2018).

---

[1] "700. Yıl'a 2 milyon dolar" [2 million dollars for the 700th anniversary], *Milliyet*, 10 February 1999 https://www.milliyet.com.tr/the-others/700-yila-2-milyon-dolar-5257361 (30 June 2020)

The two vectors of neo-Ottomanism—one relying essentially on multicultural citizenship and pluralism and the other on the inherited Muslim-Turkish legacy of the Empire, with an orientation towards the Middle East and Islam—went side by side until the early 2010s (Karaca 2019, 286–287), when the "tolerance" and pluralism vector lost its dynamism, popularity, and credibility. Possibly, the assassination of Hrant Dink on 19 January 2007,[2] the new political context of the "Arab Spring", the brutal suppression of the Gezi Revolt, the Syrian War, and the policy of isolation in reaction to mounting regional problems all played a part in this. As "Ottoman cosmopolitanism" lost its momentum, it was "Ottoman/Turkish imperialism" and "Ottoman Islam" that largely defined neo-Ottomanism in the 2010s.

The centenary commemorations of the First World War (1914–1918) provided grounds for reformulating and exhibiting "Erdoğanian neo-Ottomanism", as a specific and selective way of remembering the Ottoman past in essentially "Sunni Muslim Turkish terms" (Doroll 2015). Paying little heed to current research or knowledge of Ottoman history, the Justice and Development Party (AKP) leadership has relied on "Ottoman nostalgics" (Yavuz 2016) to connect and mobilise the masses behind the righteous and successful ministry of Turkish Muslim grandeur and prosperity over other groups (White 2014). This chapter on the recent commemoration and memorialisation of the First World War and the "Independence War" (Greco-Turkish War, 1919–1922) in Turkey brings to light the AKP's neo-Ottomanist history politics, with particular focus on the rise of the Sunni-Muslim-Turkish imperial legacy and the fall of the one-man hero cult built around the "founding father", Mustafa Kemal Atatürk.[3]

The first part of the chapter provides an overview of official commemorations of the centenary of the First World War in Turkey, specifically the Battles of Sarıkamış (January 2015) and Gallipoli (April 2015), and the First Battle of Kut (April 2016). Our examination highlights four points: First, these commemorative events were organised around isolated

---

[2] On 19 January 2007, Hrant Dink, the founder and the chief editor of the Armenian-Turkish weekly newspaper AGOS and the most vocal and visible member of the remaining Armenian community in Turkey, was assassinated on a busy street in Istanbul in front of his office. The murder was widely reported, both in national and international media, putting the AKP government under pressure regarding its treatment of religious minorities (Ayata 2012, 14–15).

[3] For a discussion of non-official centenary events, see Maksudyan 2019.

"victories" and Muslim "martyrdom", consciously avoiding a complete historiography of the war, which resulted in catastrophe for the Ottoman Empire. Second, in line with the current government's neo-Ottomanist tendencies, the centenary events aimed to challenge Kemalist historiography by reducing the exaggerated visibility of Atatürk and highlighting the role of religious faith and Muslim solidarity under "Turkish leadership". Third, the commemorations consciously omitted the existence of non-Muslim soldiers in the Ottoman army during the First World War and also aimed to suppress and silence the centenary of the Armenian Genocide. Finally, the events were completely gender-blind, and by equating suffering and martyrdom with masculinity, they accentuated the invisibility of women in the narratives of war.

In the second part of the chapter, we trace other realms where women who fought in the First World War and the "Independence War" are becoming increasingly visible: those of culture, education, and cityscapes. Once completely silenced and erased from national memory, these "heroines" have made an epic entry to the public sphere in the 2000s. We trace the change in the culture of commemoration evident in memorials, schoolbooks, and popular culture, arguing that the flourishing of these heroines has significant indications. First, it points to a change in the perception of women's role in war efforts. Replacing the anonymous altruistic rural mother who carried ammunition to the front (Kancı and Altınay 2007), these new representations show uniformed women carrying weapons themselves, hence changing women's role from that of assistance to active participation. Second, they showcase the shift from a narrative of struggle whose singular protagonist was Mustafa Kemal towards a more diversified and pluralistic account of heroism and suffering. Finally, their militarist and nationalist tone forms a perfect continuum with the long-existing "myth of the military nation" (Altınay 2004), which, by definition, is exclusionary and hostile to non-Turkish and non-Muslim citizens in many ways. In that sense, inclusion of women is less a matter of diversity as in the first vein of neo-Ottomanism, than reinforcing a Turkish-Muslim nationalism as in its current form.

Re-envisaging the Empire through the Centennial Commemorations of the First World War

The centennial of the First World War triggered a large wave of commemorative events worldwide. Official commemorations in Turkey focused largely on "victories" during the war (in the context of Battle of Gallipoli [Çanakkale] and the First Battle of Kut) and on Muslim masculine "martyrdom" (on all occasions). The concept of "martyrdom" had been formulated in the context of Islam and the declaration of holy war (*jihad*) against the Allies in November 1914, fought singularly by men with a masculinist notion of heroism.

Despite being on the losing side in the war, Turkish nationalist historiography and memory regards the Battle of Gallipoli (1915) as a victory, one that was a pivotal precursor to the "Independence War" and the creation of the modern state of Turkey in 1923 (Aksakal 2014; Yanıkdağ 2017; Gürcan and Johnson 2016). The exaltation of the "Turkish victory" in Gallipoli was used not only to obscure the Ottomans' eventual defeat in the war, but also to stress the "anti-imperialist character" of the prospective nation state. Commemorations in Gallipoli had been taking place since the immediate aftermath of the battle in 1916 (Sınmaz Sönmez 2015), accelerated by the grand opening of the Çanakkale Şehitler Abidesi (Gallipoli Martyrs' Memorial) in 1960. Even though the battle has always been part of the Kemalist cannon of memory, the AKP government shifted the emphasis slightly and commemorated the Gallipoli campaign as part of a "struggle of Muslim martyrs against Christian invaders" (Lüküslü 2016).

The centenary commemorations started on 14 March 2015 with the visit of President Recep Tayyip Erdoğan to the Gallipoli Peninsula to place a wreath on the Martyrs' Memorial and to "pray upon the graves of martyrs".[4] On the 18 March Martyrs' Day in 2015, Prime Minister Ahmet Davutoğlu also led a series of commemorative events "to mark the sacrifice made by Ottoman soldiers" and remark the debt of the country to the "quarter of a million" Ottoman soldiers "who sacrificed themselves".[5] In

---

[4] "Cumhurbaşkanı Erdoğan, Çanakkale Şehitler Abidesi'ni Ziyaret Etti" [President Erdoğan visited the monument of martyrs in Çanakkale], issued by the Office of Turkish President, 14 March 2015, https://www.tccb.gov.tr/haberler/410/29707/cumhurbaskani-erdogan-canakkale-sehitler-abidesini-ziyaret-etti (16 May 2019).

[5] "Turkey starts programme of events to mark Centenary of Gallipoli campaign", *Centenary News*, 19 March 2015, http://www.centenarynews.com/article/turkey-starts-programme-of-events-to-mark-centenary-of-gallipoli-campaign (4 April 2019).

the opening ceremony a gold medal bearing the words "Çanakkale Impassable" was pinned to the Turkish flag, which was then raised, representing the "253,000 martyrs".[6] The Minister for Culture and Tourism, Ömer Çelik, noted that an extensive ceremony would "make the world hear our [Turkey's] voice".[7]

Within the scope of the 100th anniversary of the "Çanakkale Victory", the Prime Minister's Office ordered all public institutions (ministries, universities, schools, hospitals) to serve a lunch menu on 18 March 2015, composed of the dishes supposedly eaten by the soldiers at the front a hundred years ago: wheat soup, grape compote, and bread. The printed menus noted that these items were served "to commemorate our sacred martyrs with mercy and gratitude".[8] Designed to create empathy and identification with the suffering of the soldiers by turning their poverty and the dire conditions of the campaign into lived experience, the menu was, however, not popular among students in schools and universities; moreover, the veracity of the menu has been challenged by a few historians. Yet, the practice was retained after the centenary and is still followed at annual commemorations.

In his speech at the 18 March ceremony, Prime Minister Davutoğlu reminded listeners of an upcoming and international Gallipoli commemoration. He said that the "nations fighting both on the side of Turkey and against it" would meet in April 2015. Doubtlessly referring to efforts being made to have the Armenian genocide recognised, he noted that some people were "trying to create a culture of hatred through 1915", while he would prefer "to leave aside the feelings of hatred, grudge and vengeance".[9] The Gallipoli commemorations on 24/25 April, Anzac Day, were among the biggest centenary events of 2015, since the campaign played a crucial role in shaping national identities not only in Turkey, but

[6] "Büyük Zafer 100. yılında törenlerle kutlandı" [The 100th anniversary of the big victory has been celebrated with ceremonies], *Habertürk*, 19 March 2015, https://www.haberturk.com/gundem/haber/1055358-canakkale-zaferinin-100-yildonumu-cesitli-etkinliklerle-anildi (16 May 2019).
[7] http://basin.kulturturizm.gov.tr/TR-132055/kultur-ve-turizm-bakani-omer-celik-18-mart-sehitleri-an-.html (16 May 2019).
[8] "Başbakanlık'ta 'Çanakkale Menüsü'" [The 'Gallipoli menu' at the office of the presidency], *Yeni Şafak*, 18 March 2015, https://www.yenisafak.com/gundem/basbakanlikta-canakkale-menusu-2104817 (16 May 2019).
[9] "Davutoğlu: Milletimiz mertçe savaşır" [Davutoğlu: Our people fight bravely], *Yeni Şafak*, 18 March 2015, https://www.yenisafak.com/gundem/davutoglu-milletimiz-mertce-savasir-2104830 (16 May 2019).

also in Australia and New Zealand (Beaumont 2015).[10] The ceremony on 24 April 2015 took place in the Martyrs' Memorial. President Erdoğan and numerous guest leaders entered the ceremony area through a corridor of soldiers wearing the "historical uniforms" of "Turkish soldiers" at Gallipoli (Fig. 7.1).[11] The ceremony was attended by 16 heads of state, as well as other state representatives, such as presidents of parliament, vice-presidents, prime ministers, ministers, and ambassadors. French President François Hollande and Russian President Vladimir Putin, although invited to Gallipoli, attended the Armenian genocide commemoration in Yerevan instead.[12]

In 2016, the AKP government discovered and commemorated another First World War "victory". The Siege of Kut'ül Amare between 3 December 1915 and 29 April 1916 was an episode involving the Ottoman Empire and Great Britain, ending with the surrender of British soldiers (Çetinsaya 2017). During a talk on 28 April 2016, President Erdoğan noted that there had been an attempt to erase the victory of Kut'ül Amare from the "nation's memory" and from the pages of history. Erdoğan announced that the victory would be "officially commemorated" on its centenary the following day (29 April), under his own auspices and those of the Prime Minister and the Chief of General Staff, with a pompous ceremony "to commemorate the glory and to honour the martyrs and heroes".[13] On 29 April 2016, Turkey's official news agency (Anadolu Ajansı) published a series of news items (including an infographic) wherein it presented the siege of British-occupied Kut in Mesopotamia in the winter of 1916 as a

[10] *Centenary News*, 26 March 2015, http://www.centenarynews.com/article?id=3286 (4 April 2019).
[11] "Çanakkale'de görkemli anma töreni" [Splendid commemoration in Çanakkale], *TRT Haber*, 24 April 2015, https://www.trthaber.com/haber/gundem/canakkalede-gorkemli-anma-toreni-180633.html (16 May 2019).
[12] The countries represented included the United Kingdom, Albania, Azerbaijan, Bosnia and Herzegovina, Djibouti, South Sudan, Ireland, Montenegro, Qatar, Macedonia, Mali, Niger, Pakistan, Senegal, Somalia, Turkmenistan, Afghanistan, Sudan, Australia, New Zealand, Moldova, Romania, and Syria.
World leaders join Gallipoli commemoration in Turkey, *Aljazeera*, 24 April 2015, https://www.aljazeera.com/news/2015/04/world-leaders-remember-gallipoli-centenary (16 May 2019).
[13] "Cumhurbaşkanı Erdoğan: Tedavülden kaldırılıp tarihin tozlu raflarına havale edildiler" [President Erdoğan: They have been put on the dusty shelves of the past], *Anadolu Ajansı* (*AA*), 28 April 2016, https://www.aa.com.tr/tr/turkiye/cumhurbaskani-erdogan-tedavul-den-kaldirilip-tarihin-tozlu-raflarina-havale-edildiler/563210?preview=1 (19 May 2016).

Fig. 7.1 Soldier with the "historical uniform" of the First World War Ottoman infantry. (Sibel Hürtaş, "Çankkale ve Öteki Şehitler" (Çanakkale and other martyrs), *Al-Monitor*, 27 March 2015)

"forgotten" victory and the "second most important Ottoman victory after the Battle of Çanakkale (Gallipoli)".[14] The government and pro-ruling party publications circulated a conspiracy theory to explain the "conscious negligence" in remembering the siege, specifically comparing it to the great importance attributed to the Battle of Gallipoli. In order to make up for "a hundred years of oblivion", the centenary of Kut was to be

[14] See, Kut'ül Amare, "Bağımsızlık ve hürriyet aşkının destanı" [An epic of love of independence and freedom], *AA*, 29 April 2016, https://www.aa.com.tr/tr/turkiye/kutul-amare-bagimsizlik-ve-hurriyet-askinin-destani/563536 (4 April 2019); "Kut'ül Amare zaferi Rusları da etkiledi" [Kut victory also influenced the Russians], *AA*, 29 April 2016, https://www.aa.com.tr/tr/dunya/kutul-amare-zaferi-ruslari-da-etkiledi/563654 (4 April 2019); "Kut'ül Amare Zaferi'ni İngilizler bize un"utturdu [The English made us forget the victory of Kut], *AA*, 29 April 2016, https://www.aa.com.tr/tr/dunya/kutul-amare-zaferini-ingilizler-bize-unutturdu/563531 (4 April 2019); "100. Yılında Unutulan Zafer: Kut'ül Amare" [Forgotten Victory in the 100th Anniversary: Kut'ul Amare] (infographic), *AA*, 29 April 2016, https://www.aa.com.tr/tr/info/infografik/1019 (4 April 2019).

commemorated in an extravagant manner. The Ministry of Culture and Tourism was charged with the organisation of numerous events to mark it, including the publication of prestige books, maps, and graphic novels, organising exhibitions and symposiums, and creating digital media.[15]

The ceremony, organised "under the auspices of the Presidency" at Lütfi Kırdar International Convention and Exhibition Centre, mainly featured a "theatre play", curiously named "Kut'ül Amare Dramatic Staging with Documents" (Kut'ül Amare Belgeli Dramatik Gösterimi). Along with President Erdoğan, the guests included high-level politicians, military personnel, and bureaucrats. Several community leaders from southern Iraq and the current governor of the city of Kut, Malik Halef, also attended the ceremony.[16] After a performance by 38 janissary musicians and 72 actors, President Erdoğan, the Governor of Kut, and the Minister of Culture and Tourism took to the stage. President Erdoğan was presented with the flag of the 6th Army, which "won the victory" at Kut; the governor then made a short speech, subsequently presenting the president with the "soil of Kut, watered with martyr's blood".[17] This was followed by a long speech by Erdoğan referring to the main tenets of the government's commemorative centenary politics. The program ended when the Iraqi community leaders, whose "grandfathers were martyred in Kut", presented him with a flag with the crescent and the star, symbolizing the Turkish flag.

Prime Minister Davutoğlu also spoke, promising that they would "keep [alive] the spirit of Kut'ül Amare until doomsday" and that Kut'ül Amare would not be "forgotten again until doomsday".[18] As promised, the Kut "fever" has continued beyond its centennial in 2016. The office of the presidency, the government with its various ministries, and the ruling party's municipalities have organised numerous meetings and panels, as well

---

[15] The Ministry of Culture and Tourism published a short clip for the centenary, "Kut'ül Amare hafızalardan silinmeyecek" [Kut'ül Amare won't be erased from the memories], issued by *AA*, 29 April 2016, https://youtu.be/X91JjJ8NMlo (16 May 2019).

[16] "Kut'ül Amare Zaferi'nin 100.yılı için görkemli anma programı" [Splendid commemoration for the 100th anniversary of the Kut'ül Amare victory] *AA*, 29 April 2016, https://www.aa.com.tr/tr/turkiye/kut-ul-amare-zaferinin-100yili-icin-gorkemli-anma-programi/563907 (16 May 2019).

[17] Ibid.

[18] "Tarihi 1919'dan başlatanlar milletimizin hasmıdır" [Those who start the history from 1919 are the enemy of our people], *Yeni Şafak*, 30 April 2016, https://www.yenisafak.com/gundem/tarihi-1919dan-baslatanlar-milletimizin-hasmidir-2459219 (16 May 2019).

as publishing several special issues and books about the campaign in 2017 and 2018. In 2017, the "victory" was added to the Turkish history curriculum (8th grade) under the heading, "National Revival: Steps to Independence", and the anniversary of the victory was inserted into the national education calendars.[19] Before the 2016 discovery of the siege, Kut'ül Amare had only attracted the academic interest of a limited number of historians. Since its glorious entry into the public sphere, however, more than 20 popular history books and novels have been published, including children's historical fiction.

Suffering, Martyrdom, Victimhood

Commemoration of the First World War in Turkey has always depended on contemporaneous political settings and dynamics, which at times overshadowed actual experiences of the war and its aftermath. Remembrance of devastating defeats or Ottoman failures has not been part of Kemalist memory politics (Arcan 2017; Lüküslü 2016). Sarıkamış presents an important exception as it has long been remembered as a tragic defeat caused by the high ambitions of Mustafa Kemal's rival, Enver Pasha. Since 2002, AKP rule has provided a strong Islamic setting for the commemoration of the war, and Sarıkamış, framed in terms of sacrifice and martyrdom, has become particularly useful for an Islamist re-imagination of late Ottoman history. In this sacralised recasting, martyrdom, a concept charged with masculinity, has a more important emotive value than victory itself (Lüküslü 2016).

The official commemoration of the Battle of Sarıkamış was an AKP government novelty, initiated for the first time in 2013. Taking place in the winter of 1914–1915, close to the current Armenian border, it constituted a devastating defeat of Ottoman forces by the Russian military. In a Ministry of Youth and Sports project, "Youth on the Trail of Martyrs" (*Gençlik Şühedanın İzinde*), tens of thousands of young people were brought to Sarıkamış, Çanakkale, Malazgirt, and Dumlupınar to commemorate the martyrs (of different battles) in 2013. Sarıkamış and Çanakkale are First World War fronts, whereas Malazgirt is the site of "the entry of the Turks to Anatolia" in 1071, and Dumlupınar refers to the

---

[19] "Kitaplardan İsmet İnönü çıktı Kut-ül Amare girdi" [İsmet İnönü got erased from textbooks whereas Kut'ül Amare is now covered], *Sözcü*, 17 January 2017, https://www.sozcu.com.tr/2017/egitim/kitaplardan-ismet-inonu-cikti-kut-ul-amare-girdi-1626476/ (4 April 2019).

final victory of the Turkish national forces in 1922.[20] On the 99th anniversary of the Battle of Sarıkamış (January 2014), the Ministry organised a second memorial march for the fallen soldiers, entitled "Turkey is Walking with its Martyrs".[21] Finally, during the centennial anniversary of Sarıkamış, a reported 30,000 people met in the Kızılçubuk village of Kars, despite heavy weather conditions, to commemorate "the fallen of Sarıkamış". The number of fallen soldiers has tended to rise with the approach of the centennial; earlier references mentioned 22,000 martyrs, which became 60,000 in 2015,[22] rising in 2016 to 90,000.[23]

The centennial commemoration in 2015 entailed an 8.5 km walk in the Allahuekber Mountains that lasted for two hours. During the march to the newly built ceremonial area in front of the Sarıkamış Martyrs' Memorial, the crowds used slogans with Islamic references suggested by the ministry (Fig. 7.2).[24] Important political figures, such as the Parliament Speaker, the Minister of the Interior, and the Minister of Youth and Sports, were present at the commemoration, followed by purportedly a hundred thousand people. The Ministry of Youth and Sports declared that they want "all members of society" to appreciate the "spirit of Sarıkamış". The commemorative march, he announced, is a "meaningful journey" to connect Turks with their national history and their martyred ancestors. The

[20] "Gençlik Şühedanın İzinde: Dumlupınar'dan Zafertepe'ye" [Youth On the Trail of Martyrs: From Dumlupınar to Zafertepe], *T24*, 20 August 2013, https://t24.com.tr/haber/genclik-suhedanin-izinde,237430 (4 April 2019).

[21] "Binlerce Genç, Sarıkamış'ta Ecdadın İzinde Yürüdü" [Thousands of Youth walked on the trail of martyrs in Sarıkamış], *Ministry of Youth and Sports*, 5 January 2014, http://www.gsb.gov.tr/HaberDetaylari/3/3798/binlerce-genc-sarikamista-ecdadin-izinde-yurudu.aspx (4 April 2019).

[22] "Sarıkamış Harekatının 100. yılında anma yürüyüşü" [Memorial march on the 100th anniversary of the Sarıkamış operation], *CNN Türk*, 5 January 2015, https://www.cnnturk.com/video/dunya/sarikamis-harekatinin-100-yilinda-anma-yuruyusu (4 April 2019).

[23] "Sarıkamış Şehitleri 101. Yılında Anıldı" [Sarıkamış Martyrs were commemorated on the 101st Anniversary], *Hürriyet*, 6 January 2016, http://www.hurriyet.com.tr/sarikamis-sehitleri-101-yilinda-anildi-37223066 (4 April 2019).

[24] These were, "Asımın Nesli Asrın Yürüyüşünde" [Asım's generation at the March of the Century], "Gök Allahuekber, Yer Allahuekber" [Sky Allahuekber, Earth Allahuekber]. "Asım'ın Nesli Asrın Yürüyüşünde", *İHA*, 4 January 2015, https://www.iha.com.tr/haber-asimin-nesli-asrin-yuruyusunde-426210/ (16 May 2019).

Fig. 7.2 Poster for the centennial Sarıkamış commemorations prepared by the Ministry of Youth and Sports. The poster slogans read, "Asım's generation at the March of the Century"; "Sky Allahuekber, Earth Allahuekber"

Sarıkamış commemoration has since been included in the national commemorative calendar.[25]

In his classic work on war commemorations, George Mosse (1990) underlines the creation of "The Myth of the War Experience" as an essential element of sacralising wars, making them meaningful, and producing the narrative that all those who died at the behest of other—more powerful—men, did not fall in vain. Therefore, ceremonies, films, and reenactments that bring "the war experience" closer always have a religious tone. Through this myth, Mosse (1990, 7) argues, "the memory of the war was refashioned into a sacred experience which provided the nation with a new depth of religious feeling, putting at its disposal ever-present saints and martyrs, places of worship and a heritage to emulate". In Turkey, making a great defeat meaningful, glorifying all those lives that were lost—not even to war but to insufficient preparation—and creating a narrative of victories in the midst of defeat, requires religious discourse to be tightly

[25] On the 104th anniversary (2019), several ministers, soldiers, and thousands of people walked in heavy snow. See "Şehitler böyle anıldı" [Martyrs were remembered like this], *CNN Türk*, 6 January 2019, https://www.cnnturk.com/video/turkiye/sehitler-boyle-anildi (4 April 2019).

braided with nationalism and masculinity, as the Sarıkamış commemorations attest. Yet, although, following Mosse, nationalism can in itself be read as religion, there is also a detectable turn towards Islam as *the religion* in the war commemorations of the last two decades.

The greater salience of religious interpretation is widely visible in the recasting of the victory at Gallipoli, which during the 2000s has somehow shifted from a "Turkish nationalist victory" towards "an Ottoman victory based on religious faith" (Baykut 2016). As part of the centenary events, the Presidency of Religious Affairs (*Diyanet*) organised commemoration of the martyrs in mosques in 81 cities and 957 districts. During the morning prayer at Grand Mosque of Bursa (Bursa Ulu Camii), 253,000 *hatims* (full recitations of the Qur'an) were dedicated to the 253,000 martyrs.[26] During the Gallipoli ceremonies of 24 April 2015, the President of Religious Affairs, Mehmet Görmez, was the first speaker, taking the floor even before Prince Charles and President Erdoğan. After reciting the Quran, he said a long prayer for the martyrs of Çanakkale.[27]

Bringing masculine patriotism and Muslim faith together was also clearly conveyed in the controversial governmental campaign video, "The Prayer" (*Dua*), which was broadcast by the Turkish Presidency on 20 April 2015 to mark the 100th anniversary of the Battle of Gallipoli.[28] The video begins with soldiers—who came to the battlefield from across the Ottoman Empire—giving their names and combat readiness, interspersed with images of their unborn grandchildren, also from various regions of contemporary Turkey. Then the voice of President Erdoğan begins to recite an Islamic-toned patriotic poem by the nationalist poet Arif Nihat Asya. The video continues with images of Erdoğan praying at the Çanakkale Martyrs' Memorial and laying a commemorative wreath at the grave of one of the Ottoman soldiers in the symbolic cemetery (Thys-Şenocak 2018, 212).

[26] "Bursa Ulu Camii'nde Çanakkale Şehitleri İçin 253 Bin Hatim Duası Yapıldı" [253 hatim prayers have been prayed for the Gallipoli martyrs at the Ulu mosque in Bursa], *Haberler*, 18 March 2015, https://www.haberler.com/bursa-ulu-camii-nde-canakkale-sehitleri-icin-253-7087953-haberi/ (16 May 2019).
[27] "Çanakkale'de görkemli anma töreni" [Splendid commemoration in Çanakkale], *TRT Haber*, 24 April 2015, https://www.trthaber.com/haber/gundem/canakkalede-gorkemli-anma-toreni-180633.html (16 May 2019).
[28] "Turkish President Erdoğan's Gallipoli 'prayer' stirs debate", *Hürriyet Daily News*, 21 April 2015, www. hurriyetdailynews.com/turkish-president-erdogans-gallipoli-prayer-stirs-debate-81350 (6 July 2020).

The commemoration of the siege of Kut, likewise, was filled with Islamic references. The government recommended "1001" full recitations of the Quran for the martyrs of Kut to be performed in the religious vocational schools across the country. Their students were also expected to lead Islamic memorial services (*Mevlid*) in mosques.[29]

In sum, the centennial commemorations stressed the suffering and victimhood of the Muslim soldiers, especially in the centenary events organised around the Gallipoli and Sarıkamış campaigns. Whether in the form of terrible weather conditions (Sarıkamış) or the poor quality of the food (Gallipoli), military life was narrated as a pious form of misery to reach the sacred honour of martyrdom, which is reserved to men; hence offering an only slightly revised version of masculine heroism. As we discuss below, the AKP government also pursued a quantitative competition involving "Muslim losses" set against Armenian genocide victims. The great number of human losses in Gallipoli and Sarıkamış—which surprisingly increase on a yearly basis—are presented as the Turkish "equivalents" of the Armenian genocide.

Imperial Visions

The commemoration of the First World War may also be seen as part of the AKP's larger neo-Ottomanist aspirations. As we have illustrated, the new narratives stress Turkey's religious ties with the Muslim world. Both Gallipoli and Kut are presented as Muslim victories against great Christian powers. Moreover, the "leading role" of the Turks or the "historical legacy" of leadership in the Middle East is constantly highlighted. This neo-Ottomanist perspective seeks to privilege Turkish leadership and a paternalistic position over "other Muslims".

Erdoğan noted in his speech at the centenary of "the forgotten victory of Kut" that the name Turk, at the time, "did not refer to a certain nation (*kavim*), but referred to all Muslims".[30] The commemoration of Kut, therefore, purposefully highlighted Muslim solidarity and unity under the Ottomans by focusing on the support of local Muslim Arabs, together

---

[29] "Görkemle kutlansın" [May it be celebrated with splendour], *Hürriyet*, 17 April 2016, http://www.hurriyet.com.tr/gundem/gorkemle-kutlansin-40089900 (4 April 2019).

[30] "Tarihi 1919'dan başlatanlar milletimizin hasmıdır" [Those who start the history from 1919 are the enemy of our people], *Yeni Şafak*, 30 April 2016, https://www.yenisafak.com/gundem/tarihi-1919dan-baslatanlar-milletimizin-hasmidir-2459219 (16 May 2019).

with the sympathetic position of Indian Muslims in the British army. A moderately popular TV series, *Mehmetçik, Kut'ül-Amare*, was also produced by the state channel in the aftermath of the centenary. It is a propagandistic work that feeds into nationalist populism with a strong attachment to militarism, Islamic identity, and neo-Ottomanism. The president and his government have embraced *Mehmetçik, Kut'ül-Amâre* publicly and enthusiastically. Indeed, the first episode of the series was screened in the conference hall of the presidential complex (Onaran 2022).

The new official interpretation of Kut marginalised the rise of Arab nationalism—which, in the past, Kemalists interpreted as treachery and betrayal (Çiçek 2012)—as a plot by Christian Western powers against the unity of the Muslims.[31] Erdoğan claimed that remembrance of Kut'ül Amare corrected "an important defect (*arıza*) of the official [Kemalist] history discourse", that relied on the lie that "Arabs stabbed us in the back", whereas, during the siege "the people of Kut acted like a part of the Ottoman army, giving martyrs for the cause".[32] Certainly, reframing Arab involvement in the First World War anew also served pragmatic political ends at the height of Syrian migration to Turkey and the increasing xenophobia targeting the refugees. Acquitted of being historical traitors, Arabs were elevated to the status of brothers-in-arms, in Erdoğan's words. As a successful attempt to contain racist tendencies and animosities within the nationalist segments of the society, Battle of Kut commemorations contributed to the legitimation of recent Arab presence in the country.

The Invisibility of Non-Muslim Soldiers and Genocide Denialism

In line with the government's neo-Ottomanist emphasis on "Muslim martyrdom", elaborate centenary observances ignored the presence of non-Muslim soldiers in the Ottoman lines. Centenary observations of the Gallipoli campaign became another occasion to emphasise the invisibility of non-Muslims in the AKP's official history narrative. Non-Muslim soldiers who lost their lives were not saluted during the ceremony and their names were removed from the list of martyrs issued by the Defence Ministry (Hürtaş 2015). As the faith-based narrative, resting on the collective sacrifices of devout Muslim martyrs, explained the "victory" behind Gallipoli, the Peninsula became an Islamic pilgrimage route and a space of

[31] Ibid.
[32] Ibid.

prayer (Thys-Şenocak 2018). In this formula, non-Muslim Ottoman troops, specifically Greeks, Armenians, and Jews, were excluded from both history and the memory of the battle.

The centenary commemoration of the First World War was also characterised by denialism in order to silence and obscure the centenary of the Armenian genocide (Adjemian and Nichanian 2013). In 2015, the government used the Gallipoli centenary occasion to deflect international attention and criticism of Turkey's official stance on the Armenian genocide (Macleod 2017, 98), as 2015 was also the centenary of the genocide and a year of international demands for recognition. Armenia issued a declaration on 29 January 2015, demanding that Turkey recognise the killing of Armenians during the First World War as genocide. In his declaration on 12 April 2015, Pope Francis described the mass killings of Armenians as "the first genocide of the twentieth century". Following the Pope's statement, the European Parliament MEPs backed a resolution on 15 April 2015 urging Turkey to use the centenary to "come to terms with its past" and to "recognise the genocide".[33]

In 2010 the Minister of Foreign Affairs, Davutoğlu, had already noted that 1915 might mean "genocide" to Armenians but, for the Turks, "it meant Gallipoli".[34] Predictably, denialist calculations determined Turkey's 2015 international commemoration of the Battle of Gallipoli. The government used the centennial to distract domestic and global attention away from Genocide Remembrance Day (24 April 2015)[35] by pushing the

---

[33] Armenian genocide centenary: "MEPs urge Turkey and Armenia to normalize relations, issued by European Parliament", 15 April 2015, https://www.europarl.europa.eu/news/en/press-room/20150413IPR41671/armenian-genocide-centenary-meps-urge-turkey-and-armenia-to-normalize-relations (6 July 2020).

[34] " A Conversation with Ahmet Davutoglu", *Council on Foreign Relations*, 14 April 2010, https://www.cfr.org/event/conversation-ahmet-davutoglu-0 (27 March 2019); Murat Yetkin, "Davutoğlu: Ermeni diasporasıyla temas istiyoruz" [Davutoglu: We want contact with the Armenian diaspora], *Radikal*, 26 March 2010, http://www.radikal.com.tr/yazarlar/murat-yetkin/davutoglu-ermeni-diasporasiyla-temas-istiyoruz-987815/ (27 March 2019)

[35] The day signifies the round-up of Armenian notables in Istanbul for deportation (and murder) in 1915.

international observance from 18 March[36] to 24/25 April.[37] The deliberate attempt to overshadow the genocide centenary was a denialist strategy to overwrite Armenian suffering with an emphasis on the suffering of Ottoman *cum* Turkish soldiers at Gallipoli (Leupold 2017, 215; Aybak 2016, 136; Macleod 2017). While sidelining genocide commemorations in 2015 with Gallipoli, the government propagated another "victory" in 2016—that of the siege of Kut—to be commemorated on 23 April 2016. Here the government killed two birds with one stone. Not only was the national holiday celebrating the anniversary of the opening of the Grand National Assembly in 1920 overshadowed, but also Genocide Remembrance Day.

Around the same time, the Ministry of Foreign Affairs organised an exhibition entitled, "In Lieu of a Pomegranate: Time to Remember, Not to Forget, in Turkish-Armenian Relations" (7–29 April 2016) at the *Tophane-i Amire* exhibition hall of Mimar Sinan Fine Arts University. In dire contrast to its title, the event was preoccupied with forgetting and denying the genocide through methods of silencing, trivialisation, and euphemism (Türkyılmaz 2016). In her interview with the weekly Armenian newspaper, AGOS curator Güzin Erkan described the exhibition's intention with reference to the tolerant, pluralist, and convivial dimensions of neo-Ottomanism. Erkan underlined that the exhibition illustrated "the contribution of Armenian people to this society", in order to focus on "co-existence" and "positive stories" and not "get stuck in 1915" (Diler 2016).

---

[36] The government passed a new law for the "Çanakkale Martyrs' Day" commemorations, specifically indicating the date 18 March: "18 Mart Şehitler Günü ve 19 Eylül Gaziler Gününde Yapılacak Törenler Hakkında Yönetmelik", http://www.mevzuat.gov.tr/Metin.Aspx?MevzuatKod=7.5.5792&sourceXmlSearch=&MevzuatIliski=0 (27 March 2019).

[37] Robert Fisk, "The Gallipoli centenary is a shameful attempt to hide the Armenian Holocaust", 19 January 2015, *The Independent*, https://www.independent.co.uk/voices/comment/the-gallipoli-centenary-is-a-shameful-attempt-to-hide-the-armenian-holocaust-9988227.html (27 March 2019)

The exhibition, welcoming its visitors with Davutoğlu's "just memory"[38] and Erdoğan's "condolence message" from 2014,[39] reflected the centenary version of denialism by equalising the perpetrators and the victims as "victims of the same tragedy" (Yetkin 2022). Taner Akçam notes that the concept of "just memory" strengthened the politics of Turkish martyrdom in the First World War. In this constellation, Gallipoli and Sarıkamış are presented as Turkish "equivalents" to the genocide, whereby "Muslim losses" are put into competition with the Armenian genocide victims (Akçam 2010). In sum, the centenary denialism mainly relied on "the tragedies that befell the Turkish and Muslim people who had lost their lives in WWI", as the Ministry of Foreign Affairs wrote in its response to Pope Francis.[40]

Construction of Femininities through War Commemoration

In the grand official ceremonies surrounding the centennial commemorations we hardly ever come across a mention of gender. In Turkey, as elsewhere, militarism and masculinity are so tightly interwoven and naturalised (Sjoberg and Via 2010; Nagel 1998; Selek 2012; Sümbüloğlu 2013) that during the massive events politicians did not bother to refer to the women who took part in the war in various capacities, even for the sake of political correctness. The equation of martyrdom and heroism with masculinity prevailed silently by virtue of the omission of women from the historical narrative. However, in the same period, the image of the woman warrior also entered the public stage, although much more humbly and certainly more locally. The discovery of heroines of the First World War and the "Independence War", and their public acknowledgement, has indications

---

[38] Davutoğlu first used the concept in 2010, "A Conversation with Ahmet Davutoğlu", *Council on Foreign Relations*, 14 April 2010, https://www.cfr.org/event/conversation-ahmet-davutoglu-0 (27 March 2019). Later, he wrote an article about the concept in 2014. Ahmet Davutoğlu, "Turkish-Armenian Relations: Is a 'Just Memory' possible?" *Turkish Policy Quarterly* (2014).

[39] "Turkish PM offers condolences over 1915 Armenian massacre", *The Guardian*, 23 April 2014, https://www.theguardian.com/world/2014/apr/23/turkey-erdogan-condolences-armenian-massacre (27 March 2019)

[40] "Press Release Regarding the Statements Delivered During the Liturgy in Vatican on April 12, 2015", http://www.mfa.gov.tr/no_-110_-12-april-2015_-press-release-regarding-the-statements-delivered-during-the-liturgy-in-vatican-on-april-12_-2015.en.mfa (16 April 2019)

for the perceived social position of women in the patriarchal social order and also the entanglement of militarism and masculinity; but, when it comes to revising Turkish nationalism as the foundational premise of the Turkish Republic, they fall short of providing a fresh perspective. These women and their life struggles have become useful narrative devices and representations only insomuch as they serve "the myth of the military nation" (Altınay 2004), celebrated throughout the centennial events, by pluralising its constituents.

Memorials for Heroines

Until around the twenty-first century, unlike the unknown soldier monuments that constitute the norm in Europe (Kreiser 2002), Turkish Republican war memorials have been built around one constant figure, that of Mustafa Kemal Atatürk (Gür 2013). In his person, he embodied the new regime, as well as the "Independence War" that led to the establishment of the nation-state. In the earliest victory monuments, he is either situated on a huge pillar or stands in the forefront. In the earliest monuments raised in Istanbul, Samsun, and Ankara, he is depicted alone, on his horse (Gür 2013). Later, figure compositions were introduced in a few major monuments. In the Taksim monument, which was erected in 1928, the figure composition on the northern side refers to the "Independence War". Atatürk is depicted in his uniform, followed by anonymous heroes of the war. Among them, we see a woman sitting on the ground holding a small child in her arms, with an expression of suffering on her face. Right behind him is another woman, stepping forward with urgency and determination. Although without a weapon or a uniform, she is apparently part of the war effort. The male figures are of all walks of life, armed and eagerly pushing forward.

In Ankara's famous equestrian Atatürk Memorial of 1927, Mustafa Kemal Atatürk is placed on a huge pillar. The design by Heinrich Krippel focuses on him as "the incarnation of the victorious Anatolian people" (Kreiser 2006, 192). At the foot of the pillar there are three figures: two male soldiers actively looking at the horizon and a woman in a rural attire. The woman is carrying artillery ammunition on her back and is situated behind the main statue. On the reliefs of the main pillar, there is another woman with her baby wrapped against her body, pulling a heavy oxcart loaded with ammunition. This female figure, dressed in generic rural clothing and either carrying ammunition on her back or pulling an oxcart, almost always with a baby included in the scene, has, for long, been the embodiment of women's contribution to the "Independence War" in the national imagination.[41] She is to be found in school books and in reliefs all around the country: emblematic of sacrifice and service, but also of women's expected support role in war (next to male "lead actors"). With the new millennium, representations of women have started to change, although there is a detectable persistence of the image of the mother carrying ammunition. However, she is no longer anonymous. She has multiple names and many stories.

Klaus Kreiser (2002) starts his article on public monuments in Turkey with the famous epigraph from Benedict Anderson: "A society that suddenly wants to raise statues is a changing society." Kreiser's focus is on the debates about public statues that rarely and, over almost fifty years, only gradually broke the monopoly of Atatürk statues in Turkey. He reads these debates as indicative of a change towards a more pluralistic society, one moving slowly away from the one-man regime of the early Republic. Anderson's claim holds even better today. Since the early 2000s, we have been witnessing a pluralisation of memorials, busts, and public statues in Turkey. Some are rather abstract and symbolic, while others depict historical figures within a wide range, from sportsmen to scientists. A similar trend is observable in the monuments dedicated to war commemoration. Sculptures of local war heroes are being raised in their hometowns as well as in major metropolitan centres.

As illustrated above, the mother-child duo has been a staple of nationalist memorialisation of the wars that led to the collapse of the Ottoman Empire and the foundation of the Turkish Republic. It is therefore no surprise that Şerife Bacı (Sister Şerife) is the most popular figure, with statues erected in her honour not only in her hometown Kastamonu and its districts, but also in Istanbul. According to the most disseminated account, Şerife Bacı died in 1921 while carrying ammunition from the Black Sea coast to the military forces inland. Her baby was found alive under a quilt that protected both her and the artillery ammunition that was loaded on the oxcart, beside which Şerife Bacı froze to death. Her

---

[41] The figure was also "reproduced" for the ten-year commemorations of the Republic on 29 October 1933. In the "procession of villagers", there was in the front a village woman who pulled an oxcart laden with boxes of munitions, with a gun on her shoulder (Öztürkmen 2001, 61). In fact, all through the 1930s the significant contribution of the "Turkish women" to the "national struggle" was always stressed. It was claimed that "she distinguished herself through bravery and service" during the war (Cumhuriyet 1934).

mythical story of martyrdom inspired the figure of the unknown woman to be found in many early memorials, but her name remained inscribed in local history. The first memorial that included her was erected in 1990, and was again dominated by the overarching presence of Mustafa Kemal standing on a pillar (Fig. 7.3, top left); but at least she was positioned at the front with her famous oxen and the loaded cart. The countless memorials that were dedicated to her after the turn of the millennium, however, do not contain Mustafa Kemal, nor is Şerife Bacı anonymised.[42] She appears on her own, with her oxen and baby, occasionally accompanied by local old men or young boys. However, she is still the symbol of the double sacrifice of a woman—sacrificing her own life for her country and for her child—and is still positioned on the lesser-valued backstage of the war.

The first large-scale statue of a woman without the presence of Atatürk was erected in 1994 in Erzurum (Fig. 7.3, top right). It depicts and commemorates the local war heroine, Nene Hatun, who fought in the Russo-Turkish War of 1878–1979 as a young woman and lived until the age of 98 in the same city. In the memorial, she was shown with a baby on her back, her arms raised, and a rifle in her left hand. The monument caused controversy, as local historians claimed that she attended the war with an axe, leaving her infant child behind at home.[43] Indeed, the child constitutes part of the legend, as she is reported to have said, "A Turkish child would survive without a mother but couldn't survive without a homeland."[44] Positioning love for the country over maternal love, the story has proved instrumental in creating a national consciousness that glorified militarism (Kancı and Altınay 2007), but it also implied an

---

[42] For a few examples see, "Şehit Şerife Bacı Anıtı" [Şerife Bacı Monument], İnebolu Belediyesi http://www.inebolu.bel.tr/inebolu-detay.asp?Id=102&ineboludetay=sehit-serife-baci-aniti; "Şehit Şerife Bacı Anıtı" [Martyr Şerife Bacı Monument], Seydiler, Kastamonu https://www.tskgv.org.tr/tr/sehit-serife-baci-sehitler-aniti; "Şerife Bacı Anıtı" [Şerife Bacı Monument], Ayazağa, İstanbul https://www.yasamgazetesi.com.tr/ozel-haber/bu-millet-senin-gibi-kahramanlara-minnettardir-serife-baci-aniti-ayazagada-acildi-h172061.html; "Şerife Bacı Anıtı" [Şerife Bacı Monument], Gaziosmanpaşa Istanbul http://www.gophaber.com/haber-sehit_serife_baci__kar_ustunde_cephane_tasiyor...-11765.html (7 July 2020)

[43] "Tarihe adını kahramanlığıyla yazdıran Nene Hatun'un heykeli tartışmaya neden oldu" [The statue of Nene Hatun, who made her name written in history with her heroism, caused controversy], HaberTurk, 11 May 2017 https://www.haberturk.com/yerel-haberler/haber/53573170-tarihe-adini-kahramanligiyla-yazdiran-nene-hatunun-heykeli-tartismaya-neden-oldu (7 July2020)

[44] Ibid.

Fig. 7.3 *Top left:* The memorial of Atatürk and Şerife Bacı in Kastamonu, sculpted by Tankut Öktem between 1985 and 1990; the memorial stands in the city centre ("Atatürk ve Şehit Şerife Bacı Anıtı" [Atatürk and Şerife Bacı Monument], Kastamonu Belediyesi (7 July 2020)). *Top right and bottom right:* Nene Hatun Memorial, with the rifle (1994–2018) and with the axe (as of 2018). *Top right and bottom right*: Nene Hatun Memorial, with the rifle (1994–2018) and with the axe (as of 2018). *Bottom left:* Monument of Gördesli Makbule in Gördes, Manisa, courtesy of Hilal Alkan, 20 May 2019

transgression: a woman leaving aside her designated citizenly role as a mother to take an active part in the fight. It is precisely this aspect that the monument erases by putting the baby on Nene Hatun's back. After much controversy and many years, in 2018 the rifle was exchanged for an axe; however, the baby remained (Fig. 7.3, bottom right). A high-ranking local state official explained during the opening ceremony that they were aware that "Nene Hatun did not fight carrying her baby", but that they "wanted to remind everybody that she had children".[45]

Including children in public statues as reminders of women's designated position in Turkey's citizenship regime (Kancı and Altınay 2007) was dropped by the turn of the millennium, especially in memorials erected as part of the centennial commemorations. Here, local heroines are often depicted in uniform, with weapons in their hands and ammunition belts crossing their chests. It is only their headgear that gives away their local origins. Children are excluded from these statues and women appear simply as warriors. Examples of such monuments include Dağköylü Fatma Çavuş (Sergeant Fatma of Dağköy) in Samsun, Kamalı Fatma (Dagger Fatma) in Adana, Halime Çavuş (Sergeant Halime) in Kastamonu and Istanbul, and Adile Hala (Aunt Adile) in Mersin. While these memorials are part of a trend in which Anatolian cities are re-discovering their "past histories" and "forgotten hero(in)es", in an effort to commercialise and create sights of interest in their cityscapes, the representation of women not as mothers but as warriors is striking.

The memorial of "Martyr Makbule Hanım"[46] in Manisa, Gördes, has a special place among these woman warrior memorials. In this statue, erected in 2017 as a centrepiece in the park named after her, she is mounted on an energetically rearing horse (Fig. 7.3, bottom left). This is a rather exceptional representation, given that equestrian statues have been, for long, singularly reserved for Atatürk; even that commemorating his closest companion and presidential successor, İsmet İnönü, planned for Taksim Istanbul, caused a major controversy in the 1940s and was only placed somewhere else after 40 years of delay (Kreiser 2002). Yet now, in line

---

[45] "Nene Hatun heykelindeki 24 yıllık hata düzeltildi" [The mistake on Nene Hatun's memorial has been corrected after 24 years], *Hürriyet*, 12 December 2018. https://www.hurriyet.com.tr/gundem/nene-hatun-heykelindeki-24-yillik-hata-duzeltildi-41049068 (18 June 2020).

[46] "Milli Mücadele Kahramanı Şehit Makbule Hanım" [The Hero of the Independence War Martyr Makbule Hanım], *Gördes Kaymakamlığı*, 27 June 2019. http://www.gordes.gov.tr/milli-mucadele-kahramani-sehit-makbule-hanim (8 July 2020).

with one of the main tenets of neo-Ottomanism, a place of honour that was once reserved for Atatürk is curiously occupied by a local female fighter in Western Anatolia. Makbule Hanım's statue invites a revision of masculinist accounts of war by pluralising heroism.

Popularisation

The presence of these newly found heroines is certainly not limited to memorials; they have also become important elements of popular culture. In 2016, the public broadcaster TRT released a series titled, *Yüzyıllık Mühür* (A Hundred-Year-Old Seal), to commemorate the Battle of Gallipoli, with special emphasis on women. Several biographies in a similar vein have been written by enthusiastic non-academic authors in the last twenty years. In 1999, a local Aydın researcher and writer, Sabahattin Burhan, published a historical novel entitled *Çete Ayşe* (Bandit Ayşe), narrating the heroism of the famous local women fighter Ayşe, who lived in an Aydın village. This was followed by Gonca Elmas Akay's *Kara Fatma* (Black Fatma) (2010), İlknur Bektaş's *Milli Mücadelede Bir Üsteğmen Kara Fatma* (Black Fatma: A Lieutenant in the National Struggle) (2013), and Mehmet Dağıstanlı's *Ben Kara Fatma* (I, Black Fatma) (2018). These books provide a detailed (albeit fictionalised) account of the life of Lieutenant Fatma Seher Erden, who fought on various fronts in the First World War and the "Independence War". Due to the efforts of author İlknur Bektaş, the Turkish Red Cross restored her once missing grave in Istanbul in 2014.[47] Bektaş continued to write on the topic of female heroines in her collection *Milli Mücadelenin Cesur ve Kayıp Kadınları* (The Brave and Missing Women of the National Struggle) (2017) and *Milli Mücadele Kahramanı Nazife Kadın* (Heroine of the National Struggle: Maid Nazife) (2020). During the same period, another non-academic author, Tuba Emlek, published *Milli Mücadele Kahramanı Kahraman Kadınlar* (The Heroines of the National Struggle) (2017).

Similarly, Nene Hatun has received increased interest in the last decade. Except for two children's books that were published in 1959 and 1982, all 17 book titles that focus on the war deeds of Nene Hatun came out after 2010. It is striking that children are the target audience of over two-thirds

---

[47] "'Kara Fatma'ya 59 yıl sonra anıt mezar" [After 59 years, there is a memorial tomb for 'Kara Fatma'], *Anadolu Ajansı*, 14 June 2014 https://www.aa.com.tr/tr/yasam/kara-fatmaya-59-yil-sonra-anit-mezar/151164 (26 June 2020).

of these books, along with numerous other children's books and graphic novels which have been produced on war heroines. Nezahat Onbaşı (Corporal Nezahat), Tayyar Rahmiye (Flying Rahmiye), Kılavuz Hatice (Guide Hatice), Halime Çavuş, Kara Fatma, Binbaşı Ayşe (Major Ayşe), Asker Saime (Soldier Saime) and Şerife Bacı all appear in children's books, often targeting primary school age, in colourful and dramatic visual and narrative representations. Some of the illustrations in these books are also to be found on posters and puzzles.

The case of Kara Fatma is of particular importance here, showcasing the politics of this popular/commercial memory work (Fig. 7.4). In her work on "Kara Fatma(s)", Zeynep Kutluata (2006, 2007), for example, identifies several different female warriors in the late Ottoman and post–First World War context on whom the character may be based. She argues that, with the "genre" of Kara Fatma, "we are talking about a folkloric myth, a heroine in the land of Anatolia" (Kutluata 2006). This figure, built on multiple historical realities, has been claimed by various conflicting parties in the last two decades. Mehmet Bayrak (2002) unearthed archival records identifying two of these figures as female Kurdish notables. Yet, the only Kara Fatma who is now in circulation in popular culture is Fatma Seher Erden who fought in the "Independence War". She is represented singularly as a Turkish heroine.

Heroines in the Curriculum and Education

This mushrooming of pedagogical material is in line with both neo-Ottomanist revivalism as well as deliberate government efforts to shift the focus of the national mythology of independence in the school curricula from the persona of Atatürk to more local, ordinary, and dispersed figures from all over Anatolia. In their review of teaching about the "national struggle" (Milli Mücadele) at primary-school level, Şimşek and Çakmakçı (2019) found that from 1931 to 2005, the only names that are mentioned in this context were Atatürk and his commanders, İsmet İnönü, Fevzi Çakmak, and, depending on the political climate of the time, Kazım Karabekir. In 2005, a local commander of militia in Antep, Şahin Bey, appeared in the schoolbooks for the first time. After 2012 women figures have also found a place in the curriculum alongside many other male local heroes (Şimşek and Çakmakçı 2019, 203); "Knowing National Struggle Heroines" has been added as a "learning objective" at both primary and high school levels. Şerife Bacı (1900(?)–1921) is again the first to enter,

Fig. 7.4 A widely circulating picture of Kara Fatma, Fatma Seher Erden ("Kurtuluş Savaşının Kahraman Kadın Askeri: Kara Fatma" [The heroic female soldier of the Independence War: Kara Fatma], *CNN Türk*, 28 April 2017

followed by Gördesli Makbule Hanım (1902–1922) and Tayyar Rahmiye Hanım (1890–1920) (T.C İnkılap Tarihi ve Atatürkçülük Dersi Öğretim Programı 2018; Sosyal Bilgiler Dersi Öğretim Programı 2018).

The inclusion of "National Struggle Hero(in)es" in the new curriculum is indicative of a new politics of history. First, it reflects pedagogical changes in the school curricula and history education, which now emphasise local settings and conditions in order to appeal to and motivate students from all over Turkey (Şimşek and Çakmakçı 2019, 204). The populist character of the government's political discourse is obvious in this attempt to reach all corners of the country through the "life stories" of new heroes and heroines (Sosyal Bilgiler Dersi Öğretim Programı 2018, 14). Second, we see a change in the way gender is represented in schoolbooks, placing particular emphasis on the presence of women "in all aspects of life", including war (accomplished by the interventions of the feminist movement and as part of the EU accession process) (Karakuş et al. 2018). However, although gender-balanced representations can be seen as a step towards diversifying pedagogical role models, they do not necessarily challenge the basic tenets of acceptable femininity and hegemonic masculinity in the patriarchal heteronormative symbolic order. Moreover, the biographies of heroines in the schoolbooks only cover the particular time period when they fought or assisted the war effort. It is as if they did their part then peacefully returned home or, preferably, fell as martyrs.

Reflecting the inscriptions on their memorials, schoolbook accounts represent these heroines as embodying an unthreatening femininity in a very masculinist, militarist tale, as if they had bracketed their womanhood while heroically fighting and falling "like men". Actually, this bracketing of femininity is presented as their major accomplishment, or rather the precondition of their inclusion into the national mythology a hundred years later, the primary evidence for this being the narrative that emphasised the prioritisation of patriotism over maternal love. They are, therefore, accepted into proper citizenship in Turkey—which has from its inception relied on the masculine (read also as soldiers, because "every Turk is born a soldier" and soldiering is the realm of men) as the norm— by becoming *honorary males* in an exceptional time period in their life courses.

Nothing illustrates this point better than the life story of Halime Çavuş. A young woman from Kastamonu, Halime (Kocabıyık) fought in the "Independence War" dressed as a young male soldier. She became famous after she met Atatürk, who noticed that she was a girl with apparent surprise and appreciation. Halime was later injured and had to retire early. After the war she was invited to the presidential residence and was awarded a medal and a pension. She lived in her village until her death in 1976, always wearing her military uniform and shaving her non-existent facial hair (Milliyet 2004), thus refusing to give up her hard-won honorary male status (Fig. 7.5).

The change in gender representations has not radically shifted the notion of acceptable/respectable femininity or hegemonic masculinity; neither have the locality and plurality of local heroines necessarily produced diversity. In the schoolbooks, these figures are invariably represented as Muslim-Turkish women (even in the case of Kara Fatma) and their heroism is a showcase, or evidence, of the heroism of Turkish women in general, a representation that is in line with the general frame Kenan Çayır identifies in his work on schoolbooks. According to Çayır (2015), despite the comprehensive curriculum reform of 2005, which was also an

Fig. 7.5 Halime Çavuş in a photograph published in the national newspaper *Milliyet* on 30 August 2004. The photo caption reads, "Halime Çavuş tells her memories of the 'Independence War' to her visitors"

effort to implement EU norms, textbooks still preserve an ethno-religious national identity. Ethnic and religious minorities, when not represented as historical and present threats to national unity, are addressed within the discourse of tolerance, which reproduces the presumption of unequal citizenship (Çayır 2015).

The new wave of memorialising the wars of the last century, and heroic female figures who had been completely absent from the official narrative for almost eighty years, has significant implications. First of all, it has certainly made women's active participation in the war visible, particularly with a shift from the figure of the altruistic mother to the female fighter. Second, new memorials and school curricula, as well as increasing cultural production connected with the heroines, suggest a pluralisation of heroism and citizenship that has marked Turkey's social and political life in the early 2000s. Atatürk is no longer the single signifier of the nation(alist) state, a fetish that embodies and "reproduces the overpowering image of a unified statehood" (Navaro-Yashin 2002, 197). These new memorials provide fresh symbolic links with the past, and supply novel and essential elements of a foundational national mythology (Lowenthal 1985) that go beyond the "monoculture" (Kreiser 2002) of Atatürk. In that sense they fit perfectly into the neo-Ottomanist agenda and line of cultural production, and enlarge its coverage. Furthermore, and also in line with the narrowing down of neo-Ottomanism from a cosmopolitan, multicultural ideal to nostalgia for a golden age of national glory, the plurality of these female fighters is strictly limited to Muslimness and Turkishness. In these recent accounts, women's participation in the war effort is framed as a patriotic fight in defence of the homeland that is defined by these two characteristics, thus serving to re-emphasise ethno-religious national identity, while acknowledging diversity only in a very limited way.

CONCLUSION

The late 1990s and early 2000s in Turkey witnessed the emergence of revisionist accounts of late-Ottoman and early-republican history and feminist historiography. These critical accounts, also partially in dialogue with the diversity and pluralism aspects of a prevalent discourse on Ottoman cosmopolitanism, were quickly hijacked, cleared off their critical content, and massed to be refurbished as the AKP's new politics of history. In the context of the centennial commemorations of the First World War, a selective way of remembering the Ottoman past through "Turkish imperial rule" and the protection of "Muslim faith" largely defined neo-Ottomanism. Commemorative events were centred around the role of Islam and solidarity under Turkish leadership, and consciously omitted non-Muslim soldiers and ethnic violence against non-Muslims. The incorporation of mythical narratives of women warriors into the centennial memorialisation fever indicated a pluralisation of heroism to a certain level, and a shift in the notion of gendered citizenship that assigns men to soldiering and women to motherhood. This can, however, be seen as a negligible shift, as women's participation in war was always bracketed as an exceptional act of heroism under extraordinarily dire conditions. Moreover, this new wave of heroic representations reflected the same obsession with "Muslim martyrdom" and homogeneous ethno-religious identity, along with the neo-Ottomanist aspiration to undermine the hero cult around Mustafa Kemal. The AKP's sacralisation of history through a predominantly faith-based narrative, highlighting prayer (instead of technology), sacrifice (instead of reward), and martyrdom (instead of heroism), has also rhymed perfectly with the government's ideological necropolitics in the post–15 July (2016) coup context.

References

Adjemian, Boris and Mikaël Nichanian. 2013. Du centenaire de 14-18 à celui de 1915. *Études arméniennes contemporaines* 2: 65–88.

Akçam, Taner. 2010. What Davutoğlu Fails to Understand. *The Armenian Weekly*, online. Accessed March 27, 2019. https://armenianweekly.com/2010/05/19/akcam-davutoglu/.

Aksakal, Mustafa. 2014. Introduction. *International Journal of Middle East Studies* 46 (4) [Special Issue on World War One]: 653–656.

Altınay, Ayşe Gül. 2004. *The Myth of the Military-Nation: Militarism, Gender, and Education in Turkey*. New York: Palgrave Macmillan.

Arcan, H. Esra. 2017. Homeland Memory: Construction of Memory Politics and the Media in Turkey Related to World War I. In *Current Debates in Public Relations, Cultural & Media Studies*, ed. Emrah Doğan and Ercan Geçgin, 481–504. London: IJOPEC Publication.

Ayata, Bilgin. 2012. Tolerance as a European Norm or an Ottoman Practice? An Analysis of Turkish Public Debates on the (Re)Opening of an Armenian Church in the Context of Turkey's EU Candidacy and Neo-Ottoman Revival. In *KFG Working Paper Series 41, Kolleg-Forschergruppe (KFG) "The Transformative Power of Europe*. Berlin: Freie Universität Berlin.

Aybak, Tunç. 2016. Geopolitics of Denial: Turkish State's 'Armenian Problem'. *Journal of Balkan and Near Eastern Studies* 18 (2): 125–144.

Bayrak, Mehmet. 2002. *Geçmişten Günümüze Kürt Kadını [Kurdish Women from the Past to the Present]*. Ankara: Özge Yayınları.
Baykut, Sibel. 2016. The Re-contextualization of the Battle of Gallipoli through Commemorations. *Intercultural Understanding* 6: 7–15.
Beaumont, Joan. 2015. Commemoration in Australia: A Memory Orgy? *Australian Journal of Political Science* 50 (3): 536–544.
Çayır, Kenan. 2015. Citizenship, Nationality and Minorities in Turkey's Textbooks: From Politics of Non-recognition to 'Difference Multiculturalism'. *Comparative Education* 51 (4): 519–536.
Çetinsaya, Gökhan. 2017. Kut al-Amara. In *1914–1918-online. International Encyclopedia of the First World War*, ed. Ute Daniel, Peter Gatrell, Oliver Janz, Heather Jones, Jennifer Keene, Alan Kramer and Bill Nasson. Berlin: Freie Universität Berlin.
Çiçek, M. Talha. 2012. Erken Cumhuriyet Dönemi Ders Kitapları Çerçevesinde Türk Ulus Kimliği İnşası ve 'Arap İhaneti' [Turkish National Identity Formation and the 'Arab Betrayal' within the frame of school books of the Early Republican Era]. *Divan: Disiplinlerarası Çalışmalar Dergisi* 32: 169–188.
Çolak, Yılmaz. 2006. Ottomanism vs Kemalism. Collective Memory and Cultural Pluralism in 1990s Turkey. *Middle Eastern Studies* 42 (2): 587–602.
Cumhuriyet. 1934. Bugünkü Türk Kadını: İstiklâl Harbindeki Yararlık ve Cesaretile Temayüz Etmiştir [Turkish Woman Today: She Distinguished Herself through Service and Bravery during the Independence War], July 25, p. 7.
Diler, Fatih Gökhan. 2016. Derdimiz tüm olayı 1915'e kilitlemeden, o dört yıllık zaman diliminde anlamak [Our Problem is Understanding These 4 Years before Making Everything About 1915] *AGOS*, online: Accessed March 27, 2019. http://www.agos.com.tr/tr/yazi/15087/derdimiz-tum-olayi-1915-e-kilitlemeden-o-dort-yillik-zaman-diliminde-anlamak.
Doroll, Courtney Michelle. 2015. *The Spatial Politics of Turkey's Justice and Development Party (AK Party): On Erdoğanian New Ottomanism*. Unpublished PhD. Dissertation. Tucson: University of Arizona.
Ergin, Murat, and Yağmur Karakaya. 2017. Between Neo-Ottomanism and Ottomania: Navigating State-Led and Popular Cultural Representations of the Past. *New Perspectives on Turkey* 56: 33–59.
Fisher-Onar, Nora. 2009. Echoes of a Universalism Lost: Rival Representations of the Ottomans in Today's Turkey. *Middle Eastern Studies* 45 (2): 229–241.
Furlanetto, Elena. 2015. 'Imagine a Country Where We Are All Equal': Imperial Nostalgia in Turkey and Elif Shafak's Ottoman Utopia. In *Post-Empire Imaginaries?: Anglophone Literature, History, and the Demise of Empires*, ed. Barbara Buchenau, Virginia Richter and Marijke Denger, 159–180. Leiden: Brill.
Göknar, Erdağ. 2006. Orhan Pamuk and the 'Ottoman' Theme. *World Literature Today* 80 (6): 34–38.

Gür, Faik. 2013. Sculpting the Nation in Early Republican Turkey. *Historical Research* 86 (232): 342–372.

Gürcan, Metin and Robert Johnson, ed. 2016. *The Gallipoli Campaign: The Turkish Perspective*. London & New York: Routledge.

Hürtaş, Sibel. 2015. Gallipoli Centenary Marks Another Snub for Turkish Minorities. *Al-Monitor*, online. Accessed July 5, 2020. https://www.al-monitor.com/pulse/originals/2015/03/turkey-gallipoli-war-other-m.html#ixzz6RRYVBtNd.

Kancı, Tuba and Ayşe Gül Altınay. 2007. Educating Little Soldiers and Little Ayşes: Militarised and Gendered Citizenship in Turkish Textbooks. In *Education in 'Multicultural' Societies. Turkish and Swedish Perspectives*, ed. Marie Carlson, Annika Rabo and Fatma Gök, 51–70. London & New York: I.B. Tauris.

Karaca, Banu. 2019. 'When Everything Has Been Said Before…': Art, Dispossession, and the Economies of Forgetting in Turkey. In *Women Mobilizing Memory*, ed. Ayşe Gül Altınay, María José Contreras, Marianne Hirsch, Jean Howard, Banu Karaca and Alisa Solomon, 285–302. New York: Columbia University Press.

Karakuş, Emel, Esra Mutlu and Yelkin Diker Coşkun. 2018. Toplumsal Cinsiyet Eşitliği Açısından Öğretim Programlarının İncelenmesi [Analysing Curricula in terms of Gender Equalityity]. *Kadın Araştırmaları Dergisi* 17: 31–54.

Konuk, Kader. 2011. Istanbul on Fire: End-of-Empire Melancholy in Orhan Pamuk's Istanbul. *The Germanic Review: Literature, Culture, Theory* 86 (4): 249–261.

Kreiser, Klaus. 2002. Public Monuments in Kemalist and Post-Kemalist-Turkey. *Journal of Turkish Studies (Essays in Honour of Barbara Flemming*. Guest Ed. Jan Schmidt). 26 (2): 43–60.

———. 2006. War Memorials and Cemeteries in Turkey. In *The First World War as Remembered in the Countries of the Eastern Mediterranean*, ed. Olaf Farschid, 183–197. Egon: Würzburg.

Kutluata, Zeynep. 2006. *Gender and War during the Late Ottoman and Early Republican Periods: The Case of Black Fatma(s)*. Master Thesis. Istanbul: Sabancı University.

———. 2007. Geç Osmanlı ve Erken Cumhuriyet Dönemi'nde Toplumsal Cinsiyet ve Savaş: Kara Fatma(lar) [Gender and War during the late Ottoman Empire and the Early Republican Turkey: the Kara Fatma(s)]. *Feminist Yaklaşımlar [Feminist Approaches]* 2: 73–90.

Leupold, David. 2017. Authentische Gewaltgeschichten oder verzerrte Spiegelbilder? Die türkische und armenische Geschichtsdeutung von 1915 im Lichte des Nationalmythos. In *Geschichte als Ressource. Politische Dimensionen historischer Authentizität*, ed. Barbara Christophe, Christoph Kohl and Heike Liebau, 211–240. Berlin: Klaus Schwarz Verlag.

Lowenthal, David. 1985. *The Past is a Foreign Country*. Cambridge: Cambridge UP.
Lüküslü, Demet. 2016. Creating a Pious Generation: Youth and Education Policies of the AKP in Turkey. *Southeast European and Black Sea Studies* 16 (4): 637–649.
Macleod, Jenny. 2017. The Gallipoli Centenary: An International Perspective. In *War Memory and Commemoration*, ed. Brad West, 89–106. New York & London: Routledge.
Maksudyan, Nazan. 2019. Centenary (Turkey). In *1914–1918-online. International Encyclopedia of the First World War*, ed. Ute Daniel, Peter Gatrell, Oliver Janz, Heather Jones, Jennifer Keene, Alan Kramer, and Bill Nasson. Berlin: Freie Universität.
Milliyet. 2004. Kurtuluş Savaşının Elifleri [The Elifs of the Independence War]. *Milliyet* (30 Ağustos Özel Sayısı), August 30.
Mills, Amy. 2011. The Ottoman Legacy: Urban Geographies, National Imaginaries, and Global Discourses of Tolerance. *Comparative Studies of South Asia, Africa and the Middle East* 31 (1): 183–195.
Mosse, George L. 1990. *Fallen Soldiers: Reshaping the Memory of the World Wars*. Oxford: University Press.
Nagel, Joane. 1998. Masculinity and Nationalism: Gender and Sexuality in the Making of Nations. *Ethnic and Racial Studies* 21 (2): 242–269.
Navaro-Yashin, Yael. 2002. *Faces of the State: Secularism and Public Life in Turkey*. Princeton, NJ: Princeton University Press.
Onaran, Burak. 2022. New Histories for a New Turkey: The First Battle of Kut (1916) and the Reshaping of the Ottoman Past. In *The Politics of Culture in Contemporary Turkey*, ed. Pierre Hecker, Ivo Furman and Kaya Akyıldız. Edinburgh: Edinburgh University Press.
Öztürkmen, Arzu. 2001. Celebrating National Holidays in Turkey: History and Memory. *New Perspectives on Turkey* 25: 47–75.
Riexinger, Martin Thomas. 2014. The Ottoman Empire as Harmonious Utopia: A Historical Myth and its Function. In *Islamic Myths and Memories*, ed. Izchak Weismann, Mark Sedgwick and Ulrika Mårtensson, 35–52. Farnham: Ashgate.
Selek, Pınar. 2012. *Sürüne Sürüne Erkek Olmak* [Becoming a Man Through Boot Camp] Istanbul: İletişim Yayınları.
Şimşek, Ahmet, and Emre Çakmakçı. 2019. Cumhuriyet Dönemi İlkokul Tarih Ders Kitaplarında Millî Mücadele [The Independence War in Primary School History Textbooks in the Republican Period]. *CTAD* 15 (30): 189–227.
Sınmaz Sönmez, Cahide. 2015. Çanakkale Savaşlarını Anma ve Kutlama Etkinlikleri (1916–1938) [Commemorations of the Gallipoli Campaign (1916–1938)]. *Çanakkale Araştırmaları Türk Yıllığı* 19: 173–195.
Sjoberg, Laura and Sandra Via. 2010. Introduction. In *Gender, War and Militarism: Feminist Perspectives*, ed. Laura Sjoberg and Sandra Via. Westport, CT: Praeger.

Sosyal Bilgiler Dersi Öğretim Programı. [Social Sciences Curricula] 2018. Ankara: T.C. Milli Eğitim Bakanlığı Yayınları, online: Accessed July 9, 2020. http://mufredat.meb.gov.tr/Dosyalar/201812103847686-SOSYAL%20B%C4%B0LG%C4%B0LER%20%C3%96%C4%9ERET%C4%B0M%20PROGRAMI%20.pdf.

Sümbüloğlu, Nurseli Yeşim. 2013. Giriş: Türkiye'de Militarizm, Milliyetçilik ve Erkek(lik)lere Dair Bir Çerçeve [Introduction: A Frame About Militarism, Nationalism and Men/Masculinities in Turkey] In *Erkek Millet Asker Millet: Türkiye'de Militarizm, Milliyetçilik ve Erkek(lik)ler [Male Nation Soldier Nation: Militarim, Nationalism and Men/Masculinities in Turkey]*, ed. Nurseli Yeşim Sünbüloğlu. Istanbul: İletişim Yayınları.

T.C İnkılap Tarihi ve Atatürkçülük Dersi Öğretim Programı. [The Curriculum for the History of the Revolution and Kemalism] 2018. Ankara: T.C. Milli Eğitim Bakanlığı Yayınları, online. Accessed July 9, 2020. http://mufredat.meb.gov.tr/Dosyalar/201812104016155-%C4%B0NKILAP%20TAR%C4%B0H%C4%B0%20VE%20ATAT%C3%9CRK%C3%87%C3%9CL%C3%9CK%20%C3%96%C4%9ERET%C4%B0M%20PROGRAMI.pdf.

Thys-Şenocak, Lucienne. 2018. *Divided Spaces, Contested Pasts: The Heritage of the Gallipoli Peninsula*. Abingdon: Routledge.

Tokdoğan, Nagehan. 2018. *Yeni Osmanlıcılık: Hınç, Nostalji, Narsisizm* [Neo-Ottomanism: Resentment, Nostalgia, Narcissism]. Istanbul: İletişim.

Türkyılmaz, Yektan. 2016. Tarih Vertigosu, Hafıza Hipnozu: Nar Niyetiyle Hatırlamak [Vertigo of History, Memory Hypnosis: Remembering 'In Lieu of a Pomegranate']. *AGOS*, online. Accessed March 27, 2019. http://www.agos.com.tr/tr/yazi/15089/tarih-vertigosu-hafiza-hipnozu-nar-niyetiyle-hatirlamak.

White, Jenny. 2014. *Muslim Nationalism and the New Turks*. Princeton, NJ: Princeton University Press.

Yanıkdağ, Yücel. 2017. Ottoman Empire/Middle East. In *1914-1918-online. International Encyclopedia of the First World War*, ed. Ute Daniel, Peter Gatrell, Oliver Janz, Heather Jones, Jennifer Keene, Alan Kramer and Bill Nasson. Berlin: Freie Universität.

Yavuz, M. Hakan. 1998. Turkish Identity and Foreign Policy in Flux. The Rise of Neo-Ottomanism. *Critique: Critical Middle Eastern Studies* 7 (12): 19–42.

———. 2016. Social and Intellectual Origins of Neo-Ottomanism: Searching for a Post-National Vision. *Die Welt des Islams* 56 (3–4): 438–465.

Yetkin, Eren Yıldırım. 2022. *Violence and Genocide in Kurdish Memory: Exploring the Remembrance of the Armenian Genocide through Life Stories*. Leverkusen-Opladen: Verlag Barbara Budrich.

CHAPTER 8

The New Ottoman Henna Nights and Women in the Palace of Nostalgia

Petek Onur

Dressed in an ostentatious kaftan, the 21-year-old bride is sitting on a velvet couch in a small dressing room decorated with pink oriental patterns. With her in the room, which is also a DJ cabin and kitchen, are her mother, two bridesmaids who double as dancers, and the event organiser. While the bride is being shown the choreography of the first dance, evening *ezan* echoes from the Ottoman mosque in this historic neighbourhood of Ankara. After the *ezan*, she will step into the palace of nostalgia for her henna night, which will be an evening of a revitalised tradition inspired by Ottoman palaces and Oriental imageries of history.

How can we understand this kaleidoscopic scene from contemporary Turkey? Any attempt to answer this question will inevitably lead to a discussion of neo-Ottomanism as a particular perception of the past, a vision for the future, and a political ideology but, much more than these, as a cultural trend that involves the creative agencies of a variety of actors. In

P. Onur (✉)
Department of Cross-Cultural and Regional Studies, University of Copenhagen, Copenhagen, Denmark
e-mail: petek.onur@hum.ku.dk

© The Author(s), under exclusive license to Springer Nature Switzerland AG 2023
C. Raudvere, P. Onur (eds.), *Neo-Ottoman Imaginaries in Contemporary Turkey*, Modernity, Memory and Identity in South-East Europe,
https://doi.org/10.1007/978-3-031-08023-4_8

the last decade neo-Ottomanism has been essential in the political strategies of the ruling AKP (Justice and Development Party, Adalet ve Kalkınma Partisi), expressing the aim of revitalising the power and the glory of the Ottoman Empire in contemporary Turkish society. It redefines Turkish identity with nationalist and Islamic references to history, in opposition to Western, secularist, and republican ideals, and suggests a male-dominant imperial system as grounds for the legitimacy of a gender hierarchy.

This chapter, based on fieldwork exploring the new Ottoman henna nights in Turkey, firstly asks how authenticity and tradition are created as elements of the restorative nostalgia of neo-Ottomanism and, secondly, how women perceive and experience this new tradition and understand its symbolism in regard to their gender roles and status. It claims that, within the processes of constructing and spreading the tradition, claims of authenticity, aesthetics, and the use of history should be considered in relation to a longing for the past. Henna night, a long-standing wedding tradition, which has regained its significance and popularity with a neo-Ottoman touch, stands out as a striking example, particularly in how it revitalises the imperial palace atmosphere with spatial designs, costumes, dances and entertainment, and various visualised details of the harem world.

The theoretical conceptualisations of nostalgia by Svetlana Boym provide the conceptual basis of the study's problematic, which is the relationship between cultural heritage, nostalgia, and the uses of history. The dressing room described above is the backstage and gateway to an evening designed to fulfil the longing for a past shaped by the imaginaries and desires of organisers and customers, and it is right at the centre of this relationship. In her seminal study of nostalgia, *The Future of Nostalgia*, Svetlana Boym (2001) defines the concept as "a longing for a home that no longer exists or has never existed. Nostalgia is a sentiment of loss and displacement, but it is also a romance with one's own fantasy" (Boym 2001, Introduction, para. 4). Boym suggests that these feelings develop due to "an incurable modern condition" arising from the rapid growth of processes connected to globalisation, progress, and modernisation (ibid., Introduction, para. 5). It is not an individual but a collective state of mind that involves a "yearning for a different time—the time of our childhood, the slower rhythms of our dreams. In a broader sense, nostalgia is rebellion against the modern idea of time, the time of history and progress" (ibid., Introduction, para. 11). She defines two types of nostalgia that apply to the relationship between people's past, imagined community, home, and perception of self: restorative nostalgia and reflective nostalgia.

Reflective nostalgia focuses on "longing and loss, the imperfect process of remembrance" (ibid., Chapter 4, para. 2). Those who are captured by reflective nostalgia are very much aware of the fact that time is irreversible, that their home is lost. By contrast, restorative nostalgia dwells upon *nostos*, or returning home, and involves a desire to reconstruct the home lost in the past.

Boym claims that, when nostalgia is articulated to the sphere of politics, romance becomes an essential part of nation building. Accordingly, she argues that the reconstruction of the home, the nation, requires the claims of absolute truth and the revitalisation, or invention, of traditions and symbols. Therefore, for the formation of national identities and movements, and for religious revivalism, restorative nostalgia is central to approaches to the past (Introduction, para. 21–22). Boym emphasises that in restorative nostalgia, "the past is not supposed to reveal any signs of decay; it has to be 'freshly painted' in its 'original image' and remain eternally young" (2001, Chapter 5, para.1). Thus, restorative nostalgia manifests itself in attempts to rebuild the past and history in order to create a common national and religious collective identity, a national memory, and official accounts of history, which leave no space for uncertainties or grey areas. She connects her argument to Eric Hobsbawm's (1983) concept of "invented traditions" which is based on the argument that traditions in modern societies are much more formalised and ritualised than those in traditional societies. In the face of the speed and scale of modernisation, the new traditions tend to be more conservative and fixed. Besides, Hobsbawm argues, the stronger the ties with the past, the more selective its presentation becomes (Hobsbawm 1983, 2–5). According to Boym, an invented tradition provides a relaxing code to ease the feelings of the loss of social bonds and attachments, a code that shows itself in the form of restorative nostalgia by rebuilding the symbols of home and its rituals in order to conquer and spatialise time (Boym 2009, 77, 88). The longing for the power and glamour of the Ottoman era, as the home lost in the past, becomes manifest in the invention of traditions and symbols which visualise that period, as well as reconstructions of history. According to these conceptual grounds, neo-Ottoman henna nights as an invented tradition belong to the sphere of restorative nostalgia, representing endeavours to rebuild the Ottoman home.

Just like nostalgia, the notion of authenticity is a product of the modern age and its socio-political transformations (Bendix 1997). It is a quest that "requires collective work to discover, recognize and authorise the 'real thing', as well as a collective effort to thrust away its opposite" (Fillitz and Saris 2012, 2). It is also a search for the genuine generated by "the anxiety that arises from the fear that modern life is by its nature inauthentic—even counterfeit or spurious" (Upton 2001, 299). Hence, it comprises claims of truth. The authenticity is constructed, approved, consumed, and, in the case of traditions, performed in the alienating world of modernity. But who has the power to authenticate? Who makes the claims of truth and genuineness? Where is the agency of its consumers and performers? These questions are also central to a critical analysis of the new henna nights as cultural repercussions of a political ideology, analysis that dwells upon the ideology's multidimensional and versatile circulation.

Studies that focus on the impact of neo-Ottomanism have been increasing as the ideology further diffuses into social and cultural life with the involvement of both political and civil actors. Esra Özyürek has drawn attention to the political uses of memory in the Turkish public sphere by both secular and Islamist actors who turned public memory into a battleground throughout the history of the Turkish Republic (2006). Jenny B. White's (2012) comprehensive discussion addresses the role of this ideology in the dynamics of the new nationalist-Islamist politics, while Onur Bakıner's (2013) analysis of the majoritarian conservatism in neo-Ottomanism shows that the strategy continues to be a building block in political mobilisation. The cultural and spatial practices and uses of history and neo-Ottomanism are relatively new but flourishing areas of research. Museums such as Miniatürk and the Panorama 1453 History Museum in Istanbul, opened in the AKP period, come to the fore as popular examples of spatial reconstructions of history.[1] Zafer Çeler calls these endeavours "pseudo historicism", which initially gained official status through the AKP's 2005 project entitled "From Tradition to Future", which transformed modern school buildings into Ottoman-Seljuk-style buildings. He notes that similar transformation projects followed for justice palaces (court houses), police headquarters, and local government and municipality buildings (Çeler 2019, 14–15). Batuman's (2019) work also dwells upon and illustrates the politics of new Islamist nation-building with architectural examples from the AKP era and Nora Fisher-Onar (2018) discusses the politics of space in the construction of Ottoman-Islamic imaginary in Istanbul with a nationalist formula.

[1] See Öncü (2010), Bakiner (2013), Bozkuş (2014), and Ergin and Karakaya (2017). For a general discussion of spatial practices see Dorroll (2015).

While setting the stage with spatial transformations, the political actors of neo-Ottomanism have also been following a strategy of creating cultural symbols to mobilise the masses with feelings of resentment, nostalgia, and narcissism (Tokdoğan 2019). These strategies have had their greatest impact thanks to the TV series and movie productions with Ottoman themes that have reached millions of viewers in Turkey, the Middle East, and the Balkans. *Magnificent Century* (*Muhteşem Yüzyıl*), which depicts the glorious years of the reign of Süleyman the Magnificent and his wife Hürrem Sultan, followed by *Resurrection: Ertuğrul* (*Diriliş: Ertuğrul*), which narrates the story of the foundation of the Ottoman State, gained incredible popularity and became the most influential reflections of neo-Ottomanism in contemporary popular culture. A decade after the first broadcast of *Magnificent Century* the trend continues with further historical TV series and box office movies. Their visualisations, imaginaries, and aestheticisation of power, heroism, glamour, and glory have been so strong that they have generated in their audience emotional bonds with Ottoman history (Ergin and Karakaya 2017).[2] Moreover, they opened up new fields of consumption in everyday life and its celebrations, by means of a variety of market offerings for enthusiasts of restorative nostalgia. Last but not least, the representations of history in this setting function to legitimise particular forms of masculinities and femininities, which are shaped by a nationalist-Islamist patriarchy. While the Ottoman roots of Turkish society are highlighted, the patriarchal authority of the sultans and military heroes are presented as the ideal shape of masculinity in both *Magnificent Century* and *Resurrection: Ertuğrul*. Meanwhile, *Magnificent Century* defines women's role as that of a concubine and their place as the harem, a segregated space full of luxury and glamour but with no connection to the outside world. By contrast, *Resurrection* depicts women as having a rather more equal status with men as advisors, leaders, friends, and warriors (Güler 2018); however, the popularity of these female characters remains far behind that of the female characters of *Magnificent Century*, especially the public fascination with Hürrem Sultan.

---

[2] For a discussion of these productions, see Ergin and Karakaya (2017). See also Suner's (2011) analysis of box office movies with Ottoman themes.

Transformation of Customs: Spaces, Symbols, and Womanhood

The dynamic intersections of the spatial, cultural, political, emotional, and gender dimensions of neo-Ottomanism, which feed from a Turco-Islamic, as well as an Orientalist perspective on history has directly led to revitalisations and inventions of traditions in recent years. Many traditions, which had lost their status and significance in the rapid modernisation, Westernisation, and secularisation processes of the Turkish Republic, especially in the cities, started to be re-embraced by urbanites from all social classes as opportunities to express feelings of nostalgia, aspirations for power and status, and neo-Ottoman identity. Henna nights are among those traditions which gained a new outlook, symbolism, and style. They have a rooted history and critical place in wedding ceremonies in Turkish culture—as in India, the Middle East, and North Africa—with the clothes of the brides, the henna songs, and other customs varying from one region to another and constituting a rich cultural heritage. During the rapid modernisation and urbanisation of the early Republican era, the henna night tradition became associated with rural life and backwardness for the new, young, educated urbanites but it continued to be an essential part of wedding celebrations in small towns and villages. Despite diverse local variations, there are common aspects of henna nights. Mostly, female relatives, friends, and neighbours of the bride and her family are invited as guests to the bride's family home in the few days before the wedding. In some regions men are also invited. The guests sing folk songs and dance and are served a meal. The bride, her head covered with a red scarf, sits in the middle of the room; the henna paste, prepared from henna powder and water in advance, is spread on her palms, a gold coin is placed on them by the mother and/or mother-in-law and they are then wrapped in handkerchiefs. The henna stains the skin with its reddish colour, symbolising blood and sacrifice in this rite of passage from girlhood to womanhood (Ustuner et al. 2000). This interpretation, which is widely shared by attendees of henna nights, old and new, "voices a very strict traditional and religious norm which defines the woman's body as an object belonging to the husband", dictating that girls can only transition to womanhood through marriage and that premarital sex is out of the question (Ustuner et al. 2000, 210). The henna paste is offered to the guests after the bride. During the ceremony, the bride is expected to cry; if she does not, it is considered an augur of bad luck and also a sign of her eagerness to leave her home and get married.[3]

Those who migrated from rural areas to cities did not leave their traditions behind and thus henna nights continued to be a part of wedding celebrations in the cities. In addition to holding them in households, henna nights are also organised in the interior and exterior common areas of apartments, streets, coffee houses, and wedding halls. In the 2000s, the children of urban middle and upper-middle-class couples who had rejected henna nights for their own wedding celebrations rediscovered them thanks to the newly expanding wedding sector. However, these gatherings—held in homes, hotels, restaurants, and cafés—were rather modern and largely considered an opportunity for the bride to have fun with her friends and family. The emergence of Ottoman-style henna nights corresponds to the release of *Magnificent Century* in 2011–2014, which was followed by *Magnificent Century: Kösem* (*Muhteşem Yüzyıl: Kösem*) in 2015–2017. Despite the fact that these productions were harshly criticised by the AKP and conservatives in society (Arsan and Yıldırım 2014), their role in getting broader sections of society to remember Ottoman history and its cultural codes, and making them a part of the quotidian life, cannot be ignored. *Resurrection: Ertuğrul* has been the most successful production among the other TV series that followed the Ottomanist trend and has been mostly watched by a nationalist and conservative audience. The imaginaries of the Ottoman era on TV have resulted in the association of prestige, status, and magnificence with palace life, and authentic gender roles with the representations of sultans and warriors in these series. The recent form of henna nights provides a perfect opportunity to observe how these cultural codes are put into practice as part of wedding celebrations.

The historic centre of Ankara (the Citadel region and the neighbourhoods that surround it), which has gone through processes of neglect and decadence, restoration and regeneration, also became the birthplace of the new henna houses, which offer specially decorated places and organisation services for henna nights. Most of these are located in the Hamamarkası neighbourhood, which was largely demolished and re-built in accordance

---

[3] The information about the henna night tradition is gathered from the interviews, personal observation and experiences, and related studies in the field of folklore Turkey, which is very rich and diversified. For some examples, see Korkmaz (1999), Göde (2010), Taşkıran and Şar (2016), Karaca (2016), and Dülger (2019).

with its classical architecture within the scope of the urban regeneration plan of Altındağ Municipality.[4] The goal of this study has been to understand and analyse the construction of the new henna tradition, with a special focus on the space and atmosphere of palace nostalgia which it creates, and how it symbolises womanhood. For this purpose fieldwork was conducted in April–November 2019, which comprised interviews with seven women who had a henna night and four henna house owners in Hamamarkası—and one in the Çayyolu district of Ankara in order to compare the impact of location. All interviewed brides were university graduates; two of them had a master's degree. Central to fieldwork was observation of nine henna nights held in two henna houses in Hamamarkası and in three other districts of the city. To gain a broader picture of the place of henna rituals in the wedding sector, in-depth interviews were also conducted in Istanbul with the owner of the largest wedding fair organisation company and the first specialised henna night organiser in Turkey. Visual and textual materials on the web pages and social media accounts of the henna houses constitute the study's secondary data.

Creating a Space: Mansions, Alternative Spaces, and Creative Actors

The first spaces to be specially decorated and designed for Ottoman henna nights were in some sixteen new mansions in Hamamarkası—a rather small region of a few streets rebuilt in 2012–2019—with new ones about to be opened at the time of research. The first, opened by Altındağ Municipality, attracted wedding organisers and entrepreneurs and swiftly became a lucrative business. The henna houses look rather simple on the outside (Fig. 8.1) but their interior decorations are very glittery and colourful (Fig. 8.2).

The predominance of gold plating and the vivid colours of red and turquoise are noticeable at first sight, all of which are associated with the aesthetics of Ottoman palace decorations. Furthermore, decorative details suggesting authenticity, such as kaftans, tughras, helmets, satin and velvet textiles, replicas of orientalist paintings, and mirrors are all meticulously chosen by the owners of the henna houses to recreate the atmosphere of the Topkapı Palace—the sultans' residence from 1478 to 1853—as

---

[4] For more detail on the transformation of the area and the recent nostalgia culture see Onur (2018).

8 THE NEW OTTOMAN HENNA NIGHTS AND WOMEN IN THE PALACE... 217

Fig. 8.1 The current outlook of Hamamarkası, with its rebuilt mansions, is in stark contrast with the demolished neighbourhood preceding it: an area of urban decay with neglected houses, poverty, and high crime rates. (Photograph by author)

represented in TV series and orientalist art. In this setting a throne for the bride is a must and the more flamboyant it is, the better. In front of the throne there is a dance floor while guests are seated along the walls on *sedi*rs, Turkish-style sofas.

> We visited henna houses here and tried to apply what we saw in others. Certainly, they [the TV series] influenced us. The throne, the lights, the costumes... They influenced us in terms of decorations.... and people can suggest many things, the new generation. We also consider these. (Emrah, henna house owner in Hamamarkası, personal interview, 05.10.2019)[5]

Most attendees at henna nights are women, with the mansions holding 100–120 guests. The groom and other men wait outside the main room,

[5] Interviews conducted in the period 08-11.2019. All interviewees' names are anonymised.

Fig. 8.2 Interiors of henna houses in Hamamarkası compete with one another in adopting imageries of Ottoman luxury and authenticity. (Photograph by author)

sometimes in the garden or in the doorway, until they are invited in for the henna ceremony. There is a dressing room for the bride and the dancers/bridesmaids, and a small kitchen. One mansion also has a *masjid* (prayer room). The houses offer their small courtyards for henna nights during the summer, should their customers prefer. The courtyards lack the intense harem atmosphere of the interiors but the presence of thrones reminds the bride and the guests of Ottoman nostalgia.

An exception to the neo-Ottoman trend in Hamamarkası is the Kalıpçızade mansion, which has preserved its museum-like authenticity as it was personally restored by its owners, the Kalıpçı family, thus remaining outside of the municipality's regeneration project. The family had lived there for three generations before eventually moving out and repurposing the building to operate as a venue for *ferfene*s,[6] weddings, engagements, henna nights, and other private events. The owners had been very critical of the new Ottoman henna nights for several years, finding them kitsch, inauthentic, and disrespectful of tradition, but finally adopted some elements themselves, such as the throne, palace costumes, and the henna night program, in order not to lose potential customers.

It is no surprise that other places in Ankara where henna nights are held, such as modern henna houses and wedding halls, have also been attempting to create harem-like spaces for their customers. One of these places is Ihlamur Kasrı (Linden Palace) at the heart of Keçiören, a predominantly conservative district in Ankara (Fig. 8.3). It is a large complex comprising several wedding halls with the capacity to host 200–400 guests.

Another venue for henna nights, which I observed outside Hamamarkası, was in Çayyolu, a suburban district of Ankara with a largely secular, Republican population. It was opened by Leyla and Sermet, who sold their henna house in Hamamarkası and opened a new one here with an Indian theme, encouraged by what they saw as a promising potential customer base. It is a large space in a modern apartment with the capacity for 200–300 guests. In a personal interview for my previous study of nostalgia culture in Ankara, Leyla had explained that *Magnificent Century* and Hürrem Sultan had inspired the decoration and henna costumes (Onur 2018, 160). Yet this new henna house seems to be rather influenced by an Indian imperial-style imaginary, copied from other Indian-themed henna nights. Two brides and another organiser mentioned in the same series of interviews that Indian and Gypsy[7] henna nights had emerged as alternative themes, even though their contents and programme resemble one another. In one of the upper-class neighbourhoods of Ankara there is also a henna costume shop particularly catering to Indian-style henna nights.

---

[6] *Ferfene* is a tradition of winter public dinners where people exchange ideas, disseminate knowledge on a particular subject, sing folk songs, and dance. It is part of Ankara's intangible cultural heritage.

[7] Acknowledging the differences in approaches to the usage of the terms Gypsy and Roma, I prefer to use Gypsy when it is used by the respondents and the henna organisers.

Fig. 8.3 Ihlamur Kasrı bears a very strong resemblance to the Ottoman-Seljuk architectural projects of the AKP era. (Photograph by author)

The third place outside Hamamarkası was a henna house located in Oran district of Çankaya, another predominantly secular, Republican district of the city. Although it is a detached house with modern architecture, the interior is decorated to evoke Turkish-Ottoman authenticity and a more modest level of glamour (Fig. 8.4). Unlike the other henna places, a full dinner with alcohol is served, and men and women can sit together throughout the night if they prefer. Colours of blue and gold, and velvet and satin textiles are used in decoration, with a combination of *sedir* and table settings.

Istanbul, the capital city of the Ottoman Empire, offers well-off families a choice of places to experience heritage and nostalgia. Çırağan Palace, Sait Halim Paşa Yalısı,[8] and a few other historic mansions and small palaces on the Bosporus, which have been turned into hotels or hospitality venues, are the perfect places for luxurious henna nights and weddings. Furthermore, Mehmet, the founder of the first henna-party company and the trendsetter in the sector explained that, if his wealthiest customers

---

[8] *Yalı*, which literally means coast, is a specific, historical, architectural form of residence on the coastline of the Bosphorus built in the Ottoman era. A *yalı* is a two or three-storey building right beside the sea with a small garden and a small pier.

Fig. 8.4 A velvet sofa with satin pillows is preferred here as the bride's throne. (Photograph by author)

request it, his company can transform the halls of five-star hotels into Çırağan Palace or any other specific historic mansion/*yalı* by covering the walls with traditional fabrics and bringing in furniture and decorative items.

Proliferating companies like Mehmet's in the wedding sector provide a wide range of options in decorations, bridal costumes, party favours, and program features. Mehmet told me that during the early years, his company used floor cushions for an authentic seating touch but in recent years, it has started to offer various thrones, which Mehmet designs. He noted that now none of the brides would prefer to sit on the floor, explaining that they had been influenced by the decorations in the *Magnificent Century*, especially in the early 2010s when customers started to demand the ambience that they saw on the TV series. This was also affirmed by Sena, who has organised the largest wedding fair in Istanbul since 2002; both noted, however, that the Ottoman trend in henna nights has been in decline in Istanbul since 2016 and almost none of their customers now request the theme.

The annual wedding fair in Istanbul and Mehmet's company are the major actors in the henna sector that determine the trends—mostly according to popular culture, global fashions, and their own creative ideas—aiming to offer novelties every year. However, the organisers in

Ankara follow a more consistent style, one which has roots in the neo-Ottoman transformation in Hamamarkası. One of the most essential features of the reconstruction of the henna-night tradition is creating a space that evokes the lost home, the Ottoman heritage associated with imperial palaces of Istanbul, meanwhile claiming the space's authenticity. Accordingly, the henna spaces are aestheticised to ensure that the bride and the guests find themselves caught up in a sultan's harem entertainment and yet the imaginaries of this entertainment closely resemble orientalist depictions of the harem in Western art and in the TV series.

TOOLS AND SIGNS OF AUTHENTICITY, TRADITION, AND HERITAGE EMBEDDED IN ENTERTAINMENT

The organisers design the henna nights so to ensure the bride and the guests experience and perform authenticity, thanks to the commoditisation of the tradition and rituals. Performative authenticity, a concept which is discussed in the field of heritage tourism studies (Daniel 1996; Knudsen and Waade 2010; Zhu 2012), illuminates how the cultural and/or emotional distance between the customers and the neo-Ottoman henna tradition and its spaces is overcome. Authentication or the production of authenticity "has become a strategy to appropriate sites and places and a strategy to invest emotionally in places" and authenticity is now seen as "something experienced through the body, through performance, management and media, authenticity becomes a feeling you can achieve" (Knudsen and Waade 2010, 5). Contemplating the flow of the henna nights from this perspective reveals how the henna spaces are appropriated by the agents who construct the tradition to achieve this feeling.

For those seeking to hold a henna night in Ankara, the mansions in Hamamarkası present themselves as historic, nostalgic, traditional, and authentic options at an affordable price. It is particularly for this reason that some lower and middle-class couples prefer to have their wedding and henna night on the same day in these mansions. The set of services which are called "henna night packages" include between two and five bridesmaids/dancers, the bride's henna kaftan or *bindallı*,[9] eight to ten *bindallı*s

---

[9] *Bindallı* is the common name for traditional Turkish henna dresses or long jackets which are mostly made of velvet or satin and embroidered with gold or silver lace. The term literally means "with a thousand branches" because the decorations are mostly in flower, leaf, or branch patterns.

for the bride's friends and sisters, a tambourine and drum, the groom's scarf and fez, dried nuts and fruits, small pastries, soft drinks, tea, Turkish coffee, photo and video shoots, plastic flowers and candles, a belly dancer, a DJ, a *rengarenk* belt (adorned with long, colourful ribbons), henna tray, *lokum* (Turkish delight) and rose water, and an artist who draws Indian henna patterns on the guests' hands. Pricing ranges from just the rent of the mansion to the all-inclusive luxury package. The organisers who were interviewed stated that prices as well as lifestyles determine a bride's preferences. For instance, veiled women of conservative families and upper-middle-class, highly educated, professional women who are in their 30s omit the dancers and the belly dance show, and the latter group's henna nights are rather simple and modest. The most demanding customers are brides in their early 20s with lower levels of education who do not work, either for personal reasons or because they are unemployed. Erdem, a henna house owner, mentioned that some of these women wanted to wear three or four different kaftans on the night. Most of the interviewees also emphasised the role of social media, particularly Instagram posts by friends and celebrities, in clients' decisions about the style and novelties in the program. Ultimately, a customised package is shaped by numerous social, economic, and cultural factors, meaning that the brides are also significant actors, shaping the tradition with their preferences.

Henna nights mostly begin at 19.00, although afternoons can be preferred. In an all-inclusive "deluxe" or "Kösem Sultan" package the guests are welcomed by bridesmaids dressed in their *bindallı*s and served *lokum* (Turkish delight) and rose water at the entrance and, when they are seated, Ottoman sherbet is served. The sherbet is ready-made in the henna mansions in Hamamarkası while in more expensive places it is handmade. In Ihlamur Kasrı, where the henna night was organised by a henna event company, the sherbet was served in glasses, which were placed on a special cage-like skirt worn by one of the bridesmaids. A henna artist who will stay throughout the night starts to visit the tables, asking guests if they would like to have Indian henna on their hands, arms, and sometimes ankles. The Indian henna style is preferred for its lesser permanence, fast and practical application, and aesthetic patterns. Meanwhile, the bride has a photoshoot, which takes place outside the hall, mostly in specially decorated spots or on the street if the organisation is in Hamamarkası.

After the photoshoot the bride is prepared by her mother, close friends, and the organiser in the dressing room while the organiser explains the flow of the evening. Then the bridesmaids, who will be dancers for the rest of the event, demonstrate the choreography of the opening dance which they will perform with the bride. The organiser also asks if the family has a special henna tradition, which they want to perform, and mostly they receive a "no" from the bride's mother. After the arrival of the guests, the henna night begins with the opening dance by the bride and the dancers. In several high-society henna nights in Istanbul in 2018 the brides were brought to the hall in an open palanquin called a *tefur* carried on the shoulders of male dancers, and at the henna night of famous model Esin, the bride came to the building on horseback. Large, flashy, satin shawls, ribbons, or hand fans are used, which seem to be inspired by Chinese fan dances (Fig. 8.5, top) The choreographies, costumes, and show music are almost the same at most of the henna nights. After the first dance the bride sits on her throne and the music continues while the food and beverages are served. The bride chats with the guests who come to sit on the smaller sofas or floor cushions beside the throne as if to enact a scene from a nineteenth-century painting of harem life. The dancers invite the guests to dance throughout the night; an empty dance floor seems to be an indication of a lack of entertainment and, therefore, a less successful event. Popular songs for henna nights are modernised folk songs, Oriental dance songs in Arabic, and Turkish pop songs of the 1990s, which recently became very popular among the youth as "oldies but goldies". At the henna nights of Azeri and Kurdish families, their own folk music was played and most of the guests took part in folk dances throughout the night. The dancers perform another 4–5-minute dance show with different costumes and accessories 30–40 minutes after the opening.

At around 20:00–20:30, the dancers and friends take the bride back to the dressing room and she gets prepared for the henna ceremony. If the bride has been wearing another dress, she dons her kaftan or *bindallı*. The friends and sisters also wear their *bindallı*s, which are plainer than the bride's, and gather up candles and/or flowers; the organisers prepare the henna tray. They all enter the hall to the sounds of *Yüksek Yüksek Tepeler*, the best-known henna folk song. The bride is seated on a chair in the middle of the dance floor and the dancers and the friends encircle her, singing the song. The groom enters the hall at this point accompanied by a dancer playing a drum, his brothers, and close friends. This intrusion into the female environment is called the *damat baskını* (groom's raid). He is seated next to the bride and a bridesmaid enters the hall, dancing while holding a red gauze scarf. Red is also preferred in *bindallı*s for its symbolic meanings and on this occasion it resonates with the colour of

8 THE NEW OTTOMAN HENNA NIGHTS AND WOMEN IN THE PALACE... 225

Fig. 8.5 *Top*: The opening dance show in Ihlamur Kasrı. The bride has taken her place on the gilt throne surrounded by other gilt Turco-Islamic ornaments. The large screen at the back welcomes the guests with a photograph of red roses and candles. (Photograph by author). *Middle*: Couple dancing after the henna ceremony to an Ankara folk song. (Photograph by author). *Bottom*: Filiz and her husband are joining a Romani dance. (Photograph by Uygar Bulut)

henna and thus with blood, sacrifice, and virginity. The dancer covers the bride's head with the gauze and a green scarf is put around the groom's shoulders. A star and crescent are embroidered on the scarves, symbolising the Turkish flag, while the green colour symbolises Islam. An elderly woman from the family of the bride or groom is invited to spread henna on the hands of the couple, who refuse to open their hands; meanwhile the mothers of the couple are invited to the dance floor. The bride's mother puts a gold coin in the groom's palm and the groom's mother puts a gold coin in the bride's palm and then the woman on henna duty puts a small amount of henna in each palm and wraps their hands with a handkerchief. Most couples do not want the henna, finding it too traditional, conservative, or rural, and choose to wear symbolic bracelets of red plastic flowers instead. After the ceremony, the couple dances alone on the dance floor for a song or two until other guests join them (Fig. 8.5, middle).

Henna houses also add their special touches to the ceremony. Emrah's house asks the bride to break a terracotta jug, Leyla and Sermet ask the groom to let out a yell and the bride to drop her handkerchief in response, to resemble a pre-modern way of communication between lovers. At the Kalıpçızade mansion, they ask the couple to spread butter onto a tree in the garden and then hammer in a nail to wish for a smooth and happy as well as solid and long-lasting marriage. The person who applies the henna may say a prayer and wish the couple good luck. In Çayyolu, Leyla makes a small speech, which is also commonly repeated in the ceremonies:

> Do you know when henna is applied? To the young men who are about to go to their military service, for them to sacrifice themselves for their country; to the sheep to be sacrificed, for them to sacrifice themselves for Allah; and to the newly-wed brides, for them to sacrifice themselves to their husbands and families.

Yüksek Yüksek Tepeler (*On High Hills*) as rendered by pop singer Candan Erçetin is played again during the ceremony and after that *Kına Gecesi* (*Henna Night*), a song by another pop singer Yeşim Salkım, is played rather than local folk songs.

A belly dance show follows or precedes the henna ceremony. The groom and his male friends and family members can stay and dance until the end of the night (Fig. 8.5, middle) or leave after the ceremony. Later on, the bridesmaids/dancers wearing colourful long skirts present a Romani dance show (Fig. 8.5, bottom). Towards the end of the henna night, there is a final entertainment for the bride and guests, called *rengârenk* (colourful). The bride dons the beribboned *rengarenk* belt and each guest around her takes one long ribbon and dances to Sertap Erener's *Rengârenk*, a Turkish cover of *Ringa Ringa*, a popular song on the soundtrack of the Indian movie *Slumdog Millionaire*. The dance is influenced by Erener's video of it,[10] in which she dances in a long colourful skirt, and her dance in the Eurovision song contest.[11] Henna nights mostly end with pop music, and one of the henna houses plays a popular rock song. The entertainment is finished by 22:00 in Hamamarkası because of local regulations, and by 23:00 in other places, and guests start to leave after taking a photo with the bride. At some henna nights party favours of the night are given to the guests before the farewell.

Certain adjustments which are made for strictly conservative families whose women members and guests are veiled were observed in the fieldwork and also mentioned by the organisers. These include omitting all dance shows, holding women-only events—extending to staff and photographers—choosing kaftans or *bindallı*s according to the veiling style and preferences,[12] and collecting guests' smartphones at the reception desk.

The organisers design and customise the henna night tradition to make the brides feel they are more than special, thanks to the thrones and crowns; the brides are also the centre of attention, unlike the wedding when they share attention with the groom. What makes contemporary henna nights different are their playfulness and imageries of how to be sultan of the harem, merged with a diversity of claimed-to-be authentic symbolism blended with Ottoman nostalgia. This range of symbolism indicates restorative nostalgia, which essentially bears a dimension of power and authority. In *Simulacra and Simulations*, Jean Baudrillard

---

[10] https://www.youtube.com/watch?v=KctSHOFo2ig, (03.08.2022).
[11] EurovisionFanTV (n.d.) https://www.youtube.com/watch?v=cJksu8XxZCo (15.10.2020).
The official video of the song was shot in a historic Turkish bath and Topkapı Palace: https://www.youtube.com/watch?v=bRAjf9rFA58 (15.10.2020). It was harshly criticised and first censored and then banned by the state television for the scenes associated with lesbianism and drug abuse.
[12] Sometimes the styling can go to extremes. The organiser at the Kalıpçızade mansion told me about a veiled bride, dressed by her mother early in the morning that summer, who fainted and was hospitalised at the end of the night because her kaftan and the layers of skirts underneath were too heavy and her stockings and scarves too tight.

suggests a strong causality between the decline of power and the increase in the collective demand for signs that resemble power as a form of substitute.

> When it has totally disappeared, we will logically be under the total hallucination of power—a haunting memory that is already in evidence everywhere, expressing at once the compulsion to get rid of it (no one wants it anymore, everyone unloads it on everyone else) and the panicked nostalgia over its loss. (Baudrillard 2006, 23)

Baudrillard argues that the simulation of power is left when actual power does not exist anymore and the demand for signs of power emerges. In the field of politics, signs of power are now mass produced and consumed like commodities (2006, 26). In Turkey, the increasing demand for the symbols which are thought to represent power should be understood as an expression of mourning for the loss of the sovereign power of the Ottoman Empire. Furthermore, the demand, supply, and consumption of the symbols take place in a nationalist-Islamist political framework that guides the neo-liberal economy in which the wedding sector operates. Lastly, it is also clear that the particular playfulness in the nostalgia for the Ottoman era and the performances of authenticity exhibits a self-orientalism in its emulations of harem entertainments as depicted in Western Orientalist art. The resemblances of the aesthetic features of the night and the performances of the actors to these depictions may not be intentional but are incontrovertible.[13]

NEW MEANINGS, NEW WOMANHOODS

Watching the mesmerising henna nights described above has left the impression on me that they must provide an incomparable experience for the brides, with all their imperial nostalgia. Furthermore, it is apparent that the tradition has gained a new meaning that differs from its old connotations of self-sacrifice, sad farewell to the family home, and bridal virginity. Therefore, one of the most significant interview questions concerned the meaning of henna and the henna night for the bride. Responses mentioned the protection it provides from bad luck and the evil eye, the way it

---

[13] I would like to thank Kerem Öktem for his contribution of the concepts of playfulness and self-orientalism.

symbolises the beginning of a new life for women, its links to Turkmen culture and unification with nature, and the fact that it was an opportunity for informal entertainment before the wedding and the sanctification of marriage. The common statement the brides made about the experience was, "We had so much fun"; indeed, some interviewees mentioned that they had more fun at the henna night than at their wedding. This emphasis shows that joy and fun has a central place in the contemporary henna nights. Brides rarely touched on concepts like sadness, nostalgia, and devotion to family—a strong indication that the new experiences have become a completely contradictory phenomena to the previous understandings of the practice.

> I said I didn't want to cry, I didn't want those sayings or songs [made] for crying, [although] I think it is in the tradition. An emotionality over the woman's transition from old to new roots and adaptation. I rejected that. I thought that in fact it had to be a celebration. (Filiz, bride, personal interview, 11.10.2019)
>
> I didn't see it as a big process. I took it as a party with a concept. ... It wasn't the day of my life. It wasn't very boring either. All the dancers, costumes, and such. ... It's something like, "Why do you wear a wedding dress in your wedding?" It is a formality. (Özlem, bride, personal interview, 26.08.2019)

Özlem, who had her henna night in Oran, also unsympathetically suggested that the popularity of henna nights had to be due to the preference for women-only entertainment, which is related to the increasing Islamic conservatism in society. On the other hand, she told that she, as the daughter of a Kemalist Republican family, had a mufti wedding before the official wedding and she found it more meaningful and spiritual than her other wedding rituals and ceremonies.

The second question was why henna nights are preferred over modern alternatives such as a bachelors' or engagement party. Pressures by mothers came up as one of the dominant reasons.

> The decline [in demand] already began in 2017–2018. The new generation does not want henna. 80% of [the parties] are at the will of the mothers or mothers-in-law or friends. They [the brides] do not want traditional things very much. (Mehmet, henna organiser in Hamamarkası, personal interview, 05.10.2019)

I wanted a simple marriage ceremony but I have friends from the sector. One of them is a henna organiser, one of them is the owner of a very important magazine, *Evleniyoruz* (*We're Getting Married*) ... They said, "We cannot let you have a simple wedding ceremony. We will have hamam, henna, we will get spoiled." Then I surrendered. My mother also wanted it very much; she wanted to invite her friends. We had a few arguments with her because of this. (Esin, bride, personal interview, 02.11.2019)

People want to host their guests in flamboyant and luxurious places. I think the mothers' influence counts a lot in this. I'm sure that a bride and a groom from the new generation would prefer a country wedding. I think that social pressures cause this. ... In one in three couples I clearly observe that it is the mothers who want henna. It is a tradition. Even if they [parents] don't have enough money, they get credit, sell their car and make a henna [night] and wedding. (Mine, henna organiser in Hamamarkası, personal interview, 10.10.2019)

Organising the henna night is traditionally the responsibility of the bride's mother; thus, it is also an opportunity for the bride's family to demonstrate wealth and status, a performance, which can be measured against the wedding, which is organised by the groom's family. This combines the traditional codes and customs of wedding preparations and celebrations of the past with the concerns of creating a wealthy and prestigious image of the family. The bachelor party option rarely replaces a henna night in this context because of the inappropriateness of inviting elderly family members to such an event. Ostentatious celebrations have turned into status symbols and a wedding on its own is not seen as sufficient in this regard.

Another pressing concept to be discussed is the agency of the women within the boundaries of a reinvented tradition. Filiz particularly addressed the issue by stating that in the past women did not have a say in their henna nights, which were defined by devotion and sacrifice, but now their views are taken into account, while the dancing and having fun make them feel powerful. Therefore, restorative nostalgia in this context becomes a tool of empowerment and freedom. Some interviewees also stated that the costumes, a henna crown or tiara, the throne, and other features that created the Ottoman palace atmosphere, made them feel like a sultan themselves. The expansion of the henna sector in connection with the wedding sector and the resulting diversification in products and services on offer are important factors generating these feelings and self-perceptions. Henna nights have become more sophisticated over time thanks to the expanding sector and the creation of a demand for novelties. Mehmet explained that he could hardly find authentic henna items to use in his first show at the 2008 wedding fair. Today, however, the henna sector boasts thousands of henna organisers, styling specialists, dancers, photographers, owners of henna houses and other venues, henna artists, providers of food and beverages, kaftan and *bindallı* tailors, manufacturers of hundreds of items used in a henna night such as plastic flowers, candles, tableware and other decorations, drums and tambourines, dance costumes, thrones and other furniture, henna trays, and all kinds of bridal accessories. Women who find themselves in a decision-making position in this world of glamour tend to experience a sense of empowerment, even though it may be just an illusion. Furthermore, the joy and fun involved in consuming the nostalgic items and services boost the sense of freedom.

Nonetheless, nostalgia for a lost or imagined past is also a dominant feeling among the brides, with the space being the main determining factor. It is particularly expressed by those women who had their henna night in Hamamarkası. Berna observed that she had always dreamed of having a photo album just like her grandparents' and Hamamarkası was the perfect location for her. Zeynep too mentioned that the historic atmosphere of the locale and the mansions were a determining factor in her choice, besides the affordable prices and the opportunity to have the henna night in a garden. Filiz's henna night was at Kalıpçızade mansion (Fig. 8.5) because of the couple's reflective nostalgia. As she told me, "We love the past. That's why we found a Vosvos [Volkswagen Beetle] for our wedding. … For the henna night, I found a very old second-hand gypsy dress which had been really worn." That was the reason why she chose that place without hesitation:

> Because the atmosphere was nice, the courtyard, the place was an old house; some people had lived there… [the owner was born there] It is magnificent! The life experiences of all those people… so that place really impressed us. I said OK without talking about the price. I felt that I belonged there to that extent. (Personal interview, 11.10.2019)

Her second reason was her objection to the women-only entertainment offered by other henna houses. She finds them "wanna-be Ottoman" and insulting to women, and thus sought an authenticity which was compatible with her modern Turkish Alevi-Bektashi identity.[14]

Esin's henna night is a significant case for observation and discussion due to its widely spread codes of meaning in the intersections of popular culture, heritage, politics, power, and gender relations. The henna night, which Mehmet organised in a country club in Istanbul, began with her short horseback ride to the hall; she and her husband wore sultan costumes designed by a famous fashion designer and, as a reference to Hürrem Sultan and Süleyman the Magnificent in the harem in the TV series, she kissed the skirt of her husband's kaftan. As expected, the night made the headlines of the magazine press and social media for a long time, some of which criticised its Ottoman nostalgia and symbols of women's submissiveness. In my interview with her, Esin explained that the event was her friends' gift and she wanted to thank them with publicity, and so made those gestures she "learned from Hürrem". Creating a scene with codes of traditionalism, patriarchy, Ottoman heritage, and nostalgia, the reception and dissemination of these cultural codes via all kinds of media will, in turn, encourage the continuation of neo-Ottoman henna nights and the reproduction of the related symbolism of gender roles. As Mehmet stated, "Recently, high society's interest in henna nights has increased. The henna [event] we did for Esin drew the attention of many celebrities." He added that he was proud to revitalise this tradition.

The Future of Nostalgia

The new Ottoman henna night is a reconstructed tradition in contemporary Turkey's social, economic, political, and cultural context. It is the outcome of neo-Ottoman politics and a product of popular culture and the burgeoning wedding sector, as well as being deeply connected with the social dynamics of decades of rural to urban migration and the changing cityscape and city culture. Discussions of women's gender roles, status, and empowerment find fuel in elements of new henna nights, which, in addition to, and perhaps despite, all the vitality of these issues, come to the fore as a fascinating form of entertainment and playfulness with their restorative nostalgia for the Ottoman era. The tendency to standardise henna nights with common constructions of authenticity and aesthetic

---

[14] She explained that in Alevi-Bektashi culture men and women come together in worship and entertainment.

preferences leads to a loss of local variations in customs and traditions—already almost forgotten—and, thus, cultural diversity, replacing it with Orientalist representations and imageries of Ottoman heritage. The actors in the process whom this chapter examines, namely, the organisers and the brides, perceive it as new, yet authentic entertainment, but there is also an aspect of self-Orientalism, of perceiving the Turkish culture through a Western lens. The change at stake reminds us that forgetting and remembering are active processes in the case of traditions, play a determining role in self-definitions, and generate a sense of belonging to the cultural heritage of a nation. While the sweeping trend of Ottoman henna nights has almost ended in Istanbul, it seems that it will have a longer life in Ankara, with the addition of occasions such as university graduation, baby's *mevlut*[15] and sixth-month celebrations, and boys' circumcision ceremonies, with minor adaptations. This offers a further field to examine and analyse in order to understand ongoing changes in the tradition.

The influence of the transformation of henna nights on gender, womanhood, and women's self-perceptions has two main aspects. Firstly, the expansion of the sector and the diversification of services and goods in the market give women the message that they are in power on the henna night from the point that they start to invest in symbols of power: a kaftan, a crown, bridesmaids, and everything that is designed to remind her she is the sultan of the night. Yet it is evident that this power is both illusionary and temporary as well as class-bound. The glamour and power symbols of a henna night in an Ottoman palace in Istanbul are not comparable with a lower-class henna night in Hamamarakası or a small wedding hall. While the bride in the former is "getting spoiled", it is a matter of budget whether all the desirable trappings of a dream wedding and henna night may be fulfilled in the latter. Although both may be designed with the purpose of creating a common illusion, what the less wealthy families experience tends to be a replica of a replica.

The construction of tradition and modernity is the second aspect that determines the self-definition and self-perception of women. The conservatism of AKP politics is diffusing into society in creative and sometimes

[15] *Mevlud* or *Mevlid* is a poem written by Süleyman Çelebi who was an imam in Bursa in 1409. The poem narrates Prophet Muhammed's life and it is recited on the day of the prophet's birth (*Mevlid Kandili*) and other sacred days, for praying for a new-born baby's health, at funerals and anniversaries of a loved one's death, and other special occasions significant in a person's life. (*Türkiye Diyanet Vakfı İslam Ansiklopedisi, Mevlid*, https://islamansiklopedisi.org.tr/mevlid%2D%2Dsuleyman-celebi, (22.01.2021).

subtle ways and this becomes evident in the increasing significance attributed to marriage and, accordingly, wedding celebrations. Old traditions are revitalised and added to the assemblage of more modern ones to form a long list of occasions and events to announce and celebrate the couple's new life: proposal, betrothal celebrated among the nuclear families directly involved, a larger engagement party, bride's hamam, henna night, religious marriage (known as imam marriage or mufti marriage), bachelor party or girls' night out, wedding, and, finally, honeymoon. The conservative pressures on couples, especially women, to get married remain strong or are even strengthening, and the celebrations serve the function of convincing the couples, particularly women, that marriage is a fascinating and magnificent stage in life. Popular culture, social media, conservative politics, all agree on this point. It is the case whether you are a famous model who has lived an independent life for twenty years or a young woman who has never heard of a henna night being held in her family before.

The rapid pace and unstable nature of social changes and long-lasting crisis in Turkey and its unique experiences of modernity as a post-imperial country generate a further longing for the past or its imaginaries, if in diverse ways. Enabling us to dwell on the impact of this contemporary form of nostalgia on women's status and gender roles, henna nights will seemingly continue to be a subject of analysis.

Acknowledgment This chapter is based on the research entitled "Yeni Osmanlı Kına Geceleri ve Saray Nostaljisi İçinde Kadınlar" ("New Ottoman Henna Nights and Women in Palace Nostalgia"), which received Sabancı University, Gender and Women's Studies Center of Excellence, 2018 Şirin Tekeli Research Award. I am deeply grateful and honoured to receive this award.

References

Arsan, Esra and Yasemin Yıldırım. 2014. Reflections of Neo-Ottomanist Discourse in Turkish News Media: The Case of The Magnificent Century. *Journal of Applied Journalism & Media Studies* 3 (13): 315–334.

Bakiner, Onur. 2013. Is Turkey Coming to Terms with Its Past? Politics of Memory and Majoritarian Conservatism. *Nationalities Papers* 41 (5): 691–708.

Batuman, Bülent. 2019. *Milletin Mimarisi: Yeni İslamcı Ulus İnşasının Kent ve Mekân Siyaseti*. İstanbul: Metis.

Baudrillard, Jean. 2006. *Simulacra and Simulation*. Ann Arbor: The University of Michigan Press.

Bendix, Regina. 1997. *In Search of Authenticity: The Formation of Folklore Studies*. Madison: University of Wisconsin Press.

Boym, Svetlana. 2001. *The Future of Nostalgia*. New York: Basic Books, Amazon Kindle E-Book Edition.

Bozkuş, Şeyda Barlas. 2014. Rethinking Nationalism in the Case of 1453 Conquest Museum in Istanbul. *Global Media Journal: Turkish Edition* 4 (8): 1–12.

Çeler, Zafer. 2019. Pseudo-Historicism and Architecture: The New Ottomanism in Turkey. *Journal of Balkan and Near Eastern Studies* 21 (5): 493–514.

Daniel, Yvonne Payne. 1996. Tourism Dance Performances Authenticity and Creativity. *Annals of Tourism Research* 23 (4): 780–797.

Dorroll, Courtney M. 2015. *The Spatial Politics of Turkey's Justice and Development Party (AK Party): On Erdoganian Neo-Ottomanism*. Unpublished PhD dissertation, School of Middle Eastern and North African Studies. Tucson: University of Arizona.

Dülger, Cansu. 2019. İzmir Ödemiş'te Kına Gecesi Âdetleri. *Folklor Akademi Dergisi* 2 (1): 53–68.

Ergin, Murat and Yağmur Karakaya. 2017. Between Neo-Ottomanism and Ottomania: Navigating State-Led and Popular Cultural Representations of the Past. *New Perspectives on Turkey* 56: 33–59.

EurovisionFanTV. *Sertap Erener—Everway That I Can* (Turkey—Final—Eurovision Song Contest 2003). Accessed October 15, 2020. https://www.youtube.com/watch?v=cJksu8XxZCo.

Fillitz, Thomas and A. Jamie Saris. 2012. Authenticity Aujourd'hui. In *Debating Authenticity: Concepts of Modernity in Anthropological Perspective*, ed. Thomas Fillitz and A. Jamie Saris. Oxford: Berghahn Books.

Fisher-Onar, Nora. 2018. Between Neo-Ottomanism and Neoliberalism. In *Istanbul: Living with Difference in a Global City*, ed. Nora Fisher-Onar, S.C. Pierce, and E. Fuat Keyman, 1–21. New Brunswick, NJ: Rutgers University Press.

Göde, Halil A. 2010. Kına Türküleri Üzerine. *Folklor/Edebiyat* 16 (64): 163–180.

Güler, Elif. 2018. The Symbolic Restoration of Women's Place in Turkey's Resurrection. *Studies in Popular Culture* 40 (2): 97–116.

Hobsbawm, Eric J. 1983. Introduction: Inventing Traditions. In *Invention of Tradition*, ed. Eric J. Hobsbawm and Terence Ranger, 1–14. Cambridge: Cambridge University Press.

Knudsen, Britta Timm and Anne Marit Waade. 2010. Performative Authenticity in Tourism and Spatial Experience: Rethinking the Relations between Travel, Place and Emotion. In *Re-Investing Authenticity: Tourism, Place and Emotions*, ed. Britta Timm Knudsen and Anne Marit Waade, 1–19. Berlin: De Gruyter.

Korkmaz, Kürşat M. 1999. Elli Yıl Önceki Gaziantep'te Gelin ve Damat. *Milli Folklor* 11 (43): 77–82.

Sertab Erener, *Rengârenk*. Accessed August 03, 2022. https://www.youtube.com/watch?v=KctSHOFo2ig

Öncü, Ayşe. 2010. Narratives of Istanbul's Ottoman Heritage and Competing Political Claims to its Present. In *Spatial Conceptions of the Nation: Modernizing Geographies in Greece and Turkey*, ed. Nikiforos Diamandouros, Caglar Keyder and Thalia Dragonas, 205–228. London: IB Tauris.

Onur, Petek. 2018. Re-creating Nostalgia: Urban Culture in Citadel, Hamamönü and Hamamarkası Neighbourhoods of Ankara. *Ankara Araştırmaları Dergisi* 6 (2): 145–166.

Özyürek, Esra. 2006. *Nostalgia for the Modern: State Secularism and Everyday Politics in Turkey*. Durham, NC: Duke University Press.

Sertab Erener. *Everyway That I Can Album Version*. Accessed October 15, 2020. https://www.youtube.com/watch?v=bRAjf9rFA58.

Suner, Asuman. 2011. Between Magnificence and Monstrosity: Turkishness in Recent Popular Cinema. *New Perspectives on Turkey* 45: 123–154.

Taşkıran, Elif Gizem and Sevgi Şar. 2016. Geçmişten Günümüze Kına. *Mersin Üniversitesi Tıp Fakültesi Lokman Hekim Tıp Tarihi ve Folklorik Tıp Dergisi* 6 (2): 30–37.

Tokdoğan, Nagehan. 2019. *Yeni Osmanlıcılık: Hınç, Nostalji, Narsizm*. İstanbul: İletişim.

Türkiye Diyanet Vakfı İslam Ansiklopedisi, Mevlid. Accessed January 22, 2021. https://islamansiklopedisi.org.tr/mevlid%2D%2Dsuleyman-celebi.

Upton, Dell. 2001. Authentic Anxieties. In *Consuming Tradition, Manufacturing Heritage: Global Norms and Urban Forms in the Age of Tourism*, ed. Nezar AlSayyad, 298–306. London: Routledge.

Ustuner, Tuba, Güliz Ger and Douglas B. Holt. 2000. Consuming Ritual: Reframing the Turkish Henna-night Ceremony. *Advances in Consumer Research* 27 (1): 209–214.

White, Jenny. 2012. *Muslim Nationalism and the New Turks*. Princeton: Princeton University Press.

Zhu, Yujie. 2012. Performing Heritage: Rethinking Authenticity in Tourism. *Annals of Tourism Research* 39 (3): 1495–1513.

CHAPTER 9

Post-truth and Anti-science in Turkey: Putting It into Perspective

Hande Eslen-Ziya

The rise of right-wing populism, with its attacks on left-leaning politicians, mainstream media, academics, and scientists has led to increasingly authoritarian politics throughout the world. As outlined by Mede and Schäfer (2020, 473), populism produces a struggle between "an allegedly virtuous people and political elites which are portrayed negatively". According to Edis (2020, 4), an important commonality among right-wing populists is their "opposition to a 'liberal elite' that derives its power from its education and professional status". Mudde and Rovira Kaltwasser (2013, 2018) define populism as a set of morally charged ideas leading to conflict over political decision making between the so-called lay person and the elite. Populism's anti-elitism targets not only politicians but also, as Mede and Schäfer (473) argue, "other representatives of the alleged establishment—including scientists and scholarly institutions", following a populist rationality wherein scientists are portrayed as elites who mask the truth from

H. Eslen-Ziya (✉)
University of Stavanger, Stavanger, Norway
e-mail: hande.eslen-ziya@uis.no

© The Author(s), under exclusive license to Springer Nature Switzerland AG 2023
C. Raudvere, P. Onur (eds.), *Neo-Ottoman Imaginaries in Contemporary Turkey*, Modernity, Memory and Identity in South-East Europe,
https://doi.org/10.1007/978-3-031-08023-4_9

the people. This science-related populism, or anti-science, may be observed in attacks on universities and scientific research on climate change (Ylä-Anttila 2018), gender theory (Giorgi and Eslen-Ziya 2022; Eslen-Ziya 2020, 2022), and vaccination (Davis 2019), wherein experts are framed as "less trusted than ordinary people" (Motta 2018, 483). Such a lack of trust in the opinion of experts and intellectuals and the "trust in the wisdom of ordinary people" (Oliver and Rahn 2016, 198) leads to anti-intellectualism—a new form of knowledge production and science in the post-truth world (Merkley 2020; Williamson 2019).

In this new form of science—or pseudo-science—knowledge is produced in relation to right wing and conservative populist discourses. Gender theory is one strand of scientific knowledge defied by the populists, who create and use pseudo-scientific knowledge to challenge gender theory and gender equality. Turkey, with its recent stepping back on rights and freedoms (Korkut and Eslen-Ziya 2018; Eslen-Ziya and Erhart 2015) is a representative case of illiberal authoritarian right-wing populist governance under the leadership of Recep Tayyip Erdoğan and the AKP (Adalet ve Kalkınma Partisi, Justice and Development Party). In this chapter, I present emerging conceptualisations on gender and women's issues in Turkey by dissecting the distorted scientific arguments that have been created and moulded into populist discourses, outlining their content, and discussing the alternative orientations and conceptualisations of gender and women's issues that are appearing. I then relate these developments and discourse settings to gender equality and women's rights discourses.

Contextualising the Turkish Case

Despite the progressive changes in the early 2000s, after almost two decades we can now observe a subsequent stepping back in terms of rights and freedoms in Turkey (Korkut and Eslen-Ziya 2018; Eslen-Ziya and Erhart 2015), in addition to a rapid polarisation between AKP supporters and its opponents, one of the marks of the populist ideology in Turkey. According to Keyman (2014, 29), since 2011 "every election [the] AK Party won resulted in increasing polarization in terms of secularism, ethnicity and religion [...] as Erdoğan and the AKP have become stronger, polarisation [has] widened and deepened". The "us vs. them" divide created by the populist ideology became most evident during the Gezi Park protests, when Erdoğan declared the protestors to be looters (çapulcu). By classifying them as "irresponsible citizens", he marginalised the urban, middle-class, educated elite taking part, who were in fact there as common citizens conscious of their rights and freedoms (Korkut and Eslen-Ziya 2018). Nine years after the protests, polarisation remains constant in Turkish populist politics.

Throughout the rapid polarisation and deterioration of rights under the influence of predominantly conservative norms (Saraçoğlu and Demirkol 2015), the Turkish government has continued to adopt populist discourses involving Islamist elements of neo-Ottomanism, nationalism, and conservatism. Indeed, the Ottoman-Islamist past dominates the discursive narratives of the government (Coşar and Yeğenoğlu 2011). The "social and political order under the party's rule maintained by a new set of norms and values", as argued by Korkut and Eslen-Ziya (2016, 13), serves as a counter-conduct, a counter-narrative (Cebeci 2016). It was via these narratives that the AKP's populism set the rules for the majority's understanding of politics. Indeed, these narratives function as the discursive governance (Korkut and Eslen-Ziya 2011, 2016, 2018) whereby the AKP government opposes gender equality, among many other things. Such governance also allows for public agenda-setting through active sense-making—a process in which the media and public discourse play critical disseminating and legitimating roles, particularly in restrictive political settings (Burul and Eslen-Ziya 2018, 2020), such as Turkey.

Much as institutionalised Islam (Korkut and Eslen-Ziya 2018) and neo-Ottoman nostalgia now dominate the discursive governance, so has anti-genderism as a counter-narrative of gender started to evolve. By neo-Ottomanism, I imply the production of a discursive redefinition of gender roles and duties with reference to Islam and familialism (Korkman 2016), which simultaneously materialises in academic persecution and self-censorship in critical gender studies. In this chapter I demonstrate how the AKP government, instead of attacking gender studies altogether, pursues the creation of an alternative gender discourse, opening the way for a new discursive governance. I argue that, by combining the Ottoman heritage with Sunni-Islamic identity under the branding of a 'New Turkey', the AKP also opens a space for populism and neoliberal economic vision. This chapter therefore argues that the anti-gender movement in Turkey has the ambition to become an alternative field of knowledge production containing patriarchal discourses and traditional gendered identities.

NEO-OTTOMAN POPULISM

The AKP's populist governance has captured scholarly attention (Elçi 2019; Selçuk 2016; Yabancı 2016) that mostly focuses on its election slogans, including Erdoğan's "us vs. them" rhetoric and conspiracy theories about the West as the imagined external enemy. Narratives such as the national will/power contrasted with the elites of the so-called old Turkey clearly depict the populism used by the AKP government (Mudde and Rovira Kaltwasser 2013; Yabancı 2016). This chapter, by taking gender as a key pillar of populist discourse, presents the backlashes related to women's rights and gender equality within the government-supported troll-scientific realm.

Troll science, as defined by Eslen-Ziya (2019, 2020), is based on (distorted) scientific arguments (Kuhar 2015) moulded into populist discourse, creating an alternative narrative of conceptions of gender equality. Like troll accounts that post superfluous and even off-topic messages on social media to provoke, distract, and start arguments, troll science produces narratives that diverge from the scientific facts (as in the case of climate change and vaccination debates). The public normative order of the AKP government in the New Turkey is creating conservative, troll-scientific discourses on gender theory and what it means to be women and men.

Eslen-Ziya (2020) argues that, like the role of social media trolls in the spread of fake news, troll science is produced by rejecting scientific facts or accepting false facts and conspiracy theories (Szabados 2019, 208) and sharing in circles that further disseminate such beliefs; Eslen-Ziya et al. (2019) refer to such circles as "emotional echo chambers" in which common emotions are "echoed" back and forth and shared by others. This, in turn, not only helps disseminate beliefs into larger circles, it also allows emotions to be echoed back to their producer(s). In response, emotions become stronger as well as more ideological. In this case then, troll-scientific arguments, by spreading fake information, are attached to emotions that enable them to be acceptable in certain circles—in this specific case, ideologically conservative ones.

The so-called academic articles published in KADEM's *Kadın Araştırmaları Dergisi* (JWS—Journal of Women's Studies) are good examples of this. JWS, the official, academic periodical of the Women and Democracy Association (KADEM), is a peer-reviewed journal that publishes research on gender and women's studies. What is significant about

JWS is that it was created by President Erdoğan's daughter, Sümeyye Erdoğan-Bayraktar, in 2013, with the "aim [of conserving] the essential values of women in Turkey",[1] "and formulating common public awareness in societies in terms of women's rights and equal opportunities with the family and in social roles" (KADEM mission statement). The articles published by JWS are valuable in realising the discursive aspects of AKP populism. They also help us further illustrate how populism shapes wider state-society relations, as such ideological discourses help create the emotional echo chambers (Eslen-Ziya et al. 2019). Through these echo chambers discourses get distributed and accepted by the ideologically conservative groups. It is through these emotional echo chambers that ideological discourses interact with collective social actors and help contribute to the populist politics regime under AKP's hegemony.

GENDER UNDER THE RULE OF AKP

According to Szabados (2019, 220), science and research expenditure in Turkey increased from 0.48% of the gross domestic product in 2003 to 0.88% in 2015. This increase may seem surprising to some; however, as I demonstrate in this chapter, occurring as it has in the period since the AKP came to power, it is used to support the ideological discourse that the government aims to disseminate. As Szabados (2019, 220) argues, the attitude of the regime in Turkey toward science is controversial and ideological. For example, it is now Erdoğan who elects the members of the Turkish Academy of Science, making it a reflection of Turkish politics. In 2009 the national science-funding agency banned an article on Darwin's birth[2] and the publication of any books on evolutionary theory, including school textbooks. Furthermore, in 2019 the Turkish Ministry of Education cancelled gender equality programmes in schools.[3] While all these strategies exemplify the anti-science turn of the AKP government, I am more interested in studying what is happening in parallel through the development of alternative scientific discourses, referred to here as troll science.

---

[1] http://kadem.org.tr/kadem-hakkinda/. Accessed on 4.11.2019.
[2] https://www.nature.com/news/2009/090310/full/news.2009.150.html Accessed on 4.11.2019.
[3] https://ahvalnews.com/gender-equality/turkeys-educational-authorities-cancel-gender-equality-programmes Accessed on 4.11.2019.

According to Kandiyoti (2016, 105), policing gender norms and imposing familialism constitute the central nodes of AKP ideology and practice in at least two crucial domains: promoting gender as a marker of difference and the employment of policies that promote (neo-)conservative familialism. Erdoğan has made many public statements—"I do not believe in gender equality";[4] "Have at least three children";[5] "Do not delay marriage! Do not be too picky in choosing a spouse"[6]—that clearly depict the use of gender as a public discourse to impose family values, and "shor[e] up populism that privileges gender as a marker of difference, pitting an authentically national 'us' against an 'anti-national' (*gayri-milli*) 'them'" (Kandiyoti 2016, 105). Hence, I argue that under the AKP regime gender serves as a key pillar for the populist discourse, further strengthened via troll-scientific discussion. This is one of the main reasons why gender studies or gender research has not simply been dismissed from the academic agenda as it has been in many parts of Europe;[7] rather, they have been re-defined within the anti-gender movement.

In Turkey, gender studies programmes and gender theory itself is criticised as non-academic, ideological (Kuhar and Zobec 2017), and Western, and the anti-gender movement is presented as the alternative science in the field. To this end, the content of the academic conferences and seminars organised by the government and the articles published by JWS all serve as a substitute for what they refer to as Christian and Western gender theory. Ayhan argues that anti-genderism in Turkey has become manifest due to recent political economic transformations:

> Indeed, the Turkish welfare regime has been undergoing important transformations since 2002 with changes in social security and health care, flexibility in the labour market and privatizations. The new social security law opposed fiercely by labour organizations, decreased government contribution in wages, pensions and health care and increased minimum age for

---

[4] https://www.newsweek.com/women-and-men-are-not-equal-says-turkish-president-286681. Accessed on 20.04.2020.
[5] https://www.hurriyet.com.tr/gundem/erdogan-en-az-uc-cocuk-dogurun-8401981. Accessed on 20.04.2020.
[6] https://www.milliyet.com.tr/siyaset/evlilik-konusunda-cok-secici-olmayin-1913996. Accessed on 20.04.2020.
[7] In Europe this is achieved through attacks on gender research and gender studies programmes within universities. The Central European University in Hungary, where Hungarian Prime Minister Viktor Orban banned the gender studies programme, provides a telling example.

retirement. Flexible/part time employment of civil servants was introduced through these new regulations. Privatization of state-owned enterprises, a phenomenon dating back to 1980s in Turkey, was accelerated under AKP governance, leaving thousands unemployed as a result. (Ayhan 2019, 3)

Kandiyoti (2016, 106) refers to this as the marriage between neoliberalism and (neo-) conservative familism. It is certainly the outcome of the patriarchal view that portrays women as the natural care providers and the mothers of future generations. This is where neo-Ottoman nostalgia comes into the picture with the imposed ideal of a three-generational, extended family. Korkman (2016) argues that this in turn pushes women into compulsory motherhood by limiting access to reproductive health services and/or via the publicity given to traditional gender roles, which nudges women into domestic and care-taking roles. As Yazıcı (2012) and Korkut and Eslen-Ziya (2011, 2016) claim, it is through such discursive governance that the state hands its responsibility for the social protection of children, the elderly, and the disabled to women via the discursive shift to "strengthening the family" (Yazıcı 2012, 105). Here, "we witness the paradox of the simultaneous deployment of neoliberal welfare policies with a conservative discourse that denounces neoliberalism's ideological centre, 'the West', which acts as the foil to the 'strong Turkish family' as its imagined and maligned 'Other'" (Kandiyoti 2016, 106).

Moreover, as the state diverges away from the welfare regime, family and the women within the family become the natural care providers. Hence, anti-gender discourses supported by troll-scientific articles help support these public narratives, "deliberately setting conservative discourses geared to sustain public narratives in line with traditional gender roles and identities" (Korkut and Eslen-Ziya 2018, 63). Based on this assumption, in the following section I show how—via troll science—gendered roles and women's work within the family is advocated, mirroring the neoliberal policies of New Turkey.

TROLLING SCIENCE AND GENDERED POPULIST DISCOURSE

As demonstrated by Rigney (1991), anti-intellectualism in Turkey takes three principal forms: religious anti-rationalism, populist anti-elitism, and unreflective instrumentalism. What is unique to the Turkish case, however, is the development of an anti-gender movement within the so-called academic realm; in other words, both the concept of gender and gender theory in general are being created via what appears to be a religious-rational scientific discourse. This not only opens a space for the populist narratives of the AKP government, it also provides what I call troll-scientific support through the so-called academic arguments and theories that have subsequently emerged, promoted by the application of Islamic rhetoric. KADEM and JWS play a major role in both supporting and developing such populist common-sense statements. JWS claims that its main goal is to bring new perspectives to women's issues:

> JWS, instead of taking singular approaches to women's issues, [...] aims to open up such discussions to a wider academic audience and intellectuals in the light of new and different perspectives. In addition, it aims to present criticisms and develop new concepts in light of the hegemonic discourses and analyses in women's studies in our country, while taking into account the alternative orientations and conceptualisations of the international academy in women's studies. (Albayrak 2015, 8)

JWS positions itself as a "protective shield against those who blame the values of our society for the injustices women suffer".[8] Analysis of the articles it publishes identifies two dynamics in the replication of anti-gender discourses: first, the protection of the so-called values of society (i.e., serving as a shield against those who say it is society that creates injustice for women[9]); and second, reproducing an essentialist gender ideology. While the former hinders change to the patriarchal dynamics of the culture, the latter marginalises the efforts of feminists and feminist organisations, making it impossible for them to work together.

Since 2015, JWS has published eight issues. Each starts with a note from the editor and an interview and includes about five articles on women's issues from different disciplines, such as law, political science, economy, art, anthropology, and so on, reinforcing and solidifying the journal's perceptions of gender equality and women's rights with scientific knowledge. Content analysis of the articles shows seven recurrent themes: the concept of gender equality vs. gender justice; the role of family; women in the workforce and the glass-ceiling syndrome; women's political representation; and migration, poverty, and violence. In the following section, I

---

[8] http://kadem.org.tr/kadem-hakkinda/. Accessed on 4.11.2019.
[9] KADEM mission statement.

focus on the first two of these themes: gender equality vs. justice and the role of the family, as they dominate the gender politics of the AKP.

Gender Equality vs. Gender Justice

Erdoğan brought gender equality into discussion at an International Women's Day meeting organised by KADEM on 8 March 2010 when he claimed that women are not equal to men; "Women can only be equal to women",[10] he announced.

> Women and men could not be treated equally because it goes against the laws of nature [...] Their characters, habits and physiques are different [...] You cannot place a mother breastfeeding her baby on an equal footing with men [...] You cannot make women work in the same jobs as men do, as in communist regimes [...] You cannot give them a shovel and tell them to do their work. This is against their delicate nature.[11]

His emphasis on the biological differences between women and men meant they could not serve the same functions, and that some work was not suitable for women due to their "delicate nature". He also gave a similar speech at a summit in Istanbul, stating, "Our religion [Islam] has defined a position for women: motherhood." He even criticised feminists in Turkey for discarding motherhood.

Such a rejection of feminist discourses is later supported in one of the articles analysed in this chapter. E. Sare Aydın Yılmaz, associate professor at Istanbul Commerce University and KADEM's founding president, states that feminist literature belongs to the West and cannot be embraced by Turkish culture (2014). Discarding the feminist thesis altogether by categorising it as a Western way of thinking is one of the underlying features of the anti-gender movement. We also see this in the Vatican's Pontifical Council for the Family, which asserts that feminist ideology is part of Western Colonialism:

---

[10] https://www.theguardian.com/world/2014/nov/24/turkeys-president-recep-tayyip-erdogan-women-not-equal-men. Accessed on 12.05.2021.

[11] Guardian (2014). Recep Tayyip Erdoğan: "Women not equal to men". Available online at: https://www.theguardian.com/world/2014/nov/24/turkeys-president-recep-tayyip-erdogan-women-not-equal-men. Accessed on 12.05.2021.

> [F]eminist ideology [...] known as "gender" has led to a misunderstanding of the complementary difference between men and women and a growing confusion about sexual identity that complicates the assumption of roles and sharing of tasks in the home. (Corredor 2019, 615)

The Vatican later published a Lexicon of articles that clarify the Holy See's stance on such issues. Ambiguous and Debatable Terms regarding Family Life and Ethical Questions is a compendium explaining the importance of family and life. Its editors' summary is presented below:

> This long-awaited English translation of the Lexicon will be an invaluable resource to all those who genuinely seek to understand the profound truth, goodness and beauty of marriage and family. It is a gift to the faithful and to the broader community from the Church. In response, each of us is called to reflect on how we can best use it to proclaim the authenticity of Christ's message, especially in the areas of marriage and family in the third millennium. It will greatly assist all those of good will who seriously wish to learn the truth about marriage and family and to embark on the New Evangelisation. (pro Familia, Pontificium Consilium 2003, 200)[12]

Hence, the troll-scientific discourse in the JWS can also be observed within Western religiously conservative circles. For instance, in one of the chapters of the *Lexicon*, Bishop Óscar Alzamora Revoredo (2003, 465) stresses that "differences between men and women, beyond the obvious and not anatomical ones, do not correspond to a fixed nature, but are products of the culture of a certain country or epoch". In other words, he argues, gender theory unsettles the so-called moral fabric of society as it encourages people to "'invent' him/herself" (Alzamora Revoredo 2003, 465) by erasing the so-called natural differences between women and men. Resonating with both President Erdoğan's and the Vatican's populist anti-gender, anti-feminism discourses, Yılmaz (2015) also discusses how women and men cannot be equal, as it is against their nature. In parallel with the right-wing rhetoric of the West, she opposes the gender concept as a social construct and defines it as being biologically predetermined. Gender then becomes a rhetorical device used by either the AKP government (or the Vatican) to "counter gender and sexual equality policy" (Corredor 2019, 616) and advance political goals.

---

[12] https://www.amazon.com/Lexicon-Ambiguous-Debatable-Regarding-Questions/dp/1559220503. Accessed on 08.11.2019.

This religious nationalism (Edis 2020, 8), with its "populist revolt against secular expertise, aiming to delegitimise liberal elites" provides support for "religiously-coloured pseudo-science". According to Edis (2020), religious conservatists use creationism and evidence of divine creativity to challenge science in general, specifically targeting gender theory and evolution:

> Such creationism ranges from an emphasis on literal interpretations of sacred texts to the intelligent design movement that presents a more scientific image. In any case, varieties of creationism are classic pseudo-sciences [...] much of the case for creationism depends on portraying established scientific expertise as corrupt. (Edis 2020, 8)

As creationists emphasise authority and loyalty, and traditional social roles are authoritarian in nature, they approach professional claims to neutral expertise with suspicion (Edis 2019), and construct their own form of authority. In fact, the development of troll-scientific arguments is their way of building such institutional authority. Resembling the Vatican's populist resistance to evolution, populism in Turkey is also constructed within Turkish academia via its anti-secularism discourses and endorsement of creationism. Likewise, this trend is observed in the anti-gender and troll-scientific discourses presented in JWS. As Edis (2000) argues, this Turkish form of Islamic creationism is closely resembling Christian examples of right-wing religious conservatism, but in the Turkish case, right-wing populist resistance to elite expertise has been more visible:

> Turkish right-wingers have not only built alternative institutions and supported pious intellectuals affirming popular beliefs, but in a political environment shaped by decades of conservative rule they have made considerable progress towards becoming the new mainstream. Right-wing populism has made few inroads into American educational institutions and intellectual high culture. In contrast, in Turkey and in some other populous middle-income Muslim countries such as Malaysia and Indonesia, religious populists have established an alternative, pious form of modernity. (Edis 2020, 8)

The Turkish revolt against secular expertise evident in Yılmaz's articles produced gender justice rhetoric around the same time as Erdoğan claimed that women and men are not and cannot be equal. This clearly indicates a relationship between troll-scientific developments and right-wing populist rhetoric used by the government. Furthermore, Yılmaz in her article, titled "A New Momentum: Gender Justice in the Women's Movement", published in the *Turkish Policy Quarterly*, articulates that she is writing her articles as a response to feminist scholars and the women's movement's claims that women and men are equal:

> Why men and women acquire different roles and statuses in social life has been among the topics that have been constantly discussed to date. The concept of equality created in this context emphasises that there should be no difference between the two genders and that women and men should be treated equally without being subjected to any distinction in both social and private life. But the concept of equality cannot explain the current situation on this issue as necessary, and ignores the fact that women and men are different by creation. However, the attitude of men and women to life and their expectations and powers are also different. (Yılmaz 2015, 112)

Yılmaz emphasises her opposition to feminist scholars in Turkey who, she says, are failing to acknowledge the differences between men and women. She further argues that feminists in Turkey have "created a homogenous image of women, thus ignoring the differences among them" (Yılmaz 2015, 108). This, she argues, causes women to lose their female identity: "in the quest for equality, the endeavour was to make women exist through masculinisation, and thus women were detached from the female identity" (Yılmaz 2015, 108).

According to Yılmaz, introducing the notion of gender justice/gender equity and abandoning the concept of gender equality will help develop an understanding of the differences both among women and between women and men. Otherwise, she argues, the universalistic, Western feminist demands for gender equality and women's rights will cause more harm than good. This clearly is an Islamic interpretation of being a woman and/or man where differences are attributed to nature (*fitrat*). Within Islamic doctrine, women and men are defined as different by nature while at the same time complementary (Toker 2009), which implies that they must take different and gendered social roles and duties. In this respect, gender justice becomes a concept highlighting the gender-based division of labour wherein duties are naturally assigned to either women or men, giving rise to a gendered division of labour in which a woman is expected to be a good mother and carer to the family. This leads us to the concept of family mainstreaming, which emphasises the importance of family and the role of women within the family at the expense of gender equality.

FAMILY MAINSTREAMING

In 2019, just before International Women's Day on 8 March, the Turkish Family Assembly distributed anti-gender statements via Twitter and Facebook. The slogans included, "Stop the global war on the family", and "The terrorism of gender equality and homosexuality is a crime against humanity". The Assembly demanded the annulment of the Istanbul Convention and repeal of Act. No. 6284 that aims to end violence against women. It also claimed the restoration of men as heads of the family. This anti-gender campaigning developed around three major issues: the protection of family, the Istanbul Convention, and the role of men within the family. Gender and gender equality were perceived as a threat to the family unit. The views reflected neo-Ottoman nostalgia for the three-generational, extended family.

Korkut and Eslen-Ziya's (2018) analyses of Friday *hutbes* (sermons) reveal a similar pro-family narrative with distinctive roles and duties attributed to both women and men. They show how the emphasis on family in the *hutbes* serves to preserve the neo-Ottoman, traditional, and patriarchal structure of families. Similarly, in an earlier study, Korkut and Eslen-Ziya (2016) trace political discourse in relation to population politics and Erdoğan's three-children slogan—"For a young population, citizens should always have three children [...], scientifically even two children suggest decline."[13]—suggesting that it constructs a traditional and subordinate female subjectivity.

Defining women by familial roles, with a primary responsibility to be a wife and give birth, pushes woman into compulsory motherhood and domestic and care-taking roles (Korkman 2016). Within the same family, on the other hand, the man enjoys control over the bodies and sexuality of his female relatives: daughters, sisters, wives, and mothers. The discursive shift is made in the name of "strengthening the family" (Yazıcı 2012, 105) and creating the "strong Turkish family" (Kandiyoti 2016, 106). This robust Turkish family narrative is also evident in the troll-scientific discourses analysed. Tekin's (2017) quotation below clearly feeds into the Turkish populist political discourse in the New Turkey:

---

[13] NTV (2009) Erdoğan: İş işten geçmeden en az 3 çocuk [Erdoğan: Before it is too late at least 3 Children]. Available online at, http://www.ntv.com.tr/turkiye/erdogan-is-isten-gecmeden-en-az-3-cocuk,ZEQhCeWHVkS06lEDhd72Ng. Accessed 7 June 2019.

As a matter of fact, family, women, sex, intimacy [...] many concepts, categories and structures today are the subject of multidimensional debate and destruction. Finally, the age of marriage is delayed, family building is not encouraged, divorce (rates) are increasing, privacy is weakening; society is becoming an anomie. In the history of mankind, the family is heterosexual but now [the] legal status of homosexual marriages and even adoption of children is desired by these families thus family is being subjected to deconstruction and it is one of the important discussion topics in today's world [...] The results obtained with the deconstruction show those weaknesses: First; human is living in the universe, which is given to him and the qualities of the male and female categories are more natural in terms of building a family. The opposite is to force the human nature to the nature's opposite.... (Tekin 2017, 14)

Defining family as the sacred unit in which women have reproductive responsibilities clearly places them within the private sphere. Moreover, in the claim that the opposite constitutes a challenge to human nature, we observe gender mainstreaming being replaced by family mainstreaming (Çakar 2014). While gender mainstreaming is about evaluating the different implications for people of different genders at all policy and legislative levels, family mainstreaming is just the opposite; it creates a single typology of women: mothers and wives. Family mainstreaming represents only heterosexual people and heterosexual families, with the goal of promoting population growth. Placing the family, but not the single individual, at the core of demographic growth appropriates the critical gender studies discourse.

The differential and essentialist roles assigned to women and men, according to Yılmaz (2015, 110), do not cause hierarchy: "The fact that the duty to administer the family has been laid upon men does not generate a hierarchical order in any case, and does not prevent equality between women and men as human beings and subjects of God." On the contrary, she argues, gender justice "will provide the fair and proper sharing of roles in favour of women" (Yılmaz 2015, 112). However, defining women as mothers with the primary responsibility for childbearing and child rearing not only assigns them the responsibility for raising the "future of Turkey" (Korkut and Eslen-Ziya 2018, 63), it also allocates state responsibility for social protection to families. This, according to Kandiyoti (2016), reflects the neoliberal transformation of employment and welfare regimes. The neoliberal and right-wing populist discourses of New Turkey are cultivating the public narrative through discursive governance, religious sermons, and new troll-scientific arguments. The discursive governance is implemented through academic conferences, seminars, and publications, turning the anti-gender movement into an alternative field of knowledge production.

Troll science is thus being used to provide scientific material to support or justify gender inequalities (Kuhar 2015) and institutionalise pro-government, conservative, and patriarchal discourses. Hence, with the significant gender backlash, the New Turkey can be observed as setting an agenda at the academic level through a troll science that references Islam and Islamic discourses. Edis (2020, 4), who discusses the power of conspiracy theorists to affect political discourses, argues that with the advancement of digital media technologies, this false information spreads quickly and widely:

> Conspiracy theorists are not just convinced that the American government is hiding evidence of space aliens; conspiracy theories have started to seriously affect political discourse. In the United States, many Republicans worry about a Deep State that schemes to block President Trump; many Democrats think the Trump presidency is a Russian plot. In Muslim countries, conspiracy theories about the CIA, Jews, or Freemasons are never far from the popular political imagination. And so, it goes across the globe. The internet lowers the cost of dissemination for crank notions, and the echo chambers and information bubbles promoted by social media give pseudo-science an ideal environment to flourish.

I add to Edis's argument that it is not just the information that is shared but also the emotions attached to them. In other words, I argue that the discourses that have a reference to Islam are indeed ideological discourses loaded with emotions that create emotional echo chambers (Eslen-Ziya et al. 2019), thus enabling their swift distribution among and acceptance by ideologically conservative groups. Troll-scientific arguments that spread fake information and invoke religious arguments and ideologies become emotionally loaded and easily accepted in ideologically conservative circles. They become so intertwined that rejection of troll science becomes a rejection of the Islamic doctrine; hence, no one dares to question the former without being accused of questioning the latter (Eslen-Ziya 2020). In other words, the Islamist ideology dominates the gender narrative through both the discursive definitions in troll-scientific arguments and the emotional echo chambers that impact on the everyday practices of women and men. Thus, troll science is part of the attempt to integrate religious doctrine with science and/or academia, with aims to traditionalise the everyday life of men and women entirely.

To conclude, the AKP government not only hesitates to further the EU-membership project (Patton 2007; Kardas 2008; Zihnioglu 2013), as of 2011 it has taken a completely new turn with anti-gender discourses. In fact, one of the important aims of the anti-gender movement is to create alternative troll-scientific knowledge to support the right-wing populist and conservative ideology of the governments in power. In this chapter, I demonstrate how, via the introduction of troll science to support anti-gender and conservative discourses within the newly emergent anti-scientific academia, the AKP government is furthering its neoliberal-conservative regulation of three main policy areas: reproduction, sexuality, and the family.

Conclusion

In this chapter I have outlined the emerging conceptualisations of gender and women's issues in Turkey, visible in the concurrently created so-called scientific arguments supporting them. I have accomplished this by linking troll-scientific developments to intensifying right-wing populism. I have scrutinised these distorted scientific arguments moulded into right-wing religious populist discourses and outlined emerging troll perspectives and alternative orientations towards and conceptualisations of gender and women's issues. I then related this conservative emphasis on traditional understandings of religious doctrines to troll-scientific discourses refuting academic scholarship on gender equality and women's rights. Based on a combination of religious discourse and scientific articles, such discourses explicitly argue that the preservation of the "natural" union between men and women is essential both for the well-being of children and the development of "healthy" societies.

The use of gender and gender theory by right-wing populists as a rhetorical device for political purposes and the advancement of political goals runs counter to gender and sexual equality policies, creating a gender backlash at all levels of society. This new, alternative, and so-called scientific discourse "regenerates the issues of family and marriage as an ideological battleground of contemporary cultural wars" (Kuhar 2015, 90), and stimulates an ever-increasing intolerance of critical thinking. The ideological battleground becomes, in turn, the emotional component of discourses produced by the troll science that enables emotional echo chambers (Eslen-Ziya et al. 2019) and the fast distribution and acceptance of such discourses by ideologically conservative groups. In other words, the troll-scientific arguments that spread fake information are connoted with religious arguments, such as creationism, and emotionally loaded ideologies that facilitate their easy acceptance in certain circles: in this specific case, ideologically conservative ones. The two become so intertwined that rejection of troll science becomes a rejection of the Islamic doctrine, and hence no one dares to question the former for fear of being accused of questioning the latter.

The troll science in Turkey that is embedded in Islamic creationism serves as a threat not only to science but also to the very secular system of the Republic. As similarly argued by Sayin and Kence (1999, 29), Islamic creationism, unlike "Christian creationism, […] is a critical part of the rise of an extreme religious movement and has actively contributed to the decline of democratic reforms and progress in scholarship and research in the Turkish Republic". This is clearly observable in the political rhetoric of President Erdoğan and AKP officials.

REFERENCES

Albayrak, Şule. 2015. Editorial Notes. *KADEM Kadın Araştırmaları Dergisi KADEM Journal of Women's Studies* 2: 2 (Dec.).
Alzamora Revoredo, Oscar. 2003. An Ideology of Gender: Dangers and Scope. In *Lexicon: Ambiguous and Debatable Terms Regarding Family Life And Ethical Questions*, Pontifical Council for the Family, ed. Joseph Meaney, 465–482. Virginia: Human Life International.
Ayhan, Tutku. 2019. KADEM's 'Gender Justice' or the Momentum of Anti-genderism in Turkey. Accessed 15 October 2020. https://blogs.lse.ac.uk/gender/2019/04/29/kadems-gender-justice-in-turkey/.
Burul, Yeşim and Hande Eslen-Ziya. 2018. Understanding 'New Turkey' Through Women's Eyes: Gender Politics in Turkish Daytime Talk Shows. *Middle East Critique* 27 (2): 179–192.
———. 2020. Understanding 'New Turkey' through Women's Eyes: Gender Politics in Turkish Daytime Talk Shows. In *Media and Politics in the Southern Mediterranean: Communicating Power in Transition after 2011*, ed. Roxane Farmanfarmaian, 300–314. London: Routledge.
Çakar, Nigar Demircan. 2014. Neden Toplumsal Cinsiyet Adaleti? [Why Social Gender Justice?]. *KADEM Kadın Araştırmaları Dergisi KADEM Journal of Women's Studies*. Accessed 12 May 2021. http://kadem.org.tr/neden-toplumsal-cinsiyet-adaleti/.

Cebeci, Münevver. 2016. De-Europeanisation or Counter-conduct? Turkey's Democratisation and the EU. *South European Society and Politics* 21 (1): 119–132.

Corredor, Elizabeth S. 2019. Unpacking 'Gender Ideology' and The Global Right's Antigender Countermovement. *Signs: Journal of Women in Culture and Society* 44 (3): 613–638.

Coşar, Simten and Metin Yeğenoğlu. 2011. New Grounds for Patriarchy in Turkey? Gender Policy in the age of AKP. *South European Society and Politics* 16 (4): 555–573.

Davis, M. 2019. Globalist War against Humanity Shifts into High Gear: Online Anti-vaccination Websites and 'Anti-public' Discourse. *Public Understanding of Science* 28 (3): 357–371.

Edis, Taner. 2019. Cosmic Conspiracy Theories: How Theologies Evade Science. In *Theology and Science: From Genesis to Astrobiology*, ed. Richard Gordon and Joseph Seckbach, 143–165. Hackensack, NJ: World Scientific.

———. 2000. The Rationality of an Illusion. *The Humanist* 60 (4): 28.

———. 2020. A Revolt Against Expertise: Pseudoscience, Right-Wing Populism, and Post-Truth Politics. *Disputatio* 9 (13): 1–29.

Elçi, Ezgi. 2019. The Rise of Populism in Turkey: A Content Analysis. *Southeast European and Black Sea Studies* 19 (3): 387–408.

Eslen-Ziya, Hande. 2019. Right-wing Populism in New Turkey: Leading to all New Grounds for Troll-science in Gender Theory. Paper presented in Populism, Religion and Gender: Tensions and Entanglements Workshop. University of Bergamo, 4–5 December 2019.

———. 2020. Right-wing Populism in New Turkey: Leading to all New Grounds for Troll-science in Gender Theory. *HTS: Theological Studies* [special issue Gender, Justice, Health and Human Development]. 76 (3): 1–9.

———. 2022. Knowledge, Counter-knowledge, Pseudo-science in Populism. In *Populism and Science in Europe*. (Palgrave Studies in European Political Sociology), ed. Hande Eslen–Ziya and Alberta Giorgi. London: Palgrave Macmillan.

Eslen-Ziya, Hande and Itir Erhart. 2015. Towards Post-heroic Leadership: A Case Study of Gezi's Collaborating Multiple Leaders. *Leadership and Authority in a Crises-constructing World Leadership*. 11 (4): 471–488.

Eslen-Ziya, Hande, Aidan McGarry, Olu Jenzen, Itir Erhart and Umut Korkut. 2019. From Anger to Solidarity: The Emotional Echo-chamber of Gezi Park Protests. *Emotion, Space and Society*. 33: 100632.

Giorgi, Alberta and Hande Eslen-Ziya. 2022. Populism and Science in Europe. In *Populism and Science in Europe* (Palgrave Studies in European Political Sociology) ed. Hande Eslen–Ziya and Alberta Giorgi. London: Palgrave Macmillan.

Kandiyoti, Deniz. 2016. Locating the Politics of Gender: Patriarchy, Neo-liberal Governance and Violence in Turkey. *Research and Policy on Turkey* 1 (2): 103–118.
Kardas, Şaban. 2008. Turkey under the Justice and Development Party: Between Transformation of 'Islamism' and Democratic Consolidation? *Critique: Critical Middle Eastern Studies* 17 (2): 175–187.
Keyman, E. Fuat. 2014. The AK Party: Dominant Party, New Turkey and Polarization. *Insight Turkey* 16 (2): 19.
Korkman, Zeynep Kurtuluş. 2016. Politics of Intimacy in Turkey: A Distraction from 'Real' Politics? *Journal of Middle East Women's Studies* 12 (1): 112–121.
Korkut, Umut and Hande Eslen-Ziya. 2011. The Impact of Conservative Discourses in Family Policies, Population Politics, and Gender Rights in Poland and Turkey. *Social Politics* 18 (3): 387–418.
———. 2016. The Discursive Governance of Population Politics: The Evolution of a Pro-birth Regime in Turkey. *Social Politics. International Studies in Gender, State & Society* 23 (4): 555–575.
———. 2018. *Politics and Gender Identity in Turkey: Centralised Islam for Socio-Economic Control* (Routledge Studies in Middle Eastern Politics). London and New York: Routledge.
Kuhar, Roman. 2015. Playing with Science: Sexual Citizenship and the Roman Catholic Church Counter-narratives in Slovenia and Croatia. *Women's Studies International Forum* 49: 84–92.
Kuhar, Roman and Aleš Zobec. 2017. The Anti-gender Movement in Europe and the Educational Process in Public Schools. *CEPS Journal* 7 (2): 29–46.
Mede, N.G and M.S. Schäfer. 2020. Science-related Populism: Conceptualizing Populist Demands toward Science. *Public Understanding of Science* 29 (5): 473–491.
Merkley, Eric. 2020. Anti-intellectualism, Populism, and Motivated Resistance to Expert Consensus. *Public Opinion Quarterly* 84 (1): 24–48.
Motta, Matthew. 2018. The Dynamics and Political Implications of Anti-intellectualism in the United States. *American Politics Research* 46 (3): 465–498.
Mudde, Cas and Cistóbal Rovira Kaltwasser. 2013. Exclusionary vs. Inclusionary Populism: Comparing Contemporary Europe and Latin America. *Government and Opposition* 48 (2): 147–174.
———. 2018. Studying Populism in Comparative Perspective. *Comparative Political Studies* 51 (13): 1667–1693.
Oliver, J. Eric and Wendy M. Rahn. 2016. Rise of the Trumpenvolk: Populism in the 2016 Election. *The ANNALS of the American Academy of Political and Social Science* 667 (1): 189–206.
Patton, Marcie J. 2007. AKP Reform Fatigue in Turkey: What Has Happened to the EU Process? *Mediterranean Politics* 12 (3): 339–358.

Pro Familia, Pontificium Consilium. 2003. *Lexicon: Ambiguous and Debatable Terms Regarding Family Life and Ethical Questions*. Bologna: Edizioni Dehoniane.

Rigney, Daniel. 1991. Three Kinds of Anti-intellectualism: Rethinking Hofstadter. *Sociological Inquiry* 61 (4): 434–451.

Saraçoğlu, Cenk and Özhan Demirkol. 2015. Nationalism and Foreign Policy Discourse in Turkey under the AKP Rule: Geography, History and National Identity. *British Journal of Middle Eastern Studies* 42 (3): 301–319.

Sayin, Ümit and Aykut Kence. 1999. Islamic Scientific Creationism: A New Challenge in Turkey. *Reports of the National Center for Science Education* 19 (6): 18–20.

Selçuk, Orçun. 2016. Strong Presidents and Weak Institutions: Populism in Turkey, Venezuela and Ecuador. *Southeast European and Black Sea Studies* 16 (4): 571–589.

Szabados, Krisztian. 2019. Can We Win the War on Science? Understanding the Link between Political Populism and Anti-Science Politics. *Populism* 2 (2): 207–236.

Tekin, Mustafa. 2017. Gender and Justice from the Deconstruction to Reconstruction. In *International Social Gender Justice Congress: Women and Family*. Istanbul: KADEM.

Toker, İhsan. 2009. Eşitlik ve Adalet Kavramları Çerçevesinde Müslüman Kadınlarda Toplumsal Cinsiyet Örüntüleri. *Ankara Üniversitesi Sosyal Bilimler Enstitüsü Dergisi* 1 (1): 142–165.

Williamson, Timothy. 2019. In the Post-truth World, We Need to Remember the Philosophy of Science. Accessed 12 May 2021. https://www.newstatesman.com/2019/01/post-truth-world-we-need-remember-philosophy-science.

Yabancı, Bilge. 2016. Populism as the Problem Child of Democracy: The AKP's Enduring Appeal and the Use of Meso-level Actors. *Southeast European and Black Sea Studies* 16 (4): 591–617.

Yazıcı, Berna. 2012. The Return to the Family: Welfare, State and Politics of the Family in Turkey. *Anthropological Quarterly* 85 (1): 103–140.

Yılmaz, E. Sare Aydın. 2014. Eşitlik Üstü Adalet [Justice above Equality]. *Kadın ve Demokrasi Derneği*, 13 December 2014.

———. 2015. Kadın Hareketinde Yeni Bir İvme: Toplumsal Cinsiyet Adaleti. *Turkish Policy Quarterly.* 13 (4): 107–115.

Ylä-Anttila, Tuukka. 2018. Populist Knowledge: 'Post-truth' Repertoires of Contesting Epistemic Authorities. *European Journal of Cultural and Political Sociology* 5 (4): 356–388.

Zihnioglu, Ozge. 2013. *European Union Civil Society Policy and Turkey: A Bridge Too Far?* London: Palgrave Macmillan.

CHAPTER 10

Mixed Marriage Patterns in Istanbul: Gendering Ethno-religious Boundaries

Özgür Kaymak

Rum Orthodox, Jews, and Armenians have been the building blocks of Istanbul's economic, political, spatial, and cultural history.[1] However, throughout the history of the Republic, Turkey's non-Muslims have negotiated a political space shaped by the largely unfulfilled promise of equal citizenship and the everyday experience of members of an unwelcome minority. Consequently, demographically, these communities have been shrinking and today make up only about 0.001% of the population, while continuing to be an important part of urban daily life, culture, and social structure.

---

[1] I thank the anonymous reviewer for the careful readings and acute criticisms from which I benefited in various drafts.

Ö. Kaymak (✉)
MEF University, Istanbul, Turkey
e-mail: kaymako@mef.edu.tr

© The Author(s), under exclusive license to Springer Nature Switzerland AG 2023
C. Raudvere, P. Onur (eds.), *Neo-Ottoman Imaginaries in Contemporary Turkey*, Modernity, Memory and Identity in South-East Europe,
https://doi.org/10.1007/978-3-031-08023-4_10

257

After coming to power in 2002, the Justice and Development Party (Adalet ve Kalkınma Partisi, AKP) declared its strong commitment to international human rights and, in its first years in government, passed several reform packages with regard to non-Muslim minority communities, developing hitherto absent positive dialogue with them. Furthermore, the political elites of the AKP adopted the rhetoric of multiculturalism, tolerance, and pluralism. All these developments raised the hopes and expectations of non-Muslim communities, although the AKP's approach was often framed by nostalgic reference to an imagined and tolerant Ottoman past instead of the EU's framework of human and minority rights. In other words, the enhancement of the legal rights of non-Muslim communities during the EU accession process was justified by the neo-Ottomanist understanding of the AKP in the first decade of the party's rule, which was based on a logic of benevolent toleration rather than a notion of rights. Furthermore, the increasing authoritarianism of the government since 2011, in conjunction with the freezing of EU negotiations, the deterioration of human rights protections, and the halting of policies aiming to improve the status of non-Muslim communities, led many analysts as well as community members to conclude that minorities were being instrumentalised by the AKP in accordance with their political interests.

As the governing party's emphasis on the Sunni-Muslim character of the nation and de-secularisation of the public and cultural spaces has intensified, the public and academic debates about multiculturalism, pluralism, and hybrid identities of the early 2000s have waned. However, it is within this shifting national political context of the last twenty years that "mixed marriages" have been increasing in Turkey: that is, marriages and relationships between those who are citizens of the Turkish Republic yet have different religious beliefs from the Sunni Muslim majority and are legally considered a "minority", with individuals from other ethno-religious groups, predominantly those belonging to the Muslim majority. Through a gender analysis of the (re)construction of ethno-religious boundaries within mixed marriages, this study shifts the focus from the practices of agents who have adopted the neo-Ottomanist narrative and understanding to shine a light on cases of boundary crossing within the private sphere rather than the political/public sphere, where new hybrid identities and means of co-existence are being negotiated.[2]

Focusing on the meanings and representations of mixed marriages within the Rum Orthodox, Armenian, and Jewish communities in Turkey—whose numbers have been dwindling at a rate that threatens their continued existence in the country—provides a unique opportunity to interrogate how social cleavages and the sensitivities of ethno-religious boundaries are being transformed. It also facilitates investigation of the circumstances under which these boundaries are crossed within the context of the conservative and Islamist discourse of the AKP. Here I analyse the family as the primary space wherein ethnic and religious practices are socially built, and underline the contradictions and complexities involved in mixed marriage relationships from a gender perspective.

Based on data collected from extensive fieldwork conducted between May 2018 and December 2019, we show that non-Muslim individuals within mixed marriages are, on the one hand, developing ways to preserve their ethno-religious identities in their daily lives and resist assimilation, while, on the other, they remain integrated into the society at large; therefore, I argue that pluralism, recognition, multiculturalism, and the means of co-existence crystallise in the private rather than the public and political spheres. Semi-structured in-depth interviews were conducted with 51 individuals from Rum, Armenian, and Jewish communities in Istanbul, from different age groups (from 25 to 73 years of age), social classes, and genders. Respondents, reached by the snowball sampling method, included 37 women and 14 men in total: 19 from Rum, 14 from Armenian, and 18 from Jewish communities who, at the time of the interview, were either married to their partner or at different stages before marriage, such as marriage promise or engagement.[3] We also conducted two focus group interviews. The majority of the respondents were considered to be middle class. Acknowledging the fact that it was not possible to identify a single perspective among Rums, Jews, and Armenians based in Istanbul, we aim to reflect a range, all of which are a substantial part of the general picture.

---

[2] This study draws on part of the field work conducted in 2019 by Dr Özgür Kaymak and Dr Anna Maria Beylunioglu for the book entitled *Kısmet Tabii, Rum, Yahudi ve Ermeni Toplumlarında Karma Evlilikler* (For Sure It Is Faith, Mixed Marriages in Rum, Jewish and Armenian Communities, İstos, 2020).

[3] Although in the social scientific literature the mixed LGBTQ+ families are also considered in this context with increasing frequency, the sample here is limited to heterosexual couples with traditional forms of marriage.

Because of the confidentiality principle, we have personally transcribed the conversations that we recorded. Interviews were also conducted with religious officials and leading figures from the Chief Rabbinate in Turkey, the Armenian Patriarchate, and the Greek Orthodox Church in order to gain an understanding of community leaders' positions on the issue and how they differ from those of ordinary individuals.

The starting point and main problematic of this study was to gain understanding of mixed relationship/marriage processes and their dynamics, best understood through individual experience. As emphasised by Touraine (2000), qualitative research should focus on the personal perspectives of individuals in order to grasp the mechanisms that form the basis of social relations.[4] Studies using identity narratives as empirical tools provide us with a deep pool of knowledge about how individuals perceive and interpret social reality and shape their behaviour accordingly (Yuval-Davis 2011). With this in mind, in-depth personal interviews were conducted with women and men in mixed marriages, or those who have had—or are still in—mixed relationships, in order to obtain their life stories. This approach adopts the personal as an epistemological tool and uses individual experiences to reveal the meaning of mixed marriage, to understand it, and to record daily life experiences into history.

In the rest of the chapter, I begin by outlining the socio-political history of non-Muslim communities in Turkey since the founding of the Republic, focusing on their second-class treatment despite the founding principle of secularism, before discussing how the relationship between the state and non-Muslim communities has been re-shaped under the AKP. I then briefly address the concepts which are the focus of the chapter, such as tolerance and multiculturalism. Finally, I present a statement of the main issues raised by the study and an analytical assessment based on the conceptual and theoretical background.

---

[4] Alain Touraine is considered as one of the most important contemporary sociologists. Touraine's work has mainly focused on the individual-society relationship. The French social thinker argues against the idea that all we can do is to agree on mutual tolerance and respect for personal freedom; instead, he suggests a construction of an active self. Touraine asserts that the only way to prevent the destruction/erosion of identity in a globalised world is for individuals to develop a personal life-project, which he calls the "Subject". To become a subject, the individual constructs itself as an actor—as we can follow in the interviewers' comments throughout this research—forming a stable point of reference in a world of permanent and uncontrollable change.

Conditions for the non-Muslim Communities in Republican Turkey

The relationship between the state and non-Muslim communities[5] has been a sensitive issue since the founding of the Turkish Republic in 1923. Although the constitution stated the principle of secularism, whereby the state was ostensibly required to distance itself from all religious beliefs equally, Islam had always played an important role in the formation of Turkish identity. After the founding of the Republic, despite contradicting the aim of the secular state, non-Muslim citizens continued to be defined as minorities with reference to their religious identity and excluded from the national identity. Throughout the history of the Republic, assimilationist, and discriminatory pressure from state and society has been rife, and, as a result, the population of non-Muslim communities has been shrinking dramatically. Today, it is estimated that there are approximately 2,500 Rums, 14,000 Jews, and 60,000 Armenians in Istanbul, the most populous city in Turkey with a population of 15.5 million.[6]

A state-centric modernisation project has been imposed on non-Muslim communities through various cultural, economic, and political practices since the establishment of the Republic. The impetus behind these policies was to create a national bourgeoisie and a homogeneous society in which being Sunni-Muslim was defined as the main element of "being Turkish". The first implementation of this project was realised through the population exchange between Greece and Turkey in 1923, which resulted in an

---

[5] The Treaty of Lausanne (1923) established the legal basis of religious minority rights (Articles 37–43)—in Turkey, this applies to "non-Muslim communities/minorities", namely, the Rum Orthodox, Jewish, and Armenian communities—and is still technically in force today.

[6] Information gathered from interviews with community leaders in December 2020. Ottoman censuses (1911–1912) claim that 17% of the total population of Anatolia was non-Muslim (this ratio corresponds to 3 million among the total population of 17.5 million) (Canefe 2007, 90). Until the census in 1965, "population by religion" was determined, except for the 1950 census. The total population of the country according to Turkey's first census conducted in 1927 was 13.5 million of which 110,000 were Greek, 77,000 Armenian, and 82,000 Jewish. By 1927, the ratio of non-Muslims in the general population had decreased to 2%. According to results of the first census, Greek was Turkey's 4th largest language, while in 1965 this ratio was down to 1.5% (Dündar 2000, 58).

enormous decrease in the size of the Rum Orthodox[7] population. Moreover, the laws passed during the 1930s in order to regulate the economic and societal sphere set "being a Turk" as the minimum criterion for economic participation. It was common to see newspaper advertisements underlining the state's propaganda and encouraging the use of "domestic goods" as well as speaking Turkish. The cornerstone of the economic handover was the Capital Tax (Wealth Tax) implemented in 1942. Considering that non-Muslims comprised 87% of the payers of this special tax, which was implemented to cover the expenses of the Turkish government during the Second World War, the financial burden fell disproportionately on non-Muslims (Aktar 2012, 145). Turkification policies were not limited to the exclusion of non-Muslims from the economic and societal spheres; they also included spatial arrangements. The 1934 pogrom that took place in Thrace—considered to be the first antisemitic action in the Turkish Republic—constitutes a striking example (Bali 2012). In June 1934, Jewish houses and workplaces were subjected to intense violence and destruction, which resulted in the Jewish community's forced emigration from the territory. After the 1934 pogrom, the September 6-7 pogrom of 1955 targeted Istanbul's Rum community as well as other non-Muslim groups. As a result of these, by 1955 the number of non-Muslims in Turkey had fallen to below 1% of the population. In other words, non-Muslims were actually removed from Turkish society. This enormous decrease in their population caused non-Muslim societies to live much more closed within their communities and to draw strong boundaries with the wider society. They have begun to feel distrust, fear, and reservations towards the state and the society in general. Especially for those who are sixty years old and above today, discriminations and inequalities that they experienced created a heavy burden in their familial and community collective memories. Therefore, as we will analyse in the next section, mixed marriages constituted a redline and was a great taboo until the last 10-15 years.

Turkification policies continued through to 1964 when the Turkish government cancelled the 1930 "Treaty of Commerce and Navigation"

---

[7] The author acknowledges the interchangeable use of Rum, Greek, Hellen, Byzantine, and Grec. Rum Orthodox is used here—to differentiate it from Greek Orthodox denoting those of Greek nationality—to refer to those who stayed in the Ottoman Empire after 1821 and then automatically became, first, Ottoman subjects and then citizens of the Turkish Republic in 1923.

between Greece and Turkey, in parallel with the escalation of the conflict between Turks and Greeks in Cyprus. Greeks residing in Istanbul were deported,[8] and 30,000 Rums—including those who were married to Greek nationals—had to leave Turkey within 6–7 months; this resulted in the complete disappearance of the local Rum Orthodox population in Istanbul (Örs 2019).

Apart from the Turkification/ anti-minority policies summarised above, non-Muslims have encountered countless difficulties and extrajudicial practices limiting their civil and religious freedoms since the founding of the Republic. The most striking of these violations took place after Turkey's military intervention in Cyprus in 1974 when Rum citizens were treated as "hostages";[9] limitations were also put on non-Muslims' civil and religious rights. Provisions of the Law on Foundations, the Turkish Civil Code, and the Municipality Law restricted the property that Christian communities could possess and prevented non-Muslims from legating their properties to religious foundations. The state also interfered with the election procedures of both administrative authorities and religious bodies, while teaching religion was limited for non-Muslim minorities. The Rum Orthodox Theology School was closed by the state in 1971 and remains unopened. Moreover, a legal framework that would enable non-Muslim individuals to be formally recognised, along with constitutional protections to secure their religious freedoms, are absent (Beylunioglu 2015). Religious minorities were also subject to discrimination in many other fields in their daily lives, from university entrance exams to recruitment in government institutions.

NON-MUSLIMS UNDER THE AKP RULE

Since the AKP came to power in 2002, debates with regard to freedom of religion and the rights of religious minorities have become more significant. In its first years, the AKP declared a strong commitment to

---

[8] The Treaty of 1923 allowed Greek citizens resident in Istanbul before 30 October 1918 to become *etabli*, meaning that they were part of the Istanbul Rum community without the need for Turkish citizenship.

[9] Rums suffer from this "reciprocity mentality". The Reciprocity Principle is based on Section Three of the Treaty of Lausanne which refers to the "parallel obligations" of Greece and Turkey towards their Muslim and non-Muslim communities. However, drawing on the most negative sense, both Turkey and Greece implemented this principle in order to penalise individuals and use them as a tool to send a message to their respective states (Oran 2008).

international human rights standards, continued the EU reform process initiated by the previous government, and passed five reform packages before 2004, including certain changes with regard to non-Muslim minority[10] communities. The government's reconciliatory approach to non-Muslims culminated in the reintroduction of the Law of Foundations in 2006. The AKP's special interest in recasting the parameters of religious freedom was welcomed by most non-Muslim minority representatives due to the AKP's positive emphasis on the "richness" of different cultures in comparison to the Kemalist tradition of opposing the enhancement of non-Muslims' rights (Beylunioglu 2017). However, the AKP's approach to freedom of religion in general and the rights of non-Muslim communities in particular was not fully compatible with the EU's human rights framework, and the positive dialogue with non-Muslim communities slowly lost its focus with the resurgence of the "Ottoman model".

Even during the height of Turkey's accession process, Turkish lawmakers frequently referenced the Ottoman Empire and its tolerant approach towards non-Muslim minorities, more specifically the *millet* system in which people of different religions co-existed and were tolerated under the superiority of Islam,[11] although statements by some government representatives harboured traces of hate speech against non-Muslims.[12] The exclusionary attitude became more pronounced after 2011, however, when the AKP government and its leader, Recep Tayyip Erdoğan, began

---

[10] The term "minority" has a delicate history in Turkey, and a negative connotation in popular imagery. Here, the term "minority" is used in both its legal and sociological frameworks.

[11] In the *millet* system of the polyethnic and multireligious Ottoman Empire, Greek Orthodox, Armenians, and Jews were all recognised as self-governing units and allowed to impose restrictive religious laws on their own members. For various theological and strategic reasons, the Ottomans allowed these minorities not only the freedom to practice their religion, but a more general freedom to govern themselves in internal matters. On the other hand, while the Christian and Jewish *millets* were free to run their internal affairs, their relations with the ruling Muslims were tightly regulated. The Ottomans accepted the principle of religious tolerance, where that is "understood to indicate the willingness of a dominant religion to co-exist with others" (Braude and Lewis 1982). About the *millet* system also refer to Ortaylı (2012), İnalcık (2014).

[12] Cemil Çiçek's (Minister of Justice at the time) claim about Armenians' "stabbing us in the back" took place in a conference at Istanbul Bilgi University in 2005, https://www.hurriyet.com.tr/gundem/justice-minister-cicek-conference-on-armenians-like-a-stab-in-the--back-to-turkish-people-38732614. Minister of Defence Vecdi Gönül's statement on 10 November 2008 can be also considered in this context: "Could we still be a nation state if Rums and Armenians continued to exist in this land?", https://www.milliyet.com.tr/siyaset/bakandan-tehlikeli-sozler-1014564. (October, 2015).

to emphasise "Islam" as the absolute priority of the state.[13] The EU began to be perceived as a subpar alternative to the Ottoman model of tolerance for diversity and co-existence, especially after 2011. The state disregarded and ignored many EU-led policies, and non-Muslims have by and large claimed to have not noticed substantive improvements in their daily lives (Kaymak 2017).

While in 2015 the state commemorated the Holocaust and allowed the celebration of Hanukkah in public space for the first time, and in 2015 the Directorate General of Foundations decided to build a new church, the Syriac Orthodox church, for the first time in the history of the Turkish Republic—signalling an increasing positive dialogue between non-Muslim communities and the AKP government—most of the non-Muslim communities' problems remained unsolved. Moreover, the murder of Yasef Yahya[14] just before the November 2003 Istanbul synagogue attacks, the murders of Roman Catholic priest Andrea Santoro in October 2006 and Hrant Dink in 2007,[15] and the Zirve Publishing House massacre[16] are indications of continued threat towards non-Muslim minorities today.[17]

---

[13] "Erdoğan: Bizim Tek Derdimiz Var, İslam, İslam, İslam (Erdoğan: We Have Only One Concern, Islam, Islam, Islam)", Available at http://bianet.org/bianet/siyaset/166454-erdogan-bizim-tek-derdimiz-var-islam-islam-islam. (31 July 2015). Actually, the deterioration of basic rights in Turkey did not occur in an abrupt shift around 2011. The EU Commission's 2006 Progress Report contains a powerful critique of Turkey's failure to live up to standards on democratic governance and human rights; see EU Commission, *Turkey 2006 Progress Report*, https://ec.europa.eu/neighbourhood-enlargement/sites/near/files/pdf/key_documents/2006/nov/tr_sec_1390_en.pdf.

[14] Yasef Yahya was murdered in his dental office in Şişli, Istanbul in August 2003. The murderers were captured following the attack on the Masonic Lodge in Kartal in March 2004. They confessed that they killed Yahya because he was Jewish.

[15] The assassination of Hrant Dink, the most important public figure in Armenian identity awareness, on 19 January 2006 in front of the Agos newspaper building in Şişli, Istanbul, traumatised the Armenian community.

[16] The Zirve Publishing House murders, called "the missionary massacres" by Turkish media, took place on 18 April 2007, in Malatya, Turkey. Three employees of the Bible publishing house were attacked, tortured, and murdered by five Muslim assailants.

[17] In a highly worrisome development, on 29 May 2020 the Hrant Dink Foundation released a written statement for the press announcing that Rakel Dink—wife of late journalist Hrant Dink—and the attorneys of the Hrant Dink Foundation had received death threats via email, accusing the foundation of telling "tales of fraternity", demanding Armenians to leave the country, and threatening Rakel Dink and the foundation's lawyer with death. Two days later the suspect who sent the threatening mails in question was caught; http://bianet.org/english/minorities/225629-two-suspects-who-threatened-hrant-dink-foundation-face-up-to-26-years-in-prison?bia_source=rss, 12 June 2020; https://hrantdink.org/en/announcements/2414-public-statement. Accessed 17 June 2020.

Another point that needs to be underlined is that Turkish Jews have been compelled to confront increasingly pervasive antisemitism, especially during the last decade of AKP rule. The Anti-Defamation League's (ADL) world ranking of the most antisemitic countries, puts Turkey first with 69%, Iran second with 56%.[18] According to the Survey on Social and Political Trends in Turkey conducted by Kadir Has University, 37% of the respondents stated they did not want to have a Jewish neighbour.[19] Moreover, according to the Istanbul-based Hrant Dink Foundation's Media Watch on Hate Speech Report, Jews are the fourth most often targeted group by hate speech while Rums are second and Armenians fifth.[20] Rising antisemitism in Turkey is a dominant factor, if not the primary one, for the migration in recent years of Turkish Jews to Israel as well as to other countries (Kaymak 2019).

Moving beyond Tolerance

Most of the non-Muslim respondents in this study hold the opinion that their communities have been ignored by the state due to their miniscule populations in comparison to the Sunni-Muslim majority. Many stated that their decreasing numbers, due to social, cultural, and political oppression and eventual migration, create a picture where their numbers are not even sufficient to be the subject of such a political agenda today. Although acknowledging that the AKP government returned some of their rights during the EU accession process, many respondents also raised their concerns about being instrumentalised for the political interests of the government as part of the democratisation process. Non-Muslims increasingly respond (Kaymak 2017) that today they are considered "disliked entities", and promotion of their multicultural identity by the government in recent years was merely window-dressing. The most up-to-date and striking development in this regard is the recent issue of turning the Hagia Sophia

---

[18] Valansi, Karel. "Ira Forman: "Yükselen Antisemitizmden Endişeliyiz" [Ira Forman: We are worried about rising anti-Semitism]. *Şalom*. (11 July 2014). http://www.salom.com.tr/haber-91384-ira_forman__yukselen_antisemitizmden_endiseliyiz_.html.

[19] Haligua, Eli. "Toplumun %31,7'si Musevi komşu istemiyor" [31.7% of society do not want a Jewish neighbour]. 2 February 2018. *Avlaremoz*. http://www.avlaremoz.com/2018/02/02/toplumun-17si-musevi-komsu-istemiyor-2/. (10 June 2018).

[20] https://hrantdink.org/tr/asulis/faaliyetler/projeler/medyada-nefret-soylemi/2134-medyada-nefret-soylemi-mayis-agustos-2019-raporu-yayimlandi [Hate speech in media]. (7 April 2020).

museum into a mosque, which has caused serious debates in both national and international media and in political platforms. In July 2020, a top Turkish court revoked the 1934 decree by Mustafa Kemal Atatürk, founder of the Turkish Republic, which had turned Hagia Sophia into a museum; its reconversion to a mosque was an indispensable dream of Turkey's Islamists. In the Islamist political tradition of President Erdoğan and his AKP, Atatürk's experiment in secular republican governance was a foreign imposition, and Hagia Sophia's status as a museum a seal on the country's spirit (Koru 2020). Therefore, the idea was always that opening the Hagia Sophia for prayers would mark the maturation of Islamist power and cement its gains. Various authorities of the Greek and Russian Orthodox churches voiced their indignation. The governments of the EU and the United States muttered their regrets. UNESCO released a statement warning Turkish authorities against "taking any decision that might impact the universal value of the site". Some critics lamented what they saw as a blow to Turkish secularism. "To convert it back to a mosque is to say to the rest of the world unfortunately we are not secular anymore", Nobel Prize-winning novelist Orhan Pamuk told the BBC (Tharoor 2020). Meanwhile, Turkey's Christian population are bystanders in a debate that ultimately ignores the challenges facing a shrinking community.

The interviewees sadly summarised their views on the subject to the author as follows:

> Hagia Sophia is a very strong example of how the AKP's perception of religious minorities is entirely dependent on its political interests. We didn't find the steps taken at the time sincere, anyway. If we are talking about the "multicultural mosaic nature of the country", then why is the Greek Orthodox community, which numbered hundreds of thousands during the 1940s, no longer more than 2,000 people? Where have the madam's gone…? (Rum, 35, Female)

During the interviews, interviewees aged 50 and over nostalgically emphasised the "old state of Istanbul" (referring to the 1970s–1990s), when the non-Muslim population had not yet decreased to such an extent. At this point, it is worth mentioning that the interviewees approach the change in the sociocultural climate of Istanbul from a critical perspective, noting that it has been drastically transformed by the internal migration of the last 50 years from the eastern and northern regions, and the religiously conservative articulation of public/cultural life during the AKP regime.

Non-Muslims of Istanbul see this change in the socio-demographic structure of their city as a threat to their urban, modern, secular way of life.

As Mills (2014, 299) points out, the nostalgic emphasis on minority cultures in Istanbul is generally a form of othering that tries to express the city's predominantly Turkish imagination. Nostalgia, the product of memories, emphasises the harmonious co-existence of social life among ethnic groups in the neighbourhood, shared holidays, home visits, and street friendships, thus working to conceal discriminations and exclusions. The nostalgia for cosmopolitanism supports the elimination of difference and turns minorities into a complete collective. Similarly, the respondents in the study conveyed their opinion that non-Muslim communities were being promoted as elements of folklore in support of Turkey's accession into the EU.[21] According to Marshall and Bottomore (2000, 161–164), the multiculturalist ideology of liberal discourse leads to the acceptance of minorities only from a folkloric perspective, constructing "other" cultures as exotic and perceiving them as commodities. Practicing tolerance in liberal tolerance discourse makes exclusions invisible.

The AKP's definition of tolerance is confined to the acceptance of non-Muslims under the banner of the Sunni-Muslim-Turkish nation. Ultimately, toleration in the Ottoman context, as in other imperial contexts, refers to the "absence of persecution of people but not their acceptance in the society as full and welcomed members of community" (Barkey 2008, 110). Kaya and Harmanyeri (2010) also argue that tolerance is nothing but a "myth" in Turkey, one which has been functional in concealing the mistreatment of ethno-cultural and religious communities other than the Sunni-Muslim-Turk majority.[22]

---

[21] Contrary to the common interpretation of state authorities in Turkey, the Lausanne Treaty, the founding treaty of the Republic of Turkey (1923), does not limit non-Muslim minority communities living in Turkey to the Greek, Armenian, and Jewish communities. While political elites do so, both at the discursive level and also in the implementation of the laws, not only are there Orthodox, Catholic, and Protestant denominations of these communities, there are also individuals holding numerous different religious beliefs—Syriac (Orthodox, Catholic, Protestant), Russian Orthodox, Bulgarian Orthodox, Baha'i, Yezidi, Chaldean, Jehovah's Witness—living in Turkey and, contrary to the common view, the universal interpretation of the Treaty of Lausanne, now accepted in the literature, includes all non-Muslim beliefs.

[22] For a striking article on this subject see Foti Benlisoy, "Pandeli, Uncle Tom and Tolerant Hypocrisy". https://m.bianet.org/bianet/azinliklar/135799-pandeli-tom-amca-ve--hosgorulu-riyakarlik. (15 August 2020).

Taking into consideration all these arguments, this study suggests that the increase in the number of mixed marriages in Turkey—and globally—within the last 20 years demonstrates more than the free will of the individuals concerned. It also reflects the circumstances under which ethno-religious boundaries can be crossed or strengthened, and interrelations among different social groups belonging to a nation. It thus offers a unique opportunity to evaluate the acceptance of different beliefs within a society (Rebhun 1999). When we study non-Muslim minorities in Istanbul from the perspective of the sociology of everyday life, we can say that the discourse and values of "respect, recognition and acceptance of difference-coexistence-multiculturalism"[23] are observed and experienced within the private realm rather than the public/political sphere as a result of minority communities' dwindling populations. On the one hand, minorities feel a strong sense of belonging to Istanbul despite their dramatically decreasing populations, and share similar concerns, troubles, and joys regarding their daily lives as urban, modern, secular Muslim Turks.[24] On the other hand, and in spite of their demographic disadvantages, members of non-Muslim minority communities investigated in this study seek to retain their ethno-religious cultures and identities through practicing and passing down religious traditions, rituals, and linguistic knowledge from generation to generation; they also live in an integrated way with their socio-cultural classes.[25] It is, therefore, fitting that this chapter focuses on how pluralism/multiculturalism is experienced in the private sphere within the context of mixed marriages between non-Muslim minorities and the Muslim majority, from a gendered perspective.

Mixed Marriages within Rum, Jewish, and Armenian Communities

Mixed marriages are the biggest social phenomenon of all three communities and high on the agenda of their leadership. All acknowledge the rise of out-group marriages among their members in the last 10–20 years.

---

[23] Multiculturalism is sometimes used to describe a plurality of cultural groups co-existing with all their tensions and conflicts, but in this article, multiculturalism is simply a synonym for pluralism.
[24] Major sectors of the Istanbul Rum, Jewish, and Armenian communities maintain a secular lifestyle.
[25] Duru (2015) demonstrates that individuals belonging to different groups can come to share similar values based on longstanding attachment to place and everyday practices.

However, only the Jewish leadership shared the rate of marriages of Jews of Istanbul and Muslim-Turks with the author, noting that it is approximately 45–50%. Historically, mixed marriages were the red line of Rum, Jewish, and Armenian communities in Turkey, although there were exceptions. The main reason behind resistance to the acceleration of mixed marriages has been the risk of assimilation of the person marrying outside the community to the other group, seen as higher for women, thus threatening the cultural existence of communities with already declining populations. As Turkey's Armenian Patriarchate Metropolitan observes:

> The ghetto is the only chance that minorities can become themselves. So that minorities can protect their identity and sense of belonging. Otherwise, assimilation begins. These mixed marriages started to increase in the 1990s. The environment in which there was healthy neighbourhood pressure began to disappear. The families began to decide on their own. In the past, everyone was responsible for everyone's honour. Divorce was equivalent to leprosy. (Turkey's Armenian Patriarchate Metropolitan, March 2019)

Another important reason behind resistance has been the negative historical experiences of non-Muslims throughout the history of the Republic (discussed above), and distrust, prejudice, and fear of the wider society/ state.[26] Among older non-Muslims, mixed marriages have constituted the greatest taboo. For those respondents over 60, marriages took place mostly within the community and at a young age (18–23), and out-group marriages were considered to be a "betrayal" of the community (Beylunioglu and Kaymak 2020). The majority of the respondents observed that their parents' marriages had been arranged, with partners selected mostly from the social environment of the family and community (minority schools, associations, neighbourhoods). This "betrayal" perspective of older generations crystallises in the narrative of the Rum respondent:

> Married with a Muslim Men. My family rejected me; marrying someone outside the community was the worst scenario that could happen to them in life. It was not even an option at those times. I could hardly attended to my mother's funeral; my sister and brother did not want me there. I suffered a lot... (Rum, 74, Woman)

---

[26] For more detail on non-Muslims' citizenship experiences see Aslanoglu et al. (2012), Brink-Danan (2014), Ekmekçioğlu (2016), Kaymak (2017), Maksudyan (2015), Meseri and Kuryel (2017).

Women usually got married and had children right after graduating from high school. Among non-Muslim women respondents over 60, very few had their own business or were senior managers. Working women were mainly secretaries, executive assistants, accountants, and teachers. Many stated that their mothers left work after having children. Respondents over 50 mostly led a communitarian life within their own inner public spaces ("church quarters" as they called them). In keeping with the cultural climate of the country at the time (late 1970s) they had conservative family structures, where gendered division of labour and gender roles in the domestic sphere were clearly defined and predominant. Divorce in all three congregations was a social shame for this age group and caused stigmatisation within their communities, as a 56-year-old Jewish woman respondent states "No way! Divorce was out of question. You could lose all your network within the community; few people had the courage to divorce". Due to the embarrassment of divorce to their families, couples were forced to stay married "for better or worse". A woman was not allowed to divorce even if the alternative was staying in an unhappy marriage for many years.

However, as the community leaders pointed out and the data collected in this study confirmed, mixed marriages have slowly started to occur in the last 25 years, picking up pace in the last 10 years. Contrary to the community experiences and world outlook of those 50 and over—that is, conservative, communitarian, with a high level of communal pressure—non-Muslim individuals, aged between 30–45 years, who are in mixed marriages do not socially associate themselves with their communities, and position themselves more independently. Thus, it is important to point out that, while the concept of "community" has been used in this study to identify the legal membership of the individuals interviewed, it does not necessarily reflect their own perceptions. Many individuals interviewed define themselves as "atheist-deists"; they prefer to practice their religious beliefs individually, not tied to institutions, and have secular-urban-modern lifestyles. More than half define themselves as leftist-social democrat and feminist. Being a "Rum-Jewish-Armenian" is part of their identity, but not their primary social identity. Thus, in this context, they embrace their ethnic identities culturally,[27] yet are very sensitive to gender equality. They live their traditions and customs through rituals; family

---

[27] They hold on to their ethnic identity "symbolically" in their secular and independent lifestyles; see Herbert J. Gans, "symbolic ethnicity", 2010.

gatherings for Christmas, Easter, Rosh Hashanah, and other holidays represent collective ceremonies. They are disturbed by the thought of being trapped by closed community life, and openly criticise it:

> Being a part of minority community is really challenging. It is like a big family; everyone feels responsible and see the right to intervene in everyone's life. Because of this, because of the gossip network, I did not have a serious relationship within my community. (Armenian, 45, Men)

Integrated into the wider society, they have alternative groups of friends from different social strata. Although they might have had their primary education in minority schools, most have completed high school in mixed schools, are highly educated, and almost all work. While they want their children to learn the minority language (like Greek and Armenian)[28] and ethnic heritage, to support the continuity of minority culture and social capital, they place universal values such as "happiness, conscience, tolerance and respect" at the forefront in their lives rather than community and traditional values.

Based on the fieldwork, four factors have been identified behind the recent rise of mixed marriages in non-Muslim communities in Turkey: demographics, spatial mobility, socio-economic mobility and gender equality, secularisation/pluralism.

(1) Demographics

Each year the populations of Rum, Jewish, and Armenian communities show a decrease compared to the previous year due to decreasing birth rates, increasing mortality rates, and emigration.

(2) Spatial mobility

Non-Muslim communities tried to maintain the practice of living within their ethnic enclaves until approximately the last fifteen years when people began to leave the traditional urban "minority districts" and spread into the newly formed living spaces of the city. Mixed marriages weakened

---

[28] Judeo Spanish or Ladino (Jewish Spanish) had become the living language of members of the Ottoman Jewish community, and was used as a common language in Istanbul until the 1950s. Today, it is spoken only by a small segment of people in the community, on the other hand, it is possible to observe the patterns of resurrection of Ladino nowadays. Hebrew is used by Jews of Istanbul only in religious matters.

the clustering and accelerated the spatial dispersion of communities (Kaymak 2017). Due to both factors, the ethnic marriage market is shrinking and the possibility of finding a spouse from the same community is getting smaller.

(3) Socio-economic mobility and gender equality

Reflecting Turkey's changing cultural climate, another important factor which may cause an increase in mixed marriages is that minority youth are more educated than their parents' generation; most of them have at least a university degree. Increased social mobility (higher education, a prestigious job, better income) offers minorities new opportunities to establish contacts with individuals from the wider community in their work and residential spaces; it consequently encourages border crossing between minority and majority groups (Alba and Nee 2003), as well as contact and friendships that might result in dating and marriage.

(4) Secularisation and pluralism

Fieldwork showed that young adults have a strong conviction about the growing importance of pluralism and diversity in society and prefer to live a personal religious life. Their emphasis on the secular perspective that faith and religious practice should be between God and the individual rather than based on strict communal rules makes them more open to romantic relationships with individuals of a different faith. Thus, the stigma and social tensions around mixed marriages have begun to decrease.

Gender Aspect of Mixed Marriages

Countering the predominant discourse of increasing conservatism and religiosity among the Sunni-Muslim majority in Turkey and current repressive state policies, the phenomenon of mixed marriages points to dynamics of hybrid identities in the making. Increasing numbers of non-Muslim individuals choosing to be in a relationship and form families with people outside of their own communities—crossing their ethno-religious boundaries—are negotiating new ways of co-existence with, and acceptance by, their own communities, as well as the Sunni-Muslim majority, rather than accepting the position of merely being tolerated.

Non-Muslim families are very sensitive to how their social environment would approach the issue of mixed marriage, and the reactions they would receive. In minority communities with closed and traditional structures, the mechanisms of surveillance and gossip work very strongly. Almost all the respondents stated that the symbolic pressure coming from the community acted as a powerful element of control over their parents.

However, what is more striking is the differential treatment of men and women with regard to mixed marriages conveyed by individuals interviewed; this is largely due to the fear of assimilation and dissolution among non-Muslim communities. There had been especially significant pressure on women over 60 compared to men of the same age group. Since women and mothers were associated with the private sphere and traditional gender roles, they were considered to have the main responsibility for transferring minority identity in the family. As Yuval-Davis (1997, 196) points out, women have traditionally symbolised the cultural identity and boundaries of the social group to which they belong as carriers of "the burden of ethno-cultural continuity and endogamy". The following narrative example is a good example of this:

> Our parents always used to say: "when a Rum woman marries a Muslim/Turkish man she will assimilate to the other side and lose all the contact with her family and community." Therefore, there used to be a higher social pressure on woman than men. Assimilation was the biggest fear of our parents. (Rum, 65, Woman)

In mixed families, women have an essential role in the generational transmission of cultural practices and in determining the boundaries of the collectivity (Anthias and Yuval-Davis 1989). Therefore, gender relations have an increasing and deepening importance in multi-ethnic and multicultural societies.[29] The mixed marriage experiences of Rums, Jews, and Armenians differentiate the private sphere from experiences in the public sphere as a minority individual, and deepen the gender roles in this context.[30] This makes the private sphere a more sensitive and fragile area for

---

[29] As Lerna Ekmekçioğlu stressed (2016), all kinds of reproduction in the Turkish Armenian community are the duty of women.

[30] While non-Muslims conceal their signs of minority identity in public spaces with different strategies (not wearing crosses, speaking without an accent, using their universal/Turkish names rather than the one referring to their ethnic-religious origin) in order to avoid discrimination and exclusion in everyday life practices, the private sphere is outside of state control. It is here that minority culture is protected, implemented, and transferred, and non-Muslim individuals feel they will not be discriminated against due to being a minority. For these reasons, the private spaces of the community are more "intimate, sheltered and confidential".

minorities compared to the wider society. The study revealed a greater level of unease with regard to the mixed marriages of non-Muslim women. Even though the closed and conservative structure of non-Muslim societies compared to 15–20 years ago has started to break down, families still have reservations about women marrying outside the group because of the fear that they will be estranged from their families and communities and assimilate, the children will be raised as Muslim, and in extreme cases they will be forced to convert. The reaction of the family of a 29-year-old Armenian woman to the family of her Muslim husband illustrates this point clearly: "My parents were very anxious before they met him and his family. "[They are] a very bigoted, closed family, they will take you in, they will make you try things [like the veil]; you will be very oppressed" After they met they were relieved, but they had these concerns at the beginning." Another narrative also sheds light on this matter:

> The family [Muslim/Turkish side] can be very secular and modern, still… Parents and grandparents are always hesitant about mixed relations and marriages. It is never their first choice and believe me, they can put a huge pressure on your shoulders in order for you to give up. The redline is the child: is she/he going to be Jewish or Muslim? This is the breaking point for them. (Jewish, 45, Woman)

During fieldwork, the author could only obtain information on the gender ratio of mixed marriages from Turkey's Jewish community leaders. According to these figures, the proportion of Jewish men who have married Muslim-Turkish women so far is 66% of the total of Jewish mixed marriages. No such statistics could be obtained from Rum and Armenian communities. In this context, symbolic boundaries constructed at the intersection of religion/ethnicity and gender are strong and striking, while the findings of the study indicate that women are subjected to more social pressure than men. In this case, being both a woman and a minority meant having a multiple burden: "In these kinds of marriages, the daughter is treated in a more protective manner in the family. There is a fear that the girl will be more assimilated. It's changed now, but usually that's the case. It is relatively easy for men" (Jewish, 45, Woman).

Women's narratives described in detail the intervention of the social environment and how it is reflected in their relationships, whereas male narratives did not extensively address this issue. When women brought "an outsider" into their communities' micro-socialisation spaces, they received stronger reactions, experienced more stress in getting their families and societies to accept their relationships, and discovered that the gossip mechanism worked very fast in this context. When a boyfriend is from within their own community, women can readily reveal this to their families and their environment at the beginning of a relationship. However, when they are with a Muslim-Turkish man, they prefer to keep it secret until the relationship becomes serious and they are confident about the person, or they decide to make the relationship formal. The introduction of a boyfriend to family and social circles means that he is also included in the circle, and that the relationship is accepted and approved by the society.

> Since there is no legal bond between us [Rum woman and a Muslim fiancé], I didn't want to introduce him to my community for a long time for I would receive a negative reaction. Nobody should know who your fiancé is, [if] you are with an "x", a foreign face: "The daughter of so and so is with a Turk!" Normally, if you are with someone of your own culture, you can say it with peace of mind, for example, "We are eating with Niko." So, always in secret. You always try to postpone. You can't declare him as your boyfriend, because you have to wear this [pointing to the ring]. Having him approved. Having him included in the circle. (Rum, 47, Female)

During the interviews, many examples of matchmaking were recounted which presented it as a common practice in promoting intra-group marriages in the Rum, Jewish, and Armenian communities. Another point observed during the interviews is that the person responsible for matchmaking in the family or social environment is necessarily a woman.

> Matchmaking was very strong in the community; there were women who did it well. Virtuous women. Let's say somebody, let's call her Mari, you say, "Mari, I'm thinking of this girl for my son, give it a hand and we'll get them together." They surely would have found a way. (Rum, 38, Male)

Jewish interviewees also emphasised Jewish mothers' over-controlling attitudes toward their sons, their role as the primary agent in the family in choosing the "right spouse", and their sometimes repressive and directing role in emotional relationships, with some referencing the "Jewish mom" theory.

> The "Jewish mom" is not an urban legend, but real [laughing]. They are mediators, not just in their nuclear families, but whenever someone has a

problem, has a dispute in their family life, they are summoned to Shabbat immediately. And if it is a series that goes from grandmother to mother, it is a woman who directs the familial issues. They are extremely fond of sons and they can interfere with the choice of spouses, which is a problem. (Jewish, 43, Female)

Ethno-cultural differences that are claimed to exist between non-Muslim and Muslim-Turkish communities are one of the main factors behind the negative approach to mixed marriages. We observed that people in mixed marriages suffered social discrimination, especially from family members, when they crossed ethno-cultural boundaries. This, and negative stereotypes, are based on the religious-ethnic-cultural roots of the partner. In this context, there is a widespread social understanding that non-Muslim men are considered to be more "acceptable" spouses than Turkish Muslim men. The "acceptable" male model refers to a husband who is more loyal to his home, waits on the children hand and foot, is more in accord with his spouse, more tolerant, is not macho, and does not cheat on his wife or use physical violence;[31] it is stressed that in non-Muslim families, women are not subjected to physical violence such as beatings. These communities generally associate the high rate of violence against women in the Middle East—including Turkey—with Islam, and underline that in this religion women are seen as worthless, whereas in a Jewish, Rum, or Armenian family, hands are not raised against women, who are more valued. Non-Muslim communities focus in particular on the ideological role of Islam in gender-based role patterns in the family, and male authority and hegemonic dominance more broadly. They claim that this inequality and the secondary role of women originates in religion (Kandiyoti 2007, 92), thus making the value judgment that Islam is patriarchal and anti-women's rights (ibid.: 93). On the other hand, most of our interviewees presented internal criticism of their own communities for this perception and define this general understanding regarding Turkish men as "cultural blindness".

> This perception always exists in this community, there are always reservations: the reality of brute force [among Muslim men], of not being devoted to his wife and home. In my opinion, this is not a perception, it exists. He might be very well educated, and cultured but this is family coding, society

[31] For more information on the "Jewish men make good husbands" theory, see Mcginity (2014, 35–40), Toback and Haback (1986).

coding, and I think a little bit of genetic coding, Turkish men have this "tough-guyness", saying "heeyt". That's why when their daughters want to marry a Turk, parents become more nervous. (Rum, 47, Woman)

> Of course! There is cheating, beating in our community. We are part of this [Turkish] culture, these cultural values are also embedded in the Jewish society for centuries. (Jewish, 48, Men)

Analysis demonstrated that families reacted more strongly to the possibility of a Rum, Jewish, Armenian woman marrying a patriarchal Muslim-Turkish man than a man from one of these communities marrying a Muslim woman. On the other hand, the increase in the number of Muslim brides within the communities is also attributed to demand on the part of non-Muslim men in recent years. Although a Rum, Jewish, Armenian family might initially oppose them, Muslim brides are accepted into the group as they are viewed as less spoiled than non-Muslim women in general, and as showing greater respect for the parents. It was even suggested that that some men prefer to marry a Muslim girl for these reasons.[32]

> If we are taking in nine Muslim brides, we are taking in one Muslim groom. Why would she go to a patriarchal family? Now there has been an increase in Muslim brides. The mothers-in-law who have taken a Muslim bride are very satisfied. They are very respectful they are not spoiled. I have friends who are very pleased with the Muslim bride. At first, they objected a lot, but now they defend them fiercely. (Jewish, 53, Woman)

On the other hand, Jewish male interviewers frequently stressed that Jewish women were spoiled in a family environment where the mother figure was so dominant and that this situation created a disadvantage for men in future marital life.

> I think Jewish women are more spoiled than men. In my life, men carry the stress of life. He [the Jewish man] doesn't talk much at home; he tries to meet the demands. In my mother's generation, the woman doesn't work. Even if the man's work is in crisis, women will go out and eat in restaurants. That's what the daughter sees. Boys, like Italian men, they're committed to the mother. I think the reason is what they call the "Jewish Mom" phenomenon. (Jewish, 48, Men)

---

[32] Here the views of the respondents are conveyed paying attention not to make the mistake of cultural reductionism.

Interviewees in their 30s and 40s criticised this dominant viewpoint in their families and communities, saying that they found it extremely reductionist, contradictory, and discriminatory. They reiterated that, today, this assumed cultural differentiation between a Rum, Jewish, or Armenian male and a Muslim male from a similar social class has diminished, and they gave examples of non-Muslim men starting to be "Turkified" over time.

> There were many mothers around me, around our mothers [saying], "No matter what, a Muslim man beats, cheats, and treats his wife badly." Our men were raised being called "my pasha, my son". In Muslim families, mostly, no matter how modern, it is said "he is a man, my child, put up with it". The woman is softer, mild-mannered. Now, a man who grew up being called "my pasha, my son" falls more easily for a woman who calls him "oh my pasha". Jewish men get more attention from Muslim women. Jewish women [and] Muslim men are not as compatible ... [It] is a very difficult equation. Is there no beating or contempt in our community? Of course, there is. (Jewish, 43, Woman)

Female interviewees interpreted the fact that the marriage of a woman to a Muslim man was opposed by their families due to assertions of violence, while the marriage of a man to a Muslim woman was deemed rather more acceptable as a great dilemma and discrimination. Most of the women interviewees stated that in their families this kind of ethno-cultural difference between the social groups posed a greater threat than the assimilation risk of mixed marriages.

> One day, my father confronted me and said, "I would never consent to you marrying a Muslim man." But I had a brother, he said, "He can marry a Muslim girl, I would not object to [that]." According to him, a Jewish man would be a good [marriage partner for his daughter]; he would hold the woman in high esteem; but a Muslim woman is more acceptable [for his son]. (Jewish, 49, Woman)

Concluding Remarks

Mixed or interfaith marriages demonstrate how societies are structured by ethno-religious/racial hierarchies and inequality. This chapter traces the contours of marriage and the family as central institutions for reproducing gendered, ethno-religious patterns. Nevertheless, the study also finds that intimate relationships reveal how mixed couples challenge notions of the inferiority of non-Muslim religions and Islam's superiority—and vice versa—through the everyday realities of loving and forming families across ethno-religious boundaries. It is unique in drawing on their experiences, not just to understand these relationships but also to provide a microcosm of societal dynamics and to examine the meanings of interactions between members of both stigmatised and dominant groups in the context. It also presents how both ethnicity-religion and gender, as well as other social categories, can combine to produce particular meanings.

The needs and experiences of mixed-marriage families, and their perspectives, practices, and choices, increasingly structure how religious communities, belief, and practice function in Istanbul. But they also increasingly shape how Turkish culture views concepts such as religious difference and the degree of permeability between different traditions. Based on analysis of the narratives, I argue, the social and ethno-religious boundaries are crossed within the context of neo-Ottomanist discourse of the AKP among Muslims' and non-Muslims', as individuals who lead urban, secular lifestyles with their dwindling numbers in the geography of the city. Countering the nostalgic discourses of an imagined Ottoman past, a different scenario is being played out in the private realms of non-Muslim and Muslim families, where pluralism, multiculturalism, and hybrid practices are actually being experienced through mixed marriages. On the other hand, marriage institution is embedded by gender hierarchies and roles. As this study shows, non-Muslim women carry the burden of being a "minority" more than non-Muslim men during their mixed relationships/marriages. In minority communities, gossip mechanism works very strongly. The symbolic pressure coming from the community acts as a substantial element of control over its members. Gender relations and roles have an increasing and deepening importance in minority cultures. Women are considered to have the principal responsibility for the transmission of minority identity (language, religious practices, rituals, and the like) within the family. Hence when it comes to a marriage outside of the community women experience this pressure from their parents and society more than men do because of the fear of assimilation. The other reason women are subjected to more pressure is an assumed cultural differentiation, the social understanding that non-Muslim men are considered to be more "acceptable" spouses than "patriarchal Turkish Muslim" men. Therefore, private sphere becomes a more sensitive and fragile area for minorities compared to the wider society.

REFERENCES

Aktar, Ayhan. 2012. *Varlık Vergisi ve Türkleştirme Politikaları* [Wealth Tax and Turkification Policies], 11th ed. Istanbul: İletişim.
Alba, Richard and Victor Nee. 2003. *Remaking the American Mainstream: Assimilation and Contemporary Immigration*. Cambridge, MA: Harvard University Press.
Anthias, Floya and Nira Yuval-Davis. 1989. Introduction. In *Woman-Nation-State*, ed. Nira Yuval-Davis and Floya Anthias. London: Macmillan.
Aslanoglu, Anna Maria, Foti Benlisoy and Haris Rigas. 2012. *İstanbul Rumları Bugün ve Yarın* [Rums of Istanbul, Today and Tomorrow]. Istanbul: İstos.
Bakan'dan Tehlikeli Sözler [Dangerous Terms from the Minister]. 2008. *Milliyet*, November 11. Accessed August 12, 2020. https://www.milliyet.com.tr/siyaset/bakandan-tehlikeli-sozler-1014564.
Bali, Rıfat N. 2012. *1934 Trakya Olayları* [1934 Thrace Events]. Istanbul: Libra.
Barkey, Karen. 2008. *Empire of Difference: The Ottomans in Comparative Perspective*. Cambridge: Cambridge University Press.
Benlisoy, Foti. 2012. Pandeli, Uncle Tom and Tolerant Hypocrisy. *Bianet*, January 30. Accessed August 15, 2020, from https://m.bianet.org/bianet/azinliklar/135799-pandeli-tom-amca-ve-hosgorulu-riyakarlik.
Beylunioglu, Anna Maria. 2015. Freedom of Religion and Christians in Turkey. *Turkish Policy Quarterly* 13 (4): 139–147.
———. May 2017. Recasting the Parameters of Freedom of Religion in Turkey: Non-Muslims and the AKP. In *Authoritarian Politics in Turkey: Elections, Resistance and the AKP*, ed. Bahar Başer and Erdi Öztürk, 141–156. London: IB Tauris.
Beylunioglu, Anna Maria and Kaymak Özgür. 2020. *Kısmet Tabii... İstanbul'un Rum, Yahudi ve Ermeni Toplumlarında Karma Evlilikler*. Istanbul: İstos.
Braude, Benjamin and Bernard Lewis, ed. 1982. *Christians and Jews in the Ottoman Empire: The Functioning of a Plural Society*. New York: Holmes&Meir.
Brink-Danan, Marcy. 2014. *Yirmi Birinci Yüzyılda Türkiye'de Yahudiler, Hoşgörünün Öteki Yüzü* [Jews in Turkey in the Twenty-First Century, the Other Face of Tolerance] Trans. Barış Cezar. Istanbul: Koç University Publications.
Canefe, Nergis. 2007. *Anavatandan Yavruvatana Milliyetçilik, Bellek ve Aidiyet* [Nationalism, Memory and Belonging from Motherland to Fosterland]. Istanbul: Bilgi University Publications.
Dündar, Fuat. 2000. *Türkiye Nüfus Sayımında Azınlıklar* [Minorities in National Census of Turkey]. 2nd ed. Istanbul: Çiviyazıları.
Duru, Deniz Neriman. 2015. From Mosaic to *Ebru*: Conviviality in Multi-ethnic, Multi-faith Burgazadası, Istanbul. *South European Society and Politics* 20 (2): 243–263.

Ekmekçioğlu, Lerna. 2016. *Recovering Armenia, the Limits of Belonging in Post-Genocide Turkey*. Stanford: Stanford University Press.
Erdoğan: Bizim Tek Derdimiz Var, İslam, İslam, İslam [Erdoğan: We Have Only One Concern, Islam, Islam, Islam]. Accessed July 31, 2015. http://bianet.org/bianet/siyaset/166454-erdogan-bizim-tek-derdimiz-var-islam-islam-islam.
Haligua, Eli. 2018. Toplumun %31,7'si Musevi Komşu İstemiyor [%31,7 of the Society do not Want a Jewish Neighbor]. *Avlaremoz*, February 2. Accessed June 10, 2018. http://www.avlaremoz.com/2018/02/02/toplumun-17si-musevi-komsu-istemiyor-2/.
[*Hate Speech in Media: May–August 2019 report*] Accessed April 7, 2020. https://hrantdink.org/tr/asulis/faaliyetler/projeler/medyada-nefret-soylemi/2134-medyada-nefret-soylemi-mayis-agustos-2019-raporu-yayimlandi.
İnalcık, Halil. 2014. *Türklük, Müslümanlık ve Osmanlı Mirası* [Turkishness, Islam and Ottoman Heritage]. Istanbul: Kırmızı Oda.
Kandiyoti, Deniz. 2007. *Cariyeler, Bacılar, Yurttaşlar, Kimlikler ve Toplumsal Dönüşümler* [Concubines, Sisters, Citizens, Identities and Social Transformations]. Istanbul: Metis.
Kaya, Ayhan and Ece Harmanyeri. 2010. *Tolerance and Cultural Diversity Discourses in Turkey*. Fiesole: Robert Schuman Centre for Advanced Studies, European University Institute.
Kaymak, Özgür. 2017. *İstanbul'da Az(ınlık) Olmak: Gündelik Hayatta Rumlar, Yahudiler, Ermeniler* [Being a Minority in Istanbul: Rums, Jews and Armenians in the Daily Life]. Istanbul: Libra.
―――. 2019. Turkish Jews' Perspectives on Israel. In *Jewish Studies and Israel Studies in the Twenty-First Century*, ed. Carsten Schapkow and Klaus Hödl. Washington, DC: Lexington Books.
Koru, Selim. 2020. Turkey's Islamist Dream Finally Becomes a Reality. *New York Times*, July 14. Accessed August 15, 2020. https://www.nytimes.com/2020/07/14/opinion/hagia-sophia-turkey-mosque.html.
Maksudyan, Nazan. 2015. Üç Kuşak Üç Katliam: 1894'den 1915'e Ermeni Çocuklar ve Yetimler [Three Generations, Three Massacres: Armenian Children and Orphans from 1894 till 1915]. *Toplum ve Bilim* (132).
Marshall, T. H. and Tom Bottomore. 2000. *Yurttaşlık ve Toplumsal Sınıflar, Kimlik* [Citizenship and Social Classes, Identity]. Ankara: Gündoğan Publishing.
McGinity, Keren R. 2014. *Marrying Out: Jewish Men, Intermarriage and Fatherhood*. Bloomington: Indiana University Press.
Meseri, Raşel and Aylin Kuryel. 2017. *Türkiye'de Yahudi Olmak Bir Deneyim Sözlüğü* [Being a Jew in Turkey: A Dictionary of Experience]. Istanbul: İletişim.
Mills, Amy. 2014. *Hafızanın Sokakları: İstanbul'da Peyzaj, Hoşgörü ve Ulusal Kimlik* [Streets of Memory: Landscape, Tolerance, and National Identity in Istanbul]. Istanbul: Koç University Publications.

Minister of Justice Çiçek: Conference on Armenians Like a Stab in the Back to Turkish People. 2005, *Hürriyet*, June 25. Accessed August 12, 2020. https://www.hurriyet.com.tr/gundem/justice-minister-cicek-conference-on-armenians-like-a-stab-in-the-back-to-turkish-people-38732614.

Oran, Baskın. 2008. Reciprocity in Turco-Greek Relations: The Case of Minorities. In *Reciprocity: Greek and Turkish Minorities, Law, Religion and Minorities*, ed. Samim Akgönül. Istanbul: Istanbul Bilgi University Press.

Örs, İlay. Ed. 2019. *İstanbullu Rumlar ve 1964 Sürgünü, Türk Toplumunun Homojenleşmesinde Bir Dönüm Noktası* [Rums of Istanbul and 1964 Exile, A Turning Point in the Homogenization of Society]. Istanbul: İletişim.

Ortaylı, İlber. 2012. *Ottoman Studies*. 4th ed. Istanbul: Istanbul Bilgi University Press.

Rebhun, Uzi. 1999. Jewish Identification in Intermarriage: Does a Spouse's Religion (Catholic vs. Protestant) Matter? *Sociology of Religion* 60 (1): 71–88.

Tharoor, Ishaan. 2020. The Trouble Making Hagia Sophia a Mosque Again. *Washington Post*, July 13. Accessed August 15, 2020. https://www.washingtonpost.com/world/2020/07/13/hagia-sofia-mosque-erdogan/.

Toback, Sandy and Debbie Haback. 1986. *The Jewish American Prince Handbook: From Bris to Bar Mitzvah and Beyond*. Chicago: Turnbull and Willoughby Publishers.

Touraine, Alain. 2000. *Can We Live Together? Equality and Difference*. Stanford: Stanford University Press.

Turkey 2006 Progress Report. https://ec.europa.eu/neighbourhood-enlargement/sites/near/files/pdf/key_documents/2006/nov/tr_sec_1390_en.pdf.

Valansi, Karel and Ira Forman: "Yükselen Antisemitizmden Endişeliyiz" [We are Worried About Rising Anti-Semitism]. *Şalom*. Accessed July 11, 2014. http://www.salom.com.tr/haber-91384-ira_forman__yukselen_antisemitizmden_endiseliyiz_.html.

Yuval-Davis, Nira. 1997. *Gender and Nation*. London: Sage Publications.

———. 2011. *The Politics of Belonging*. London: Sage Publications.

CHAPTER 11

Neo-Ottoman Intersections: The Politics of Gender in a Transforming Turkey—An Afterword

Nora Fisher-Onar

TWO SYMBOLIC ACTS

On March 20, 2020, the Republic of Turkey withdrew from the Council of Europe's (CoE) Istanbul Convention. Signed by 45 out of 47 CoE members, the treaty seeks "the protection of women against violence" and the promotion of "substantive equality between women and men". (Article 1). Ironically, the document had been ratified in 2011 by an earlier iteration of the very same AKP (Adalet ve Kalkınma Partisi, Justice

---

I am grateful to Kristen Sarah Biehl and Hanna Muehlenhoff for their thoughtful comments on draft versions of this chapter.

N. Fisher-Onar (✉)
University of San Francisco, San Francisco, CA, USA
e-mail: nfisheronar@usfca.edu

© The Author(s), under exclusive license to Springer Nature Switzerland AG 2023
C. Raudvere, P. Onur (eds.), *Neo-Ottoman Imaginaries in Contemporary Turkey*, Modernity, Memory and Identity in South-East Europe,
https://doi.org/10.1007/978-3-031-08023-4_11

285

and Development Party) that was now overseeing Turkey's withdrawal. At that time, the move had been read as an encouraging sign that the Islamist-rooted authorities remained committed to gender equality. The principle, after all, had been woven, albeit imperfectly (Dedeoglu 2012), into the country's legal regime, public spaces and social fabric over generations via both top-down and bottom-up mobilization.

Piquing outrage among activists and opposition political parties, the decision to withdraw from the Istanbul Convention prompted many questions. Why would a government jettison a signature move of its own tenure? And why would it choose to do so at a time when Ankara was facing increasing criticism of its economic and political performance. The move was puzzling because despite demands from ultraconservatives to rescind the legislation, surveys showed cross-cutting support for confronting violence against women across otherwise polarized Turkey.[1] What, ultimately, would be the consequences for women and gender minorities? The stakes were significant in a context where both the state—and state-aligned civil society—increasingly championed the principle of gender complementarity over equality (Atalay 2019; Eslen-Ziya, this volume), despite mounting reports of violence against women and the LGBTQ community (Sallan Gül 2013; Sansal 2021).[2]

Strikingly, the exit from the Istanbul Convention evoked very similar questions as had been articulated eight months earlier vis-à-vis another potent act of legal and cultural revisionism. On July 24, 2020, Hagia Sophia (Ayasofya) was re-opened for prayers as a dedicated mosque. The UNESCO[3] landmark had been a museum since 1935, having served as a mosque since the 1452 Ottoman conquest of Constantinople, and as the world's grandest church for much of the preceding millennium. The decision to reconsecrate Hagia Sophia, likewise at the behest of ultraconservative civil society, meant that the broader public's experience of the site would henceforth be mediated by Islamic observance. As with the Istanbul Convention, the symbolism-drenched decision piqued questions like "why?" and "why now?" And, as with the gender legislation, the move

---

[1] "Strategies and Tools for Mitigating Polarization in Turkey," https://www.turkuazlab.org/en/home/. Accessed on 27 May 2021.

[2] According to data from the advocacy group We Will Stop Femicide, over 2,000 women have been killed due to gender violence, data which echoes law enforcement numbers of 2,500. Notably, the only year in which a dip has been observed was 2011 when Turkey signed the Istanbul Convention (Eski 2020).

[3] United Nations Educational, Scientific and Cultural Organization.

intensified anxieties among people rendered vulnerable, in this case, Turkey's small non-Muslim community, and millions of non- or loosely practicing Muslims.

Explanations for both decisions included contingent and political factors. At the circumstantial level, pressures included the constraints and opportunities faced by governments during the Covid-19 pandemic. During this period of economic and political turbulence, leaders sought to rally core constituents even at the cost of—and sometimes expressly by—alienating non-supporters. At the same time, the pandemic meant that most states and societies were by and large indifferent to drama beyond their borders. National naval-gazing meant that incumbent politicians around the world were able to pursue internal policies that otherwise might generate global outcry.

At a second, deeper level, political calculations were nested in slower moving social projects like the explicitly espoused goal of Turkey's leadership to engineer a more conservative society. A key component of this agenda has been to generate a sense of continuity with the Ottoman-Islamic past imagined as a source of justice, authenticity and grandeur (a framing of history in which women figured diminutively in public spaces, if at all). Over two decades of AKP rule, the project has found expression at the level of "high politics" and in realms like foreign policy, as well as in "everyday" attempts to recalibrate cultural codes (Fisher-Onar 2009, 2013, 2018; Fisher-Onar et al. 2018). Read in light of this longer-term project, the Istanbul Convention and Hagia Sofia decisions can be read as signposts marking the intersection of gender and Ottoman-Islamic nostalgia. The overlapping message: that AKP-dominated Ankara aims to accelerate the paternalistic, neo-conservative transformation of national consciousness.

Until this volume, however, few studies have sought to untangle the fraught relationship between gender and neo-Ottomanism even as excellent work exists on both topics in their own right. In this contribution, I aim to help close the gap by schematically surveying the evolution of the two phenomena and their study over the past century, attending, in particular, to the fine contributions to this volume. Positing neo-Ottomanism as a gendered "site of memory", my inquiry is guided by the following questions: What role does gender play in historical and contemporary attempts to construct citizenship and national belonging? In what ways—and who—does neo-Otttoman revivalism, in its many variants, (dis) empower? What are the implications for gender equality, women's rights, and LGBTQ+ activism? And what do our answers to these questions suggest, in turn, about the evolving intersection of gender and citizenship in nationalist/populist nostalgia projects around the globe?

THE NEO-OTTOMAN LACUNA OF GENDER STUDIES IN TURKEY

To begin wrapping our minds around these questions, it is imperative to recognize that the "woman question" has been topical ever since the late Ottoman period. During this tumultuous era, reformers confronted the challenge of ascendant European great powers by defensively modernizing military, economic, political and cultural governance (Kandiyoti 1991). As Ottoman state and society transformed over the course of the nineteenth and early twentieth centuries, imperial subjects were transformed into citizens. Within this context, the question of women's proper role and rights acquired resonance as attested to by multiple journals devoted to the question during the late Ottoman era (Çakır 2007).

Questions of citizenship and belonging—and their gendered implications—were reimagined with the foundation of the Republic of Turkey. Kemalist nation-state builders responded to the trauma of imperial collapse by rejecting values and practices associated with the *ancien régime*. One form which reforms took was a sort of state feminism which acknowledged legal equality in most if not all walks of public life (Sirman 1989). Thus, women in Turkey famously enjoyed the right to vote or run for office before their counterparts in some Western contexts. At the same time, women were exhorted to publicly perform the ideals of secularized, national citizenship. The role found considerable uptake among women from elite, urban backgrounds such as Atatürk's adopted daughters, Afet İnan and Sabiha Gökçen, who rendered services to the state as a nationalist historian and military fighter pilot, respectively. Yet, homegrown patriarchy, along with forms imported from the West,[4] continued to shape the gender order in public and private, urban and rural settings (Özsu 2010). As such, from the 1920s until the 1970s, the hegemonic narrative was that women had achieved equality even as hierarchies persisted in economic, social and political life (Arat 1989; Müftüler-Baç 1999). One upshot was

[4] The adoption of the Swiss civil code, for instance, was widely touted as emancipatory but, in practice, meant reinscribing the man as primary head of household among other patriarchal practices prevalent in the "West" as well as the "East" during this period (Arat 1994).

to impel politically energized women to channel their efforts towards other causes along the right/left spectrum (Çiçekoğlu 2019).

However, In 1971, and then more vociferously in 1980, military coups and ensuing purges suppressed ideological politics, especially on the left. This spurred many women to explore their voices at the intersection of gender and identity politics. For example, a number of leftist women of Turkish and Kurdish origin embraced the language of "third wave" feminist activism. The term denotes pursuit not only of equality (first wave feminism) and recognition of women's difference (second wave feminism) but also mindfulness of the ways that women's predicaments intersect with other structures like class and ethnicity (Crenshaw 2017; Diner and Toktaş 2010). Thus, Kurdish feminists critiqued their Turkish counterparts' tendency to ignore specifically Kurdish challenges, even as they were joined by left-leaning feminists in challenging the class privilege of Kemalist women's activists (Fisher-Onar and Paker 2012; Arat and Altınay 2015; Simga and Göker 2017).

During this same period, pro-religious women also sought space in public life. Their efforts were in sync with broader Islamist mobilization of newly urban migrants, seizing opportunity spaces opened up by the generals' disproportionate clampdown on the left. One site of Islamic women's mobilization was universities where headscarves had been banned by the junta as a symbol of grassroots, pro-religious activism. This ban on veiling in public institutions was a paradoxical move on the part of the putatively secularist army given its contemporaneous endorsement, in the post-coup era, of a tutelary "Turkish-Islamic synthesis" which aimed to co-opt religious energies in society (under the banner of an ethicized, religious nationalism). Pro-religious activists, however, were not persuaded, arguing that the army's prohibition on women's religious attire in state institutions was discriminatory (it impeded, for instance, women's access to higher education while allowing Islamist men to advance). Covering, its defenders argued, was not a repressive practice. Rather, it empowered by permitting pro-religious women to uphold culturally "authentic" codes of modesty and honor (*namus*), and thus to more confidently navigate the public spaces increasingly available to conservative constituencies in rapidly urbanizing Turkey. The argument was received sympathetically, in turn, by many secular, liberal feminists in an uneasy alliance. This alignment endured for as long as Islamists were in the political opposition (during much of the 1990s) or advocates for democratizing change (in the early 2000s), a period when "Islamo-liberal" arguments about religious freedom flourished (Fisher-Onar 2021b; Kadıoğlu 1994; Göle 1996; Arat 2007; Saktanber and Çorbacioğlu 2008; Alimen 2018).

Meanwhile, mobilization around the veil informed networks and practices that enabled many pro-religious women to thrive professionally, especially after the AKP came to power in 2002. Occupying positions of influence as journalists, academics, and politicians, many pro-Islamic women have sought, for their part, to support the broader goal of Ottoman-Islamic reimagination of public life. This phenomenon of "conservative women in power" has created a "dilemma", as Özcan observes (2018) for secular feminists worried about their pro-Islamic counterparts' "partners[hip] with patriarchy" (Atalay 2019; Saktanber 2002). The fear is that women's gains of recent decades—and the principle of gender equality more broadly—will be rolled back under the umbrella of religious majoritarianism. These anxieties have been exacerbated by the abrogation of the Istanbul Convention (and, indirectly, by the privileging of neo-traditional Islamic practices exemplified by the Hagia Sofia mosque conversion).

Yet the dynamics which link gender with religion are as complex as the interface with ethnicity or class. This is attested to by the multilayered motivations behind, for instance, the decision of some conservative women to unveil—motives which range from political disillusionment with the AKP's authoritarian turn, to personal and theological rationales (Kütük-Kuriş 2021). Far from a fundamental clash between binary, "secularist versus Islamist" approaches to women's roles—a dualistic frame which tends to guide the Western gaze—gender politics in Turkey are messy and multidirectional. Seeking to make sense of these fraught intersections, gender studies has flourished in conversation with a growing body of transnational feminist and LGBT/queer scholarship.[5] Gender research has helped us to better understand women's mobilization[6] and LGBTQ+ activism,[7] including in response to societal violence.[8] An expansive body of further research examines how gender interacts with: domestic politics

---

[5] E.g. Kandiyoti (2010), Parmaksız (2019), Özbay and Öktem (2021).
[6] E.g. Eslen-Ziya (2013), Koyuncu and Sumbas (2016), Kardam (2017), Coşar and Gençoğlu Onbaşi (2008).
[7] E.g. Korkman (2016), Pearce (2018), Kamasak et al. (2019), Selen (2020), Doan and Atalay (2021).
[8] E.g. Parla (2001), Kogacioglu (2004), Ataman (2011), Atuk (2020), Adak (2021).

and foreign policy,[9] neoliberal capitalism, consumerism and labor,[10] human rights,[11] migration,[12] militarism and masculinities,[13] ethnicity and nationalism,[14] sectarian and religious dynamics[15] and intersectional alliances,[16] among many other productive nodes of inquiry. As will be canvassed below, some of this work has noted the gendered implications of neo-Ottoman revival. A critical mass of gender scholarship, however, arguably foregrounds not the neo-Ottoman in general, nor the Ottoman-Islamic in particular, but the specifically Islamist thrust of revisionist nation-building.

THE GENDER LACUNA OF NEO-OTTOMANISM

Mirroring these omissions, gender has been quite a muted theme in the flourishing body of work on neo-Ottomanism as the below review reveals. Nevertheless, over the course of a century that has seen contests over gender—and the study thereof—evolve in dynamic ways, another transformation has unfolded: the gradual reimagination of the Ottoman inheritance as basis of the national project.

To make sense of neo-Ottoman nostalgia in its multiple variations, I draw on Pierre Nora's seminal notion of *lieu de memoire* as a physical site—but also discursive trope (Fisher-Onar 2015)—where "memory crystallizes and secretes itself" (Nora 2008, 7) In our post-modern age of multiple truths but no Truth, memory—and its cultivation by those who seek to steer a society—offers an organic sense of continuity with the certainties of tradition. This connection is galvanizing, even though the actual historical/empirical traditions in question have long been eclipsed

---

[9] E.g. Bilgic (2015), Kabasakal Arat (2017), Süleymanoğlu-Kürüm and Rumelili (2018), Aksoy (2018), Muehlenhoff (2019), Ataç (2021).

[10] E.g. White (2004), Potuoğlu-Cook (2006), Gökarıksel and Secor (2009), Beşpınar (2010), Acar and Altunok (2013), Altan-Olcay (2014), Savcı (2016); Onur in this volume.

[11] E.g. Coşar and Onbaşi (2008).

[12] E.g. Ozyegin (2010), Eder (2015), Gülçür and İlkkaracan (2016), Biehl and Danış (2020), Kaşka (2020).

[13] E.g. Altınay (2004), Dönmez and Özmen (2013), Gökarıksel and Secor (2009), Açıksöz (2019), Alpan (2019), Doğu (2016).

[14] E.g. Kancı and Altınay (2007), Gökalp (2010), White (2011), Al-Ali and Tas (2018).

[15] E.g. Fisher-Onar and Müfütler-Baç (2011), Mills (2018), Akboğa and Şahin (2018), Mutluer (2019), Kaymak, in this volume.

[16] E.g. Fisher-Onar and Paker (2012), Simga and Göker (2017), Çağatay (2018), Alemdar et al. (2020), Çelik and Göker (2021).

by modernizing transformation. Sites of memory thus serve the pursuit of "restorative nostalgia" (Boym 2008; Fisher-Onar 2009, 2021a; Yavuz 2020; Onur and Raudvere, in this volume) by inviting, in the case of Turkey, participation in a reinvented tradition of world historical greatness and spiritual restoration.

Yet, as philosopher of history, Michel-Rolph Trouillot (1995) aptly adds (given the persistent erasure of his forebears' Haitian revolution from our canon of modernity), memorial practices entail power dynamics. The inscription of one historiography omits or deliberately erases alternative renditions of history/memory. When it comes to Ottomanist revivalism, gender is among the dimensions by and large silenced in a story that encompasses *cultural* and *political* sites of memory.

The will to rehabilitate the Ottoman past has existed ever since early Republican nation-builders broke from Ottoman norms and institutions (which had themselves been transformed over the prior century of modernization [Mardin 1973) (Yavuz 1998). The experience of rupture via the cultural revolution of the 1920s was especially traumatic for pro-religious cadres (Ruacan 2020). Its rendering in subsequent historiography as a "narrative of victimhood" (Lord 2018, 36; Yavuz 2016, 2020) arguably entailed affinities with the experience of colonized communities around the world at the dismantling of native cosmologies (Fisher-Onar et al. 2014). To be sure, Turkey's Kemalist agents of Eurocentric modernity were internal rather than external, secularization had been well under way during the Ottomans' "long nineteenth century," and the erasure of pro-religious agencies in the early Republic was hardly as comprehensive or brutal as was the case with direct European colonization. Nevertheless, a sort of subaltern anguish at epistemological breach has taken both cultural and political forms.

Early responses included the enigmatic musings of writers like Ahmet Hamdi Tanpınar which helped to generate a literary tradition of Ottomanist nostalgia that flourishes to this day. Many such works grapple with a sense of dislocation in spiritual terms (Göknar 2019). Another prominent theme for authors in this genre—and in political neo-Ottomanism as well—has been grief at the loss of the cultural pluralism which was a key feature of the multi-faith, multi-ethnic Ottoman Empire (Barkey 2008). This hankering for a pluralist past is especially salient in the neo-Ottomanism of secular, liberal authors like Orhan Pamuk (Göknar 2006; Fisher-Onar et al. 2018). Women writers like Elif Şafak and Sema Kaygusuz have contributed to this strand of literary production but, as Chovanec (2021) argues, neither their novels nor the corpus more broadly especially attends to gender.

These challenges to Republican amnesia were paralleled by efforts within the academy, especially after the 1950 transition to democracy. Historians like Halil Inalcik and Ömer Lutfi Barkın seminally recovered knowledge of the Ottoman "golden age" (Fisher-Onar 2015). Sociologists and intellectual historians like Şerif Mardın likewise sought the structural and ideational sources of contemporary Turkish dynamics in the Ottoman period (1973). Challenges to a classical Kemalist claim—that the foundation of the Republic marked an existential rupture from the Ottoman past—soon followed as scholars probed intellectual and institutional elements of continuity between the late Ottoman and early Republican periods (Zürcher 1992; Göçek 2014; Topal 2017). As with the literary strand of neo-Ottomanism, few such studies grappled with the gendered dimensions of the empire's enduring purchase,[17] a gap commiserate with the gender-blind thrust of academic production around the world during much of the twentieth century.

These intellectual challenges to Republican amnesia were echoed in political efforts to reinstate connectivity with the past. With the dawn of multi-party politics, center right parties like the Democrat Party (*Demokrat Parti*, DP) of the 1950s, Justice Party of the 1960s and 1970s (*Adalet Partisi*, JP), and Motherland Party (*Anavatan Partisi*, ANAP) of the post-1980 period rehabilitated elements of the eclipsed era while embracing liberal (and subsequently neoliberal) economic transformation. As such, the Ottoman-Islamic heritage was often evoked in the liberal (and gender-blind) language of religious freedom. The approach was commensurate with the cosmopolitan thrust of literary neo-Ottomanism with its emphasis on the Empire as a source of tolerance and multiculturalism, as well as glory. These resonances were most prominently touted by Prime Minister/President Turgut Özal during the 1980s and early 1990s, establishing a discursive framework which the next generation of pro-religious

---

[17] Göcek's influential work engages with historical sociology, postcolonial critique and gender in both Ottoman and contemporary Turkish context without explicitly gendering the link *between* Ottoman legacies and today's gender politics. There is also a flourishing body of historical work on women and gender in the Ottoman empire, including queer approaches (see, e.g., Ze'evi 2006; Altınay 2015; Schick 2018). These works, however, tend to be concerned with Ottoman experiences *per se* and not the purchase of their memory in post-Ottoman political projects.

political actors would appropriate (Çolak 2006; Taşpınar 2008; Ongur 2015). Education and infrastructure were two further sites where center-right parties in the multi-party period sought to rehabilitate public religion in conjunction with neo-Ottoman nostalgia. An alternative secondary educational track was established for theological training (*imam hatip* schools) and religious content was incorporated into the general secondary school curriculum. Similarly, right-leaning governments pursued ambitious mosque-building programs in Ottoman-Islamic style towards (re)awakened consciousness of the imperial heritage (Batuman 2017). But while these nascent forms of neo-Ottomanism had gendered implications, not least in terms of promoting neo-traditional performances of piety in public spaces, few analysts probed the intersections.

An often overlooked thinker, for example, at the interstices of these cultural and political strands of Ottoman-Islamic revivalism was Samiha Ayverdi—leader of a modernist Sufi lodge (*Altay Ümmi Kenan Dergahı*). Yavuz (2020) documents how Ayverdi engaged the question of women's role within a prolific non-fiction and fiction *oeuvre*. She envisaged the early Ottoman empire as a site where the universal ideals of Islam were manifest in the cultural, political, legal, and everyday endeavors of society. Ayverdi thus contributed to broader efforts to "subvert" (Özyürek 2006, 157) Kemalist historiography. The goal: to cultivate memoires (in keeping with Nora's view of memory as the appropriation of history by contemporary actors) of an idealized Ottoman-Islamic habitus (in keeping with Boym's "restorative nostalgia" as revisionist praxis). Ayverdi's organizational efforts included founding the Turkish Women's Culture Association (*Türk Kadınlar Kültür Derneği*) and serving as founding and guiding figure of bodies like the Istanbul Conquest Society (*İstanbul Fetih Cemiyeti*) and the New Birth Society (*Yeni Doğuş Cemiyeti*). Her strategy of channeling the power of embodied practices towards Ottoman-Islamic recovery arguably found its apex in her organization of the now iconic Mevlana Memorial Ceremony (*Şeb-i Arus*) held annually in Konya on the anniversary of the thirteenth-century poet Rumi's passing. Via these efforts, Ayverdi also set a precedent for women's active contribution to neo-Ottoman restorative nostalgia to this day

Ayverdi's activism was overshadowed, however, by a more assertive and highly patriarchal strand of Ottoman-Islamic nostalgia evident in the mobilization among Sufi orders (*tarikat*) like the Nakşibendi which had been influential during the period of late Ottoman modernization but which were suppressed during the single-party era (1923–1950). Figures affiliated with the early movement like Necip Fazıl Kızılkürek espoused an aggressively revanchist neo-Ottomanism which has been reprised in populist narratives of Ottoman-Islamic resurgence today (Duran and Aydın 2013; Uzer 2020; Fisher-Onar 2021a, b). Open organizing became possible with the re-legalization of *tarikat* after the transition to multi-party politics (1950–present). Nakşibendi disciples went on to found Turkey's National View (*Milli Görüş*) tradition of political Islam. The movement's very name evokes a national community (*milli*) steeped in Ottoman-style religious affiliations in juxtaposition to the secular notion of *ulus* preferred by secularist nationalists (White 2011). The MG movement fielded a series of political parties which participated in coalition governments throughout the second half of the twentieth century.

In the 1980s, the MG's Welfare Party (Refah Partisi, RP) proved especially successful, as noted above, at recruiting to its grassroots organization newly urban women seeking to navigate the economic and cultural pressures of Turkey's neoliberal transformation during this period. Conservative women thus obtained experience in political mobilization. And while much women's activism was confined to the party's rank and file, several women gained prominence as parliamentarians and plaintiffs, notably in European Court of Human Rights cases which challenged the state's headscarf ban in public institutions (Cindoglu and Zencirci 2008; Kavakci Islam 2010).

Then, at the dawn of the 2000s, a moderate breakaway faction of the movement, the AKP, gained control of the government, a position the party has yet to relinquish (even as the party leadership swung hard right by the second decade of incumbency). Over the course of its tenure, the AKP succeeded in capturing the state.[18] It now wields well-funded instruments like a revamped Presidency of Religious Affairs (*Diyanet*) which is increasingly leveraged as a domestic and foreign policy tool[19] towards a reimagined Ottoman-Islamic ecosystem. In this context, scholar-turned-statesman Ahmet Davutoğlu reached out to the former imperial geography as foreign minister (2009–2014) and the prime minister (2014–2016). His multi-regional foreign policy vision was based on the presumptive "strategic depth"[20] furnished by historical and cultural connections with

[18] E.g. Kaygusuz (2018).
[19] E.g. Özturk (2021), Lüküslü (2016).
[20] Davutoğlu (2001), Murinson (2006).

the post-Ottoman Balkans,[21] the Middle East,[22] Eurasia,[23] and Africa.[24] The approach was characterized by some as an appropriation of Özal-era neo-Ottomanism in its emphasis on positive-sum pluralism,[25] while others underscored the Islamist civilizational ontology that underpinned the framework,[26] and still others emphasized the plasticity of the frame and hence its customizable thrust for the situation at hand.[27] Further research has examined the domestic/international interface[28] of historical references in policy frames from the impact of cultural neo-Ottomanism on Turkey's soft power[29] to normative accounts which advocated for infusing the doctrine with "democratic depth"[30] given's the AKP's authoritarian turn during its second decade in power.[31] However, despite the rich range of themes covered in this literature—and the persistence of neo-imperial aspirations in national and foreign policy[32] well after Davutoğlu's exit from the government—only a few studies, like Durgun's (2016) exploration of hegemonic vs. alternative neo-Ottoman masculinities, have explicitly explored the gendered thrust of Ottomanist nostalgia.

WHERE THE TWAIN SHALL MEET: GENDERING NEO-OTTOMANISM

With the ascendence of the AKP in the 2000s and especially after the turn to illiberal populism since the 2010s (İlhan Demiryol 2020), neo-Ottoman revisionism has become much more salient and thus impactful on Turkey's gender order. As in the preceding century, neo-Ottoman revivalism today and its gendered implications can be parsed at both *cultural* and *political* sites. A burgeoning body of scholarship, exemplified by the contributions to this volume, is taking on the challenge. In the process, conceptual/

---

[21] E.g. Rüma (2010), Somun (2011), Fisher-Onar and Watson (2013).
[22] E.g. Kardaş (2010), Hoffmann and Cemgil (2016).
[23] E.g. Tüysüzoğlu (2014), Sengupta (2014), Torbakov (2017), Fisher-Onar (2020).
[24] E.g. Ozkan (2010), Bacik and Afacan (2013), Langan (2017), Akca (2019).
[25] E.g. Laçiner (2003), Aras (2009).
[26] E.g. Ozkan (2014), Dalacoura (2017), Cornell (2018).
[27] E.g Fisher-Onar (2009, 2013), Öktem et al. (2012), Danforth (2014), Yanık (2016), Wastnidge (2019), Chovanec and Heilo (2021).
[28] E.g. Ergin and Karakaya (2017), Yang Erdem (2017), Hintz (2018).
[29] E.g. Al-Ghazzi and Kraidy (2013), Carney (2014), Karanfil and Eğilmez (2017).
[30] Fisher-Onar (2012).
[31] E.g. Öktem and Akkoyunlu (2016).
[32] E.g. Saraçoğlu and Demirkol (2015).

theoretical frameworks and methodologies are being refined, and empirical findings generated towards a timely, interdisciplinary research agenda on the gendered thrust of contemporary neo-Ottomanism.

On the cultural front, work on how social and commercial practices absorb and reflect neo-Ottoman "memory work" (Walton 2010) increasingly recognizes the gendered nature of imperial nostalgia. A case in point are the femininities and masculinities portrayed in Turkey's flourishing soap opera industry, especially big budget Ottoman-era romps, in which women characters reproduce—but also subvert—Orientalist and neo-traditional expectations alike (Yalkin and Veer 2018; Laurence 2019). Hailing from sociology, Ergin and Karakaya (2017; in this volume) usefully juxtapose this type of commodified "Ottomania" with "neo-Ottomanism". The former, they argue, encompasses playful and pleasure-oriented practices often associated with a feminized private sphere (albeit one where the "private" is percolating with women's political agencies as in miniseries about palace intrigues). Neo-Ottomanism, by way of contrast, is associated with state-led attempts to install a hypermasculine vision of the nation as heir of Ottoman-Islamic empire in a stern bid to revise historical and collective consciousness.

Studies of culture also attend to the power of Ottomanist referents at the interstices of private and public. Rites of passage from circumcision to marriage—and the often elaborate ceremonies which mark them—have proven particularly productive sites for inquiry (Alimen and Askegaard 2020). For example, Onur (in this volume) and Kaymak (in this volume) demonstrate the power of an ethnographic approach. Onur's contribution unpacks the enactment of neo-Ottoman (and otherwise themed) henna night packages. Parsing the marketing, consumption, and context of these elaborate celebrations, she uncovers the multiplicity of agencies which women bring to the negotiation of nostalgia. Kaymak, for her part, examines the phenomenon of inter-religious marriage under a government that arguably has pivoted over the past two decades from a more tolerant if paternalistic neo-Ottoman approach towards minorities (Beylunioglu 2017) to a less tolerant Ottoman-Islamic nationalism which privileges non-(Sunni) Muslim citizens. Yet, the "everyday" intimacies of marriage, Kaymak shows, enable constant challenge to the hierarchies which structure inter-religious relations, affirming pluralism in private if not public spaces. The two chapters thus challenge simplistic readings of gendered neo-Ottomanism as a binary battleground between secular progressives and religious reactionaries. Instead, they uncover multilayered negotiations, often at an intimate scale, which both empower and disempowe.

Another set of contributions to this volume draws inspiration from geography—a potent disciplinary site from which to assess the gendered implications of neo-Ottomanism via emplaced and embodied practices (Hammond 2020). Batuman's chapter builds on his extensive excavation of neo-Ottoman architectural idiom (2017, 2020) as a site of negotiation between the state, Islam(ism) and nationalism. Built spaces, he shows, offer a prism onto how pro-Islamic women are literally shaping public space as architects and activists for women-friendly places within religious structures. Women's role, in this regard, differs from the pre-AKP period of mosque construction which entailed an attempt by the nationalist state to absorb pro-religious energies but which silenced pro-Islamic women's voices (see the ban on veiling above).

By way of contrast, Batuman (in this volume) shows that in the AKP's "new Turkey," mosque-building has become a "signifier of distinction" for men and women alike within an emergent religious nationalism that explicitly envisages Islam as constitutive of the nation.[33] This salience is evident in massive projects like Ankara's Ahmet Hamdi Akseki Mosque the aesthetic politics of which have been highly contested. Thus, when the original architect of the project refused to deliver a complex in the Ottoman-Islamic "mega project" style favored by the government, two conservative women architects were appointed. The move, it is argued, was part and parcel of a strategy which incorporates—but also instrumentalizes—the growing demands among pro-Islamic women to shape spaces of public piety. This finding speaks again to the complex pathways via which neo-Ottoman revivalism both empowers and marginalizes women.

Öktem likewise explores the interstices of worldly ambition and public piety in his comparative account of mega mosques in Ankara and Istanbul. Channeling the incisive empathy of critical human geography, his story is populated by intriguing people who participate in—but rarely fill—these expansive religious edifices. Thus, we learn about the neoliberal and developmentalist calculus which informs the AKP's "grand [mosque] designs"

---

[33] The notion of Muslim identity, observant or otherwise, as constitutive of Turkish nationality has been salient throughout republican history as evidenced both by the country's foundational legal categories (which recognize non-Muslims as "minorities" but not non-Sunni or non-Turkish speaking Muslims), and social usage (which views being a "Türk" as synonymous with being Muslim).

from the anxious proprietor of an ill-frequented shop in the Akseki Mosque Complex. Similarly, Öktem viscerally communicates the sense of monumental stillness which engulfs the human visitor to Istanbul's massive but rarely used new Çamlıca Mosque (due to its distance from the city's economic and residential arteries). The takeaway: mega mosques are designed less to the measure of man or woman than to impress Ottoman-Islamic skylines onto cityscapes and national consciousness.

The aesthetic and affective power of neo-Ottoman curatorial and commemorative practices—and the erasures in which they are complicit—is further conveyed by the contributions of Janson, of Dorrol, and of Maksudyan and Alkan to this volume. Janson's work attends to the "visual-performative form" as political contest. His chapter maps the ways that government-endorsed celebrations of Ottoman poetry, calligraphy, and religious objects—including installations which situate the visitor within a neo-Ottoman soundscape via strategic placement of audio technology—exert a material force that transforms otherwise mundane public spaces into ritualized sites of connection with (re)imagined heritage.

Dorroll's chapter also conveys the revisionist reflex behind the repurposing of a historical prison complex in Ankara as a museum. The exhibit thus helps to exonerate the memory/history of those who faced persecution under early republican secularism (and, in so doing, condemns the Kemalist regime). In the process, Dorroll draws out the distinctiveness of "Erdoğanian neo-Ottomanism" vis-à-vis other variants of nostalgia in its privileging of hierarchical and homogenizing practices and state power despite the oft-heard rhetoric of neo-Ottoman pluralism.

Maksudyan and Alkan also register the tension between hegemonic behavior and pluralist frames. Their chapter maps overlap and divergence between today's historiography of Turkish-Muslim heroism during World War I vis-à-vis pre-AKP narratives. The finding: textbooks and annual/centennial commemorations of battles like Gallipoli today perpetuate earlier occlusion of the Young Turk Triumverate's contemporaneous annihilation of Anatolia's Armenians. The authors then unpack the gendered nature of these nationalist performances. First, they explore the framing of Turkish-Muslim martyrdom as heroism, contributing in the process to a promising if troubling literature on how traumatic military experiences shape hyperbolic yet tragic masculinities (see also Açıköz 2019). Second, Maskudyan and Alkan sift through significant shifts since the AKP came to power in representations of women's agency on the battlegrounds of memory. They note, for instance, a pluralization of female heroines and the unprecedented foregrounding of women's roles as fighters (roles which belie the presumptive privileging of neo-traditional femininities in AKP-led Turkey). Yet, while such portrayals go beyond Kemalist renditions of women's wartime contributions as altruistic mothers, the new accounts revalorize Turkish-Muslim agency to the exclusion of non-Turks and non-Muslims.

Memory politics speak, in turn, to the mobilizing—but also polarizing—power of gendered neo-Ottomanism. Eslen-Ziya's contribution to this collection takes on the question of polarization head-on, arguing that both official bodies and pro-government civil society employ epistemologically disingenuous methods—what she calls "troll science"—to delegitimize gender equality as a principle of governance. Mechanisms include social media (dis)information, and the cultivation of alterative spaces for academic knowledge production like conferences and publications which seek to naturalize complementarity (*fitrat*) rather than equality as the gender order.

Eslen-Ziya's work thus adds to another burgeoning body of literature on the gendered nature of Ottoman-Islamic populism. Populism, after all, is predicated on the construction of an "authentic" people in juxtaposition to "inauthentic elites" (Müller 2016; Aslanidis 2016) or nefarious outside forces (Balta et al. 2021). In Turkey today, the role of constitutive "Other" to the right-wing nationalist project is increasingly assigned to secular feminists and LGBTQ activists who are maligned as puppets of Western cultural imperialism along with other alleged threats like the political opposition.

Discursive demonization is backed up by governance moves like repression of LGBT and queer activism including Istanbul's once vibrant Pride parades (Pearce 2018). Similarly, moves like the replacement of the "Ministry of Women's and Family Affairs" with a body that subsumed women's concerns under the rubric of "Family and Social Services" presaged the withdrawal from the Istanbul Convention. Sundry other measures—from the Hagia Sofia mosque conversion to the gender politics of "everyday" (Gemici 2020)—seek to repackage citizenship in patriarchal, neo-conservative ways.

Ultimately, the otherization of gender activism is part and parcel of broader, pro-natalist exhortations by right-wing populists around the globe. The message to women is to prioritize reproductive contributions to the nation over individual, economic or professional advancement. Queer displays also are deemed anathema to the Turco-Islamic sensibilities of the prodigal "Ottoman son" (*Osmanlı evladı*) who arguably constitutes the new ideal citizen. In this regard, Turkey's emergent gender regime displays family resemblances with the patriarchal postures of populist leaders in places like Hungary, Poland, Brazil, and the United States, to name a few. Across these contexts, neo-traditional nostalgia for cultural "authenticity" is likewise being deployed to challenge transnational mobilization for gender equality and LGBTQ+ rights (Eksi and Wood 2019; Karakaya 2020; Öner 2020; Gökarıksel et al. 2019).

This volume's groundbreaking study of gendered neo-Ottomanism, as such, is informative not only for students of Turkey, but for the insights it offers into cross-cutting dilemmas of gender and citizenship which are (re)shaping states and societies across the globe.

REFERENCES

Acar, Feride and Gülbanu Altunok. 2013. The 'Politics of Intimate' at the Intersection of Neo-Liberalism and Neo-conservatism in Contemporary Turkey. *Women's Studies International Forum* 41(1): 14–23.

Açıksöz, Salih Can. 2019. *Sacrificial Limbs: Masculinity, Disability, and Political Violence in Turkey.* Berkeley: University of California Press.

Adak, Sevgi. 2021. Expansion of the Diyanet and the Politics of Family in Turkey under AKP Rule. *Turkish Studies* 22 (2): 200–221.

Akboğa, Sema and Osman Şahin. 2018. Perceptions of Democracy in Turkey: Gender, Ethnic, and Religious Dynamics. *Journal of Economy Culture and Society* 57: 1–28.

Akca, Asya. 2019. Neo-Ottomanism: Turkey's Foreign Policy Approach to Africa. *New Perspectives in Foreign Policy* 17: 3–8.

Akça Ataç, C. 2021. A Feminist Reading of Turkish Foreign Policy and the S-400 Crisis. *Alternatives* 46 (4): 103–119.

Aksoy, Hürcan A. 2018. Gendered Strategies between Democratization and Democratic Reversal: The Curious Case of Turkey. *Politics and Governance* 6 (3): 101–111.

Al-Ali, Nadje and Latif Tas. 2018. Reconsidering Nationalism and Feminism: The Kurdish Political Movement in Turkey. *Nations and Nationalism* 24 (2): 453–473.

Alemdar, Zeynep, Merve Akgül, Selin Köksal and Gökçe Uysal. 2020. *Women's Political Participation in Turkey: Female Members of District Municipal Councils.* Lund: Raoul Wallenberg Institute.

Al-Ghazzi, Omar and Marwan M. Kraidy. 2013. Turkey, the Middle East & the Media| Neo-Ottoman Cool 2: Turkish Nation Branding and Arabic-Language Transnational Broadcasting. *International Journal of Communication* 7: 2341–2360.

Alimen, Nazli. 2018. *Faith and Fashion in Turkey: Consumption, Politics and Islamic Identities*. London: Bloomsbury.
Alimen, Nazlı and Søren Askegaard. 2020. Religious Ritual and Sociopolitical Ideologies: Circumcision Costumes in the Turkish Marketplace. *International Journal of Fashion Studies*. 7 (2): 211–236.
Alpan, Başak. 2019. Hegemonic Masculinity in Times of Crisis: 15 July Coup Attempt and the Turkish Football. In *The Dubious Case of a Failed Coup*, ed. Feride Çiçekoğlu and Ömer Turan, 71–90. London: Palgrave Macmillan.
Altan-Olcay, Özlem. 2014. Entrepreneurial Subjectivities and Gendered Complexities: Neoliberal Citizenship in Turkey. *Feminist Economics* 20 (4): 235–259.
Altınay, Ayşe Gül. 2004. *The Myth of the Military Nation. Militarism, Gender, and Education in Turkey*. New York: Palgrave Macmillan.
Altınay, Rustem Ertug. 2015. The Queer Archivist as Political Dissident: Rereading the Ottoman Empire in the Works of Reşad Ekrem Koçu. *Radical History Review* 122: 89–102.
Aras, Bülent. 2009. The Davutoğlu Era in Turkish Foreign Policy. *Insight Turkey* 11 (3): 127–142.
Arat, Yeşim. 1989. The Patriarchal Paradox: *Women Politicians in Turkey*. Fairleigh Dickinson University Press.
Arat, Yeşim. 2012. *Rethinking Islam and Liberal Democracy: Islamist Women in Turkish Politics*. SUNY Press.
Arat, Zehra. 1994. Turkish Women and the Republican Reconstruction of Tradition. In *Reconstructing Gender in the Middle East: Tradition, Identity, and Power*, ed. Fatma Müge Göçek and Shiva Balaghi, 57–78. New York: Columbia University Press.
Arat, Yeşim. 2007. *Rethinking Islam and Liberal Democracy: Islamist Women in Turkish Politics*. New York: SUNY Press.
Arat, Yeşim and Ayşe Gül Altınay. 2015. KAMER, a Women's Center and an Experiment in Cultivating Cosmopolitan Norms. *Women's Studies International Forum* 49: 12–19.
Aslanidis, Paris. 2016. Is Populism an Ideology? A Refutation and a New Perspective. *Political Studies* 64 (1): 88–104.
Atalay, Zeynep. 2019. Partners in Patriarchy: Faith-Based Organizations and Neoliberalism in Turkey. *Critical Sociology* 45 (3): 431–445.
Ataman, Hakan. 2011. Less than Citizens: The Lesbian, Gay, Bisexual, and Transgender Question in Turkey. In *Societal Peace and Ideal Citizenship for Turkey*, ed. Rasim Ö. Dönmez and Pinar Enneli, 125–158. Lanham, MD: Lexington Books.
Atuk, Sumru. 2020. Femicide and the Speaking State: Woman Killing and Woman (Re)Making in Turkey. *Journal of Middle East Women's Studies* 16(3): 283–306.

Bacik, Gökhan, and Isa Afacan. 2013. Turkey Discovers Sub-Saharan Africa: The Critical Role of Agents in the Construction of Turkish Foreign-Policy Discourse. *Turkish Studies* 14 (3): 483–502.
Balta, Evren, Cristóbal Rovira Kaltwasser and Alper H. Yagci. 2021. Populist Attitudes and Conspiratorial Thinking. *Party Politics*. Published online. Accessed May 27, 2021. https://doi.org/10.1177/13540688211003304.
Barkey, Karen. 2008. *Empire of Difference: The Ottomans in Comparative Perspective*. Cambridge: Cambridge University Press.
Batuman, Bülent. 2017. *New Islamist Architecture and Urbanism Negotiating Nation and Islam through Built Environment in Turkey*. London: Routledge.
———, ed. 2020. *Cities and Islamisms: On the Politics and Production of the Built Environment*. London: Routledge.
Beşpınar, F. Umut. 2010. Questioning Agency and Empowerment: Women's Work-Related Strategies and Social Class in Urban Turkey. *Women's Studies International Forum* 33 (6): 523–532.
Beylunioglu, Anna Maria. 2017. Recasting the Parameters of Freedom of Religion in Turkey Non-Muslims and the AKP. In *Authoritarian Politics in Turkey: Elections, Resistance and the AKP*, ed. Bahar Başer and Erdi Öztürk, 141–156. London: IB Tauris.
Biehl, Kristen and Didem Danış. 2020. *Toplumsal Cinsiyet Perspektifinden Türkiye'de Göç Araştırmaları*. Istanbul: Türkiye'de Göç Araştırmaları.
Bilgic, Ali. 2015. 'We are Not Barbarians': Gender Politics and Turkey's Quest for the West. *International Relations* 29 (2): 198–218.
Boym, Svetlana. 2008. *The Future of Nostalgia*. New York: Basic Books.
Çağatay, Selin. 2018. Women's Coalitions beyond the Laicism-Islamism Divide in Turkey: Towards an Inclusive Struggle for Gender Equality? *Social Inclusion* 6 (4): 48–58.
Çakır, Serpil. 2007. Feminism and Feminist History-Writing in Turkey: The Discovery of Ottoman Feminism. *Aspasia* 1 (1): 61–83.
Carney, Josh. 2014. Re-Creating History and Recreating Publics: The Success and Failure of Recent Ottoman Costume Dramas in Turkish Media. *European Journal of Turkish Studies. Social Sciences on Contemporary Turkey* 19. Online. Accessed May 27, 2021. https://doi.org/10.4000/ejts.5050.
Çelik, Ayşe Betül and Zeynep Gülru Göker. 2021. Dialogue in Polarized Societies: Women's Encounters with Multiple Others. *New Perspectives on Turkey* 64: 31–54.
Chovanec, Johanna. 2021. Review of Hakan Yavuz Nostalgia for the Empire: The Politics of Neo-Ottomanism. Oxford University Press, 2020. *Middle East Critique* 30 (2): 111–126.
Chovanec, Johanna and Olof Heilo, ed. 2021. *Narrated Empires: Perceptions of Late Hapsburg and Ottoman Multinationalism*. London: Palgrave Macmillan.

Çiçekoğlu, Feride. 2019. The Secular Army or the New Ottoman Fantasy? Negotiating Hegemonic Masculinity in the Image of İstanbul. In *The Dubious Case of a Failed Coup*, ed. Feride Çiçekoğlu and Ömer Turan, 91–121. London: Palgrave Macmillan.

Cindoglu, Dilek and Gizem Zencirci. 2008. The Headscarf in Turkey in the Public and State Spheres. *Middle Eastern Studies* 44 (5): 791–806.

Çolak, Yilmaz. 2006. Ottomanism vs. Kemalism: Collective Memory and Cultural Pluralism in 1990s Turkey. *Middle Eastern Studies* 42 (4): 587–602.

Cornell, Svante E. 2018. Erbakan, Kısakürek, and the Mainstreaming of Extremism in Turkey. *Current Trends in Islamist Ideology*, June 4. Online. Accessed May 27, 2021. https://www.hudson.org/research/14375-erbakan-k-sak-rek-and-the-mainstreaming-of-extremism-in-turkey.

Coşar, Simten and Funda Gençoğlu Onbaşi. 2008. Women's Movement in Turkey at a Crossroads: From Women's Rights Advocacy to Feminism. *South European Society and Politics* 13 (3): 325–344.

Crenshaw, Kimberlé W. 2017. *On Intersectionality: Essential Writings*. New York: The New Press.

Dalacoura, Katerina. 2017. 'East' and 'West' in Contemporary Turkey: Threads of a New Universalism. *Third World Quarterly* 38 (9): 2066–2081.

Danforth, Nicholas. 2014. Multi-Purpose Empire: Ottoman History in Republican Turkey. *Middle Eastern Studies* 50 (4): 655–678.

Davutoğlu, Ahmet. 2001. *Stratejik Derinlik*. İstanbul: Küre Yayınları.

Dedeoglu, Saniye. 2012. Equality, Protection or Discrimination: Gender Equality Policies in Turkey. *Social Politics* 19 (2): 269–290.

Diner, Cagla and Şule Toktaş. 2010. Waves of Feminism in Turkey: Kemalist, Islamist and Kurdish Women's Movements in an Era of Globalization. *Journal of Balkan and Near Eastern Studies* 12 (1): 41–57.

Doan, Petra L. and Ozlem Atalay. 2021. After the Life of LGBTQ Spaces: Learning from Atlanta and Istanbul. In *The Life and Afterlife of Gay Neighborhoods: Resurgence and Renaissance*, ed. Alex Bitterman and Daniel Baldwin Hess, 261–285. London: Palgrave Macmillan.

Dönmez, Rasim Özgür and Fazilet Ahu Özmen. 2013. *Gendered Identities: Criticizing Patriarchy in Turkey*. Washington DC: Lexington Books.

Duran, Burhanettin and Cemil Aydın. 2013. Competing Occidentalisms of Modern Islamist Thought: Necip Fazıl Kısakürek and Nurettin Topçu on Christianity, the West and Modernity. *The Muslim World* 103 (4): 479–500.

Durgun, Doğu. 2016. Home is Where You Make it? Gender and Ahmet Davutoğlu's Strategic Vision in the Middle East. *Geopolitics* 21 (3): 628–660.

Eder, Mine. 2015. Turkey's Neoliberal Transformation and Changing Migration Regime: The Case of Female Migrant Workers. In *Social Transformation and Migration: National and Local Experiences in South Korea, Turkey, Mexico and Australia*, ed. Stephen Castles, Derya Ozkul and Magdalena Arias Cubas, 133–150. London: Palgrave Macmillan.

Eksi, Betul and Elizabeth A. Wood. 2019. Right-Wing Populism as Gendered Performance: Janus-Faced Masculinity in the Leadership of Vladimir Putin and Recep T. Erdogan. *Theory and Society* 48 (5): 733–751.

Ergin, Murat and Yağmur Karakaya. 2017. Between Neo-Ottomanism and Ottomania: Navigating State-led and Popular Cultural Representations of the Past. *New Perspectives on Turkey* 56: 33–59.

Eski, Beril. 2020. Turkey Femicides are Rising. *Think, NBC News*, August 14. Online. Accessed May 27, 2021. https://www.nbcnews.com/think/opinion/turkey-femicides-are-rising-erdogan-poised-make-violence-worse-ncna123668.

Eslen-Ziya, Hande. 2013. Social Media and Turkish Feminism: New Resources for Social Activism. *Feminist Media Studies* 13 (5): 860–870.

Fisher-Onar, Nora. 2009. Echoes of a Universalism Lost: Rival Representations of the Ottomans in Today's Turkey. *Middle Eastern Studies* 45 (2): 229–241.

———. 2012. 'Democratic Depth': The Missing Ingredient in Turkey's Domestic/Foreign Policy Nexus? In *Another Empire? A Decade of Turkey's Foreign Policy under the Justice and Development Party*, ed. Kerem Öktem, Ayşe Kadıoğlu and Mehmet Karlı, 61–76. Istanbul: Istanbul Bilgi University Press.

———. 2013. Historical Legacies in Rising Powers: Toward a (Eur)Asian Approach. *Critical Asian Studies* 45 (3): 411–430.

———. 2015. Between Memory, History, and Historiography: Contesting Ottoman Legacies in Turkey, 1923–2012. In *Echoes of Empire: Memory, Identity and Colonial Legacies*, ed. Kalypso Nicolaïdis, Berny Sebe and Gabrielle Maas, 141–154. London: I.B. Tauris.

———. 2018. Between Neo-Liberalism and Neo-Ottomanism: The Politics of Imagining Istanbul. In *Istanbul: Living with Difference in a Global City*, ed. Nora Fisher-Onar, Susan C. Pearce and E. Fuat Keyman, 1–24. New Brunswick, NJ: Rutgers University Press.

———. 2020. Making Sense of Multipolarity: Eurasia's Former Empires, Family Resemblances and Comparative Area Studies. *Qualitative and Multi-Method Research*. 17–18 (1): 15–19.

———. 2021a. Afterword: Remembering Empire: Between Civilizational Nationalism and Post-National Pluralism. In *Narrated Empires: Perceptions of Late Habsburg and Ottoman Multinationalism*, ed. Johanna Chovanec and Olof Heilo. London: Palgrave Macmillan.

———. 2021b. Turkish-Islamist Synthesis 2.0: Continuity and Change in Turkey's National Project and Foreign Policy. *Harvard Journal of Middle Eastern Politics and Policy*. 53–56. https://jmepp.hkspublications.org/wp-content/uploads/sites/17/2021/09/210930JMEPPFinalDraft.pdf.

Fisher-Onar, Nora and Meltem Müftüler-Baç. 2011. The Adultery and Headscarf Debates in Turkey: Fusing 'EU-niversal' and 'Alternative' Modernities? *Women's Studies International Forum* 34 (5): 378–389.

Fisher-Onar, Nora and Hande Paker. 2012. Towards Cosmopolitan Citizenship? Women's Rights in Divided Turkey. *Theory and Society* 41 (4): 375–394.
Fisher Onar, Nora and Max Watson. 2013. Crisis or Opportunity? Turkey, Greece and the Political Economy of South-East Europe in the 2010s. *Southeast European and Black Sea Studies* 13(3): 407–420.
Fisher-Onar, Nora, James H. Liu and Mark Woodward. 2014. Critical Junctures? Complexity and the Post-Colonial Nation-State. *International Journal of Intercultural Relations* 43A: 22–34.
Fisher-Onar, Nora, Susan C. Pearce and E. Fuat Keyman, ed. 2018. *Istanbul: Living with Difference in a Global City*. New Brunswick, NJ: Rutgers University Press.
Gemici, Basak. 2020. Populist Authoritarianism at the Urban Micro-level: Social Discomfort of Doing "Normal" in Daily Istanbul. *Contending with Polarization in Contemporary Turkey*, Middle East Studies Association Annual Meeting, October 14. Online.
Göçek, Fatma Muge. 2014. *Denial of Violence: Ottoman Past, Turkish Present, and Collective Violence against the Armenians, 1789–2009*. Oxford: Oxford University Press.
Gökalp, Deniz. 2010. A Gendered Analysis of Violence, Justice and Citizenship: Kurdish Women Facing War and Displacement in Turkey. *Women's Studies International Forum*. 33 (6): 561–569.
Gökarıksel, Banu and Anna J. Secor. 2009. New Transnational Geographies of Islamism, Capitalism and Subjectivity: The Veiling-Fashion Industry in Turkey. *Area* 41 (1): 6–18.
Gökarıksel, Banu, Christopher Neubert and Sara Smith. 2019. Demographic Fever Dreams: Fragile Masculinity and Population Politics in the Rise of the Global Right. *Signs: Journal of Women in Culture and Society* 44 (3): 561–587.
Göknar, Erdağ. 2006. Orhan Pamuk and the "Ottoman" Theme. *World Literature Today* 80 (6): 34–38.
Göknar, Erdağ. 2019. *Orhan Pamuk, Secularism and Blasphemy: The Politics of the Turkish Novel*. London: Routledge.
Göle, Nilüfer. 1996. *The Forbidden Modern: Civilization and Veiling*. Ann Arbor: University of Michigan Press.
Gülçür, Leyla and Pinar Ilkkaracan. 2016. *The 'Natasha' Experience: Migrant Sex Workers from the Former Soviet Union and Eastern Europe in Turkey*. London: Routledge.
Hammond, Timur. 2020. Making Memorial Publics: Media, Monuments, and the Politics of Commemoration following Turkey's July 2016 Coup Attempt. *Geographical Review* 110 (4): 536–555.
Hintz, Lisel. 2018. *Identity Politics Inside Out: National Identity Contestation and Foreign Policy in Turkey*. Oxford: Oxford University Press.

Hoffmann, Clemens and Can Cemgil. 2016. The (Un)Making of the Pax Turca in the Middle East: Understanding the Social-Historical Roots of Foreign Policy. *Cambridge Review of International Affairs* 29 (4): 1279–1302.

İlhan Demiryol, Gaye. 2020. Populism in Power: The Case of Turkey. In *Turkey in Transition: Politics, Society and Foreign Policy*, ed. Ebru Canan Sokullu, 101–120. Bern: Peter Lang.

Kabasakal Arat, Zehra. 2017. Political Parties and Women's Rights in Turkey. *British Journal of Middle Eastern Studies* 44 (2): 240–254.

Kadioğlu, Ayşe. 1994. Women's Subordination in Turkey: Is Islam Really the Villain? *The Middle East Journal* 48 (4): 645–660.

Kamasak, Rifat, Mustafa Ozbilgin, Sibel Baykut et al. 2019. Moving from Intersectional Hostility to Intersectional Solidarity: Insights from LGBTQ Individuals in Turkey. *Journal of Organizational Change Management* 33 (3): 456–476.

Kancı, Tuba and Ayşe Gül Altınay. 2007. Educating Little Soldiers and Little Ayşes: Militarised and Gendered Citizenship in Turkish Textbooks. In *Education in 'Multicultural' Societies: Turkish and Swedish Perspectives* (Transactions), ed. Marie Carlson, Annika Rabo and Fatma Gök, 51–70. Istanbul: Swedish Research Institute in Istanbul and London: I.B. Tauris.

Kandiyoti, Deniz. 1991. End of Empire: Islam, Nationalism and Women in Turkey. In *Women, Islam and the State*, ed. Deniz Kandiyoti, 22–47. London: Palgrave Macmillan.

———. 2010. Gender and Women's Studies in Turkey: A Moment for Reflection? *New Perspectives on Turkey* 43: 165–176.

Karakaya, Yağmur. 2020. The Conquest of Hearts: The Central Role of Ottoman Nostalgia within Contemporary Turkish Populism. *American Journal of Cultural Sociology* 8 (2): 125–157.

Karanfil, Y. Gökçen and D. Burcu Eğilmez. 2017. Politics, Culture and Media: Neo-Ottomanism as a Transnational Cultural Policy on TRT El Arabia and TRT Avaz. *Markets, Globalization & Development Review* 2 (2), Online. Accessed May 27, 2021. https://digitalcommons.uri.edu/mgdr/vol2/iss2/4/.

Kardam, Nüket. 2017. *Turkey's Engagement with Global Women's Human Rights*. London: Routledge.

Kardaş, Şaban. 2010. Turkey: Redrawing the Middle East Map or Building Sandcastles? *Middle East Policy* 17 (1): 115–136.

Kaşka, Selmin. 2020. Exploring 'Women' and 'Gender': Trajectories of Migration Research in Turkey. In *Women, Migration and Asylum in Turkey: Developing Gender-Sensitivity in Migration Research, Policy and Practice*, ed. Lucy Williams, Emel Coşkun and Selmin Kaşka, 23–47. London: Palgrave Macmillan.

Kavakci Islam, Merve. 2010. *Headscarf Politics in Turkey: A Postcolonial Reading*. London: Palgrave Macmillan.

Kaygusuz, Özlem. 2018. Authoritarian Neoliberalism and Regime Security in Turkey: Moving to an 'Exceptional State' under AKP. *South European Society and Politics* 23 (2): 281–302.

Kogacioglu, Dicle. 2004. The Tradition Effect: Framing Honor Crimes in Turkey. *Differences: A Journal of Feminist Cultural Studies* 15 (2): 119–151.

Korkman, Zeynep Kurtuluş. 2016. Politics of Intimacy in Turkey: A Distraction from 'Real' Politics? *Journal of Middle East Women's Studies* 12 (1): 112–121.

Koyuncu, Berrin and Ahu Sumbas. 2016. Discussing Women's Representation in Local Politics in Turkey: The Case of Female Mayorship. *Women's Studies International Forum* 58: 41–50.

Kütük-Kuriş, Merve. 2021. Moral Ambivalence, Religious Doubt and Non-Belief among Ex-Hijabi Women in Turkey. *Religions* 12 (1): 33.

Laçiner, Sedat. 2003. Özalism (Neo-Ottomanism): An Alternative in Turkish Foreign Policy? *Yönetim Bilimler Dergisi* 1 (1–2): 161–202.

Langan, Mark. 2017. Virtuous Power Turkey in Sub-Saharan Africa: The 'Neo-Ottoman' Challenge to the European Union. *Third World Quarterly* 38 (6): 1399–1414.

Laurence, Larochelle Dimitra. 2019. 'Brad Pitt Halal' and the Hybrid Woman: Gender Representations and Religion through Turkish Soap Operas. *ESSACHESS—Journal for Communication Studies* 12 (24): 61–78.

Lord, Ceren. 2018. *Religious Politics in Turkey: From the Birth of the Republic to the AKP*. Cambridge: Cambridge University Press.

Lüküslü, Demet. 2016. Creating a Pious Generation: Youth and Education Policies of the AKP in Turkey. *Southeast European and Black Sea Studies* 16 (4): 637–649.

———. 1973. Center-Periphery Relations: A Key to Turkish Politics? *Daedalus* 102 (1): 169–190.

Mills, Amy. 2018. Cosmopolitanism as Situated Knowledge: Reading Istanbul with David Harvey. In *Istanbul: Living with Difference in a Global City*, ed. Nora Fisher-Onar, Susan C. Pearce and E. Fuat Keyman, 97–111. New Brunswick, NJ: Rutgers University Press.

Muehlenhoff, H.L. 2019. Neoliberal Governmentality and the (De) politicisation of LGBT Rights: The Case of the European Union in Turkey. *Politics* 39 (2): 202–217.

Müftüler-Bac, Meltem. 1999. Turkish Women's Predicament. *Women's Studies International Forum* 22 (3): 303–315.

Müller, Jan-Werner. 2016. *What is Populism?* Philadephia: University of Pennsylvania Press.

Murinson, Alexander. 2006. The Strategic Depth Doctrine of Turkish Foreign Policy. *Middle Eastern Studies* 42 (6): 945–964.

Mutluer, Nil. 2019. The Intersectionality of Gender, Sexuality, and Religion: Novelties and Continuities in Turkey during the AKP Era. *Southeast European and Black Sea Studies* 19 (1): 99–118.

Nora, Pierre. 2008. *Pierre Nora en Les lieux de mémoire*. Montevideo: Ediciones Trilce.
Öktem, Kerem and Karabekir Akkoyunlu. 2016. Exit from Democracy: Illiberal Governance in Turkey and Beyond. *Southeast European and Black Sea Studies*, 16(4): 469–480.
Öktem, Kerem, Ayşe Kadıoğlu and Mehmet Karlı, ed. 2012. *Another Empire? A Decade of Turkey's Foreign Policy under the Justice and Development Party*. Istanbul: Istanbul Bilgi University Press.
Öner, Selcen. 2020. 'Europe' of Populist Radical Right and the Case of *Lega* of Salvini: Pioneer of a 'Parochial Europe'? *European Politics and Society*. Online. Accessed May 27, 2021. https://doi.org/10.1080/23745118.2020.1842700.
Ongur, Hakan Ovunc. 2015. Identifying Ottomanisms: The Discursive Evolution of Ottoman Pasts in the Turkish Presents. *Middle Eastern Studies* 51 (3): 416–432.
Özbay, Cenk and Kerem Öktem. 2021. Turkey's Queer Times. *New Perspectives on Turkey* 64: 117-130.
Özcan, Esra. 2018. Conservative Women in Power: A New Predicament for Transnational Feminist Media Research. In *Feminist Approaches to Media Theory and Research*, ed. Dustin Harp, Jaime Loke and Ingrid Bachmann, 167–181. London: Palgrave Macmillan.
Ozkan, Mehmet. 2010. What Drives Turkey's Involvement in Africa? *Review of African Political Economy* 37 (126): 533–540.
Ozkan, Behlül. 2014. Turkey, Davutoglu and the Idea of Pan-Islamism. *Survival* 56 (4): 119–140.
Özsu, Umut. 2010. 'Receiving' the Swiss Civil Code: Translating Authority in Early Republican Turkey. *International Journal of Law in Context* 6 (1): 63–89.
Özturk, Ahmet Erdi. 2021. *Religion, Identity and Power: Turkey and the Balkans in the Twenty-first Century*. Edinburgh: Edinburgh University Press.
Özyürek, Esra. 2006. *Nostalgia for the Modern: State Secularism and Everyday Politics in Turkey*. Durham, NC: Duke University Press.
Ozyegin, Gul. 2010. *Untidy Gender: Domestic Service in Turkey*. Philadelphia: Temple University Press.
Parla, Ayse. 2001. The 'Honor' of the State: Virginity Examinations in Turkey. *Feminist Studies* 27 (1): 65–88.
Parmaksız, Pınar Melis Yelsalı. 2019. Thirty Years of Gender and Women's Studies in Turkey. *Women's Studies International Forum* 77: 102279.
Pearce, Susan C. 2018. Performing Pride in a Summer of Dissent: Istanbul's LGBT Parades. In *Istanbul: Living with Difference in a Global City*, ed. Nora Fisher-Onar, Susan C. Pearce and E. Fuat Keyman, 160–176. New Brunswick, NJ: Rutgers University Press.
Potuoğlu-Cook, Öykü. 2006. Beyond the Glitter: Belly Dance and Neoliberal Gentrification in Istanbul. *Cultural Anthropology* 21 (4): 633–660.

Ruacan, Ipek. 2020. Fear, Superiority, Self-Identification and Rejection: Turks' Different Attitudes to Europe since the Late Ottoman Era. *Journal of Balkan and Near Eastern Studies* 22 (5): 684–700.

Rüma, İnan. 2010. Turkish Foreign Policy towards the Balkans: New Activism, Neo-Ottomanism or/so what? *Turkish Policy Quarterly* 9 (4): 133–140.

Saktanber, Ayşe. 2002. *Living Islam: Women, Religion and the Politicization of Culture in Turkey*. London: I.B. Tauris.

Saktanber, Ayşe and Gül Çorbacioğlu. 2008. Veiling and Headscarf-Skepticism in Turkey. *Social Politics* 15 (4): 514–538.

Sallan Gül, Songül. 2013. The Role of the State in Protecting Women against Domestic Violence and Women's Shelters in Turkey. *Women's Studies International Forum* 38: 107–116.

Sansal, B. 2021. LGBTQ Rights in Turkey: Do Not Touch My Body! In *Human Rights in Turkey. Philosophy and Politics—Critical Explorations*, ed. H. Aydin and W. Langley, vol. 15. Cham: Springer. https://doi.org/10.1007/978-3-030-57476-5_7.

Saraçoğlu, Cenk and Özhan Demirkol. 2015. Nationalism and Foreign Policy Discourse in Turkey under the AKP Rule: Geography, History and National Identity. *British Journal of Middle Eastern Studies* 42 (3): 301–319.

Savcı, Evren. 2016. Who Speaks the Language of Queer Politics? Western Knowledge, Politico-cultural Capital and Belonging among Urban Queers in Turkey. *Sexualities* 19(3): 369–387.

Schick, Irvin Cemil. 2018. Sultan Abdülhamid II from the Pen of his Detractors: Oriental Despotism and the Sexualization of the Ancien Régime. *Journal of the Ottoman and Turkish Studies Association* 5 (2): 47–73.

Selen, Eser. 2020. 'The Public Immoralist': Discourses of Queer Subjectification in Contemporary Turkey. *International Journal of Communication* 14: 5518–5536.

Sengupta, Anita. 2014. *Myth and Rhetoric of the Turkish Model: Exploring Developmental Alternatives*. New Delhi: Springer.

Simga, Hülya and Gülrü Göker. 2017. Whither Feminist alliance? Secular Feminists and Islamist Women in Turkey. *Asian Journal of Women's Studies* 23 (3): 273–293.

Sirman, Nükhet. 1989. Feminism in Turkey: A Short History. *New Perspectives on Turkey* 3: 1–34.

Somun, Hajrudin. 2011. Turkish Foreign Policy in the Balkans and 'Neo-Ottomanism': A Personal Account. *Insight Turkey* 13 (3): 33–41.

Süleymanoğlu-Kürüm, Rahime and Bahar Rumelili. 2018. Diplomaside Kadın ve Egemen Maskülenlik: Değişen Normlar ve Pratikler. *Uluslararası İlişkiler Dergisi* 15 (57): 3–18.

Taşpınar, Omer. 2008. *Turkey's Middle East Policies: Between Neo-Ottomanism and Kemalism*. Washington, DC: Carnegie Endowment for International Peace.

Topal, Alp Eren. 2017. Against Influence: Ziya Gökalp in Context and Tradition. *Journal of Islamic Studies* 28 (3): 283–310.

Torbakov, Igor. 2017. Neo-Ottomanism versus Neo-Eurasianism? Nationalism and Symbolic Geography in Postimperial Turkey and Russia. *Mediterranean Quarterly* 28 (2): 125–145.
Trouillot, Michel-Rolph. 1995. *Silencing the Past: Power and the Production of History*. Boston, Beacon Press.
Turkuazlab, 2020. Dimensions of Polarization in Turkey. Survey. Accessed May 27, 2021. https://www.turkuazlab.org/en/dimensions-of-polarization-in-turkey-2020/
Tüysüzoğlu, Göktürk. 2014. Strategic Depth: A Neo-Ottomanist Interpretation of Turkish Eurasianism. *Mediterranean Quarterly* 25 (2): 85–104.
Uzer, Umut. 2020. Conservative Narrative: Contemporary Neo-Ottomanist Approaches in Turkish Politics. *Middle East Critique* 29 (3): 275–290.
Walton, Jeremy F. 2010. Practices of Neo-Ottomanism: Making Space and Place Virtuous in Istanbul. In *Orienting Istanbul: Cultural Capital of Europe?* ed. Deniz Göktürk, Levent Soysal, and Ipek Tureli, 88–103. London: Routledge.
Wastnidge, Edward. 2019. Imperial Grandeur and Selective Memory: Re-Assessing Neo-Ottomanism in Turkish Foreign and Domestic Politics. *Middle East Critique* 28 (1): 7–28.
White, Jenny B. 2002. *Islamist Mobilization in Turkey: A Study in Vernacular Politics*. Seattle: University of Washington Press.
———. 2004. *Money Makes Us Relatives: Women's Labor in Urban Turkey*. London: Routledge.
———. 2011. *Islamist Mobilization in Turkey: A Study in Vernacular Politics*. Seattle: University of Washington Press.
Yalkin, Cagri, and Ekant Veer. 2018. Taboo on TV: Gender, Religion, and Sexual Taboos in Transnationally Marketed Turkish Soap Operas. *Journal of Marketing Management* 34 (13–14): 1149–1171.
Yang Erdem, Chien. 2017. Ottomentality: Neoliberal Governance of Culture and Neo-Ottoman Management of Diversity. *Turkish Studies* 18 (4): 710–728.
Yanık, Lerna K. 2016. Bringing the Empire Back In: The Gradual Discovery of the Ottoman Empire in Turkish Foreign Policy. *Die Welt des Islams* 56 (3–4): 466–488.
Yavuz, M. Hakan. 1998. Turkish Identity and Foreign Policy in Flux: The Rise of Neo-Ottomanism. *Critique: Journal for Critical Studies of the Middle East* 7 (12): 19–41.
———. 2016. Social and Intellectual Origins of Neo-Ottomanism: Searching for a Post-National Vision. *Die Welt des Islams* 56 (3–4): 438–465.
———. 2020. *Nostalgia for the Empire: The Politics of Neo-Ottomanism*. Oxford: Oxford University Press.
Ze'Evi, Dror. 2006. *Producing Desire: Changing Sexual Discourse in the Ottoman Middle East, 1500–1900*. Berkeley: University of California Press.
Zürcher, Erik J. 1992. The Ottoman Legacy of the Turkish Republic: An Attempt at a New Periodization. *Die Welt des Islams* 32 (2): 237–253.

Index[1]

A

Adalet ve Kalkınma Partisi, Justice and Development Party (AKP), 4, 5, 7, 8, 12, 13, 15, 23–25, 23n14, 58, 68, 70, 71, 77, 88, 90, 92, 100, 101, 103, 104, 110–112, 115–121, 125–129, 131–147, 140n9, 149, 150, 155, 156, 156n2, 159, 160, 163, 163n8, 165, 167, 168, 171, 177, 177n2, 179, 181, 184, 188, 189, 203, 204, 210, 212, 215, 220, 233, 238–246, 252, 253, 258–260, 263–268, 280, 285, 287, 290, 295, 296, 298, 299

Aesthetic, aesthetics, 2, 6, 9, 12, 13, 27, 58, 59, 61, 72, 73, 84, 89–91, 210, 216, 223, 228, 232, 298, 299

Affect, 57–92, 251

Ahmet Hamdi Akseki Mosque, Ankara, 136n7, 160–162, 164, 164n10, 171

Ankara
 Ahmet Hamdi Akseki Mosque, 136n7, 160–162, 164, 164n10, 171
 Altındağ Municipality, 100, 107–110, 116, 119, 216
 Anıtkabir, 68, 132, 133, 148
 Çankaya district, 220
 Çayyolu district, 216, 219, 226
 Citadel, 215
 Hacıbayram Mosque, 131–133
 Hamamarkası, 215–220, 222, 223, 227, 229–231
 Keçiören district, 219
 Kocatepe Mosque, Ankara, 132, 136n7, 143, 158, 159

---

[1] Note: Page numbers followed by 'n' refer to notes.

Ankara (*cont.*)
Library of the Nation (Millet Kütüphanesi), 127, 147
Melike Hatun Mosque, 134, 136, 137, 141, 150
Mosque of the Nation (Millet Camii), 127, 147
North Ankara Mosque Complex, 131, 132n3, 141, 142, 150
Oran district, 220
Presidential Complex (Cumhurbaşkanlığı Külliyesi), 127, 131, 141, 141n10, 146–150, 149n16
Ulus Square, 132, 135, 136
Wonderland Eurasia (theme park), 12
Anti-gender, 239, 242–247, 249, 251, 252
Antisemitic, 262, 266
Architecture, architectural, 4, 6, 18, 70, 77n3, 89, 99, 104, 105, 125–150, 155–171, 176, 212, 216, 220, 220n8
See also Mosque; Monument; Ottoman-Seljuk architecture
Armenian, 23, 177n2, 184, 190, 190n35, 191, 257, 259, 259n2, 261, 261n5, 261n6, 264n11, 264n12, 265n15, 265n17, 266, 268n21, 269–279, 269n24, 274n29, 299
genocide, 178, 180, 181, 188, 190, 192
See also Multicultural; Non-Muslims
Aslan, Yusuf, 111
Atatürk, Mustafa Kemal, 22, 103, 133, 136, 138, 139, 141, 146, 148, 177, 178, 193, 195, 197–199, 202, 203, 267, 288
See also Kemalism
Atıf, İskilipli Mehmed Hoca, 110

Authenticity, performative authenticity, claims of authenticity, 4, 8, 11, 15, 17, 40, 41, 43, 46–48, 108, 210–212, 216, 218–220, 222–228, 232, 246, 287, 301
Authoritarian, authoritarianism, 7, 12n5, 20, 27, 53, 61, 62, 66, 90, 130, 237, 238, 247, 258, 290, 296

B
Bindallı (kaftan), 222–224, 222n9, 227, 231
Boym, Svetlana, 11, 14, 128, 129, 138, 144, 148, 210, 211, 292, 294

C
Calligraphy, 57, 59, 60n2, 76, 80, 84, 88, 164, 176, 299
See also Aesthetics
Çamlıca Mosque, Istanbul, 131, 141, 144–146, 144n13, 150, 165, 169, 170, 299
Çanakkale, 179, 184, 187
Centenary, centennial, 37, 177–193, 177n3, 197, 203, 204, 299
Ceremony, 14, 137, 146, 167, 180, 181, 183, 189, 197, 214, 218, 224–226, 230
See also Ritual
Chamber of Architects, Ankara Branch (Mimarlar Odası Ankara Şubesi, TMMOB), 100, 105, 109, 120, 136
Christian, Christianity, 12, 14, 39, 41, 43–45, 48–50, 69, 179, 188, 242, 247, 253, 263, 264n11
See also Multicultural; Non-Muslims
Çırağan Palace, Istanbul, 220, 221

INDEX 315

Clean, cleansing, 109, 114–117, 129
Commemoration, commemorative events, culture of commemoration, 36, 37, 57–92, 111, 117, 121, 139, 176–204, 191n36, 299
See also Forgetting; Memory; Remembrance
Cosmopolitan, cosmopolitanism, 52, 126, 127, 203, 268, 293
Cultural turn, 63
Curricula, curriculum, 72, 176, 184, 199–203, 294

D
Davutoğlu, Ahmet, 179, 180, 183, 190, 192, 295, 296
Denialism, 189–192
Devotion, 58–61, 72, 73, 75, 77, 81, 87, 88, 90, 91, 229, 230
See also Piety
Dink, Hrant, 177, 177n2, 265, 265n15, 265n17
Directorate General of Foundations (Vakıflar Genel Müdürlüğü), 265
Dirt, 108, 114–118
See also Unclean
Discourse, 3, 4, 8–10, 12–17, 20–23, 25, 27, 35, 38, 39, 48, 49, 53, 65, 69, 72, 167, 186, 189, 201, 203, 238–247, 249–253, 259, 268, 269, 273, 280
Discursive governance, 239, 243, 250, 251
Diyanet (Presidency of Religious Affairs), 13–15, 20, 27, 72, 75, 129, 132, 136n7, 137, 142, 144, 146, 160–164, 163n9, 187, 295

E
Emotions, feelings, 8, 25, 26, 39, 40, 43, 70, 108, 109, 180, 186, 210, 211, 213, 214, 222, 230, 231, 240, 251
Erdoğan, Recep Tayyip, 6, 7, 13, 14, 19–26, 37, 42, 48, 57–59, 70, 104, 126, 127, 137, 138, 140, 144, 146, 149, 166–170, 179, 181, 183, 187–189, 192, 238, 240–242, 245–247, 249, 253, 264, 267
European Union (EU), 21, 163n8, 176, 201, 203, 258, 264–268
Eyüpsultan Mosque, Istanbul, 75

F
Femininity/femininities, 11, 38, 192–203, 213, 297, 300
Feminism, 23, 288, 289
First World War (WWI), 7, 175–204, 299
See also Gallipoli, the battle of; Kut, the First Battle of and the Siege of Kut'ül Amare; Sarıkamış, the battle of
Forgetting, 44, 45, 68, 99–121, 191, 233
See also Memory; Remembrance

G
Gallipoli, the battle of, 179, 182, 187, 190, 198
Gender
equality, 17, 19–21, 23, 163, 238–242, 244–249, 252, 271–273, 286, 287, 290, 300, 301
justice, 17, 21, 22, 244–248, 250
theory, 238, 240, 242–244, 246, 247, 252

Gezi Park, Istanbul, 107, 121, 140
  protests, 238
Gezmiş, Deniz, 111
Greek, 257, 259, 259n2, 261–263,
  261n5, 261n6, 262n7, 263n8,
  263n9, 264n12, 266, 267,
  269n24, 270, 272, 274–279
Greek, Rum, 262n7
  See also Multicultural; Non-Muslims

H
Hagia Sofia, Istanbul, 287, 290, 300
Harem, 17, 18, 24, 41, 42, 45, 46,
  51, 210, 213, 218, 222, 224,
  227, 228, 232
Hegemonic, hegemony, 25, 27, 37,
  38, 53, 101, 138, 149, 156,
  165–171, 201, 202, 241, 244,
  277, 288, 296, 299
Henna, henna night, 209–234, 297
Heritage, 4, 6, 11–17, 19, 22–26,
  41, 44, 45, 58–62, 64, 68, 75,
  85, 91, 92, 103, 105, 126, 135,
  136, 138, 141, 150, 168, 176,
  186, 210, 214, 219n6, 220,
  222–228, 233, 272, 293,
  294, 299
Hero, 14, 24, 41, 49, 117, 193, 194
  hero cult, 177, 204
  heroines, 178, 192–203, 299
  heroism, 24, 25, 34, 38, 111, 117,
    179, 188, 192, 195n43, 198,
    202–204, 213, 299
  See also War heroines
Hırka-i Şerif Mosque, Istanbul, 88
Historiography, 4, 61–63, 66, 68, 74,
  90, 138n8, 178, 179, 203, 292,
  294, 299
Holocaust, 64, 265
Holy war (*jihad*), 179
Honorary male, 201, 202

I
Identity, 2, 7, 8, 10, 13, 15–17, 19,
  22, 26, 27, 38, 39, 43, 44,
  61–63, 65, 99, 103, 118, 120,
  127–129, 135, 137, 138, 149,
  157, 159, 176, 180, 189, 203,
  204, 210, 211, 214, 232, 239,
  243, 246, 248, 258–261, 260n4,
  265n15, 266, 269–271, 271n27,
  273, 274, 274n30, 280,
  289, 298n33
Impurity, 40, 118
İnan, Hüseyin, 111
Independence War, War of
  Independence, 177–179, 192,
  193, 198, 199, 201, 202
Islam, Islamic, Islamism, Islamist,
  4–18, 12n5, 20–23, 25–27, 35,
  36, 38–43, 48, 49, 57–92,
  126–132, 134, 136–138, 138n8,
  146, 148–150, 155–171, 176,
  177, 179, 184, 185, 187–189,
  204, 210, 212, 226, 229, 239,
  244, 245, 247, 248, 251, 253,
  259, 261, 264, 265, 265n13,
  267, 277, 280, 286, 289–291,
  294–296, 298
Istanbul, 1, 3, 8, 12, 17–19, 21,
  24, 36, 37, 46, 57, 66–77,
  88, 102, 126, 127, 129,
  129n1, 131, 135–141,
  144–146, 163n9, 165, 166,
  168, 177n2, 190n35, 193, 194,
  197, 198, 212, 216, 220–222,
  224, 232, 233, 245, 257–280,
  299, 300
  Çamlıca Mosque, 141, 144–146,
    144n13, 165, 299
  Çırağan Palace, 220, 221
  Eyüpsultan Mosque, 75
  Gezi Park, 140
  Hagia Sofia, 287, 300

INDEX 317

Hagia Sophia, 12–14, 27, 34, 59, 67–70, 89, 90, 286
Hilye-i Şerif ve Tesbih Museum, 76
Hırka-i Şerif Mosque, Hırka-i Şerif Museum, 88
Mimar Sinan Mosque, 165, 166
MiniaTürk, 12, 212
Panorama 1453 Museum, Istanbul, 70, 90
Sait Halim Paşa Yalısı, 220
Taksim Monument, 193
Taksim Mosque, 127
Taksim Square, 135, 138
Topkapı Palace, Topkapı Palace Museum, 59, 60n2, 67–69, 75, 89, 142, 216, 227n11

J
Jewish, 259, 259n2, 261n5, 261n6, 262, 264n11, 265n14, 266, 266n19, 268n21, 269–273, 269n24, 275–279, 277n31
See also Multicultural; Non-Muslim
Jihad, *see* Holy war

K
Kaba, Kabe, 58n1, 68, 75, 84
KADEM (Woman and Democracy Association), 21, 240, 241, 244, 245
Kaftan, 18, 43, 209, 216, 222–224, 227, 227n12, 231–233
Kemalism, 58, 70, 118, 119, 121
Kısakürek, Necip Fazıl, 6, 110, 111
Kocatepe Mosque, Ankara, 136n7, 143, 158, 159
Kut, the First Battle of and the Siege of Kut'ül Amare, 181
Kutlu Doğum Haftası (Holy Birth Week), 71, 76

L
LGBT & queer activism, 300

M
Male gaze, 65
Martyr, martyrdom, 143, 178–181, 179n4, 183–189, 185n21, 186n25, 187n26, 192, 195, 201, 204, 299
See also Sacrifice
Masculinity, masculinity, hegemonic masculinity, 11, 38, 50, 178, 184, 187, 192, 193, 201, 202, 213, 291, 296, 297, 299
Materiality, 62–66, 68
Mecca, 68, 72, 84
Media, 1n1, 4–6, 8, 15, 22, 23, 23n14, 25–27, 36, 37, 45, 71, 72, 160, 164, 170, 177n2, 183, 216, 222, 223, 232, 234, 237, 239, 240, 251, 265n16, 266n20, 267, 300
Medina, 10, 82
Memorial, 64, 178, 185, 193–198, 197n45, 198n47, 201, 203, 292
Memory, 8, 19, 23, 25, 35, 37, 58–60, 66–77, 88–91, 99–121, 125, 138n8, 179, 183n15, 184, 186, 190, 202, 211, 212, 228, 262, 268, 287, 291, 292, 293n17, 294, 299, 300
collective memory, 8, 27, 35, 100, 102–103, 115, 262
Islamic memory, 188
national memory, 178, 211
Ottoman memory, 67, 90–92, 104
performative memory, 59
social memory, 59, 63, 67, 76, 88
See also Forgetting; Memorial; Politics of history; Remembrance; Sacralisation of history

Mevlid, mevlut, Mevlid-i Nebi, 58, 59, 60n2, 71, 72, 75, 77, 78, 88, 89, 91, 188, 233, 233n15
Militarism, militarist, 25, 178, 189, 192, 193, 195, 201, 291
Millet, milli, 16, 17, 156, 156n2, 167, 168, 171, 264, 264n11, 295
Mimar Sinan Mosque, Istanbul, 165–167
Mimicry, 129, 155, 158–160, 165, 167, 171
Miniatürk (theme park), Istanbul, 12, 60n2, 71, 212
Minorities, 115
Modernity, 61, 125, 212, 233, 234, 247, 292
Monument, monumental, 12, 70, 75, 100, 131, 135, 136, 138, 141, 147n14, 156, 159, 160, 162, 165, 168, 179n4, 193–195, 197, 299
See also Architecture
Mosque
  Ahmet Hamdi Akseki Mosque, Ankara, 136n7, 160–162, 164, 164n10, 171, 298, 299
  Çamlıca Mosque, Istanbul, 131, 141, 144–146, 150, 165, 169, 170, 299
  Eyüpsultan Mosque, Istanbul, 75
  Hacıbayram Mosque, Ankara, 131, 132
  Hırka-i Şerif Mosque, Istanbul, 88
  Kocatepe Mosque, Ankara, 132, 136n7, 143, 157–160
  Melike Hatun Mosque, Ankara, 134, 136–138, 141, 150
  Mosque of the Nation (Millet Camii) Ankara, 147
  North Ankara Mosque Complex, 131, 132n3, 141, 142, 144, 150
  Taksim Mosque, Istanbul, 127, 139, 140, 150
  See also Architecture
Muhammad, Prophet, 81
  devotion of, 58–60, 72, 73, 77, 81
  rose of, 59, 60, 71, 72, 77, 81, 82, 91, 92
  See also Devotion; Piety
Multicultural, multicultural heritage, multicultural citizenship, 5, 12, 14, 19, 38, 43–45, 63, 104, 105, 176, 177, 203, 258–260, 266–269, 274, 280
Multi-ethnical, 12, 16, 40, 274, 292
Multi-faith, 292
Museology, museum studies
  new museology, 60, 62–66, 68, 90
Museum, 102–103
  Hilye-i Şerif ve Tesbih Museum, Istanbul, 60n2, 76, 79, 82, 91
  memory in, 67, 70, 102–103
  nationalism in, 60–66
  Panorama 1453, Istanbul, 60n2, 70, 212
  religion in, 60–66
  Topkapı Palace Museum, Istanbul, 59, 60n2, 68, 69, 75
  Ulucanlar Prison Museum, Ankara, 99–121
Muslim solidarity, 178, 188

N
Nationalism, nationalist, 187
  Arab, 189
  Turkish, 9, 34, 35, 58, 175, 179, 193, 210
Neo-liberal, neo-liberalism, 9, 10, 37, 228
Non-Muslims, 16, 19, 23, 138n8, 141, 156n2, 178, 189–192, 204, 257–275, 268n21, 274n30, 277–280, 287, 298n33, 300

INDEX 319

Nostalgia
  reflective nostalgia, 210, 211, 231
  restorative nostalgia, 11, 14, 15, 70, 128, 138, 210, 211, 213, 227, 230, 232, 292, 294
  See also Boym, Svetlana

O
Orientalism, Orientalist art, 217
Ottoman-Seljuk architecture, 127, 136, 212, 220
Özal, Turgut, 104, 132, 175, 176, 293

P
Panorama 1453 Museum, Istanbul, 70
Performance, 59, 60, 67, 72, 163n9, 183, 222, 228, 230, 294, 299
Piety, 8, 68, 137, 294, 298
  See also Devotion
Pluralism, 104, 176, 177, 203, 258, 259, 269, 269n23, 272, 273, 280, 292, 296, 297, 299
  See also Multi-cultural; Non-Muslim
Politics of history, 175–204
  See also Memory; Sacralisation of history
Popular culture, 4, 8, 9, 13, 24, 25, 27, 33, 34, 37, 38, 47, 53, 63, 104, 178, 198, 199, 213, 221, 232, 234
Populism, populistic, 7, 171, 189, 237–242, 247, 252, 296, 300
Presidency of Religious Affairs, *see* Diyanet
Public culture, public space, 6, 13, 18, 19, 34, 59, 60, 63, 67, 71–76, 91, 92, 100–102, 104, 105, 115, 130, 131, 138, 149, 150, 163, 165, 265, 271, 274n30, 286, 287, 289, 294, 297–299

Pure, purity, 7, 8, 12, 45, 51, 79, 86, 101, 117, 118, 121, 129

Q
Quran, 36, 58n1, 68, 69, 72, 80, 85–87, 89, 91, 111, 187

R
Refah Parisi (RP) (Welfare Party), 130, 176, 295
Religious faith, 178, 187
  See also Devotion; Muslim solidarity; Piety
Remembrance, 8, 11, 100–102, 116, 117, 119–121, 184, 189, 211
  See also Forgetting; Memorial; Memory; Monument; Politics of history; Sacralisation of history
Republic, republicanism, 2, 15, 35, 37, 84, 100, 102, 121, 126, 132, 135, 137, 149, 194, 194n41, 253, 257, 260, 261, 263, 270, 292, 293
Ritual economy, ritual, 6, 8, 14, 18, 58–60, 62, 67–69, 71–73, 75, 78, 88, 90, 91, 126, 130, 137, 143, 146, 149, 163, 167, 180, 181, 183, 186, 187, 189, 197, 211, 214, 216, 218, 222, 224, 226, 229, 230, 233, 294, 297
  See also Ceremony
Rum, *see* Greek; Greek, Rum

S
Sacralisation of history, 204
  See also Forgetting; Memory; Politics of history; Remembrance

Sacrifice, 184, 189, 194, 195, 204, 214, 226, 230
  See also Martyrdom
Sait Halim Paşa Yalısı, Istanbul, 220
Sarıkamış, the battle of, 177, 184, 185
Secular, secularism, 7, 8, 19, 22–24, 34, 35, 59, 62, 68–71, 84, 91, 99, 100, 103, 112, 115, 116, 119, 126, 128, 131, 136–138, 141, 149, 156n2, 157, 158n4, 160, 165, 167, 212, 219, 220, 238, 247, 253, 260, 261, 267–269, 269n24, 271n27, 273, 275, 280, 289, 290, 292, 295, 297, 299, 300
Self-orientalism, 228, 228n13, 233
Space, 6, 8, 11, 13, 17–19, 26, 34, 38, 59–61, 63, 67–71, 84, 89, 91, 92, 99–101, 104, 105, 112–118, 120, 121, 126, 130, 131, 137, 138, 141, 149, 150, 156, 157, 163–165, 163n9, 171, 189, 211, 213–222, 231, 239, 244, 251, 257–259, 265, 271–273, 274n30, 275, 286, 287, 289, 294, 297–300
Sufi, Sufism, 14, 15, 81, 81n6, 85, 87, 294

T
Taksim Mosque, Istanbul, 127, 138–141, 150
Taksim, Istanbul, 131, 135–141, 197
  Taksim monument, 193
Tesbih (prayer beads), 76
Tezhipçi (illuminator), 85
Tolerance, 24, 175, 177, 203, 258, 260, 260n4, 264n11, 265, 268, 272, 293

Topkapı Palace, Istanbul, 67–69, 89, 142, 216, 227n11
Topkapı Palace Museum, 59, 60n2, 68, 69, 75
Tradition, 11, 15, 17, 20, 49, 51, 57–60, 62, 65, 77–85, 77n3, 88, 127, 142, 157, 164, 168–171, 209–212, 214–216, 215n3, 219, 219n6, 222–230, 232–234, 264, 267, 269, 271, 280, 291, 292, 295
Trauma, 64, 128, 149, 288
Turkish-Islamic synthesis, 132, 176, 289
TV series
  Magnificent Century (Muhteşem Yüzyıl): Hürrem Sultan and Süleyman the Magnificent, 5, 24, 25, 34, 39–53, 213, 215, 219, 221, 232
  Payitaht: Abdülhamid, 7, 25
  Resurrection: Ertuğrul (Diriliş Ertuğrul), 24, 25, 34, 39–41, 48–53, 213, 215

U
Ulucanlar Prison, Ankara, 99, 100, 105, 109–111, 115, 116, 118–121
Unclean, 117, 118
  See also Dirt; Impurity

V
Valentine's Day, 72, 73, 91

W
War heroines, women warriors, 195, 199, 204

Wedding
  celebrations, 214, 215, 234
  fair, 216, 221, 231
  sector, 215, 216, 221, 228, 230, 232
Woman and Democracy Association
  (Kadın ve Demokrasi Derneği,
  KADEM), 21, 22n12, 240, 241,
  244, 244n9, 245

Womanhood, 17, 38, 201, 214–216, 228, 233

Y
"Yüksek Yüksek Tepeler" ("On High Hills"), traditional henna night song, 224, 226

Printed in the United States
by Baker & Taylor Publisher Services